Nicholson's

GUIDE TO IRELAND

Robert Nicholson Publications

Also available:

Nicholson's Guide to England and Wales
Nicholson's Guide to Scotland
Nicholson's Historic Britain

A Nicholson Guide

First published 1983

© **Robert Nicholson Publications Limited 1983**

Maps © Robert Nicholson Publications Limited
Touring maps based on the Northern Ireland
Ordnance Survey map with the sanction of the
controller of Her Majesty's Stationery Office; and the
Ordnance Survey by permission of the Minister of
Finance, Republic of Ireland.

Text and drawings: Richard Reid

The publishers would like to thank the Bord Fáilte
(Irish Tourist Board) and the Northern Ireland
Tourist Board for providing the photographs, and
gratefully acknowledge the friendly assistance of
both boards, the Irish Embassy and the Royal Irish
Academy.

Robert Nicholson Publications Limited
17–21 Conway Street
London W1P 6JD

Great care has been taken throughout this book to be
accurate, but the publishers cannot accept
responsibility for any errors which appear.

Typeset in England by
Rowland Phototypesetting Ltd
Bury St Edmunds, Suffolk

Printed and bound in Great Britain by
Blantyre Printing & Binding Co Ltd
Blantyre, Glasgow

ISBN 0 905522 71 0

Contents

  5 **Touring maps**
 13 **Architectural glossary**
 15 **Irish-English glossary**
 17 **Introduction**
 37 **Northern Ireland**
 63 **Western Ireland**
 89 **Eastern Ireland**
127 **Southern Ireland**
155 **Index**

How to use this guide

Ireland has been divided into four geographical regions for the purposes of this guide, as shown on the diagrammatic map overleaf. The boundaries follow those of the historic provinces of Connacht, Munster, Leinster and Ulster except where these conflict with the modern political boundary of Northern Ireland. Each section is conveniently separated into a wide range of topics to cover all interests, and each entry is alphabetically listed and clearly map-referenced to make planning an itinerary easy.

The full-colour touring maps have been numbered 1–8 to facilitate quick reference. Each map reference in the text gives the map page number first, and then the map co-ordinates.

IRELAND

DONEGAL

LONDONDERRY

ANTRIM

NORTH

TYRONE

ULSTER

FERMANAGH

ARMAGH

DOWN

MONAGHAN

SLIGO

LEITRIM

CAVAN

LOUTH

MAYO

WEST

CONNACHT

ROSCOMMON

LONGFORD

MEATH

GALWAY

WESTMEATH

DUBLIN

OFFALY

EAST

KILDARE

LEINSTER

LAOIS

WICKLOW

CLARE

TIPPERARY

KILKENNY

CARLOW

WEXFORD

LIMERICK

KERRY

MUNSTER

SOUTH

WATERFORD

CORK

© RNP 1983

- - - - - County Boundaries
——— "Guide-section" Boundaries
——— Historic Boundaries

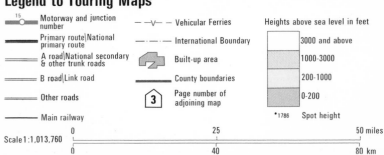

Legend to Touring Maps

15 Motorway and junction number

——— Primary route\National primary route

——— A road\National secondary & other trunk roads

——— B road\Link road

——— Other roads

——— Main railway

— —v— Vehicular Ferries

— · — · — International Boundary

Built-up area

County boundaries

3 Page number of adjoining map

Heights above sea level in feet

3000 and above

1000-3000

200-1000

0-200

•1786 Spot height

Scale 1:1,013,760

0   25   50 miles

0   40   80 km

© RNP 1983

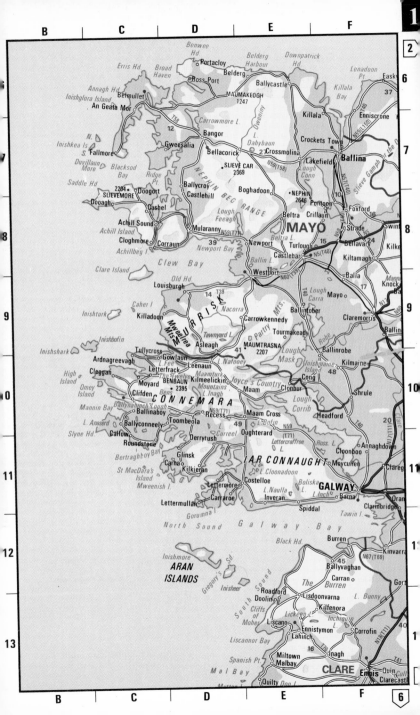

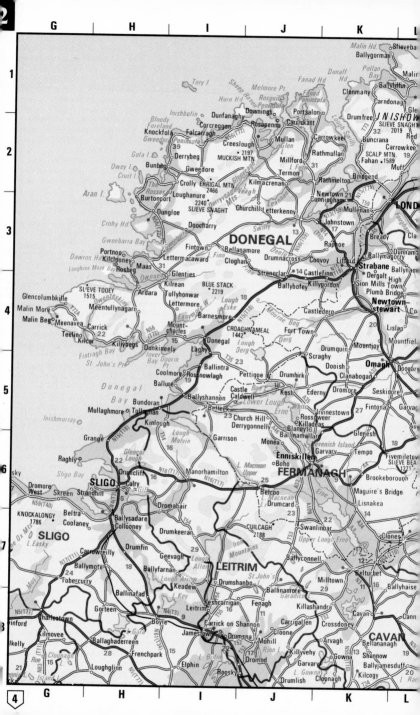

2

1

Malin Hd. Shevebe
Ballygorman
Malin

Tory I. Pollan
Fanad Hd. Dunaff Bay Ballyliffin
Melmore Pt Hd. Clonmany
Sheep Haven Bay Rosguill Carndonagh
Horn Hd. Peninsula Fanad INISHOW
Inishbofin Dunfanaghy Downings Peninsula Drumfree SLIEVE SNAGH
Bloody Corcreggan Rosapenna Portsalon Lough Swilly T73 2019
Foreland Knockfola Falcarragh Carrickart SCALP MTN. Red
Gweedore Peninsula Mullan Carrowkeel Buncrana 32 19
2 Gola I. 39 Creeslough Carrowkee
Derrybeg Glen Rathmullan Fahan 1589 Carrowke
Owey I. Bunbeg Gweedore 2197 Millford L. Fern 31 Muff
Cruit I. MUCKISH MTN Termon Rathmelton Bridgend
The Crolly ERRIGAL MTN Kilmacrenan Newtown 21 Mullenan LOND
Aran I. Rosses Loughanure 2466 Veagh Cunningham T59 Cla
Burtonport 2240 Churchill Letterkenny St. Johnstown 17 Lifford Dunnam
3 Dungloe SLIEVE SNAGHT Mts Swilly 13 Raphoe Bready
Crohy Hd. Doocharry Bellanamore Convoy Lifford Ballymagorry
Gweebarra Bay Fintown **DONEGAL** Drumacross Strabane
Portnoo Lettermacaward Finn Cloghan Stranorlar 14 Castlefinn Dergalt High
Dawros Hd. Kilclooney Maas 31 Glenties Ballybofey Killygordon Sion Mills Town Plumb Bridge
Loughros More Bay Rosbeg Owenea Kilrean BLUE STACK Newtown
Ardara Tullyhonwar 2219 stewart
4 Glencolumbkille SLIEVE TOOEY Lettermore Lough 18 Castlederg 20 Lislap
Malin More 1515 Meentullynagarn Barnesmore Eske Mountfiel
Malin Beg Meenavea Mount- CROAGHNAMEAL Fort Town Mountjoy Omagh
Teelin Carrick charles 2240 1442 Derg Drumquin Dooish
Kilcar 22 Killybegs 15 Donegal Lough Scraghy Clanabogan
Fintragh Bay Dunkineely Laghy Derg Drumhirk Dromore Seskinore
St. John's Pt Inver Doorin T35 23 Ballintra Pettigoe Irvinestown Fintona Garvag
Bay Coolmore Rossnowlagh Castle Boa I. 18 Rossweer 27 Au
5 Donegal Ballure 19 Caldwell Kesh Killadeas
Bay Bundoran Ballyshannon Belleek Lower Lough Ederny Blaney16 Glenesh 18
Inishmurray Mullaghmore Tullaghan 23 Church Hill Erne Whites Monea Ballinamallard Tempo Fivemiletow
Grange Kinlough Derrygonnelly Garvary SLIEVE BEA
Glencar Lough Garrison **Enniskillen** 1721
6 Raghly Lough 22 Melvin Manorhamilton Belcoo Boho FERMANAGH Brookeborough
sky Sligo Bay Drumcliff 16 Upper 25 L. Macnean Maguire's Bridge
Dromore Calry L. Macnean Drumcard Lisnakea
West Skreen Strandhill **SLIGO** Gill Dromahair 14
N59(T40) CUILCAGH Swanlinbar Clones
KNOCKALONGY Beltra Ballysadare Drumkeeran 2188 Upper Lough Erne 12
7 1786 Coolaney Colloney Iron Ballyconnell Belturbet
SLIGO Geevagh 29 Mountains 11 16 Ballyhaise
L. Easky Carrowreilly Drumfin Lough St. John's Milltown
Ballymote 18 Ballyfarnan Allen 29 Cavan
Tobercurry 24 Keadew LEITRIM Killashandra Crossdoney CAVAN
Ballinafad Key Drumshanbo Ballinamore Garadice Arvagh
Gorteen Leitrim Keshcarrigan Fenagh 11 Bellananagh
8 nford Charlestown N4(T3) Carrick on Shannon Cloone Carrigallen Shannow
Kilmovee Boyle Jamestown Drumsna Mohill Killyvehy Gowna 13 19
lkelly Ballaghaderreen Elphin Rinn L. Garvary Ballyjamesduff
21 Frenchpark 15 Roosky Dromod L. Gowna Kilcogy
Loughglinn Drumlish Cloonagh T24

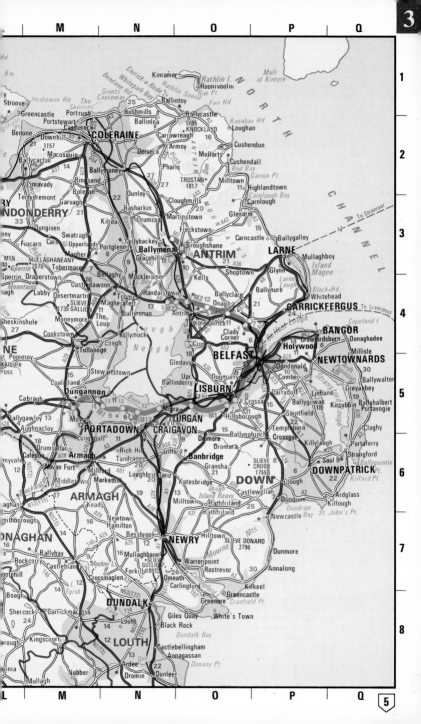

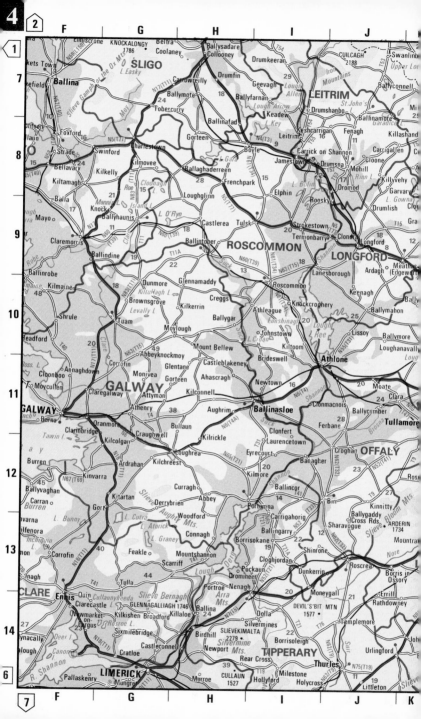

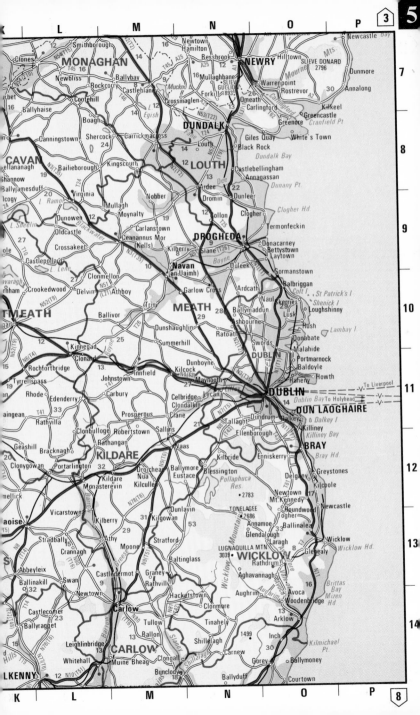

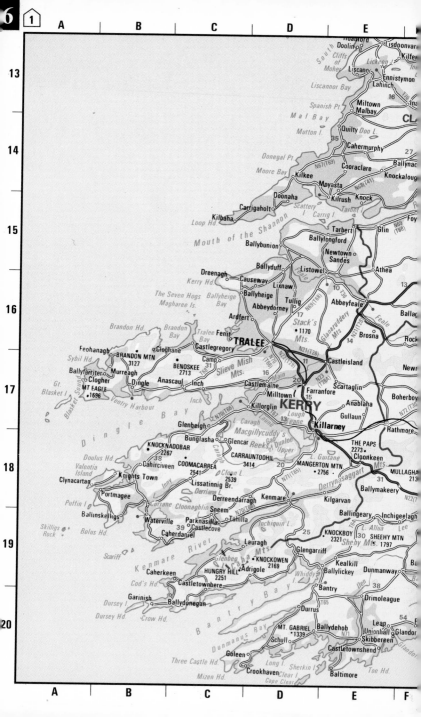

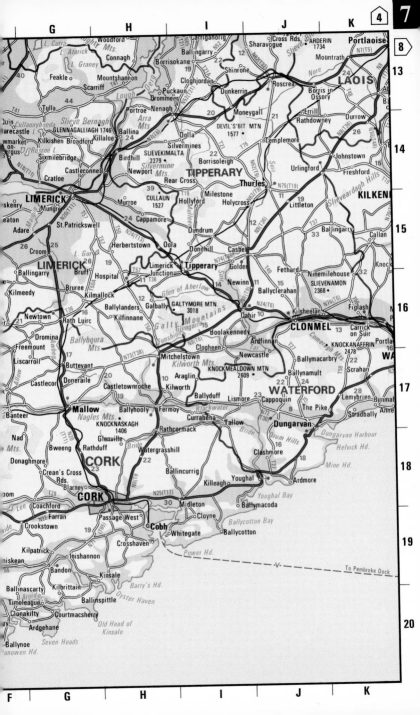

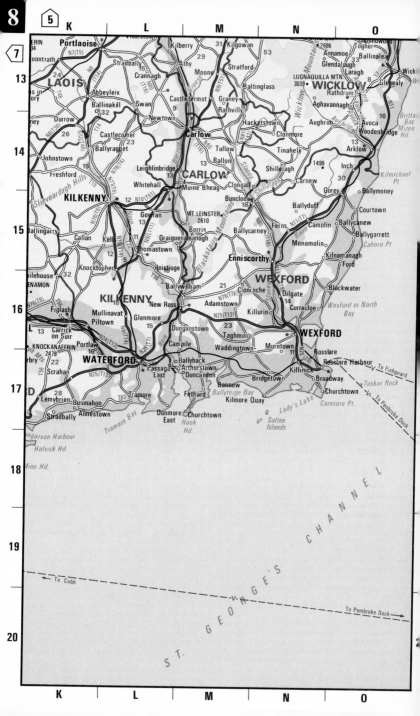

Architectural glossary

Abutment Structure that resists the thrust of an arch or vault.

Ambulatory 'A place for walking'; an arcade; aisle behind the altar at the east end of a church.

Antae Pilasters at the projecting ends of a portico.

Apse Large domed or arched recess at the end of a church.

Arcade Series of arches on columns.

Ashlar Stones hewn square and laid in regular patterns with fine joints.

Ashlaring Upright timbers used in an attic to break the acute angle between roof and floor.

Bailey Fortified enclosure; open area within a castle. Also called a ward.

Baroque 17thC Italian style; lavishly ornamented, dynamic spatial effects.

Barrow Earth burial mound.

Bas-relief Carving projecting slightly from base, used for ornamentation.

Bastion Projection from outer wall of a castle or fortification.

Bawn Fortified enclosure adjoining a castle or tower house.

Beehive hut Small corbelled stone hut in the shape of an old-style beehive.

Bell-cote Bell turret, usually at the west end of a towerless church.

Blind arcade Succession of arches along a wall, typically Romanesque.

Buttress Mass of stone or brick built against a wall to support it.

Cairn Burial mound made of rubble.

Cantilever Structural piece projecting beyond the line of support.

Castellated Decorated like a castle, with turrets, battlements, etc.

Chancel East end of church, where the altar is normally placed.

Chapter house Assembly building attached to church or cathedral.

Choir Section of church where services are sung, usually east end.

Classical Style inspired by that of ancient Greece and Rome.

Colonnade Row of columns supporting a frieze and cornice.

Corbel Supporting projection.

Corinthian Column style with fluted shaft and bell-shaped capital.

Cornice Projecting ornamental moulding on a wall, door or window.

Crenellated With battlements.

Cupola Small domed roof or domed turret on a roof; inside of a dome.

Curtain wall Outer wall of a castle.

Decorated Second stage of English Gothic, early 14thC. Characteristic: geometrical tracery.

Doric Column style with inclined projections at the base of the cornice.

Dressings Worked, finished stones.

Early English First stage of English Gothic, 13thC. Characteristic: lancet windows with little or no tracery.

Earthwork Prehistoric defence of concentric ditches on a hilltop.

Edge moulding English Gothic ornament of semicircular section.

Façade Main face of a building.

Fan-vaulting Vault of inverted concave cones, overlaid with curved ribs to produce a fan-like pattern.

Fenestration Arrangement of the windows.

Folly Architectural joke or oddity.

Frieze Decorative band, especially above a door or window.

Gable Triangular part of the wall at the ends of a ridge roof.

Georgian Style of the period 1714–1830; neo-Palladian.

Gothic Style including Early English, Decorated and Perpendicular. Characteristic: pointed arch and vault.

Gothic Revival Revival of Gothic style in 18thC and 19thC.

Hill fort Fortified hilltop settlement, typical of the Iron Age.

Hip External angle formed by joining of sloping roof pieces.

Ionic Column style with a spiral scroll on the capital and basal moulding.

Jacobean Style popular 1603–1625; blend of Gothic and classical forms.

Keep Massive inner tower of a castle.

Lancet Tall, narrow, pointed window.

Machicolation Projecting parapet on a castle wall, with openings for dropping missiles on attackers.

Motte Steep earth mound topped by a keep and surrounded by a deep ditch.

Mouldings Projecting or recessed bands used to ornament a flat surface.

Nave Main body of a church.

Neoclassical Revival of classical style in 18thC and 19thC.

Oratory Chapel for private prayer.

Palladian 16thC Italian style

Pallisade   Protective fence of stakes.

Parapet   Low protective wall on a bridge, cornice or balcony.

Pargetting   Ornamental plasterwork, incised or modelled with patterns.

Pavilion   Building connected by wings to a main block; projection.

Pedestal   Base for a column or statue.

Pediment   Triangular gable crowning façade or finishing a sloping roof.

Perpendicular   Third stage of English Gothic, 15thC. Characteristic: strong vertical tracery, large windows.

Piano nobile   Raised main floor of a Renaissance building.

Piazza   Open area amid buildings.

Pier   Square column, used to support a beam, lintel or arch.

Pilaster   Rectangular column, projecting slightly from a wall.

Presbytery   Part of a church reserved for clergy, usually in the eastern arm.

The text introduced to the British Isles in the 17thC. Characteristic: symmetry and pedimented central block.

Regency   Early 19thC style. Characteristic: elegant bow-fronted terraces.

Rococo   Fanciful interior decorative style. Characteristic: plant motifs.

Rotunda   Circular domed building.

Rustication   Rough stonework with deep joints.

Sedilia   Series of seats for the clergy on the south side of the chancel.

String course   Horizontal moulding.

Stucco   Plaster or cement on a façade.

Tessellation   Floor or wall mosaic.

Timber-framing   Wooden frame filled in with plaster, brick, stone, etc.

Tracery   Ornamental carving.

Transept   Transverse arm of a church.

Triforium   Gallery above nave arcades.

Vault   Arched roof or ceiling.

Vernacular style   Native or local style.

Victorian   Style popular 1830–1901; Gothic Revival and neoclassical.

Wattle and daub   Interlaced twigs and clay.

Fine Romanesque portal at Clonfert Cathedral, Co Galway

Irish–English glossary

The words given in bold type are Irish words, which are followed on occasion by common anglicisations in italics. Both the Irish language and its anglicised version contain many variants, so this list necessarily presents only a selection of forms.

Abha, (genitive: **abhann**)   River.
Achadh   Field; a land.
Aill (also **faill**)   Cliff.
Aonach   Fair; assembly.
Ard   Height; hill; high.
Áth (genitive: **átha**)   Ford.

Baile, *bally*   Town; townland; home.
Balla (also **falla**)   Wall.
Bán, *bawn*   Plain; field; white.
Beag, *beg*   Small.
Béal, *bel*   Mouth.
Bealach, *ballagh*   Way; passage.
Bean sí, *banshee*   Fairy-woman, traditionally a harbinger of death.
Beann (also **binn**), *ben*   Peak; headland.
Bearna   Gap.
Buaile, *booley*   Small grazing field; milking place in summer pasturage; hence, a hill dwelling.
Buí   Yellow.
Bullán (also **bollán**), *bullaun*   Large round stone; bowl.
Bun   Base; foundation.

Caiseal, *cashel*   Bulwark; stone fort.
Caol, *keel*   Narrow.
Carraig, *carrick*   Rock.
Cathair, *caher*   City; stone fort.
Ceann, *ken*   Head; headland.
Cill, *kil*   Monastic cell; church; churchyard.
Cloch, *clogh*   Stone.
Clochán (also **clachán**)   Stepping-stones; an old stone structure.
Cluain, *clon*   Meadow; watershed.
Cnoc, *knock*   Hill.
Coire, *corrie*   Cauldron; whirlpool; hence, mountain pool, cirque.
Crannóg   Wooden frame; lake dwelling.
Cúl   Back.
Curach   Coracle (light boat of tarred canvas stretched over a frame of laths), still made in the south.
Currach (also **corrach**)   Marsh.

Dáil Éireann   Lower House of the Irish legislature.
Dair (genitive: **dara**), *dare*   Oak.
Dearg, *derg*   Red.
Doire, *derry*   Oak wood; grove; thicket.
Domhnach, *donagh*   Sunday; a church reputedly founded by St Patrick.

Drom (dative: **druim**)   Back; ridge; possibly the origin of *drumlin*, a hillock.
Dubh   Black.
Dún, *doon*   Fort.

Eaglais, *aglish*   Church.
Eanach, *annagh*   Marsh.
Eas (genitive: **easa**)   Waterfall.

Feart, *fert*   Mound; tumulus; grave.
Feis   Festival; assembly.
Feis cheoil   Musical festival with competitions.
Fianna   Legendary warrior bands led by Fionn Mac Cumhaill (*Finn McCool*). The Fenians took their name from the Fianna.
Fir (plural of **Fear**)   Men.
Fir bolg   Pre-Gaelic invaders of Ireland, possibly a branch of the Belgae mentioned by Caesar.
Fleadh cheoil   Festival of traditional Irish music.

Gaeltacht   Irish-speaking district, or all Irish-speaking districts together.
Gallán, *gallaun*   Standing stone; menhir; monolith.
Gallóglach, *gallowglass*   Soldier retained by Irish chiefs up to the 16th century.
Garda (plural: **gardaí**)   Policeman; police force.
Gleann, *glen*   Valley.
Grianán   Summer house; palace.

Inis (genitive: **inse**), *ennis*   Island; river meadow; milking place.

Lios, *liss*   Ring fort; fairy fort.
Loch, *lough*   Lake; fjord; the sea.

Magh, *moy*   Plain.
Mainistir, *monaster*   Monastery; abbey.
Maoil, *mull*   Rounded summit.
Móin (genitive: **móna**)   Moor; bogland; peat.
Mór, *more*   Big; great.
Mná (plural of **bean**)   Women.
Muc, *muck*   Pig.

Ogham   Early alphabet, composed of 20 characters made up of vertical or diagonal strokes crossing a continuous horizontal line, chiefly found on standing stones marking pre-Christian burials.
Oileán, *illaun*   Island.

Oireachtas   The Irish legislature.

Poitín, *poteen*   Illicitly distilled spirits, generally made from potatoes.

Ráth   Fairy fort; ring fort.
Rinn   Point; promontory.
Ros, *ross*   Wood; wooded headland; promontory.
Rua, *roe*   Red (-haired); reddish-brown.

Sceilg, *skellig*   Steep rock; crag.
Sean, *shan*   Old.
Seanad Éireann   Upper House of the Irish legislature.
Sliabh (plural: **sléibhte**), *slieve*   Mountain.
Sráid, *strad*   Street; village.
Suí, *see*   Seat

Taoiseach   Leader; chief; the Prime Minister of Ireland.
Teachta Dála   Member of the Dáil or Lower House of the Irish legislature (abbrev.: **TD**).
Teampall   Protestant church; temple; graveyard.
Tír, *tyr*   Country; a land.
Tobar (also **tiobraid**), *tober*, *tubber*   Well.
Tóchar, *togher*   Causeway; culvert.
Tráigh (also **trá**)   Beach.
Tuaim (genitive: **tuama**)   Tumulus.
Tuama   Tomb; tombstone.
Tuatha Dé Danann   Legendary pre-Celtic people.
Tulach, *tully*   Hillock; mound.
Turlach, *turlough*   Winter lake, dry or marshy in summer.

An example of Ogham script, from the 'Book of Ballymote'

Introduction to Ireland

The westernmost island of the European continental shelf, Ireland covers 32,524 square miles, is 302 miles long and over 189 miles across at its widest point. A land of mild winters and temperate summers, it is generally an easy-going place with a friendly nature.

There are 32 counties, divided historically into four provinces: Munster, Leinster, Ulster and Connacht. Six of the nine counties of Ulster—Antrim, Armagh, Down, Fermanagh, Londonderry and Tyrone—make up Northern Ireland. The population is over 4,730,000, of whom about a third live in Northern Ireland.

A central limestone plain, covered with peat bogs and drained by the River Shannon, underlies most of the country and along the coast tower mighty hills and mountains. To the south and south west, a huge belt of red sandstone and shale is carved into spectacular rocky gorges and wooded valleys by beautiful winding rivers. In Co Galway and Co Mayo, to the west, are magnificent mountain ranges of granite, quartzite and igneous rock and the central plain slides gently down to the sea between Sligo and the southern edge of Co Donegal. North of Carlingford Lough in the east are the granite Mountains of Mourne, balanced by the Wicklow Mountains south of Dublin; the north east of the country is filled with a huge basaltic plateau enhanced by the nine Glens of Antrim.

Lough Gill, from Co Leitrim

There are over 3,000 miles of breathtaking coastline, 9,000 miles of rivers and some 800 lakes; the abundance of water partly explains the lush rolling grasslands that cover so much of the country and give it the name of the 'Emerald Isle'. The largest lake in the British Isles is Lough Neagh, to the west of Belfast, which covers 153 square miles; the highest mountain is 3,414-foot-high Carrantuohill, near Killarney in Co Kerry; and the longest river is the Shannon, which traverses 230 miles.

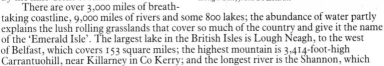

Renvyle, Connemara Co. Galway.

Once the home of the saints and scholars of early Christian Europe, Ireland is a country rich in prehistoric remains, distinctive Celtic high crosses, famous Romanesque monasteries, powerful Anglo-Norman castles, sturdy Plantation bawns and handsome Palladian mansions. It also offers some of the finest horse racing in the world; lakes, rivers and coastal seas teeming with fish; and some of the most exhilarating walking country to be found anywhere.

Ireland is a lyrical land, washed by sea and ocean and edged with dramatic cliffs or curving scimitars of dune-backed beach. It is a land of myths and legends and undying memories. Visitors can still find tranquillity in its leaf-shaded glens, along the banks of its trout-filled rivers or on the slopes of its heather-covered mountains.

Climate

Listening to the Irish discussing the weather invariably conjures up pictures of endless rain and this is not far from the truth. The rain has its advantages however: if the climate were Mediterranean, Ireland would surely be packed with visitors from coast to coast and would lose much of its rugged and peaceful charm. Even in the rain, its lush green pastures and mountains veiled in mist are memorable; when the clouds lift and a shaft of sunlight washes across valley or mountainside the effect is breathtaking.

Irish weather tends to be consistent throughout the country as the land mass is relatively small. The climate is equable and the winters invariably mild, snow being rare except on the highest peaks. There is generally a soft, south westerly wind warmed by the drifting waters of the Gulf Stream, which wash the island's coast on both sides. The coldest months are January and February, when temperatures drop to 39°F–45°F (4°C–7°C), and the hottest are July and August, with temperatures ranging from 61°F–75°F (16°C–24°C). The sunniest months are May and June with up to 6½ hours of sunshine a day and the driest month is normally April. The driest area is a narrow coastal strip around Dublin and the sunniest is the country's extreme south eastern tip. Even in the driest areas, average annual rainfall can reach 30 inches; in the centre of the country the range is 30–45 inches and in the low-lying areas, 45–60 inches. Humidity ranges from 70–90 percent.

History

Prehistoric Ireland (6000BC–AD1stC)
During the Ice Age, a wide neck of land connected Ireland with England whilst an even wider plateau connected England to the continent. After the thaw (c10,000BC), hunters began to arrive from Scandinavia; they settled first along the seashore and in the wooded Bann Valley, where flint was in plentiful supply, and gradually spread. By 6000BC, Ireland was at last cut off from Britain, and by 3000BC the nomadic life of the hunter gave way to that of the farmer. New colonists came from the Middle East in search of land to cultivate; they were vastly more sophisticated than their predecessors and formed a distinct culture. They manufactured simple flat axes, decorative pottery vessels and ornaments made from gold gleaned from the Wicklow rivers. They built wedge-shaped gallery graves, chamber tombs and great stone circles for religious ceremonies. By about 1200BC a new influx of settlers from the continent brought with them tools and weapons, including a short, heavy sword and protective bronze and leather shields. They lived in wattle and daub huts, often grouped in stockades on crannogs.

In 600BC, towards the end of the Irish Bronze Age, the first Celtic invaders arrived from the Mediterranean lands. A diverse group of peoples linked by a common language and led by powerful clan chiefs, they were armed with superior iron weaponry and had long dominated central and western Europe. By 150BC the Celts were firmly established in a series of small kingdoms.

Early Celtic Ireland (5thC BC–AD6thC)
Late Iron Age Ireland was a land of hill forts and chariot-riding warlords. The first to settle were the Nemedians. They were overrun by the Fromorian pirates, followed by the Firbolgs; they were defeated by the Tuatha dé Danaan, magic-practising tribes of the goddess Dana, who were later driven underground by the Milesians, giving rise to the tales of leprechauns in Celtic mythology. The clan chiefs lived in ring forts or lake dwellings while their clansmen lived on farms, often protected by an earthen rampart and stockade. The high point of Celtic culture was the introduction of La Tène style, named after a site in Switzerland. Characterised by remarkably sophisticated abstract decorative work applied to metalwork and stone, it reached Ireland by the 2ndC BC.

Pre-Christian Ireland was an agricultural country of some 500,000 people divided up into about 150 small local kingdoms called *tuatha*. Left alone by the Romans despite the conquest of Britain, the numerous kingdoms fought each other for survival and supremacy. The two key institutions of Irish life were the *fine* or joint family, which catered for social needs, and the tuath, which was primarily concerned with political issues. In each tuath, authority was in the hands of a king elected by the most powerful nobles; his primary functions were to lead his clansmen in war and to preside over the *óenach*, a regular assembly of the tuath where public and private matters were decided and sporting contests held. These small pastoral communities were often grouped together, with the king of the dominant tuath having authority over all of them. These groups, in turn, were later gathered into five principal kingdoms: Connacht in the west, Munster in the south west, South Leinster in the south east, Leinster in the centre and east and Ulster in the north. By the 5thC, Niall of the Nine Hostages and his descendants, the Uí Néill, ruled over the midlands and the north and promoted themselves as *ard-rí* (over-kings). Every three years a great assembly was held at Tara, 'the capital of the Irish'. Here games and poetry competitions were presided over by the Uí Néill over-king. It was not until the Viking hordes swept through Ireland, however, that the high kingship became a reality: Máel Sechnaill I, of the southern Uí Néill, killed Thorgestr of the Vikings in AD845 and seized the reins of power.

The dawn of Christianity (AD5thC–8thC)
The first country outside the Roman world to be won over to the new Christian faith, Ireland became a refuge for scholars from occupied Gaul following the Barbarian breakthrough of the Rhine frontier in AD407. In AD431 a bishop was appointed to Ireland from Rome but it was a Romanised British Celt, St Patrick, who was to fasten Christianity in the Irish heart. After escaping slavery in Ireland, St Patrick fled to Gaul and apprenticed

Statue of St Patrick, Saul, Co Down

himself to St Germanus at Auxerre. In AD432 he returned to convert the Irish and established a church in Armagh, near Emain Macha, capital of the ancient kingdom of Ulster. Despite considerable opposition (especially from the druids) huge numbers of converts embraced Christianity. Within a century new monasteries had ousted the old patrician foundations to become the centres of learning. A 6thC monastic community would be upward of 100 monks, leading a life of self denial, with frequent fast days. The scriptures were studied and often committed to memory and many monks had extensive knowledge of Latin classical authors as well as a lively interest in contemporary writings. Many monks were skilled smiths, producing fine metalwork such as the 8thC Ardagh Chalice, now in the National Museum of Ireland; others were scribes, creating beautiful illuminated manuscripts such as the 7thC 'Book of Durrow' or the early

Ardagh Chalice, Dublin

9thC 'Book of Kells', both in Trinity College, Dublin. These men spread both their religion and their learning far and wide; many travelled to Britain and the Continent, founding monasteries as they went. This gentle holy place must have seemed an easy conquest to the warring Norsemen who invaded in the late 8thC.

The Viking wars (9thC–10thC)
The Vikings were traders as well as pirates, great craftsmen as well as seamen of legendary skill. Having colonised the islands of Shetland and Orkney, a band of helmeted warriors armed with heavy swords and iron spears alighted from their longships on the

beach of Lambay Island in AD795. This was the beginning of two centuries of looting and pillaging. In AD839 the great Viking chief Thorgestr navigated a fleet into Lough Neagh and in 841 occupied Armagh, the ecclesiastical capital. The same year the Vikings established the first of their fortified settlements beside the Liffey, which would eventually grow into Dublin. In AD845 Máel Sechnaill I slew Thorgestr and became king. Following his death in AD862, Ireland was plunged into 150 years of anarchy.

Brian Boru (926–1014)
Ireland was reunited against the Vikings in the 11thC by a Munster soldier-king, Brian Boru. A legendary resistance leader and the most famous king in early Irish history, he and his brother had already routed the Norsemen at Limerick in AD964. Norse power collapsed in Munster by AD978 and a year later Boru was in control of the south. In AD997 he defeated the King of Tara, who then joined forces with him to attack the remaining Norse settlements. In 1005 Boru was acclaimed 'Emperor of the Irish' at Armagh. Only eight years later, however, the Kingdom of Leinster rebelled and joined forces with the Vikings. They confronted Brian Boru at Clontarf near Dublin on Good Friday, 1014. They were routed in the greatest battle in early Irish history but Boru and his son and grandson were slain and Ireland was once more plunged into anarchy. Rory O'Conor finally established some semblance of order between 1166 and 1198.

Church reforms (11thC–12thC)
With the Viking threat now a thing of the past, many of the Irish made pilgrimages to Rome, where reforms were taking place. This contact, combined with the influence of

Canterbury on the newly Christianised Norse towns of southern Ireland in the 11thC, created sufficient incentive for the reforming clerics. In 1111 a national synod was held at Ráith Bresail near Cashel; as a result, the old monastic organisation was replaced by 24 episcopal sees. One of the greatest Irish church reformers was St Malachy; he introduced the Cistercians to Ireland and their arrival heralded the end of the traditional Irish monasteries. He also organised the Synod of Kells in 1152, at which Ireland was given its basic diocesan organisation, which divided the country into 36 bishoprics and 4 archbishoprics. The influx of continental monastic orders also had considerable influence on Irish art and architecture. One of the most magnificent examples is the Romanesque Cormac's Chapel at Cashel, 1127–34.

The Anglo-Norman invasion (1169–71)
During the struggles for political supremacy between Rory O'Conor of Connacht and Murtough MacLochlainn, King of Ailech in the north, a personal enmity between two of their followers brought drastic consequences. Dermot MacMurrough, King of Leinster and ally of MacLochlainn, abducted Devorguilla, the wife of O'Conor's ally O'Rourke of

Arboe Cross, Co Tyrone

Breffini, in 1152. Determined to destroy MacMurrough, O'Rourke ousted him in 1166; MacMurrough sailed to France, where he sought and was given the aid of Henry II of England. The powerful Norman barons, including John de Courcy, Walter de Burgo and the Earl of Pembroke (Strongbow) rallied to his cause.

An expeditionary force landed at Bannow Bay in May 1169 and captured Wexford. This was followed by a larger expeditionary force and then by the main army under Strongbow; he landed near Waterford and took it within a few days. By 1171 many of the principal cities were in Strongbow's hands. Henry II worried lest Strongbow's successes might encourage him to set up an independent kingdom on England's flank. He landed at Waterford with a fully equipped army in 1171 prepared to assert his authority. Ireland was divided up: Strongbow was granted Leinster, John de Courcy was given Ulster and Hugh de Lacy, Meath. Henry kept Wexford, Waterford and Dublin and its environs, known as the Pale because of the wooden palisade that surrounded the area. (This is the origin of the phrase 'beyond the pale' to refer to something uncouth or uncontrollable.) This was to be England's power base in Ireland until 1921. Rory O'Conor, having pledged himself to recognise Henry II as his overlord, had his sovereignty over Connacht confirmed by the Treaty of Windsor.

The Norman occupation (1171–15thC)
Although the well-disciplined and armed Norman troops had little trouble defeating the Irish, maintaining order after the conquest presented more problems. A line of formidable fortresses was built across Co Kerry and another stretched along the coast from Cork to Bantry Bay. In Ulster, towns grew and monastic institutions were built near the forts at Carrickfergus and Coleraine. Other centres were established at Carlingford, Downpatrick, Dundrum, Dromore and Newry. The land-hungry Normans began to encroach on Gaelic lands by both legal and violent means. Alliances were made and marriages arranged between Norman knights and Irish princesses. King John visited Ireland in 1210 to establish English authority but by the mid-13thC the Norman barons controlled virtually all of Ireland.

Carrickfergus Castle, Co Antrim

English colonisation in the Middle Ages (13thC–14thC)
Colonisation brought profound changes in Ireland; towns flourished and fairs, markets and trade guilds were established. The Normans were the first to give Ireland a centralised administration, with a Chancellor of the Exchequer. A jury system was established, sheriffs appointed, Irish coinage minted and, in 1297, the first parliament of elected representatives assembled in Dublin. Between 1224 and the late 13thC there was a new influx of continental monastic orders, which established foundations throughout the island. Trade flourished; modern methods of agriculture transformed the cultivated land into a viable asset. Ports like Dublin were expanded and new ones, like Galway, planned and walled towns were built along strategic commercial routes.

The old Gaelic Brehon Law was generally enforced in those areas beyond the Pale, but those living within the Pale were subject to English Law. Many Gaelic chiefs remained stubbornly independent, mounting frequent attacks upon the colonies. With the resounding Gaelic victory at the battle of Callann in 1261, the limits of the colony within the Pale shrank as Gaelic Ireland recovered some of its lost lands. Many of the Normans became increasingly naturalised, becoming in a sense, 'Irish' chiefs. Swamped by Gaelic culture, they gradually began to adopt the language, customs and manners of the people among whom they lived. Some, like the de Burghs, who became the Burkes of Connacht, virtually 'went native' and were almost indistinguishable from their Gaelic neighbours.

In 1315 there was another concerted effort at revival by the Irish. A year after King Robert of Scotland's defeat of the English at Bannockburn, they invited his brother, Edward Bruce, to Ireland. Crowning him high-king, they set out to create a united Celtic kingdom, but at the Battle of Fachairt in 1318 Bruce was killed and the army broken. In 1366 the Kilkenny parliament drew up statutes to prohibit fraternisation with the Irish. Gaelic chieftains, now better equipped and reinforced by Scottish mercenaries, began to encroach on the Pale. The 14thC Anglo-Norman colonists sought both financial and military help from England and in 1394 Richard II landed with a powerful army at Waterford. He defeated the great Art MacMurrough of Leinster and brought to heel the remaining Gaelic chiefs. War broke out again and in 1399 Richard returned. By now things were out of hand and Richard's army was unable to tame the rebels; meanwhile Henry of Lancaster, landing in England, had seized the throne. Richard returned but was too late to save his crown. With his abdication, the English kings' lordship over Ireland ceased until the accession of the Tudors in the 15thC.

Gaelic resurgence & the Geraldine Supremacy (c1400–1534)

The Gaelic resurgence continued, particularly in the north. Eóghan O'Neill, one of the leaders of the Irish force, had by 1430 received the submission of both the Normans and the Gaels in the midlands. The assimilation of the Anglo-Normans continued, although the three great Anglo-Norman lordships—the Butlers, earls of Ormonde and the Fitzgeralds (or Geraldines), earls of Kildare and Desmond—owed loyalty to the crown. The Geraldines had married into Gaelic Irish families and could be seen, in many senses, as a bulwark of Gaelic civilisation. When the Wars of the Roses broke out in England in 1455 the Geraldines, backed by their Gaelic relatives, supported the Yorkist cause. Their arch-enemies, the Butlers, backed the Lancastrians. However all three earls were advocates of home rule: an Irish parliament not dominated by the English Crown.

With the rise of the Lancastrians under Henry Tudor in England, Ireland was once again involved in Yorkist plots. The Irish earls supported the pretenders, Lambert Simnel and Perkin Warbeck. Fearing further troubles, Henry VII sent Sir Edward Poynings to Ireland. In a series of ordinances he proscribed Irish laws, customs and dress and appointed men loyal to England as constables of the principal castles. The most repressive measure was known as Poyning's Law, forbidding Irish parliaments to meet without royal consent. The law was not repealed until the late 18th C. The Geraldines were falsely accused of treachery and in 1534 Kildare was summoned to London, leaving his eldest son, Thomas, in charge of the country. Fed a false report that his father had been executed, Thomas charged into Dublin with a band of armed men, each with a silken fringe to his helmet (hence the name 'Silken Thomas'). The rebellion was crushed by a powerful English army equipped with heavy guns. The Earl died and Silken Thomas was executed in London in 1537. The rule of the Fitzgeralds was over.

The Tudor conquest (1534–1603)

In 1541 Henry was declared King of Ireland by the Irish parliament. Unable economically to continue military rule, the king adopted a policy of unification. By a process of 'discreet persuasion', by the time of his death in 1547 he had received the submission of over 40 of the principal Gaelic and Anglo-Irish chiefs. Persuading them to abandon many of their old Gaelic ways as well as to learn English, Henry had clearly achieved his initial objective, the 'anglicising' of the peoples of Ireland. Part of this policy was religious; in 1536, the king was appointed Supreme Head of the Church in Ireland, despite considerable opposition.

Queen Mary, a Catholic, restored the old religion during her reign, but also adopted the much-debated 'Plantation' policy. The principle of this policy was the ousting of Gaelic and naturalised lords in favour of loyal British settlers, called 'Planters'. In 1556 Laois and Offaly were planted with settlers from England and Wales. Many Jesuit priests entered Ireland and by the time Elizabeth I succeeded to the throne in 1558 the Catholic community put up strong resistance to any legislation designed to make Ireland Protestant. The English seizure of Gaelic estates continued and in 1595 the Great Hugh O'Neill, Earl of Tyrone, declared war. O'Neill submitted in 1603; summoned to London and fearing execution, he fled in 1607 for exile on the Continent with over 90 of Ulster's leading families. This 'Flight of the Earls' left Ulster leaderless.

Colonisation of Ulster & the rebellion of 1641

In 1609 the Plantation of the north began in earnest. Settlers were brought in from England and the Scottish lowlands; Catholics were barred from positions of authority in both public and civil life; government was in the control of the English parliament. The bitter resentment of the Irish boiled over in the rebellion of 1641. Demanding civil and religious rights for all, and the abolition of Poynings Law, the Catholic Confederacy was formed at Kilkenny in October 1642. Backing Charles I in the English Civil War, the Confederate Army proceeded to win several victories in Ireland.

Ireland under Cromwell (1649–58)
Following his victory in the English Civil War, Oliver Cromwell landed at Dublin in 1649 with his 'New Model' army. He stormed Drogheda, massacring the garrison; he then took Wexford and laid waste Munster. The Confederation was dissolved and by 1652 the war was over. Cromwell's oppponents lost their estates and property rights; the Catholic Church was suppressed; thousands of Catholics were shipped to the West Indies; confiscated land was redistributed and Protestant settlers brought in to such an extent that Protestants now controlled the country.

Restoration & the Jacobite war (1660–1761)
The restoration of Charles II in 1660 did little to redress the wrongs of the previous decade. It was not until the succession of James II that vacancies were made for Catholics in the administration, the law and the army. The Protestants, fearing for their rights, sided with the Williamites when rebellion broke out in England; Stuart King James was backed by the Catholics. Deposed in 1688, James went to Ireland. The Irish reiterated their demands for home rule but the king insisted on retaining Poyning's Law, thus alienating even the Catholics. In 1690 the French sent 7,000 soldiers to Ireland and harried the English in the English Channel. The newly-crowned William of Orange landed at Carrickfergus and defeated James's army at the famous Battle of the Boyne. James fled. The Williamite forces took Dublin and eastern Ireland but Limerick put up an heroic defence led by Patrick Sarsfield. William returned to England but the war dragged on. A French commander, St Ruth, arrived to lead James's army (the Jacobites), now mainly composed of Irish soldiers. In June the English routed the Irish at Aughrim. Limerick surrendered with the Treaty of Limerick. The remains of the Jacobite army sailed for France and acquired the name, the 'Wild Geese'. With Ireland now defenceless and leaderless, the English conquest was at last complete. The new Irish parliament was entirely dominated by Protestants. Fearing that the 'Wild Geese' might invade again, they created the anti-Catholic Penal Laws, between 1695–1727. The social wrongs of this period were extreme: there was a famine in 1741 and a number of agrarian disturbances in Munster in 1761.

The Protestant nation (1775–1800)
The outbreak of the American War of Independence in 1775 dramatically influenced Irish politics. A Protestant Patriot Party emerged under the leadership of Henry Grattan and agitated for numerous reforms.
Westminster finally passed the first Catholic Relief Act in 1778, abolished trade restrictions in 1779 and acknowledged the legislative independence of Ireland in 1782. The revolutionary ideas of America and France spread quickly to Ireland and fear of republicanism pushed the English-controlled Dublin administration into seeking complete union with Great Britain. In October 1791, a young Protestant lawyer from Belfast, Theobald Wolfe Tone, founded the Society of United Irishmen. With their demands for Catholic emancipation and reforms of parliament rejected, the Society became increasingly revolutionary and in 1793 the Dublin government suppressed it. Wolfe Tone was sent to France to seek help and in December 1796 returned with a French fleet, but it was dispersed by bad weather and when Tone landed the following year he was caught; he later committed suicide. There followed a number of unsuccessful risings.

Statue of Wolfe Tone, Dublin

The Act of Union (1800)

William Pitt, the English prime minister, was determined to overcome the Irish parliament's resistance to the idea of Union. He secured votes by bribery and the Act of Union was passed in June 1800. Ireland became part of the United Kingdom in January the following year. The Act of Union united the Church of Ireland with the Church of England and London became the political centre. Another Irish rising was planned, led by Robert Emmet, but in July 1803 Emmet was captured and executed.

Daniel O'Connell (1775–1847)

Poverty and unemployment were widespread and George III had once more rejected pleas for Catholic emancipation. Just when he was most needed a new champion of the Catholics arose—Daniel O'Connell. The son of a smallholder from Kerry, he was called to the bar in 1798. Understanding the feelings of the peasantry, he sought to articulate their grievances and to achieve redress within the framework of the law. Elected MP for Co Clare in 1828 by an overwhelming majority, he was barred from taking his seat because he was a Catholic. The electors returned him a second time, and the government gave way. In 1829 the Emancipation Act officially opened parliament to Catholics and under the Whig (Liberal) government O'Connell secured an end to Protestant terrorism.

The Great Famine (1845–50)

Shortly before O'Connell's death in 1847, Ireland was plunged into the greatest catastrophe of its history. The potato crop, staple of the Irish diet, was blighted and the results were horrific: over 8,000 perished of starvation, typhus or cholera and many more fled penniless overseas. An unfeeling British government, ascribing the disaster to the peasants' laziness, did nothing. The exodus continued over the next 40–50 years and by 1920, over 4,400,000 emigrants had sailed for the United States alone.

The Fenians (1858)

Inspired by the ideas of Wolfe Tone, the Irish Republican Brotherhood or 'Fenians' was founded in 1858, pledged to independence through violence. A rising was attempted in 1867, but the government pre-empted it and imprisoned the leaders.

Gladstone and the Home Rule League (1869–92)

The Irish found a sympathetic ear in Gladstone. His liberalism and sense of justice led him to disestablish the Protestant State Church in 1869 and in 1870 to introduce a Land Act designed to protect Irish tenants. In the same year the Home Rule League was formed by Isaac Butt, a Protestant lawyer from Ulster. In the election of 1874, Butt's new party won over half the Irish seats and in 1877 passed to the man who was to be its true leader, Charles Stewart Parnell. The son of a country gentleman, Parnell was one of the great leaders of Irish democracy, second only to Daniel O'Connell. In 1879 he formed the Land League with Michael Davitt, a Fenian, and together they organised numerous demonstrations. Their main aims were peasant proprietorship and home rule. In 1881 a new Land Act was passed, providing for fixed tenure for tenants and fair rents; Parnell and Davitt, campaigning for more drastic measures, were imprisoned. Shortly after their release, a terrorist group called the 'Invincibles' assassinated Lord Frederick Cavendish, the new chief secretary, and his under-secretary, in Phoenix Park. Nevertheless, English opinion had become more liberal toward the 'Irish problem' and in 1885 the Ashbourne Land Act introduced state aid for farmers. In 1886 Gladstone presented his Home Rule Bill to parliament but it was rejected. The moral stance of the campaign for home rule was badly dented by Parnell's citation for adultery in 1890. In 1891 Parnell died and in 1892, with the defeat of Gladstone's second Home Rule Bill, the cause looked equally moribund.

Parnell Monument, Dublin

The growth of nationalism (1893–1914)

In 1893 the Gaelic League was founded by Hyde and MacNeill, aimed at reviving Irish culture. This was a period of great Irish literary revival. Arthur Griffith published his thesis on 'Sinn Fein' (we ourselves) in 1906, arguing that the Act of Union was illegal. With the return of the Liberals to power in Westminster that same year, home rule was once again a live issue. In 1912 yet another Home Rule Bill went before the Commons; it was passed in September 1914 but the arrival of World War I put it in abeyance yet again.

There was stubborn resistance to home rule in Ulster, led by Sir Edward Carson, a successful lawyer and MP for Trinity College, Dublin. Determined to defend the right to remain united with Great Britain, he raised an illegal army—the Ulster Volunteers. In Dublin another army, the Irish Volunteers, was set up to defend home rule. By 1914 Ireland had no less than four private armies. The Irish Republican Brotherhood, with the backing of Connolly's 'Citizens' Army', planned the Easter Rebellion of 1916.

The Easter Rebellion (1916)

Confined to Dublin, the rebellion was crushed within a week but appallingly harsh reprisals by the British government created massive public response. The republican Sinn Fein party won 73 of the total of 105 seats in the general election of 1918 and in January 1919 the Dáil declared itself free of Great Britain and began to establish its own administration. The Ulster Unionists, however, were also organising. The Anglo-Irish war that followed lasted until July 1921. Martial law was proclaimed and the Royal Irish Constabulary was reinforced by the notorious 'Black and Tans', recruited from British ex-servicemen fresh from the European front.

Partition (1921)

Britain signed a compromise treaty in December 1921, making the 26 southern counties into dominions. Six of the counties of Ulster elected by a majority to stay within the United Kingdom, with the proviso that they should have a separate parliament. Partition for the nationalists was the last straw. De Valera, who opposed the treaty, resigned as President in 1922. The Irish Republican Army (IRA) occupied the Dublin Four Courts in April 1922 and communal violence broke out in the north. In June 1922, Sir Henry Wilson, a hard-line Unionist, was assassinated by the IRA. In retaliation the Four Courts were shelled. Civil war broke out and much of the centre of Dublin was destroyed before the republicans, led by de Valera, agreed to lay down their arms in May 1923. The frontier of Northern Ireland was finally settled in 1925; meanwhile the Irish Free State became a member of the League of Nations. In 1926 de Valera formed the Fianna Fáil party (soldiers of destiny), which agreed to work within the established parliamentary system. In the 1932 election they achieved a sizable majority. The oath of allegiance to the crown was abolished and all institutional links severed. In 1937 a new constitution replaced the Irish Free State with that of Eire. Ireland finally left the British Commonwealth in 1949 to become the Republic of Ireland and was admitted to the United Nations in 1955.

In Northern Ireland, the rift between Protestant and Catholic factions continued to grow, in a population of which 40% were Catholics. Declared an illegal organisation by the Republic in 1936, the IRA nevertheless continued its sporadic bombing campaigns with a series of attacks in England during 1939. The sectarian violence of the 1960s and 1970s created an economic depression worse even than that of the 1930s. The Stormont parliament lost control and direct rule from Westminster was imposed in March 1972. Since then, sectarian riots have continued to flare in Ulster and have extended into England once more, with IRA bombings in Birmingham and London.

One history of Ireland is a story of private armies—from the early battles of the legendary Firbolgs and the Tuatha dé Danaan, to the soldier-kings like Brian Boru and the warring Norman barons. The armies these men formed were the forerunners of those of the early 20thC, such as James Connolly's Citizens' Army, Carson's Ulster Volunteers or the Irish Volunteers, which became the Irish Republican Army. Throughout its history, Ireland has been a warlike and troubled land, constantly invaded and torn with internal strife. It has suffered massacre, famine, oppression and more than its share of plain bad luck. Nevertheless it is a country of great physical beauty and has been the cradle of great literature from the earliest days; even now its enlightened tax laws encourage writers to seek its shores. The 'Irish problem', for centuries the bane of British government, has no immediately evident solution but the people and the land are still rich in much that has died in more peaceful nations.

Literary Ireland

Irish literature is primarily celebrated for lyric poetry and the short story but it is the epic sagas that raise it to the level of Greek mythology. Ireland has always been rich in orally transmitted folklore; at one time every parish had its own storyteller. This oral tradition gave rise to one of the first real vernacular literatures in Europe. Many of the sagas survive in classic illuminated manuscripts such as the 11thC–12thC 'Book of the Dun Cow', which were compiled in monastic settlements like Clonmacnois. These manuscripts tended to fall into one of three categories: those concerned with Irish culture and affairs but compiled by monks seeking self-imposed exile outside Ireland; those like the 'Book of Leinster', concerned with recording the compiler's version of Irish epics such as the 'Cattle Raid of Cooley' or the 'Great Tain'; and those produced in the years following the Norman invasion, such as the 'Book of Ballymote' or the 'Yellow Book of Lecan', which were anthologies of Irish learning. This early literature was written in Irish.

trinity college, dublin

A characteristic feature of Irish literature in the 13thC–17thC was bardic poetry. The bard, a member of an elite professional caste, composed the poems but left it to a reciter to speak them. Irish remained the dominant language until the 17thC when English, long since a rival, took over. One of the first of the great Anglo-Irish writers to write in English was satirist Jonathan Swift. Born in Dublin in 1667 and educated at Kilkenny Grammar School and Trinity College, Dublin, he became Dean of St Patrick's in 1713. The celebrated author of 'Gulliver's Travels', he also wrote a number of other social satires, such as 'The Tale of a Tub'. Oliver Goldsmith (1730–1774), son of a clergyman and author of 'The Vicar of Wakefield' and 'She Stoops to Conquer', wrote a brilliant lament for the break-up of village society in his poem 'The Deserted Village'.

The great irony of Irish literature is that many of its greatest writers were ignored or reviled by the Irish and left for exile in London and continental Europe. Richard Brinsley Sheridan (1751–1816), author of three brilliant comedies—'The Rivals', 'The School for Scandal' and 'The Critic'—left for London in 1773, where he became a Member of Parliament in 1790. Thomas Moore (1779–1852), author of 'Irish Melodies Set to Traditional Airs', left for London shortly after completing his studies at Trinity College. He became a satirist, particularly of the Prince Regent, and later wrote several biographies, including those of Sheridan and his close friend Byron. Novelist George Moore (1852–1933) was born in Mayo but after a brief period studying art in Paris he finally settled in London, where he turned his attention to literature. Dublin-born wit Oscar Wilde (1854–1900) went to Trinity College, Dublin and later Magdalen College, Oxford before finally settling in London in 1879; there he wrote 'The Picture of Dorian Gray' in 1891 and then his masterpiece 'The Importance of Being Earnest' in 1895.

There was a literary revival in the late 19thC led by figures like William Butler Yeats (1865–1939) and John Millington Synge (1871–1909), founders of the Abbey Theatre, which was opened in Dublin in 1904. Here works by numerous Irish playwrights, including Sean O'Casey (1880–1964), Samuel Beckett (1906–) and Brendan Behan (1923–1964), were regularly performed. Despite the efforts of the literary renaissance, however, writers continued to leave for London and the continent. G B Shaw (1856–1950), who was awarded the Nobel Prize for literature in 1925, left for London in 1876; his first popular stage success was 'John Bull's Other Island' in 1904. James Stephens (1880–1950), novelist and poet, also left Ireland for London, in 1925. The brilliant James Joyce (1882–1941) lived mainly in Europe from 1904 onwards. Samuel Beckett, Dublin-born novelist and dramatist, was awarded the Nobel Prize for Literature in 1969, long after he had settled in Paris. Many of these writers wrote about Ireland nonetheless; Joyce's 'Dubliners' and 'Portrait of the Artist as a Young Man', for example, are brilliant evocations of Irish life.

In the past decade there has been a notable resurgence of Irish poetry, particularly amongst the group of Ulster poets, led by Seamus Heaney and including Michael Longley, Derek Mahon and Paul Muldoon.

Myths & legends

Ireland is rich in legends, many of which explain such natural phenomena as the Giant's Causeway, Lough Neagh and the Rock of Cashel. From the early bards to Yeats's 'Mythologies', these stories have been collected and passed down through the generations and lend much to the magical, mystical feeling of Ireland. By way of example, one story tells how the devil was once in a tearing hurry to cross Co Tipperary; finding the mountains in his path, he bit a huge chunk from them to clear his way and spat it far out onto the southern plains. The hole in the mountains gave them the name of 'Devil's Bit' and the rejected mouthful is the Rock of Cashel.

Many of the legends are sad and beautiful, such as that of the Children of Lir. King Lir married a jealous woman named Aoife, who decided to drown her step-children but relented and turned them instead into swans with human voices. Thus the king learned of their fate and, mad with grief, spent the rest of his life in the trees at the water's edge. The children flew away, singing beautifully and enchanting all who heard them. They lived for 900 years, during which time it was forbidden for anyone to kill a swan in Ireland. Then with the coming of Christianity they returned to their now-ancient human bodies, were baptised and died.

More cheerful are the multitudinous tales of the leprechauns or little people. Traditionally, these mischievous folk dress in green and own a crock of gold, which can be taken by anyone able to keep their eyes fixed upon them without blinking. The leprechauns are cobblers and many stories tell of their helpfulness, but the unwary unbeliever who disturbs a fairy ráth (a small mound in the fields where the leprechauns live) or a fairy tree (the hawthorn) is liable to fairy revenge. Stories of changelings abound, too, and of a creature called a banshee that besets a house when death is near.

Ireland has its country superstitions, also: a cock-crow at midnight will bring bad luck; all visitors to a farmhouse must take a turn at the churn or the cream will never become butter. These eminently practical beliefs still live on in rural areas.

The Irish language

Although the principal spoken language in Ireland today is English, the official language of the Republic is Irish. Until 1974, a knowledge of Irish was compulsory in the Civil Service and Acts of Parliament and other official documents, street signs and placenames are still written in both languages. The widespread nationalist sentiment of the late 19thC gave birth to the Gaelic League, founded by Douglas Hyde and Eóin MacNeill in 1893.

The movement was conceived as a means of reviving the Irish language and also put new blood into such aspects of traditional Irish life as Gaelic sports, music and literature.

Like most languages, Irish has evolved over the centuries: Old Irish was spoken from cAD600–900, Middle Irish c900–1200 and Early Modern Irish c1200–1650. Modern Irish is an Indo-European language with a complex grammar, encompassing various regional dialects; it is among the earliest languages in Europe and has a rich early literature. In the early Christian era, Ireland was a country of monks and scholars and Greek—a language still almost unknown in Imperial Rome—was widely spoken by the clerics. 16thC Ireland was an entirely Irish-speaking nation but with the establishment of the English system of land tenure an English-speaking upper class grew up and the language was gradually adopted. By 1831, the shift was virtually complete and a national school system structured in favour of English was set up. Deaths and

Old manuscript, showing written Irish

emigrations resulting from the Great Potato Famine of 1845–46 tragically reduced the number of native Irish-speakers and a census of 1851 recorded that only 25% of the population spoke Irish. By 1911 the proportion had dropped to 12%.

The revival of the Irish language was a key element of state policy in 1921 and in 1925 the Gaeltacht Commission was set up to study conditions in Irish-speaking areas. In 1956 seven such districts were defined, now known collectively as the Gaeltacht. Irish can still be heard in these areas and they are also centres for traditional crafts and sports. The Donegal Gaeltacht is the largest and stretches almost uninterrupted from Fanad Head in the north to Kilcar in the south west, including also several islands such as Tory and Aranmore. The Mayo Gaeltacht includes fragments of the Curraun Peninsula and the eastern half of Achill Island, Tourmakeady in the south and Ennis in the north west. The Galway Gaeltacht is the second largest and takes in most of Connemara, the south east shore of Lough Corrib and the islands of Bealadargan, Lettermore, Lettermullen and the Aran group. Kerry Gaeltacht includes pockets of the Dingle Peninsula along the mountainous coast around Slea Head and the Ring of Kerry. Cork Gaeltacht runs from Ballyvourney in the north to Ballingeary, where the first Irish college was founded in 1904, in the south and includes Clear Island. The tiny Waterford Gaeltacht is centred around Ring, five miles from Dungarvan, where an Irish college was established in 1930. Finally, the Meath Gaeltacht is focused on the little towns of Gibbstown and Rathcairn, where Irish-speakers from the west settled in the 1930s.

Traditional music

Traditional Irish music, today found mostly in the Gaeltacht areas, was passed on originally by itinerant music and dancing masters. The oldest airs date back to the early 17thC, but it was not until 1726 that a book of Irish music was first published. In 1792 there was the great Belfast Harp Festival. Edward Bunting was commissioned to write down the various airs played. These were later published in three volumes. In 1855 George Petrie published a book of airs, including the celebrated 'Derry Air', and between 1873 and 1909 Patrick W Joyce produced another.

Until the mid-19thC, most popular ballads and songs were written in Irish and were primarily concerned with romantic, religious, political, sporting or militaristic issues. There were lullabies, laments and drinking songs, but the most prominent were love songs. Gradually more were composed in English and the popularity of broadsheet ballads began to increase.

For centuries the harp, now the national symbol, was the principal musical instrument of Ireland. Other instruments include Uilleann pipes, a refinement of Scottish bagpipes; air is pumped by using the elbow as a bellows with the bag squeezed against the musician's side. There is the bodhran, a drum made of goat skin stretched across a wooden frame. There is also the tin whistle, the fiddle—the backbone of traditional Irish dance music—the flute and accordion. The main venue for traditional Irish music is the All-Ireland Fleadh, an annual three-day music and song festival held in a different town each year. Other annual events include the Fleadh Nua, Co Clare (*May*); Fleadh Cheoil, Co Londonderry (*June*); Feis na Gleann, Co Antrim (*July*).

Food & drink

Ireland has a reputation as a land of potato-eaters and legend has it that Sir Walter Raleigh planted the first tuber in Europe here. Many Irish specialities involve this versatile vegetable—such as creamy, delicious potato soup, flavoured with chives, parsley and bacon—but there is plenty of variety to tempt the palate.

The rivers and loughs teem with salmon and trout, the lush green valleys abound with game and cattle and the spectacular coastline provides delicious shellfish. Dublin Bay prawns, also known as 'Norway lobster', are the largest British

Typical Irish breads

Sampling 'dulse' at the Lammas Fair, Co Antrim

prawn at four inches long and are extremely succulent. Cockles and lobster are found on many menus. Some of the best oysters come from Co Galway and there is a festival in their honour in Galway city every *Sep*. Salmon—grilled, poached or smoked—is one of Ireland's greatest treats, along with the more delicately flavoured salmon trout and, in season, grilse. Brown trout is also readily available and Europe's largest eel fishery is in Lough Neagh. Try also Limerick ham, traditionally oak-smoked with juniper berries.

A full Irish breakfast is not to be missed: eggs, bacon, ham, sausages, black pudding or plaice, together with Irish soda bread or potato bread. Home-made specialities like Dublin Coddle (a popular Saturday-night supper dish of bacon and sausages), bacon and cabbage or crubeens (pickled pig's trotters) can often be found in country pubs. If you're lucky enough to be in Ireland at Christmas, try spiced beef, which is marinated for a week. Hallowe'en also offers a spread of traditional dishes: colcannon is made from potatoes, onions, cabbage and cream, and contains a sixpence, a thimble, a button and a gold ring—foretelling wealth, spinsterhood, bachelordom and marriage, respectively, for those that find them; barm brack, a yeasted loaf full of spice and fruit also containing a gold ring, carrying the same prediction. Boxty pancakes, made of potatoes flavoured with caraway and fried in bacon fat, and boxty bread are two more favourites.

Dark stout is the most Irish of drinks and Guinness is the most famous variety: it can be tasted free at the Dublin brewery. Brewed with roasted malt, at its dark and creamy best it is unbeatable—especially with oysters. Irish whiskey, spelt with an 'e' to distinguish it from Scotch, is very pure and has an excellent flavour. The best whiskey comes from the Old Bushmills distillery in Co Antrim, the oldest licensed distillery in the world, and no visit to Ireland is complete without sampling their de luxe 'Black Bush'.

Co Kerry's green pastures produce flavoursome butter and cream, which are used lavishly with the delicious pastries and pies found throughout the country. One such is potato apple cake, a potato pastry stuffed with apples and cooked on a griddle.

If you happen to visit the Lammas Fair in Co Antrim do try 'dulse', a dried seaweed, or 'yellowman', a brittle pulled toffee. Another seaweed-based dish is Carrageen moss jelly, a gelatine-like substance that can be bought loose in chemists'. The taste of Ireland is certainly unique, is fun to try and rarely a disappointment.

Archaeology

The Stone Age (3000BC–2000BC)

This was the period when man ceased his wandering nomadic way of life and began to settle, to raise crops and to construct his first substantial structures. Building was of the most basic form, post and lintel, the size of span limited by the size of stone available. The major relics are Neolithic burial sites. Megalithic tombs are of two basic types, the gallery grave, generally covered by a long trapezoidal or oval cairn, and the passage grave, covered by a round mound or cairn.

Gallery graves. The gallery grave is characterised by a long chamber or gallery divided into a number of small compartments. The most elaborate of this type of grave is the *court cairn*. A characteristic of the northern half of Ireland, these are generally built in commanding hilltop positions. The plan consists of an open space or forecourt flanked by stones, used for various funerary rites. This leads into the gallery, which was closed by a large slab or door-stone. The *double court cairn* consists of two court cairns placed back to back. The *full court cairn* consists of a central, open court surrounded by galleries. Only eight examples have been discovered so far, the best of which is at Magheraghanrush, Co Sligo. A basic form of gallery grave is the *dolmen*. Often referred to as a portal tomb, the dolmen consists of a single chamber, its entrance flanked by three or more upright stones supporting a huge, flat capstone. Characteristic of the late Stone Age and early Bronze Age are the *wedge-shaped gallery graves* and the *horned cairns*. The former has a wedge-shaped plan, with a higher, broader front; the latter, a variation of the wedge-shaped gallery, is found mainly in the north, and consists of a stone-built chamber with crescent-like projections at each end resembling horns.

Portal Dolmen, near Dundonald, Belfast

Passage graves. A product of the middle Stone Age, these are roughly circular in plan with a corbelled roof supported round the edge by a kerb of heavy slabs; a low, narrow passage gives access to a central chamber. Generally grouped in cemeteries, they are of particular interest for their decorative work such as spirals, lozenges and chevrons cut on kerbstones and lintels and so forth. The passage graves of Ireland are generally found to the east and north of the central plain and are characteristic of Western Europe of the period.

The Bronze Age (2000BC–600BC)

The Bronze Age witnessed the first application of primitive metal technology and the increased importance of ritual resulted in the building of great stone circles. Wedge-shaped gallery graves and chambered cairns were also still being built.

Ring-barrows. Often associated with passage graves, they consist of a low, earthen mound edged by a bank of earth, ditch or stones, into which a number of individual cist tombs were sunk.

Stone circles. Generally dating from the late Stone Age to early Iron Age in Ireland and sometimes referred to as cromlechs, there are two main types: a circle of small stones surrounding a ring-barrow and a much larger and more impressive type known as an

axial stone circle. The latter consists of a large stone laid down lengthwise on the south west of the ring with a portal formed by two tall stones diagonally opposite it, on the far side of the ring.

Boulder-burials. Sometimes known as boulder-dolmens, they consist of a huge cover stone raised three feet off the ground by three or more flat, stepped stones.

Standing stones. Sometimes known as pillar-stones, or gallán, they are the most common of prehistoric Irish monuments. Varying in height from a few inches to over 20 feet in height, they generally indicate a boundary, mark a tomb or were used as commemorative stones. Sometimes a group of stones, often as many as 24 or more, form an alignment. Generally found in association with a stone circle, stones in alignment are usually low in height.

Holed stones. Thought to be connected with fertility rites, they are a series of stones of varying heights perforated by one or more holes.

Holed stone, Doagh, Antrim

Crannogs. Found in shallow water beside the edges of lakes, they are artificial islands built of a wooden raft that was then sunk under a hill of stones. On top were built one or more timber houses enclosed by a wooden palisade. They were built from the late Bronze Age up until the early Christian period.

Reconstructed Crannog, Craggaunowen, Co Clare.

The Iron Age (600BC–AD5thC)

With the arrival of the Celtic invaders in 600BC and the introduction of iron weapons, the inevitable increase in warfare resulted in the construction of fortified farmsteads and huge hill forts and promontory forts, instead of the great tombs characteristic of the previous ages. By 150BC the Celtic invaders were firmly established in a series of small kingdoms.

Staigue Fort, Co Kerry

Ring forts. Built from the early Bronze Age right up to the early Christian period, ring forts were really fortified farmsteads and consisted of a group of timber and wattle huts enclosed by a rampart. There are two types of ring fort—raths, which have an earth bank enclosure, and cashels, where the enclosure is of stone. Often staircases and rooms are contained within the thickness of the latter's stone wall. Many of these forts contain *souterrains*: long, narrow underground passages or galleries, often connected with domestic dwellings and used for storage as well as refuge.

Hill forts. Found mainly in the eastern part of Ireland, they consisted of large, sprawling villages built on high ground and defended by a single rampart of earth or dry stone walling, as at Tara or Navan. The latter, originally known as Emain Macha, was the legendary fortress of the Gaelic kings of Ulster.

Promontory forts. Found mainly in south and west Ireland, they are built generally on dramatic cliff-top sites, as at Dunbeg, Co Kerry or Dún Aengus on the Aran Islands.

Decorated stones. The high point of 2ndC BC Celtic Ireland is the abstract decorative work applied to both metalwork and stone and known as 'La Tène' style. Of particular interest are *carved stones* such as the Turoe Stone in Co Galway, the Castlestrange Stone in Co Roscommon and the Killycluggin Stone, originally from Co Cavan but now in the National Museum of Ireland. They are phallic-shaped sculpted granite pillars.

Ogham stone, Co Kerry

Ogham stones and pillars. Dating from the late Iron Age to the early Christian period, Ogham stones and pillars were characterised by inscriptions in Ogham, an Irish variation of the Latin alphabet. Used on memorial stones, the Ogham script recorded the name of the deceased together with a brief biography. The best examples are found in the south, especially in Kerry and Waterford.

Bullauns. Particularly common in limestone areas, they consist of bowl-like depressions in boulders or rock. Thought to have been used to prepare special ritual foods for pre-Christian fertility rites or as communal grinding-mills in early Christian Ireland.

Bullaun, Gortavoher, Co. Tipperary.

Architectural styles

Early Christian (5thC–12thC)

Ireland had been converted to Christianity to such an extent by the early 5thC that a bishop was appointed from Rome in AD431; however, it was not until the return of St Patrick, a Romanized British Celt who had at one time been a slave in Ireland, but had escaped and been educated on the Continent, that the episcopal system of church government and the monasteries were introduced. Iron Age structures such as crannogs, raths, forts and cashels continued in use. Many of the new cashels resembled Scottish brochs, but were larger in circumference and the walls were rarely more than 15 feet high, although they were up to 15 feet thick at the base, having an external batter. The entrance was usually a narrow passage. Many continued in use for several centuries; for example, the Doon Fort, an O'Boyle stronghold built on an island in Lough Doon, was still being used in the 16thC.

Clocháns. Found mainly on the Dingle Peninsula, Co Kerry, they are small stone huts, often circular in plan with a corbelled roof, shaped like a beehive. They were either simple chapels or monks' cells and are often to be found among the ruins of monasteries.

Clochan, Inishmurray, Co Sligo.

Monasteries. The early Irish monasteries were planned within an irregular walled enclosure and consisted of a number of beehive-shaped huts, which were the individual cells of the monks, surrounding one or more small churches or oratories. They were usually built of timber with wattle and daub but in the west, where timber was scarce, they were built of dry stone walling with corbelled roofs. There were generally several commemorative pillar-stones and crosses as well as little graveyards. One of the earliest surviving Irish monasteries is Skellig Michael, Co Kerry, but the most famous is the monastic complex at Glendalough, Co Wicklow, which was founded by St Kevin in the 6thC.

Churches. The earliest Irish churches were of cruck-frame construction, a primitive form of timber framing employing curved tree trunks joined at their apex and planned in one or more bays. The high, pitched roofs were covered in rushes or shingles and antae and gable finials were characteristic; because of the lack of wood on the west coast, small rectangular oratories like the Gallarus Oratory, Co Kerry, were built of dry stone walling with a rounded corbel vault giving them their distinctive upturned-boat appearance. Most of the surviving stone churches of the period date from the early 12thC. Another contemporary church is that on St MacDara's Island, Co Galway; rectangular in plan, it is built of hewn blocks of stone, larger at the base and smaller at the ridge. Of particular interest is the way the stone roof and walls of many of these churches project beyond the gable end as if in imitation of the wooden barge-boards of earlier timber churches. Also of interest: 12thC St Kevin's Kitchen, Glendalough, Co Wicklow. Characteristic features of these early churches were square-headed doorways with huge lintels and jambs leaning inwards, and small round-headed windows.

Round Towers. A combination of bell tower and refuge in times of danger, these date from the period of the Viking raids. They are tall and slender, about 80–115 feet high, tapering slightly inwards with a conical top. They are built of hewn stone, with an entrance raised high above the ground reached by a wood or rope ladder, which was quickly pulled up in the event of attack. Over 65 survive in Ireland, of which nearly a dozen are in good condition.

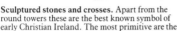

Round Tower, Glendalough C9th

Sculptured stones and crosses. Apart from the round towers these are the best known symbol of early Christian Ireland. The most primitive are the

Latin or Greek crosses inscribed on large, flattish or shaft-shaped stones. More elaborate are the *sculptured cross-slabs* in which both faces of the stone are decorated with interlaced relief patterns as a surround to the cross. Good examples are found in northern Donegal. A more elaborate development are the *high crosses*, generally placed on a stepped podium with a circle surrounding the intersection of shaft and arms. Many are decorated with scenes depicting biblical stories. Often over 16 feet high, most were built between the 7thC and 12thC.

Cross, Ahenny Co. Tipperary C8th

Detail of Moone High Cross, Co Kildare

Romanesque (11thC–12thC)

During the two centuries of the Viking wars, the moral and ethical standards of the church degenerated considerably. The necessary reforms were introduced by a series of synods instigated first by Cellach, Bishop of Armagh, and then by St Malachy, his successor. It was he who introduced the Cistercians to Ireland, the first of a series of monastic orders that were to revolutionise church architecture. Hard on the heels of these church reforms, which gave Ireland its basic diocesan organisation, came the Anglo-Norman invasion of 1169. Huge castles were constructed and new abbeys built on an unprecedented scale while yet more monastic orders began to arrive from the Continent to establish foundations.

Detail of minute, Dysert O'Dea church, Co Clare.

Characteristic features. The early Romanesque churches were small, single-chamber buildings without chancels. Gradually they increased in size with the addition of small, narrow chancels, as at Mona Incha. Roofs were steeply pitched and corbelled stone and there was often a barrel-vaulted loft space, as at St Flannan's Oratory, Killaloe, Co Clare. Decoration was especially lavish around doorways, windows and chancel arches. A typical feature was the chevron moulding, borrowed freely from Norman architecture. Other features include zig-zag ornamentation, engaged columns and tall, triangular hoods, often elaborately moulded, over many entrance portals.

Churches & cathedrals. A fine example is the decorated entrance to 12thC Clonfert Cathedral, Co Galway, which has decorative foliage work as well as human and animal heads framed in blind arcading. The most influential of all the Irish churches of this period is Cormac's Chapel, Cashel, Co Tipperary. Built 1127–34, it is one of the more spacious Irish churches of the period, famed for the elegance of its blind arcading and handsome stone roof.

Mellifont Abbey, Co Louth

Influence of continental monastic orders. The arrival of the continental monastic orders, in particular the Cistercians, had a considerable effect on Irish architecture. Characteristic, as on the continent, were large, cruciform churches and a rectangular courtyard around which were grouped ancillary buildings. The first Cistercian monastery was that of Mellifont, Co Louth, established in 1142 and closely followed by others at Boyle, Jerpoint and Ballintober.

Castles. Although the conquest of Ireland was comparatively easy for the Normans, they had a problem controlling the territory they had taken. Consequently, from the late 12thC and throughout the 13thC, the Normans built a string of great stone fortresses. There were two basic types. The first consisted of a monumental keep, as at Trim and Carrickfergus, with the addition of round towers to the corners of many keeps, a feature peculiar to Ireland. The second type, based on Norman castles in Wales such as that at Harlech, consisted of a large walled enclosure with a fortified gate-house and projecting corner towers and intermediate towers; good examples are those at Ballymote and Ballintober.

Gothic (12thC–16thC)
The transition from Romanesque to Gothic occurred much later here than in England. Whilst the Gothic was rapidly taking hold in eastern Ireland, the church builders of the west were still building in the Transitional style, with its mixture of Gothic pointed arches and Romanesque round arches. A good example of Transitional style is St Mary's Cathedral, Limerick, c1180–95. A particular hallmark of the 'school of the West' was the remarkable quality of stonework and distinctive decorative ornamentation, including fine foliage carvings; good examples are the capitals, Abbey Church, Boyle, Co Roscommon, 1161–1218 and the north doorway of the Augustinian Abbey, Cong, Co Mayo, c1225.

Characteristic features. As in England, much use was made of the pointed arch. Massive Norman pillars were replaced by groups of slender shafts. Windows increased in size and angle buttresses, set diagonally, were introduced. Window tracery was geometric in form and later curvilinear or flowing lines were introduced. Vaulting used an increasing number of intermediate ribs and carving was generally more naturalistic.

Churches, abbeys & cathedrals. The first of the purely Gothic churches to be built in Ireland were those at Inch Abbey (1187) and Grey Abbey (1193) both in Co Down. The major influence on Gothic churches of this period, built under Norman patronage, was English, the best examples of which are the cathedrals in Dublin—St Patrick's, 1220–54, and Christ Church, 12thC–13thC. Others were built in such places as Limerick, Killaloe and Kilkenny; the latter, completed in the late 13thC, has a straightforward rectangular plan with narrow transepts and a spacious choir flanked by chapels. The choir at the cathedral, Cashel (1224–89) is even larger; however, with the exception of St Patrick's, Dublin—at nearly 110 yards long the largest Irish cathedral—most are small in comparison with English and continental examples.

Parish churches. Of the few surviving medieval churches, all are small in scale and rather austerely decorated in comparison with contemporaneous English examples. Mostly they are cruciform in plan with elegant lancet windows and good examples are St Mary's, Youghal; St Mary's, New Ross; St Mutrose, Kinsale; and St Nicholas's, Galway.

Monasteries. The building programme of the various monastic orders was considerable during this period. The Cistercians continued to expand,

establishing foundations at Dunroby and Tintern Minor, both in Co Wexford, and the Augustinians built a huge priory at Athassel, Co Tipperary. There were many fine friaries, characterised by slim, tapering spires and small cloisters, built throughout the west during the 14thC and 15thC. Good examples are those at Rosserk, Sligo, Moyne and Adare. Battlemented parapets were first introduced into church architecture in the 14thC. Considerable reconstruction work was undertaken by the Cistercians in the 15thC: of particular interest are their abbeys of Holy Cross and Kilcooley, both in Co Tipperary, to which huge, squat towers were added.

Dunguaire Tower House, Co Galway

Tower houses. These are a product of the troubled times of 15thC and 16thC Ireland following the break-up of the feudal system. Generally between four to six storeys in height with a high, gabled roof, tower houses were mostly rectangular in plan with the rooms stacked vertically and reached by one or more flights of spiral stairs. Walls were thick and principal floors generally barrel-vaulted, the others more often of timber. Most stood to one side of a courtyard or bawn, surrounded by a stone wall which was sometimes turreted. One of the best preserved is the 16thC tower house at Dunguaire, Co Galway. Characteristic of early tower houses were narrow, pointed windows; later examples, as at Dunguaire, have mullioned windows with moulded hoods. Most were small in scale but some—like Caher Castle, a 15thC Butler stronghold in Co Tipperary, and Bunratty Castle, Co Clare, built 1450—are very large.

The Renaissance (16thC–17thC)
The first indication of the Renaissance in Ireland was in the application of classical ornamentation, such as pilasters and decorative floral panels in numerous tomb designs. Although many tower houses were built well into the 17thC, the concern for increased comfort led to the addition of spacious extensions to many of them.

Castles. Early 16thC Donegal Castle had a handsome manor house added to its keep in 1616 and the late 15thC Lemaneagh Castle, Co Clare, was extensively remodelled in 1643. New castles of the 17thC, whilst clearly more concerned with comfort, still incorporated some defensive features, such as projecting corner towers. Good examples are Kanturk Castle, Co Cork (1610), and Burncourt Castle, Co Tipperary (1640). Increasingly, Renaissance ideas were seen in the greater formality in planning and symmetry of façades.

Domestic buildings. Buildings like 1594 Rothe House, Kilkenny, were characteristic of the larger towns of the late 16thC, but gradually the influence of Elizabethan England began to be felt, particularly in the north, which had been planted with English settlers. Characteristics were a multiplicity of gables, the use of string courses and a proliferation of mullioned windows. A good example is the Elizabethan-style mansion added to the castle at Carrick on Suir, Co Tipperary, in 1580

Dutch influence. It wasn't until after 1660, with the restoration of Charles II, that the preference for semi-fortified houses gave way to the first purely domestic houses. The major influence came from the Dutch-inspired houses of Restoration England. Hipped roofs with wide eaves, dormer windows and use of red brick were characteristic; of the few remaining, the best example is Beaulieu, Co Louth, 1660–67.

Beaulieu, Co Louth 1660's.

The beginnings of Irish Classicism. It was with the design of the Royal Hospital, Kilmainham by Sir William Robinson in 1680–84 that Irish architecture was catapulted into the super-world of International-style Classicism. The first great classical building in Ireland, it was based on Les Invalides, Paris, and was built as a home for retired soldiers. It consists of ranges wrapped round a large courtyard. The façades are articulated by pedimented centres, with the principal façade on the north side punctuated by a square tower crowned with a spire; other details include Corinthian pilasters.

Dublin. The city began to expand rapidly from the Restoration period onwards. New streets were planned, and four new bridges built. Trinity College, established in 1592, was replanned in the Dutch-Baroque manner in the late 17thC. It was again remodelled in the mid-18thC, leaving only the library from this date. St Stephen's Green, Phoenix Park and the quays of the city were also planned at this time.

Palladian Renaissance (17thC–18thC)
Handsome public buildings were built in numerous provincial towns, such as the Barracks, Ballyshannon; the Court House, Kinsale; and the Old Custom House, Cork. The most memorable of such buildings is the Parliament House, Dublin, 1729–39: now the Bank of Ireland, it was the first public building in England or Ireland to be built wholly in the Palladian style. Designed by Sir Edward Pearce, it has a lofty, colonnaded Ionic façade with projecting wings; the curved peristyle around the sides was added later.

Country houses. During the first half of the 18thC, a number of huge country mansions were built. By far the largest was at Castletown, Co Kildare; designed in 1772 by Alessandro Galilei, the interiors

Castletown, Co Kildare.

were by Sir Edward Lovett Pearce, the major figure of Irish Palladianism. Pearce was also responsible for Bellamont Forest, Co Cavan, c1730. A handsome villa-style Palladian house, it consists of a rectangular block with a piano nobile raised above a rusticated ground storey and a pedimented portico and attic storey above. Another Pearce design is Cashel Palace, Cashel, Co Tipperary (1731), a delightful brick house; now a hotel, it was once the home of the Protestant archbishop. The Palladian style was continued with considerable gusto by Richard Castle, Pearce's one-time assistant, who designed a number of huge country houses including Russborough, Co Wicklow, 1742. An enormous Palladian mansion, this consists of a monumental centre block with an applied portico, linked to wings by low, curving colonnades.

Neoclassicism (18thC–early 19thC)
The influence of English Neoclassicism was strong on Irish architecture from the mid-18thC onwards. Characteristic features (as in England) were vast frontages of excessive regularity, punctuated at key points by pedimented porticos or crowned by domes or cupolas. The orders became a major part of the structure and much inspiration was derived from Roman classical architecture. It was an Irishman, Lord Charlemont, returning from the Grand Tour in the 1750s wishing to recreate some of the splendour of Italian classicism, who invited Sir William Chambers, the major figure in English architecture of the period, to design him a town house as well as a country villa. The house, the Marino Casino, Dublin (1759), is one of the gems of 18thC English and Irish architecture. A tiny garden house, it consists of a square basement with ground and top floor in the form of a Greek cross, the whole enriched by Greek- and Roman-style decorations. Another magnificent Neoclassical house is Mount Kennedy, Co Wicklow: designed by James Wyatt, 1772–82, it has a one-storey pedimented entry porch carried on doric columns surmounted by a huge semi-circular window.

Mount Kennedy, Co Wicklow 1772

Civic and public buildings. One of the most magnificent of Ireland's public buildings is the Four Courts, Dublin, designed 1786 by James Gandon. A combination of Baroque and Neoclassical elements, it consists of a monumental square block surmounted by a huge columned drum with a dome crowning the hall. Flanking it are monolithic wings, linked by arcaded screens. Gandon also designed the Custom House, Dublin (1781–91); it is a long, low building, punctuated at the ends and centre. The dome, carried by a high, colonnaded, square drum was inspired by Sir Christopher Wren's work at Greenwich Hospital, London.

Churches. There are few 18thC churches in Ireland but good examples exist at Ballymakenny, Co Louth and Newtownbreda, Co Down. Characteristic features of these Georgian churches are large, round-headed windows, simple rectangular plan and classical west front of three bays, punctuated by a tower and spire. Most rural churches built in the late

18thC, particularly those of the Church of Ireland, were of a simplified Gothic style. Many town churches of the early 19thC were based on Greek Temple prototypes. A good example is the Presbyterian church, Portaferry, Co Down; designed 1840 by John Millar, it is raised above a basement storey with a Doric portico back and front. The façade of Holy Trinity, Kircubbin, Co Down (1840), was modelled on an engraving of a Doric temple at Sunium. Catholic churches—unlike the Pro-Cathedral, Dublin (1815), which had a Doric portico added in 1840—turned to the Renaissance and Baroque architecture of Europe for inspiration. The Catholic clergy, mostly educated abroad, had travelled extensively in France and Italy, from where many of the ideas for their new churches came. St Mel's Cathedral, Longford (1840–93), is a case in point, with its elegant Ionic portico and elaborate sculptured pediment.

St Mary's Cathedral, Dublin.

Victorian period (1837–1901)

The railway. The last quarter of the 18thC witnessed the construction of a number of fine canal bridges and other structures related to the prevailing transport system, but it was the 19thC development of the railway that left the most indelible mark on Irish architecture. This is particularly true in Dublin, which has several magnificent stations such as Broadstone Station, designed by John Skipton Mulvany in 1850; Heuston Station, designed by Sancton Wood in 1845–6, when it was known as Kingsbridge Station; and Connolly Station, designed 1844 by William Deane Butler. The former is Graeco-Egyptian in style whilst the latter, with campanile-like towers, is in the Italianate fashion developed some 15 years earlier by Sir Charles Barry in London. Banks and other public buildings followed suit; good examples are the Custom House, Belfast (1857), and two handsome Italianate yacht clubs in Dun Laoghaire.

Churches. 19thC Ireland was an era of church-building. Unlike public and commercial buildings, for which variations of the classical style seemed most appropriate, churches were invariably built in the Gothic style. There are several by A W Pugin, the arch Gothic-revivalist. Two of interest are those at Killarney and Enniscorthy.

Civic and public buildings. Several fine classical-style courthouses were built in the early 19thC, often closing a vista with handsome porticoed front. Of interest are those at Armagh, Dundalk, Derry, Carlow and Waterford. By the late 19thC, the classical style had been usurped by a free Gothic style, as in the Guildhall, Derry, of 1887. The combination of glass and iron produced some remarkable structures, especially for railway stations and exhibition halls, and many fine warehouses and bridges were built. Good examples are the passenger shed, Heuston Station, Dublin, 1845; the palm houses, Botanic Gardens, Belfast, 1839 and Dublin, 1842–50. Unlike most other buildings, such structures were free of stylistic constraints.

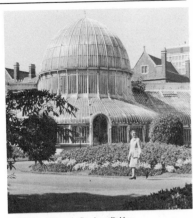

Palm house, Botanic Gardens, Belfast

20th Century

There was a gradual move away from the Gothic of late 19thC Ireland; much civic and public building was in an academic classical or Renaissance style. Early in the century there was a revival of interest in Georgian and Romanesque styles; the latter for churches, the former for libraries. Steel-framed construction produced fresh alternatives and with the profusion of new materials and the development of more sophisticated mechanical servicing almost anything could be done, and nearly everything was done.

House, Sandycove, Dublin 1937 / Michael Scott.

For a brief period the 1930s witnessed the building of a number of International-style buildings, characterised by long, horizontal bands of windows placed freely within white walls in response to specific programmatic requirements. A good example is Geragh, Sandycove, Dublin, a handsome house designed 1937 by Michael Scott, the master of modern Irish Architecture. In recent years, however, apart from one or two churches and the handsome New Library, Trinity College, Dublin, (designed 1961–67 by Ahrends, Burton and Koralek) the quality of new architecture has been depressingly poor. Since the mid-1960s there has been a strong predeliction for a banal Chicago-style frame building which has ruined many places, especially in Dublin. Here, attempts to transform a lovely Georgian town into an International city, in a misguided attempt to rid it of a certain degree of provinciality, have backfired miserably.

Traditional building

Balley & booley. 'Baile' or 'balley' is Gaelic for home-place; 'booley' means milking place or summer hill-dwelling. In summer the herdsmen and their families moved from the winter valleys to upland pastures and built a rudimentary shelter, not unlike the sheilings of Argyll or Northumberland, called a booley. It consisted generally of one large oval or rectangular room, built of sods or field stone. The roof was of bog timbers, covered with strips of sod and then thatched with heather and securely roped down. The fire was in an open hearth along one wall and there were no windows, and generally only one door. The balley, or winter home, was a more substantial dwelling.

Clachan. The name for the settlement or townland where the balley, a one-storey, one-room-deep house built of clay or loose stones, was grouped with 20–60 other houses. The clachan was planned in a fairly random pattern, the major requirement being shelter from the prevailing winds. Concerned primarily with agriculture, clachans had none of the elements associated with European villages such as a church, inn or shops.

Cruck house. Examples of cruck-framing, characteristic of housing for the peasant of medieval England, are rare in Ireland. Most examples are found in the north west. As with similar examples in the Scottish highlands and islands, they are not made of single pieces of curved timber, but of two pieces jointed at the level of the wall, the lower blade scarfed and pegged to the upper. The roofs were thatched and the walls built of solid clay or of wattle and daub.

Standard traditional house. There are three basic house types in the traditional Irish house. The first, found primarily in the east and south east, consists of a bedroom and kitchen-living room divided by a fireplace. The windows are small and there is one door, opposite the end wall of the chimney; roofs are often hipped. The second type, characteristic of the west coast, has a chimney on the gable end and two outside doors, placed opposite each other so as to control the draught. The division between bedroom and kitchen-living room was formed by a furniture partition such as a cupboard or dresser. The third type, found mainly in the north east, has chimneys on both gable ends and the entrance is protected by projecting walls, the main roof continuing as an outshot over the flanking walls.

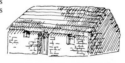

House, Duncrun townland, Co. Derry. c 1750

Weaver's house. A characteristic of many weavers' cottages, as domestic linen manufacture gradually replaced small-scale farming, was the building on of an outshot to accommodate the loom. In some instances a separate loom shop was built; in others, small lofts were built over hearth areas.

mid 19th C weavers dwelling, Ballydugan townland, Co Down

Bed recesses. Characteristic of many parts of Ireland is a bed-box in a timber frame to one side of the living room. In parts of Ulster and north west Connacht this takes the form of a bed alcove, planned to one side of the kitchen hearth and projecting out from the house in a little outshot.

House & byre. A combination of people and cattle in one unpartitioned space is characteristic of the north west and such houses generally had two entrances, with the passage between flagged. In parts of Donegal byre houses are occasionally built into steep banks, with the higher gable end being used to house cattle on the ground floor, while the space above was lofted over to create a bedroom.

Cottage, Cullybackey, Co Antrim

Stable doors. For many of the more humble dwellings, glass was a luxury; some half doors can still be seen. The lower half could be closed against wind and dirt while the top half was left open to let in light and air.

Clay housing. A characteristic of many areas, similar to the cob cottages of Devon or the Grampian region, Scotland, were houses built of clay mixed with straw and built up in layers. Spades were used to shave the walls smooth and the walls were then weather-proofed with coats of limewash. Foundations were usually of rubble.

Roofing. The more substantial houses of the settlers were constructed of rafters carried on purlins but in most houses the roof consisted of light coupled rafters with a collar. Most houses had a layer of sod strips finished with a cover of thatch, pinned to the strips. Thatch was also plastered down with clay at the eaves, gable or ridge where the thatch was most vulnerable to wind damage. Along the more

thatch roof roped down and pegged along eaves and gable end in Teelin, Co. Donegal.

inhospitable Atlantic coastline, where gale damage was at its greatest, the thatch was secured by ropes pegged to the wall tops. In parts of Co Galway thatching is taken round the chimney in a manner similar to the Black Houses on Skye.

Northern Ireland I

Antrim	Fermanagh
Armagh	Londonderry
Down	Tyrone

Ulster's past has always been a chequered one, from the time of the warring Celtic clans; marauding Vikings on their plundering raids were followed by the expeditionary forces of Anglo-Norman robber barons like John de Courcy. The most influential conflicts, however, were probably those with England. Queen Elizabeth I of England was related to the Irish O'Briens and O'Reillys, and her interest in Ireland took the form of extensive colonisation, or 'Plantation'. The frequent rebellions of the Irish aristocracy against these incursions culminated in 1607 in the 'Flight of the Earls'. The Earl of Tyrone, Hugh O'Neill, and Rory O'Donnell, Earl of Tyrconnel, set sail from Rathmullen in September for the continent; with them went the flower of Ireland's aristocracy, and their abandoned lands covered over 750,000 acres. King James I of England confiscated these lands and gave them to settlers, who came mostly from the Scottish lowlands.

It was the descendants of these 'Planters', who came to be called the 'Scotch-Irish', who emigrated a century later to the New World as pioneers on the frontier lands. Although small in number, amongst them were men who signed the Declaration of Independence, helped to draft the American Constitution and provided over a quarter of the Presidents of the United States, as well as many generals, writers and other famous men. Any list of prominent Scotch-Irish immigrants to America must include Andrew Jackson, President 1829–37, whose parents emigrated from Boneybefore, near Carrickfergus, in 1765; General Ulysses S. Grant, Federal Commander in the Civil War and President 1869–77, who was descended from a Co Tyrone family; Woodrow Wilson, President 1913–21, whose grandparents emigrated from near Strabane in 1807; General 'Stonewall' Jackson, whose grandfather emigrated from Birches, Co Armagh in 1748; General Sam Houston, first President of the Republic of Texas, whose ancestors left Ballynure, Co Antrim in 1735; Davy Crockett, hero of the battle of the Alamo, whose parents left Londonderry in the 18thC; Edgar Allan Poe, the writer, whose great-grandfather sailed from Londonderry in 1728; and Thomas Mellon, the financier, who set sail with his father from Mountjoy, near Omagh, in 1818, when he was five years old.

Nineteenth-century Europe has been described as a continent on the move; over 23 million Europeans emigrated to the United States between 1820 and 1920. One of the largest emigrations was that of 4,400,000 people from Ireland, exceeded only by over 5,500,000 from Germany. The main reason for this tragic exodus was the great Potato Famine of 1845–51; as a result of blight on the potato crop, 800,000 Irish people died of fever and starvation, and over twice as many emigrated, under miserable conditions, in the infamous 'coffin ships'.

The Government of Ireland Act of 1920 provided for the partition of Ireland and a referendum was taken. The six counties of Armagh, Antrim, Down, Fermanagh, Londonderry and Tyrone elected by a majority to remain a part of the United Kingdom. These counties formed Northern Ireland; on June 22nd, 1921, the first prime minister was chosen—Sir James Craig, son of a local whiskey millionaire. It was thought that this would be merely a temporary measure and that before long the whole of Ireland would be reunited under a single parliament, in Dublin, but this was not to be. Fifty years later, in March 1972, the Northern Ireland government at Stormont, which was struggling to say the least, was dissolved and direct rule from Westminster reinstated.

The recent 'troubles' in Belfast can thus be seen as a continuation of a long-standing conflict. Many of the Catholics in Northern Ireland seek independence from British rule and reunion with the Republic, whereas many Protestants still follow the choice of 1920

Whitewashed cottages in Glenoe, Co Antrim

and want to remain British. This religious-political dispute has erupted into a tragic and brutal civil war, which still mars the peace of this intrinsically tranquil area.

Each of Northern Ireland's counties has its own charm and, as is true throughout Ireland, breathtakingly beautiful landscape is in strong supply. Antrim, the north east corner of Ireland, has the lush, fertile Bann Valley to the west, running down to the shores of Lough Neagh, the largest lake in the UK. To the east, steep hills and rolling moorland meet the sea in a line of cliffs. The nine Glens of Antrim, a series of beautiful, narrow valleys, cascade down from the hills to the sea. The Giant's Causeway, a monumental terrace of steps some 600 feet high, wades out into the ocean on the north coast. Straddling the River Lagan on the edge of Belfast Lough is the port of Belfast, the capital of Northern Ireland. The site of an ancient river-crossing, it was here that John de Courcy built a castle in 1177, which was destroyed by Edward Bruce in 1315. The Irish linen industry began here in the 17thC, helped by an influx of Huguenot refugees in 1685; and it was here that the Society of United Irishmen was established in 1791 and where, four years later, Wolfe Tone and his colleagues climbed to MacArt's Fort, crowning Cave Hill to the north, vowing to strive until Ireland was independent. To the north east along the shore of Belfast Lough is Carrickfergus, the major port on the coast until the early 17thC, where de Courcy built one of the most formidable Anglo-Norman fortresses in Ireland.

The Giant's Causeway, Co Antrim

To the north is Londonderry, its official name given in a charter of James I but usually known as Derry. A county characterised by wild mountain landscape, it also offers the lush and peaceful Faughan Valley and beautiful beaches. Inland is Londonderry, the second city of Northern Ireland, straddling the banks of the River Foyle, where St Columba founded a monastery in AD546.

Frequently attacked, particularly by the Norsemen, who found the flourishing monastery an irresistible prey, it was not taken by the English until 1600. A Cromwellian stronghold, it was besieged by the Royalists in 1649, but Derry's most famous siege was that of 1689, when the Williamite garrison held out for 105 days against the powerful Jacobite army. There are fine Plantation towns, like Limavady, a 17thC town two miles south of the River Roe, where the melody of the 'Derry Air' was first noted down in 1851. Portstewart, on a picturesque bay in the shelter of a rocky headland, is a popular seaside resort.

To the south is Tyrone, once a part of the O'Neill earldom, a picturesque county full of whitewashed farmhouses, enhanced by Lough Neagh and the beautiful Clogher Valley. Dungannon, today a busy market centre south west of Lough Neagh, was the chief seat of the O'Neills until the 17thC. Omagh, sealed peacefully in a saddle of land wedged amongst the Sperrin Mountains, was a major battleground of 16thC and 17thC Ulster. Settled largely by Planters from the west midlands of England in the 17thC, Tyrone has several fine Plantation towns, such as Cookstown, built in the 17thC round one tree-lined street, or Moy, an estate village of the 18thC.

Fermanagh, to the south west, lies on the beautiful River Erne and its great chain of lakes. There are many delightful shady islands in the lakes, and the Cuilcagh Mountains tower along the Cavan border. To the west are limestone hills riddled with caves, and Loughs Melvin and Macnean. This was the land ruled by the powerful Maguires, whose stronghold was at Enniskillen, on an island in the River Erne. Their lands were confiscated in the 17thC. The town was granted a charter by James I in 1613, and it was then settled by English families; it was here that the Earl of Belmore built Castlecoole, one of the most beautiful houses in Ireland. By the late 19thC, Enniskillen was one of the principal bastions of the English and Scottish settlers in Ulster. It was at a school near the lake shore west of the town that Oscar Wilde was a pupil, and on Devenish Island, two miles to the north, St Molaise founded a monastery in the 6thC. It's a county of tiny villages and stark mountains, of sturdy cottages and rolling hills, and contains some of the most beautiful loughs in Ulster.

Lough Melvin, Co Fermanagh

Armagh, tucked in the south east along the borders of Monaghan and Louth is a fruit-growing country of gentle hills, rising steeply in the south to the summit of Slieve Gullion. Armagh is a county rich in history and legend. It was on a hill to the west of what is now Armagh city that Queen Macha built her royal residence in 300BC, and Navan Fort was the seat of the Ulster kings for six centuries. Armagh town has been Ireland's ecclesiastical capital for the last 1500 years; it was here that St Patrick founded his first cathedral and established a see in AD443. King Brian Boru and his son were buried here after their great victory over the Norsemen at the Battle of Clontarf in 1014. Two miles north at an ancient ford across the River Callan, Red Hugh O'Neill won a resounding victory over the English in 1598 and, despite the bloody conflicts of Moiry Pass on the border with Co Louth, had withstood the English for five years before his defeat by Lord Mountjoy in 1600.

County Down is a lush, fertile land, peppered with small hillocks called drumlins in the north. The centre is mountainous, dropping in the south to Carlingford Lough.

To the east is the Ards Peninsula, famous for lush landscape and good resorts. It is in the seaside suburb of Holywood that the 136-acre Ulster Folk Museum is to be found, with its reconstructed houses and unique collection of farm and domestic utensils illustrating the traditional Ulster way of life. To the east at the mouth of Belfast Lough is Bangor, the largest of Ireland's seaside resorts, where St Comgall founded a monastery in AD555, rebuilt by St Malachy in 1120. Other resorts include picturesque Ardglass, where King John stayed in 1210, or Newcastle—a cheery golfing resort on the edge of Dundrum Bay, with Slieve Donard blocking out a canvas of sky behind. Inland, there are a myriad smoky villages and small towns; some, like Newry, have been important since ancient times. Nestled in a gap in the hills between Dublin and Ulster, Newry has a Cistercian abbey founded in 1157, and de Courcy built a great castle here, razed by Edward Bruce in 1315.

Killyleagh Castle, Co Down

The coast

Annalong 3 P7
Co Down. Pop 900. A tiny and attractive fishing port that lies at the foot of the Mourne Mountains. One of the few places where you can still see the granite industry in operation. Good beach. Fishing trips in Dundrum Bay.

Ardglass 3 Q6
Co Down. Pop 1,000. EC Thur. It is rare to find a town with more than one castle but this fishing village, famous for its herrings, has several. It was an important port in the Middle Ages, when its citizens built themselves these small castles, which are in fact fortified houses. Jordan's Castle is now a museum and Ardglass Castle, consisting of two 15thC buildings originally built as warehouses by traders, was revamped in the Gothic style in 1789.

Ballintoy 3 N1
Co Antrim. Tiny village glued amongst the crevices of a magnificently wild stretch of coastline with a mountainous limestone headland. Rough stone cottages cling to the corkscrew road that runs down to the tiny harbour. At Magheraboy, 1¼ miles south west, is a chamber tomb, enclosed in a round cairn, called Druid Stone. To the east is the celebrated Carrick-a-Rede rope bridge, which spans a 80-foot-wide chasm between the mainland and Carrick-a-Rede Island, and is erected during the fishing season for salmon fishermen to carry their laden baskets across the breach. To the west is Whitepark Bay, a magnificent, mile-long, dune-backed crescent of beach, and facing the town lies Sheep Island.

Ballycastle 3 O1
Co Antrim. Pop 3,000. EC Wed. Important seaside resort and market town, it's really two towns in one. Spacious Upper Town, around The Diamond, is linked to the sea by a long, straight street around which the less sedate, more bustling Lower Town spreads down to the harbour. The Protestant church in The Diamond is a handsome Doric building of 1756, with Palladian window, pedimented doorway and stone spire. In Lower Town are the remains of Bonamargy Friary, founded by the Franciscans in 1500 and named after the River Margy. Crowning the cliffs west of the town are the ruins of Dunaney Castle, a 16thC MacDonnell stronghold. To the north east is Fair Head, a towering cliff of columnar basalt. To the south, beside the River Glenshesk, rises the 1,695-foot Knocklayd Mountain. It was in a cottage at Ballycastle in 1905 that Marconi made his first commercial wireless transmission. Good, mile-long sandy beach. Excellent sport fishing. Boat trips to Rathlin Island.

Bangor 3 P4
Co Down. Pop 35,000. EC Thur. MD Wed. Prosperous seaside resort forming a net of winding streets around the bays of Bangor and Ballyholme. Important ecclesiastical centre of early Christian Ireland; it was here that St Comgall, close friend of St Columba, established an abbey in the mid-6thC, where many Irish scholars and saints were educated. Repeatedly attacked by the Vikings, the abbey

Bangor, Co. Down

declined and was taken over by the Franciscans in the 15thC. It remained in Franciscan hands for nearly 150 years, and fragments of the Franciscan building, including the tower, have been incorporated into the existing Church of Ireland abbey church, built in 1832. Also of interest: several fine churches, including barn-like First Presbyterian church of 1831; 18thC Belfast Bank, Bingham Lane; Custom House, Scottish Baronial-style tower of 1637; Bangor Castle, 19thC English-style manor house in lovely grounds. Numerous rocky coves and coastal walks. Three golf courses. Open-air sea-water swimming pool.

Belfast 3 P5
Co Antrim. Pop 360,000. EC Wed, Sat. This 19thC red-brick metropolis, a product of the Industrial Revolution, is a world-famous shipbuilding centre, the capital city of Northern Ireland and the second largest city in Ireland. It straddles the winding River Lagan at the head of Belfast Lough, an ocean of inky blue twelve miles long and four miles wide.

City centre, Belfast

To the south it is surrounded by an amphitheatre of lush green hills, their slopes rich in Iron Age forts, and to the south west the River Lagan runs along the broad floor of a steep-sided, wooded valley. Running away to the west and north is the 1,000-foot-high basalt plateau of Antrim, whilst on the immediate edge of the suburbs to the north are Cave Hill (1,182 ft) and Squires Hill (1,237 ft).

History
Although occupied during both the Stone and Bronze Ages, Belfast was of little importance until the mid-18thC, overshadowed as it was in the 17thC by Carrickfergus, which was at that time the major port on the shores of Belfast Lough. Belfast started life as a cluster of forts built to guard a ford across the River Farset; the present High Street was built on the old river bed, in the 19thC. Following the invasion of Ulster in 1177, John de Courcy built a castle here, which became the focus around which the town developed. The castle itself was destroyed by Edward Bruce in 1315 and was rebuilt and razed several times more in the ensuing three centuries. Belfast was still little more than a fishing village when it was seized by the O'Neills, the Earls of Tyrone; following an unsuccessful rebellion, the land was confiscated from them in 1603 by the English and, after four years of harrassment, in 1607 O'Neill led the 'Flight of the Earls' to the continent. The lands were granted as spoils of war to Sir Arthur Chichester, who planted them with Devon men and built his own river castle. In 1613 the town was granted a charter by James I; this was later annulled,

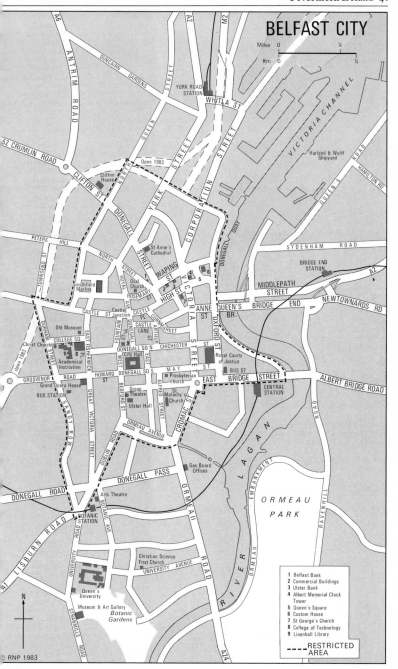

BELFAST CITY

Miles 0 ¼
Km 0 ½

1 Belfast Bank
2 Commercial Buildings
3 Ulster Bank
4 Albert Memorial Clock Tower
5 Queen's Square
6 Custom House
7 St George's Church
8 College of Technology
9 Linenhall Library

- - - - RESTRICTED AREA

© RNP 1983

but was restored in 1688. The city's status grew after the Earl of Strafford, the Lord Deputy of Charles I, bought from Carrickfergus the monopoly on imported goods, thus encouraging trade. By the late 17thC, Belfast was a prosperous market town with wharves and quays flanked with houses crowding along the banks of the River Lagan.

The fortunes of the town rapidly improved with the influx of French Huguenots fleeing the 1685 Edict of Nantes, who helped to expand the already established linen industry. By the end of the 17thC, the population had reached 2,000. Letter-press printing was established in 1696 and in 1737 the 'Belfast News Letter', the world's oldest continuously published newspaper, was founded. Cotton spinning was introduced in 1777 and became a major industry, and in 1784, following a revival of shipbuilding, a corporation was set up for the improvement of the port. Also in the 1780s Roger Mulholland, a local architect, was continuing the gradual improvement of the town, which had been started by the Earl of Donegal in 1757, by laying out a network of broad, spacious streets, such as Donegall Street. During the late 18thC and early 19thC Belfast developed as a cultural centre, with the establishment in 1785 of the Belfast Academy, 1788 the Belfast Library (in the White Linen Hall), 1815 the Belfast Academical Institution and 1845 Queen's College. In the 19thC Belfast grew swiftly. In 1810 the population was nearly 28,000, of whom over 2,000 were employed by the booming cotton industry. Trade and industry were further encouraged by the dredging of the Victoria Channel, from Belfast Lough to the port, in 1849; in 1862 the world-famous Harland and Wolff shipbuilding yard was opened, where the Titanic would later be built. In 1888 Queen Victoria granted Belfast city status. By this time the population had risen to 208,000, and by 1895 it had reached 300,000. In 1920, under the Government of Ireland Act, the city became the capital of Northern Ireland, with a population of 400,000.

Always a political hotbed, Belfast was the cradle for French revolutionary ideas in Ireland. Theobald Wolfe Tone founded the Society of United Irishmen here in 1791, aimed at ousting the English from Ulster. Throughout the 19thC and 20thC the city has been the scene of sectarian riots, and was heavily bombed during World War II. In 1964 the so-called 'tricolour riots' erupted, and in 1968 the city became once again the focus of sectarian violence. Under the Belfast Redevelopment Plan of recent years, efforts have been made to clear the city of its Victorian slums and to improve its appearance. Despite evident caring, however, the city still has an air of disquiet and continues to be a flashpoint between factions, especially in areas like the Falls and the Shankill Roads. Visitors would do well to avoid such areas; vehicle access is limited in the city centre and pedestrians are liable to search. Taxis available at the City Hall rank or by telephone. Fortunately, however, the outlying areas that have remained relatively unaffected offer many of the city's attractions, including the zoo, Belfast Castle, the Ulster Folk Museum and Stormont Castle.

Districts

The 18thC and 19thC city centred around Castle Place and Cornmarket on the west bank of the River Lagan; a series of broad streets lined with late Georgian-style houses were built in this area. Few early 19thC houses remain, however, and most of the early industrial buildings have also gone; survivors include the pedimented building of the Durham Street Weaving Company of 1834 and the 1830s Soho Foundry in Townsend Street. The port and docks also cover an extensive area, comprising seven miles of quays. Much of the city has been rebuilt since the devastating blitz of the last war, and although there is still much to be seen in Belfast, it is essentially a centre from which to visit the surrounding spectacular countryside.

Streets

The High Street was originally built along the curve of the River Farset and lined with wharves and handsome town houses. At the eastern end, by the river, is the Italianate 19thC Custom House. In the early 19thC the river was covered, making a broad and spacious street. To the west is Castle Junction, the heart of the shopping area where Belfast's principal streets meet. To the south of the High Street is Chichester Street; there is still a touch of early 19thC Belfast in Nos 7 and 9, two handsome town houses built in 1804. Bedford Street, one of a series of tree-lined avenues, was the centre of the linen industry in the 19thC and still boasts many Victorian buildings; Nos 9–15 have particularly interesting facades, with remarkable fenestration crowned by a bold Italianate cornice. Waring Street is one of the main commercial streets and has a number of fine 19thC buildings, including the Belfast Bank and the Commercial Buildings, with boldly articulated façade of 1820. Queen's Bridge was designed by Sir Charles Lanyon, the leading architect of mid-19thC Belfast, and was opened in 1841 and widened in 1886. The Gas Board Offices in Ormeau Road are also by Lanyon.

Cathedrals, abbeys & churches

St Anne's Cathedral in Donegall Street is a Romanesque basilica built 1899–1927 by Thomas Drew and W H Lynn on the site of the old parish church; with a tall, plain, rather banal nave and shallow transepts it's rather like cake without the

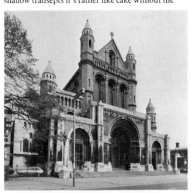

St Anne's Cathedral, Belfast

icing. In Derby Street, **St Peter's Pro-Cathedral** is a heavy-handed Gothic Revival building with twin spires, designed in a rather pompous manner by Father Jeremiah McAuley and John O'Neill in the 1860s. **Christ Church** in College Square North is a handsome red-brick Georgian building designed 1833 by William Farrel with Ionic stone main façade and an amazing three-tier pulpit by William Batt, 1878. **St Malachy's Church** in Alfred Street is a gawky Disneyland mirage of octagonal turrets and battlemented gables, designed with tongue-in-cheek audacity by Thomas Jackson in 1848; the sumptuous interior is rich in pendants and elaborate tracery-work. **St George's** in the High Street was the first Church of Ireland parish church; the main body was designed by John Bowden in 1819, with a handsome

Corinthian portico façade salvaged from the eccentric Bishop of Derry's 1788 palace at Ballyscullion, Co Derry. The **Oval Church** in Rosemary Street, an elliptical brick Presbyterian church, is by Roger Mulholland (a local architect) 1783; the exterior was crudely remodelled in 1833 but the interior has a lovely curving pulpit staircase, curved aisles, box pews and gallery. The **Christian Science First Church** in University Avenue is a weird black and white piece of 20thC vernacular by Clough Williams-Ellis, the architect of Portmeirion, Wales. **St Mark's Church** in Holywood Road, Dundela, is a red sandstone wonder with a tall, square belfry, on the top of a hill, designed by William Butterfield, the genius of English Medievalism, in 1878. The **Presbyterian Church** in May Street is a handsome classical building designed by W Smith in 1829; it has a brick and stucco façade, pediment and Ionic columns. Finally, **Knockbreda Parish Church** in Ormeau Road is an attractive building on an elegant cruciform plan, designed by Richard Castle 1747.

Castles & palaces

Belfast Castle in Antrim Road is a Scottish Baronial-style pile built in 1870 by W H Lynn, the partner of Sir Charles Lanyon. Standing in the shadows of Cave Hill, overlooking the city, it has a six-storey Balmoral-style square tower and a garden staircase reminiscent of a French chateau. Five miles east of the city centre is **Stormont Castle**, the former official residence of the Prime Minister of Northern Ireland but now used as government offices. It, too,

Stormont, Belfast

is in Scottish Baronial style, a monumental white Anglo-Palladian pastiche; built in 300 acres of gardens to the design of Sir Arnold Thornely 1921–23, it stands on rising ground at the end of an impressive avenue.

Interesting buildings

City hall in Donegall Square is a large, palazzo-style building built in 1906 by Brumwell Thomas; it has a great dome on a columned drum, corner cupolas and a handsome marble-lined entrance hall with black and white marble floor. In front is a sculptured group commemorating the victims of the Titanic disaster, and inside there is a permanent exhibition, *open Fri mornings by prior appointment.*

Clifton House in Clifton Street, also known as the Poor House or Charitable Institute, is a handsome Georgian-style pedimented brick building with an octagonal stone spire and projecting wings, designed 1774 by an amateur architect and local paper merchant, Robert Jay. The **Custom House** in the High Street at the end of Donegall Quay is a colossal Corinthian-style building, designed with considerable panache by Sir Charles Lanyon in 1857 on an E-shaped plan; it was here that Anthony Trollope, the 19thC novelist, once worked as a surveyor's clerk. In Waring Street is the headquarters of the **Belfast Bank**, originally a mid-18thC market house, transformed by Robert Taylor in 1776 into the Assembly Rooms and in the 19thC by Lanyon into the palazzo-style building (based on Barry's Reform Club, London) that we see today. The **Ulster Bank**, in the same street, is an exotic yellow stone Italianate building designed by James Hamilton, a Scottish architect, in 1860. The **Ulster Hall** in Bedford Street, now a venue for boxing, wrestling and orchestral concerts, is a

Albert Memorial Clock Tower, Belfast

monumental 1860 building by W J Barre; born in Newry, Barre was the prime mover of the Gothic Revival in Ulster. Another of his contributions to Belfast is the magnificent **Albert Memorial Clock Tower** in Queen's Square, built 1867–69. The **Royal Courts of Justice** in Chichester Street are housed in a Portland stone monolith designed in a debased classical style by J G West in 1933; they include the famous 'Four Courts'. The **Royal Belfast Academical Institution** in College Square was originally designed by Sir John Soane 1807–9, but was finally built in 1814 on a reduced scale little resembling the original plan; the **Technical College** in front of it was completed in 1907. **Queen's University** in University Road was incorporated as Belfast University in 1909. The original buildings are the red-brick neo-Tudor complex designed by Lanyon in 1849.

Parks & gardens

Barnett's Demesne, once the headquarters of the National Trust in Northern Ireland, is a thickly wooded park overlooking the River Lagan in South Belfast. In Stranmillis Road, the **Botanic Gardens**, which cover 38 acres, were established in 1829. There is a wonderful glass-domed Palm House designed by Richard Turner and Charles Lanyon in 1839, predating that of Kew Gardens in London. **Dixon Park** in the Upper Malone area is the venue for the Belfast International Rose Trials, which take place every summer. **Hazelwood Gardens**, on the wooded slopes of Cave Hill, offer fine gardens set around a large lake. Other parks are **Ormeau Park** on the banks of the river; **Musgrave Park** with tennis courts, bowling and putting greens and sports pitches; **Victoria Park**, formed from reclaimed land on the shores of Belfast Lough; and **Falls Park**, at the foot of the Black Mountain. In Antrim Road, the disused **waterworks** have been transformed into a picturesque park with waterfalls, bridges and fishing and boating facilities. **Collin Glen** in Glen Road is a marvellous wilderness of streams and dense woodland, with a bed of wildflowers covering some 50 acres on a fold of land running down from Collin Mountain. There is an attractive walk along the River Lagan towpath through the beech trees of **Minnowburn Park**, past Shaw's Bridge to the Molly Ward locks on the Stranmillis embankment.

Museums & galleries

The Belfast Transport Museum in Witham Street has an interesting exhibition that includes the

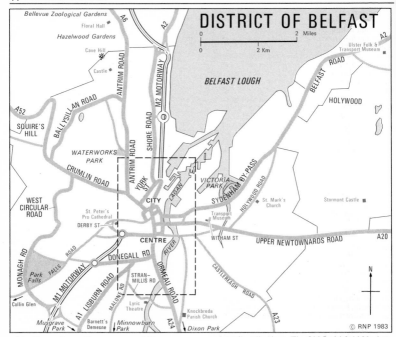

original horse-drawn Fintona tram and Maeve, a
1939 locomotive. The **Ulster Museum and Art
Gallery** in Stranmillis Road stands in the Botanic
Gardens and is an old building with a modern
extension designed 1971 by Frances Pym; it houses
an interesting collection of prehistoric axes, pottery
and spearheads, as well as a reconstructed court
cairn. The gallery includes works by Sickert,
Turner, Pissarro and other Europeans as well as the
Belfast-born Sir John Lavery and other Irish artists
such as Louis Le Brocquy, William Conor and Jack
B Yeats, the father of the poet W B Yeats. There is
also a fine natural history collection and an array of
priceless jewellery, recently recovered by divers
from the wreck of a Spanish Armada galleon found
at the Giant's Causeway. **Old Museum** in College
Square North is a handsome Greek Revival-style
building designed by Thomas Duff and Thomas
Jackson in 1831. The first of Ireland's purpose-built
museums, it is now the headquarters of the Belfast
Natural History and Philosophical Society and is
especially noted for collections of natural history and
antiquities. **Linenhall Library** in Donegall Square,
originally founded as the Belfast Society for
Promoting Knowledge, and once housed in the old
White Linen Hall, still has a superb collection of
books on Irish History and the linen trade. The
Ulster Folk and Transport Museum, evoking the
atmosphere of traditional Irish life, is a 20-minute
bus ride away near Holywood, Co Down.
Special attractions
Belfast Zoological Gardens, in Bellevue Park,
Antrim Road, Newtownabbey, houses a diverse
collection of exotic wild animals mostly in open
enclosures with 13 acres of gardens on the slopes of
Cave Hill. Llamas, lions and wolves are bred here,
and there is an aquarium, monkey house and bird

and reptile collections. The **Old Smithfield Market**,
near Royal Avenue, is a fun place to hunt for old
books and bric-a-brac. There are also numerous
large, well-equipped leisure centres.
Entertainment
In addition to the museums and parks already
mentioned, there are abundant facilities for all
sports; six 18-hole and two 9-hole golf courses, four
indoor swimming pools, two greyhound-racing
tracks and boating and sailing on Belfast Lough. The
Lyric Players Theatre specialises in poetic drama
and classics and is regarded as Northern Ireland's
National Theatre. Others include the **Arts Theatre**
in Botanic Avenue, which specialises in modern
plays, and the **Group Theatre**. The **Grand Opera
House** in Great Victoria Street was designed by
Frank Matcham in the late 19th C and recently
restored, and hosts various prestigious opera, ballet
and theatre touring companies. **Ulster Hall** in
Bedford Street is a venue for boxing and wrestling
matches as well as the home of the Ulster Orchestra,
the Belfast Operatic Society and the Belfast
Philharmonic Society. The **Queen's Film Theatre**,
in the university, shows foreign and classic films.
Floral Hall in the Hazelwood Gardens is used for
concert parties and dancing.
Shopping
The principal shopping streets are centred around
Castle Junction and include Donegall Place, Howard
Street, Fountain Street, Castle Lane, Cornmarket,
Arthur Street and Chichester Street. There are
numerous covered arcades. Many shops sell craft
products, such as wood carvings, stone and metal
artefacts and Irish jewellery. The work is produced
by a rapidly expanding cottage industry of craftsmen
working from home or in small workshops. Good
china and glass as well as textiles.

Carrickfergus 3 P4

Co Antrim. Pop 15,000. EC Wed, Sat. Once an important Belfast Lough port and 13thC stronghold of the English crown, it's an attractive, airy town with much of its 17thC atmosphere intact. The ruins of an impressive 12thC Anglo-Norman castle sit atop a rocky pedestal projecting into the lough. St Nicholas, where Louis MacNeice's father was rector, was built in the 12thC and rebuilt 1614. Also of interest: remains of 17thC town walls including north gate; 18thC houses and shops in the High Street; the Town Hall, which incorporates the fine classical façade of the former County Court House of 1779; Dalway's Bawn at Bellahill, well preserved early 17thC Planter's bawn, built in 1609 and consisting of a rectangular enclosure with three granite-built round towers.

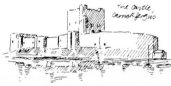

the castle carmakfergus

Cushendall 3 O2

Co Antrim. Pop 650. EC Tue. Tiny resort of attractive Georgian and Regency houses lining a handful of streets at the mouth of the River Dall. To the south is Glenariff, one of the most beautiful of Co Antrim's glens. At its foot Red Bay, a golden crescent of beach walled by sandstone cliffs, is ideal for bathing, boating and fishing. Numerous prehistoric remains in the surrounding hills.

Cushendun 3 O2

Co Antrim. Pop 150. EC Tue. Now owned by the National Trust, it's a picturesque model village of black and white English-style cottages and a hotel, built around a village green and beach as a summer resort in the early 20thC. Wedged in a wooded fold of land by the mouth of the River Dunn, it was designed for Lord Cushendun by Sir Clough Williams-Ellis, the celebrated architect of Portmeirion, Wales. Important Stone Age site.

Donaghadee 3 Q4

Co Down. Pop 3,700. EC Thur. A seaside resort that stands at the head of the Ards Peninsula, which runs south between the sea and Strangford Lough. Once a busy cross-channel port until the big ships left it for Belfast. Now the harbour is a yacht marina. Bird sanctuary on off-shore Copeland Island. Good sandy beach.

Dundrum 3 P6

Co Down. Attractive fishing village arranged as if for a picture postcard round a small harbour on the shores of secluded Dundrum Bay. Crowning a hill are the ruins of a huge 13thC Anglo-Norman castle with a giant circular keep. To the south west the horizon is blocked by the blue shadow-washed Mountains of Mourne. Good fishing in the bay. Murlough nature reserve is nearby.

Fair Head 3 O1

Nr Ballycastle, Co Antrim. These 636-foot-high cliffs look across to Scotland, only 14 miles away. The atmosphere here is really out of this world. On the cliff top are two dark lakes; one has a prehistoric fortified island said to be the haunt of underwater horsemen. Golden eagles nest here and you can enjoy a rare geophysical phenomenon looking at the curvature of the earth along the rim of the distant Atlantic.

Giant's Causeway

Giant's Causeway 3 N1

Co Antrim. A rare and famous series of cliffs that resulted from gigantic outpourings of volcanic basalt in remote tertiary times. The rock cooled as a lower layer of thousands of regular hexagonal columns and an upper layer of slim uneven prisms like a crazy architect's fantasy. This amazing piece of coast belongs to the National Trust—take the North Antrim Cliff Path, an 11-mile right of way from the Causeway to Ballintoy.

Glenarm 3 O3

Co Antrim. Pop 700. EC Wed. A picturesque seaside village spread out along the southern bank of the River Glenarm, it is one of the oldest glen villages. On the opposite bank is Glenarm Castle, an 18thC house built round an Elizabethan keep. The spectacular grounds swallow up most of a beautiful glen. Birthplace of Eóin MacNeill.

Holywood 3 P4

Co Down. Pop 8,000. EC Wed. Neat residential town six miles from Belfast on the shores of Belfast Lough. There is a ruined 14thC priory, and in the High Street stands Ireland's only maypole, still used for the occasional jig. Home of the fascinating Ulster Folk and Transport Museum.

Kilkeel 3 O7

Co Down. Pop 3,000. C Thur. Busy fishing harbour and holiday resort at the mouth of the River Kilkeel, with the Mountains of Mourne as a spectacular backdrop. To the north east is the Crawtree Stone, a portal dolmen; three miles north west is the Giant's Grave, a ruined court cairn.

Larne 3 P3

Co Antrim. Pop 18,300. EC Tue. MD Wed. Irish terminal for the ferry from Cairnryan or Stranraer. Not a resort but a good spot for a game of golf on either of the two good courses. On a strip of land to the south of the town (the Curran) great quantities of mesolithic flints have been found. Good sand beach and heated pool.

Newcastle 3 P7

Co Down. Pop 5,000. EC Thur. This is where the mountains of Mourne sweep down to the sea. Close by are Tollymore and Castlewellan Forest Parks; they offer camping caravan sites and an excellent arboretum. The beach is three miles of excellent sand, and is backed by the Royal County Down championship golf course.

Portaferry 3 Q6

Co Down. Pop 1,600. EC Thur. A tiny and picturesque village on the east side of the narrow entrance to Strangford Lough. There is a 16thC castle and an 18thC mansion, Portaferry House. Worth the few miles' trip across the turbulent narrows. Not a swimming resort but excellent fishing. Rumour has it that skate of over 180 lbs have been caught.

Portrush 3 M1

Co Antrim. Pop 4,800. EC Wed. A mile-long promontory that juts into the Atlantic, it has excellent long sandy beaches and the famous Royal Portrush Golf Course. Justifiably one of Ulster's most popular seaside resorts; good sailing, perfect swimming, bowling, tennis and putting.

Portstewart 3 M2
Co Londonderry. Pop 5,000. EC Thur. Neat little seaside resort with a good harbour and two golf courses—but you really come here for the two miles of beautiful sandy beach, and for the fishing. Thackeray used to visit here back in the 1840s.

Rostrevor 3 O7
Co Down. Pop 2,100. EC Wed. A spot that has the blandest climate in Northern Ireland due to its sheltered site on Carlingford Lough. As a peaceful centre for mountain walking, pony trekking and bathing it's hard to beat. Good little beach.

Strangford 3 Q6
Co Down. Small fishing port standing at the narrow entrance to Strangford Lough. Numerous ruined castles in area include Strangford Castle, a small 16thC tower house near the shore; Kilchief Castle, an early 15thC fortress three miles to the south. Castle Ward House, two miles west, is a fine Georgian mansion.

Warrenpoint 3 O7
Co Down. Pop 4,300. Seaport for Newry and a spacious resort, it stands at the top of Carlingford Lough. Good fishing, sports and boating facilities, and famed for its 'singing pubs'. The Old Narrow Water Castle is a three-storey tower house built around 1560 to defend the entrance to the Newry estuary; it is surrounded by a bawn wall.

Whitehead 3 P4
Co Antrim. Pop 2,600. Small seaside resort with good golf courses. Neolithic remains on nearby Muldersleigh Hill, and ruins of 17thC Castle Chichester. Two miles west stands Dalway's Bawn, a fine Plantation fortified farmhouse c1609. HQ of Co Antrim Yacht Club and of Irish Railway Preservation Society; on summer weekends enthusiasts can travel to Portrush in old coaches.

Islands & peninsulas

Boa Island 2 J5
Lower Lough Erne, Co Fermanagh. A long, thin strip of land skirting the edge of the lough, joined to the mainland at either end by a bridge. Caldragh cemetery, one of the oldest in Ireland, is the home of two strange stone figures, probably 1stC.

Carrick-a-Rede Island 3 N1
Co Antrim, 5 miles W of Ballycastle. A spot for daredevils to try their luck—a rocky island is separated from the cliffs by an 80-foot chasm: the only link is a swinging rope bridge. It's an unnerving experience to cross the bridge; and don't forget you have to make the same dizzy journey back.

Devenish Isle 2 J6
Lower Lough Erne, Co Fermanagh. Come here for an experience you can have only in Ireland—the atmosphere of exquisite Celtic melancholy. The whole island is a mass of ruins among the bracken. It is hard to imagine the richly endowed monastery in its glory. Only the thick, shattered, roofless walls give a notion of its strength. Now only cattle wander along the nave under the watchful eye of the round tower. Public ferry from Trory or Enniskillen.

Island Magee 3 P3
Co Antrim. A narrow peninsula, well wooded and once a breeding ground for goshawks. Now a lovely spot for a walk by the sea, especially along the

Gobbins, 250-foot-high basalt cliffs, once the well known haunt of witches: a black magic cult operated here until the 1960s.

Rathlin Island 3 O1
Co Antrim. A beautiful high island with buzzards breeding on the cliffs. It was here that Robert the Bruce, later king of Scotland, was inspired by the determined spider in the cave; in 1573, during the Desmond rebellion, the Earl of Essex massacred all 600 inhabitants. Now a peaceful spot and glorious wild bird sanctuary. Reach it by boat from Ballycastle.

Rathlin Island

White Island 2 J5
Castle Archdale Bay, Lower Lough Erne, Co Fermanagh. Ruined 12thC church containing eight stone sculptures built into the wall, representing Christian and pagan figures.

Inland towns and villages

Antrim 3 O4
Co Antrim. Pop 15,000. EC Wed. Quiet county town wrapped round a broad main street on the north east corner of Lough Neagh. It was once the site of an early 6thC monastery, of which a well preserved round tower with a cross incised over the entrance still stands. At the west end of the town is Antrim Castle, a 17thC house enlarged in the early 19thC but burnt in 1922 and now a picturesque ruin; remains include motte and bailey and handsome classical garden designed by Le Nôtre with fine trees and rhododendrons. Also of interest: tiny but handsome courthouse of 1726; Church of All Saints, Elizabethan structure rebuilt in 1720 with striking tower and spire added in early 19thC; four chambered cairns crowning Browndod Hill, seven miles to the north; the 92-foot-high round tower dating from the 10thC. There is a new marina on Lough Neagh and a steam railway at Shane's Castle. At Pogue's Entry is the cottage home of Alexander Irvine.

Armagh 3 M6
Co Armagh. Pop 12,500. C Wed. Site of an ancient hill fort built by the legendary Queen Macha in 300 BC, it has also been one of the most important ecclesiastical centres in Ireland for the last 1,500 years, since St Patrick built a church beside the pagan fort. The seat of two archbishops, it became an important scholastic centre. Repeatedly plundered during the Middle Ages, it was little more than a village in the 16thC and early 17thC, but the 18thC has left a handsome legacy due to the indefatigable Archbishop Richard Robinson and architect Francis Johnston, who was born here. It is

Armagh

now a handsome Georgian town. To the south is the Protestant cathedral, largely 19thC rebuilding with handsome tower and spire. To the north is the Catholic cathedral, a limestone building in the Gothic style with twin towers. Also of interest: the Mall, a long, spacious green surrounded by many fine Georgian town houses, at the end of which is the Court House, an elegant porticoed structure built in 1809; Vicars Hill, a row of handsome 18thC houses; the library, designed by Thomas Cooley in 1771 and extended in 1820; the pedimented infirmary, designed by George Ensor in 1774; the Observatory, founded by Primate Robinson in 1789; Archbishop's Palace, designed by Cooley in 1770 with fine chapel beside it of 1781. On the modern side there is a unique planetarium with space travel exhibition and a powerful public telescope.

Augher   2 L5
Co Tyrone. Pop 320. Attractive village built along the banks of the River Blackwater in the lush green Clogher Valley. At the west end of the village is Augher Castle, a Plantation stronghold built by Lord Ridgeway in 1615. A square three-storey structure, it has triangular towers projecting centrally from each side.

Aughnacloy   3 M5
Co Tyrone. Pop 730. Small market town and angling resort built along the River Blackwater near the border with Co Monaghan. In Lismore, three miles west, is Favour-Royal, a large rectangular bawn with corner towers built by Sir Thomas Ridgeway in 1611.

Ballyclare   3 O4
Co Antrim. Pop 5,200. Spacious market town on the River Sixmilewater, said to be the home of Mark Twain's ancestors. Once a centre of the linen industry, it is now primarily noted for its annual fair in early May.

Ballymena   3 N3
Co Antrim. Pop 16,500. C Wed. The birthplace of Sir Roger Casement, it is a thriving manufacturing and market town on the northern side of a dogleg in the River Braid. Founded by Scottish settlers in the 17thC, the town's prosperity dates from the early 18thC when its linen industry was first established. Of interest: the Linen Hall; St Patrick's Church of Ireland Church, a huge Gothic Revival building rebuilt in 1881; Bank of Ireland, early 19thC classical-style building; interesting 19thC commercial vernacular buildings in Mill Street and Church Street; Galgorm Castle, a Plantation fortress of 1618, 1½ miles to the south west. Numerous prehistoric remains in vicinity. Good fishing.

Ballymoney   3 N2
Co Antrim. Pop 3,760. Bustling market town on the edge of the Garry Bog (the town name means 'town of the bog' in Irish). Thought to be the home of Edgar Allan Poe's forefathers. Many fine late Georgian houses, especially in Charlotte Street. Also of interest: Masonic Hall c1775 with Italianate campanile added 1852; ruins of 1637 parish church; St Patrick's Church, built 1783; Catholic Church of Our Lady and St Patrick, built of local basalt with stained glass by Meyer of Munich; St Patrick's Parish Church, a blend of different styles with a graceful octagonal spire. Annual drama festival.

Ballynahinch   3 P6
Co Down. Pop 3,500. EC Mon, Fri. MD Thur. A small, jolly market town with colourful rows of terraced housing, laid out in the early 17thC. Many of the town's buildings were damaged during the 1798 insurrection, when British troops under General Nugent occupied the town. The United Irishmen, encamped on the surrounding heights, invaded the town and drove out the militia but were eventually routed. Of interest: 19thC Ballynahinch Mill; Montalto House, fine 18thC mansion extended in the 19thC with lovely gardens and a herd of red deer; the courthouse; St Patrick's Roman Catholic church, a large classical building; Legananny Dolmen on the southern slopes of Cratlieve Mountain, with two portal stones carrying a tapering capstone; Dunbeg, an earthen fort to the south west; Magheraknock Fort, another small hill fort three miles north. The surrounding area is rich in rounded drumlins and the 1,755-foot-high Slieve Croob sits to the south west.

Banbridge   3 O6
Co Down. Pop 7,000. Pleasant industrial market town on the Upper Bann, centring on a square that is anything but square. The Crozier Monument in the square is a curious edifice flanked by four polar bears, designed by W J Barre in 1862. Some fine Georgian buildings, including a coaching inn, still serving customers, in the 'Cut'. Early 19thC Gothic-style Holy Trinity Church features transepts by Barre, oak pews and alabaster panels.

Bushmills   3 N1
Co Antrim. Pop 1,200. Small town wedged along the banks of the River Bush, celebrated for its distillery and excellent game fishing. Of interest: Dunluce Castle, early 14thC Anglo-Norman castle standing in ruins on an outcrop of basaltic rock 2½ miles north west; the Giant's Causeway, remarkable geological collage 2½ miles to the north. Free tours of the distillery available *daily.*

Caledon   3 M6
Co Tyrone. English-style model village of neat stone cottages built along the banks of the River Blackwater by Lord Caledon in 1816. 1¼ miles south west is Caledon House, handsome Georgian mansion designed by Thomas Cooley in 1779, with Nash colonnades and domed pavilions added in 1812.

Castlederg   2 K4
Co Tyrone. Pop 1,760. Renowned salmon and trout fishing centre; also a flourishing local tweed industry. Castlesessagh, on the bank of the River Derg, is a ruined Plantation bawn c1610 by Sir John Davies.

Castlewellan   3 P6
Co Down. Pop 2,000. EC Thur. MD Mon. A tiny, elegant town laid out around two squares well planted with trees. The 18thC market house is a fine building. In a park nearby is the National Arboretum, around a Victorian-Medieval castle.

Coleraine   3 M2
Co Londonderry. Pop 16,300. EC Thur. A very handsome river port now the home of a new university. Founded as a Plantation town in 1613, it has the typical central 'diamond' plan. Textiles and whiskey are made nearby and you should see the salmon-leap, called the Cutts.

Comber   3 P5
Co Down. Pop 5,200. Attractive little linen town built round a spacious square along the north west shore of Strangford Lough. Once the site of a 12thC Cistercian abbey, replaced by the much altered Church of Ireland church in 1610.

Cookstown 3 M4
Co Tyrone. Pop 6,700. EC Wed. Laid out by a
Planter called Cook in 1609, the main feature is the
40-yard-wide High Street that runs for over a mile as
an elegant promenade. The town is now largely an
agriculture centre. Visit the Drum Manor Forest
Park close by, with its unique butterfly garden.

Craigavon 3 N5
Co Armagh. New ribbon-development linking
Lurgan and Portadown, enclosing the townships of
Brownlow and Mandeville. Brownlow Recreation
Centre has a swimming pool and roller-skating rink.

Crawfordsburn 3 P4
Co Down. Pop 500. Attractive village huddled a mile
inland in wooded seclusion at the foot of a glen.
Thatched 17thC coaching inn and Baronial-style
railway station of 1865. To the south is Clandeboye,
seat of the Marquis of Dufferin and Ava; 110-acre
country park.

Crossmaglen 3 N7
Co Armagh. Pop 1,150. Windswept border village
surrounding a huge market square. Numerous
prehistoric remains in vicinity including a
wedge-shaped cairn at Annaghmare, two miles
north, and a ring fort with souterrain at Lissaraw,
1¼ miles south. Good fishing and boating on the
nearby lakes.

Downpatrick 3 P6
Co Down. Pop 7,500. EC Thur. On the south west
corner of Strangford Lough, this is an attractive
county town with pleasant late Georgian and
Victorian buildings. Site of an early 6thC monastic
settlement harried by the Vikings, it was later
occupied by the Anglo-Normans who, using the
discovery by local clergy of the relics of St Patrick, St
Brigid and St Columba in the surrounding hills as an
excuse, transferred the see from Bangor to
Downpatrick. Parts of the 15thC choir of the
Benedictine church remain in the drastically
remodelled Protestant Cathedral of St Patrick,
designed by Charles Lilly between 1798–1812. To
the north west are the remains of an Anglo-Norman
motte-and-bailey castle. Of particular interest:
Southwell School and almshouses designed 1733 by
Sir Edward Lovett Pearce, with cupola, pedimented
entrance arch and red-brick walls dressed in stone;
impressive 19thC gatehouse of gaol; 19thC

Downpatrick Cathedral

courthouse; the ruins of the Cistercian monastery,
Inch Abbey, three miles to the south. Marking the
spot where St Patrick is said to have landed in
Ireland, 1½ miles away at the mouth of the River
Slaney at Saul stands a Church of Ireland memorial
church. Crowning a hill overlooking the lough is a
giant statue of St Patrick. Numerous prehistoric and
early Christian remains in vicinity.

Dromore 3 O6
Co Down. Pop 2,400. C Thur. Built around a market
square on the upper reaches of the River Lagan. An
important ecclesiastical centre in the early 7thC; the
present Protestant Cathedral of Christ the Redeemer
is a transformation of a mid-17thC church built to
replace the original medieval church, which was
destroyed in the rising of 1641; inside is a 6thC
gravestone, St Colman's pillow, and eight carved
misericordes in the canons' stalls. Also of interest:
large 12thC Norman motte and bailey; 9thC–10thC
high cross by the bridge across the river; ancient
stocks in the market square; Dromore House,
formerly the Bishop's Palace, built in 1781.

Dungannon 3 M5
Co Tyrone. Pop 7,500. EC Wed. An O'Neill
stronghold until the end of the 16thC, now a hilltop
market and manufacturing town, noted as the home
of Moygashel fabrics and Tyrone crystal—Northern
Ireland's answer to Waterford. Tours and shop at the
crystal factory. Good fishing in local lakes.

Enniskillen 2 K6
Co Fermanagh. Pop 9,600. EC Wed. County town of
Fermanagh, a compact nest of buildings jammed
tight on a triangular island in the middle of the River
Erne, two miles upstream from Lower Lough Erne.

Water Gate, Enniskillen

The winding main street is lined with pleasant
Georgian and Victorian buildings; a knot of tiny
streets to the north called Boston is where the aura of
old Enniskillen is at its best. Key stronghold of the
Maguires in the Middle Ages, after the north was
conquered it was granted by James I to Sir William
Cole, who established it as an important Protestant
stronghold. A rallying point during the rising of
1641, it backed the Williamite cause of 1689 at the
Battle of the Boyne.
Of interest: Enniskillen Castle, remains of 15thC
Maguire Castle (now a museum) and 17thC Water
Gate; 17thC parish church, now the cathedral, with
fine font of 1666 and the 1628 Porkrich Stone;
remains of 17thC star fort on Fort Hill with
extensive pleasure grounds and tall 19thC memorial
column to General Sir Galbraith Lowry Cole, a
veteran of the Peninsular War; Castlecoole, one of

reland's finest classical mansions, $1\frac{1}{2}$ miles south
east. On a hill to the west is Portora Royal School,
founded in 1608 by James I, where Oscar Wilde and
Samuel Beckett were educated; in the grounds are
the ruins of 17thC Portora Castle. The only town in
the British Isles to have raised two regiments, it has
also become one of Ireland's leading holiday centres,
with cruisers for hire on Upper and Lower Lough
Erne and a leisure centre. Regular international
angling contests are held, as well as other lakeland
activities.

Gracehill   3 N3
Co Antrim. Pop 500. Virtually intact Moravian
settlement established in 1746 by the Rev John
Cennick. Planned with two parallel streets and a
central square, it consists of separate houses for
unmarried brothers and sisters, a plain chapel,
schools, inn, post office and grocer's shop.

Hillsborough   3 O5
Co Down. Pop 800. EC Sat. Another Plantation
town, founded in 1650 by one Sir Arthur Hill. When
Northern Ireland had a Governor General he lived in
Hillsborough Castle, a large, mainly 19thC house.
The fort has an elegant 18thC Gothic gatehouse and
he church is well worth seeing.

Irvinestown   2 K5
Co Fermanagh. Pop 1,300. Plantation border town
founded 1618. Main shopping centre for area and
cattle market. Of interest: 1734 clock tower, all that
remains of old parish church; Necarne Castle, $\frac{1}{2}$
mile to the south, a Scottish Baronial legacy from the
Irvine family, Scotch-Irish Planters after whom the
town was named.

Keady   3 M5
Co Armagh. Pop 2,130. Once important for its linen
mills, now a quiet upland town with pleasant
wooded Keady Glen and nearby circle of fish-filled
lakes. Local centre for gaelic sports and
folk-dancing. Nearby Carnagh Forest offers
pony-trekking, fishing and a caravan site.

Killyleagh   3 P6
Co Down. Pop 2,400. EC Thur. A delightfully
unspoilt place with its own romantic castle looming
over the village and harbour on the shores of
Strangford Lough. The castle is solid, with pinnacle
roofs on each tower and a great walled park. Real
feudal splendour. Castle is not open to the public.

Limavady   3 M2
Co Londonderry. Pop 6,000. EC Thur. MD Mon. A
lovely little Georgian town, moved away from the
castle by an early Planter because it spoilt his view.
Thackeray came here and fell in love with a maid at
the inn, though he was only there for ten minutes. A
mile or so to the east is Drenagh, a cool classical
house of 1830, and ruins of 13thC church.

Lisburn   3 O5
Co Antrim. Pop 28,000. C Wed. MD Tue. A trim
town round a triangular market place. In the centre
is a statue of Gen John Nicholson who was killed in a
storming party in Delhi. Nice little Church of
Ireland cathedral in typical 1625 'Planter's Gothic',
with graves of Huguenots who developed the Ulster
linen industry.

Lisnakea   2 K6
Co Fermanagh. Pop 1,340. The second town of
Fermanagh, it clusters on a long, curving main street
with an old market place in the middle. High cross,
in the market place, is from an early monastery.
Many pleasant pubs. Of interest: early 19thC
Market House, Corn Market and Butter Market.
Main shopping centre for east Fermanagh.

Londonderry   2 K3
Co Londonderry. Pop 51,850. EC Thur. The second
city of Northern Ireland, situated on the River
Foyle. Four miles downstream, the river runs into
Lough Foyle, which in turn opens into the Atlantic
Ocean. The name 'Derry', by which all but British
officials call the city, is from the Irish 'doire',
meaning 'place of oaks'; in AD546, when St
Columba founded an abbey here, it was only a hill
crowned with trees. Nothing remains of the
pre-Plantation city; the earliest extant buildings date
from 1614, when the streets, walls and gates were
laid out by Planters from London.

History
Originally a 6thC Christian settlement, Derry was
held by the Vikings from the 9thC–12thC but
escaped Norman invasion. Continually besieged by
the Irish, it was destroyed in 1608. After the 'Flight
of the Earls', James I granted the land to the City of
London Livery Companies who, despite the efforts
of bands of Irish outlaws in the woods, rebuilt the
city, as well as building most of the surrounding
towns and villages. Derry is in classic Plantation
Town style, with cruciform street pattern, central
diamond and huge enclosing wall.
It became a naval base and garrison town, and
during the 1641 rising was a haven for hordes of
refugees. In 1649, during the Civil War, it sided with
Cromwell and was besieged unsuccessfully by the
Royalists for five months. The greatest siege of
Derry's history was that of 1688; 30,000 people
crowded into the city to escape the Jacobites and
about 7,000 of them died of starvation and disease.
Many thousands of Derrymen emigrated to America
in the 17thC and early 18thC in reaction to harsh
English laws; many famous Americans, including
Davy Crockett and Daniel Boone, came originally
from Derry families. The well known Restoration
playwright George Farquhar was also a Derry man,
born here in 1678.

Districts
Most of the original town plan survives at the heart
of the modern city, three-quarters of which lies on
the west bank of the River Foyle; it is joined to the
eastern section, Waterside, by the Craigavon Bridge,
a modern steel affair of little appeal. Probably the
best way to see the city is to take a walking tour of
the walls, mighty 20-foot-thick fortifications with
corner bastions, circling the city. There were
originally four gates, but all have been rebuilt. It is
also interesting to wander down the steep, narrow
streets outside the walls, with their quaint little
houses. Shipquay Street is the main thoroughfare;
the steepest main street of any Irish city, it retains a
Georgian character.

Cathedrals, abbeys & churches
There are two cathedrals in the city. St Columb's,
built 1628–33, is a magnificent example of Planters'
Gothic, with a tower and graceful Georgian spire. St
Eugene's in Infirmary Road was completed in 1873;
designed in flamboyant Gothic style by J J McCarthy,
it has a handsome granite spire, added in 1903.
There are many interesting churches. St Columba's,
often called the Long Tower Church, was built in
1784 on the site of an 1164 church, Templemore,
just outside the walls; it has a lavish marble altar and
stained glass by Meyer of Munich. Also of interest:
the Presbyterian Church in Great James Street, an
elegant 1837 edifice; First Presbyterian Church in
Magazine Street, with fine portico.

Interesting buildings
The city walls are perhaps the most impressive
edifice in Derry. See especially the Bishop Gate,
1789, a triumphal arch with carved heads and panels
by Edward Smyth, and the Church Bastion, with

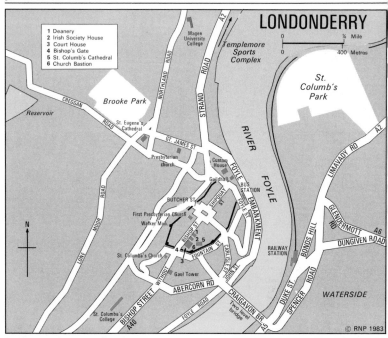

LONDONDERRY

1 Deanery
2 Irish Society House
3 Court House
4 Bishop's Gate
5 St. Columb's Cathedral
6 Church Bastion

© RNP 1983

flanking stone watchtowers. The **Walker Monument**, a Roman Doric column of 1828, commemorates the great Jacobite siege; nearby is 'Roaring Meg', a large cannon used in the siege.

Bishop Gate, Londonderry

There is a fine neoclassical **courthouse** by John Bowden, 1813, with portico modelled on the Temple of Erechtheus, Athens. The nearby **deanery** and **Irish Society's House** are two of Derry's fine Georgian buildings; stately Georgian terraces are also to be found in Clarendon Street, Queen Street and Bishop Street. The **Guildhall**, 1890, has stained glass panels depicting the city's history and a

timber-roofed banqueting hall; it is used for plays, festivals and concerts. There are also several colleges in Londonderry. **St Columb's College** in Bishop Street was built around the Earl of Bristol's 18thC Casino, and blends neoclassical and neo-Gothic styles; there is a large, disused windmill in the grounds. **Magee University College**, in the north suburbs, has a handsome neo-Gothic façade, 1865. Also of interest: **gaol tower**, 1819–24. Five miles north east is the celebrated hill fort, the **Grianán of Aileach**, originally the royal seat of the Tir Eóghain; remains consist of a massive ring fort 77 feet in diameter and 17½ feet high; it stands on the 803-foot-high Greenan Mountain.

Parks
Brooke Park is the city's main open space and provides pleasant walks. On the other side of the River Foyle lies the rolling greensward of **St Columb's Park**, affording fine views over the Inishowen peninsula.

Special attractions
The **Templemore Sports Complex** offers various facilities, including a par-3 golf course. Municipal events include the annual Irish 'feis', a competitive festival held in late *Feb*, the Foyle Festival in late *May*, and a traditional parade and ceremony commemorating the closing of the gates by the 13 apprentices in 1688, held in *mid-Aug*.

Loughbrickland   3 O6
Co Down, 3 miles SW of Banbridge. Spacious village of elegant houses around an attractive lake, noted for its trout.

Lurgan   3 N5
Co Armagh. Pop 25,000. C Wed. MD Thur. An industrious centre of the linen industry. Now joined to Portadown by an industrial zone to create

Craigavon New Town and embellished by new
Lough Neagh marina, boating lakes, ski and golf
schools and other new-town features.

Magherafelt 3 N4
Co Londonderry. Pop 4,500. Prosperous market town
radiating out from a large central square in typical
Plantation style. The 19thC Courthouse (now a
police station) is a frivolous fairy-tale building, and
the 18thC courthouse and gaol at the end of the main
street are very quaint.

Moira 3 O5
Co Antrim. Pop 760. Old-world village on a broad
main street clambering up a hill, with 18thC
blackstone houses with carriage archways and
elegant fanlights. Also a number of interesting
churches, especially St John's, 1725, at the head of
an impressive grassy avenue. Moira Demesne,
opposite the church, is an attractive park. Also of
interest: Market House, 1810; Berwick Hall, a
two-storey thatched yeoman's house, c1700.

Moy 3 M5
Co Tyrone. Pop 930. Built for the Earl of Charlemont
in late 18thC, it was modelled on Marengo in
Lombardy, with houses grouped around a long,
narrow tree-lined square.

Newry 3 N7
Co Down. Pop 20,000. EC Wed. MD Thur, Sat. One
of Ireland's oldest cities, it is a port situated
strategically in the Gap of the North. The formerly
congested centre has been extensively rebuilt, but
much pleasant and varied architecture remains,
principally along the canal—oldest in the UK and
now the scene of the annual Ulster coarse fishing
championship. Small, decorative, light-coloured
granite 19thC cathedral. Market days draw
good-humoured crowds from both sides of the
nearby border.

Newtownards 3 P5
Co Down. Pop 15,500. EC Thur. MD Mon. Neat,
handsomely planned 17thC town near Strangford
Lough, laid out by Hugh Montgomery, a Scottish
laird. Now a busy manufacturing and market centre.
At the end of Court Street are the remains of a 13thC
Dominican friary. Also of interest: elegant 18thC
town hall with cupola and pedimented entrance, set
in a giant blind arch, designed by Ferdinando
Stratford, a canal engineer from Bristol.

Omagh 2 K5
Co Tyrone. Pop 12,000. EC Wed. MD Thur, Sat.
County town of Tyrone. Good classical courthouse
and regimental museum of the Royal Inniskilling
Fusiliers. Now a centre for the Gortin Glen Forest
Park, beautiful moorland rich in waterfalls, and the
new Ulster American Folk Park. Good fishing.

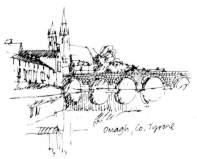
Omagh, Co. Tyrone

Portadown 3 N5
Co Armagh. Pop 22,000. EC Thur. MD Sat.
Originally a strategic settlement at the ford of the
River Bann, now a busy manufacturing town, part of
the Craigavon New Town development. Although
McGredy's—who made Portadown famous for
roses—have moved to New Zealand, the town is still
Ulster's horticultural heart. HQ of Fisheries
Conservancy, which stocks the rivers and lakes with
trout, salmon and other anglers' delights.

Strabane

Strabane 2 K3
Co Tyrone. Pop 9,500. EC Thur. MD Tue, Thur. A
busy, small town that is worth a visit only for its
associations. In the Main Street is the bow-fronted
Gray's Printing Works—John Dunlap (1747–1812)
left here after an apprenticeship to found America's
first daily paper, 'The Pennsylvania Packet'. He was
also the first printer of the Declaration of
Independence. Another employee was the
grandfather of President Woodrow Wilson, whose
cottage is now open to the public.

Tandragee 3 N6
Co Armagh. Pop 1,800. Pleasant little town on the
banks of the River Cusher; its wide main street
sweeps up to the gate of Tandragee Castle, a gothic
extravaganza now housing a potato-crisp factory.
Small Gothic-style Catholic church on the main
street is worth a look, and there are pleasant walks
along the river.

Regional features

Belleek Pottery 2 I5
Belleek, Co Fermanagh. This small village produced
superbly designed porcelain in the 19thC, from the
local feldspar. Highly glazed, intricate pieces often
resembling basket work are much prized. The 20thC
products, although hardly collectors' items, make
good souvenirs, and tours of the factory are full of
interest.

Belleek ware, co. Fermanagh

Celtic Crosses
Often to be seen just outside the villages of the
north, these great high stone crosses are relics of the
early Christian settlements of the 9thC and 10thC.
Usually sandstone with intricate carved decoration of
scenes from the Bible. Two of the finest crosses are
at Donaghmore, Co Tyrone, and the Arboe Cross
east of the village of Coagh, Co Tyrone, on the west
shore of Lough Neagh.

Fairies
It is not just the poets who knew that Ireland is the last stronghold of the fairies, many visitors come especially to find them—and they always do. A good spot to tiptoe in search of them is the Glens of Antrim. Usually fairly easy to recognise, they stand about two feet high and are, of course, dressed in green. Sometimes known as the wee folk.

Irish Tweed
Splendidly made hand-woven tweeds are produced in Ulster. They are usually thornproof and ideal for sporting wear. All kinds of tweed can be purchased in the larger shops in Belfast, some made in Ulster at Rostrevor and Hillsborough, Co Down, and at Cushendall in the Glens of Antrim.

Lambegging
A traditional Ulster custom, this consists of the banging of a large drum. Generally associated with weddings in the rural district of Ulster where the custom is for neighbours to assemble in the house of the bridal couple in the evening. Armed with horns, barrels, drums and other noisy instruments, they proceed to make bedlam, the theory being that the din will drive away any evil spirits from the vicinity of the bridal couple. These huge drums were first brought to Ulster by the Dutch Guards during the Williamite Wars of the late 17thC. The name Lambeg comes from the district in the Lagan valley, where the linen-beating hammers suggested the obvious associations.

Linen
Northern Ireland is one of the world's centres for the manufacture of damask linen. The industry has flourished since the 17thC, when Huguenot weavers arrived from France. Although most flax is now imported, you still can see the traditional methods of linen manufacture at the Ulster Folk Museum at Holywood, Co Down. Look towards the future at the world's most advanced textile laboratory at the Linen Research Institute at Lambeg, Co Antrim.

Peat
Perhaps more commonly cut and dried for fuel in the west of Ireland, peat is nevertheless still used in Ulster. On the road to Ballymoney in Co Antrim you cross one of the largest peat bogs in Northern Ireland. The Garry Bog is covered with mounds of peat that look like little houses but are in fact carefully built stacks designed to allow the peat blocks to dry. Watch out for the curiously shaped spades that the cutters use.

Pegged and round thatching
To be seen all along the north and west coasts of Ireland—the straw thatch is secured by a complete network of ropes fastened to the walls below the eaves. The roofs are often rounded to withstand gales. An older method of securing the ropes is to weight them with small boulders. The ropes are now usually made of sisal but were once made of the tough fibres of bog-fir roots. Cottages like these are to be seen around the border with Co Donegal.

The pub
Traditional Irish pubs can be found all over the province of Ulster. Although now rather dangerous places in parts of Belfast they are safe in the rural areas, and you can be assured of a warm welcome, good stout and excellent conversation. Many pubs have traditional musicians and ballad singers. A good and popular one is the Cross Keys Inn at Portglenone, Co Antrim. The seaside resort of Warrenpoint is also noted for these pubs.

Stone figures   **2 J5**
Boa Island & White Island, Lower Lough Erne, Co

Fermanagh. On Boa the visitor will find two stone idols. They have triangular shaped heads, are two-faced like Janus, and gaze out of the ferns. Thought to be 7thC, they represent some enigmatic pagan cult. There are seven equally mysterious statues on White Island.

Famous people

Chester Alan Arthur (1830–1886)   **3 N3**
Arthur House, Cullybackey, Co Antrim. Cottage home of the father of the USA (1881–85), for whom the word 'dude' was invented. Arthur Senior left for America in 1816. *Open to the public.*

Patrick Brontë (1777–1861)   **3 N6**
Loughbrickland, Co Down. Birthplace of the father of writers Charlotte, Emily and Anne; he was later rector of Haworth in Yorkshire.

John Dunlap (1747–1812)   **2 K3**
Grays Printing Press, Main St, Strabane, Co Tyrone. Said to be the house where Dunlap learnt his trade before going on to found the first American daily paper, 'The Pennsylvania Packet', and to print the Declaration of Independence. *Open summer.*

Gray's Printing Press, Strabane

Seamus Heaney (1939–)   **3 N4**
Mossbawn, Co Londonderry, 3 miles SE of Castledawson. Birthplace of the leader of the Ulster poets; the village has now been engulfed by the main road, although the house remains.

Alexander Irvine (1863–1941)   **3 O4**
Pogue's Entry, Antrim, Co Antrim. Home of this one-time newspaper boy who became a missionary in New York and wrote 'My Lady of the Chimney Corner', a classic tale of 19thC Irish life.

Francis Johnston (1761–1829)   **3 M6**
Armagh, Co Armagh. Birthplace of this eminent Georgian architect, responsible for many of Dublin's classical buildings.

C S Lewis (1898–1963)   **3 P5**
Belfast, Co Antrim. Birthplace and childhood home of the author and theologian, who lived in Dundela Avenue and Circular Road, recalled in his autobiography, 'Surprised by Joy'.

Louis MacNeice (1907–1963)   **3 P4**
Carrickfergus, Co Antrim. Childhood home of this Belfast-born poet, whose father was rector here. His unfinished autobiography, 'The Strings are False', describes the town.

Eóin MacNeill (1867–1945)   **3 O3**
Glenarm, Co Antrim. Birthplace of the distinguished Celtic scholar and founder of the Gaelic League. In 1914 he helped found and command the Irish Volunteers. His brother James was the second Governor-General of the Irish Free State.

St Patrick (AD389–460)   3 **P6**
Downpatrick, Co Down. Traditionally, the burial place of Ireland's patron saint, who landed and gave his first sermon at Saul in the year 432.

Sir Hans Sloane (1660–1753)   3 **P6**
Killyleagh, Co Down. Home of this collector of antiquities, noted for founding the British Museum.

Woodrow Wilson (1856–1924)   2 **K3**
Wilson House, Dergalt, Co Tyrone. Traditional farmhouse home of the ancestors of American President Wilson. *Open summer.*

Cathedrals, abbeys & churches

Bonamargy Friary   3 **O1**
Ballycastle, Co Antrim. Franciscan friary founded 1500, burnt 1589 but reoccupied until 1642; restored in 1931. Especially notable are the stone-roofed day room and the extensive burial vault.

The Catholic Church   3 **M5**
Moy, Co Tyrone. This church is a later addition to this curious Italianate village. It has a typical pedimented façade and a rectangular plan, which has been embellished with Gothic trappings. It is full of early 19thC conceits, narrow lancets, battlements and an amusing pinnacled bell-cote.

Devenish Abbey   2 **J6**
Devenish Island, Lower Lough Erne, Co Fermanagh. One of the most remarkable groups of ecclesiastical buildings in Ireland. On the site of a 6thC monastery there is an 81-foot-high round tower of the 9thC–10thC, perfectly preserved; the ruins of St Molaise's Church (the Teampull Mór) and house (12thC) and St Mary's Abbey (15thC).

Down Cathedral   3 **P6**
Downpatrick, Co Down. On the site of St Patrick's first stone church, built after he landed from nearby Strangford Lough in AD432. The tomb of the patron saint of Ireland is in the cathedral churchyard. The cathedral was destroyed three times in Irish wars and rebuilt.

Dungiven Priory   3 **M3**
Dungiven, Co Londonderry. On the outskirts of Dungiven, the ruins of an Augustinian priory

Tomb of Cooey-na-Gall, Dungiven Priory

church, founded 1100 by the O'Cahans, chieftains of the Derry region. Fine canopied altar-tomb, with figure believed to be Cooey-na-Gall, the 14thC O'Cahan chieftain, in Irish armour although the tomb is in medieval English style.

First (Unitarian) Presbyterian Church   3 **O4**
Crumlin, Co Antrim. An 1835 rubble and basalt church with a brick tower that is sturdy and unusual. The shape is octagonal, while inside a horseshoe gallery dominates; yellow pine pews remain. Very pretty Gothic organ.

Grey Abbey   3 **Q5**
Greyabbey, Co Down. The ruins on the shore of Strangford Lough of a Cistercian abbey founded in 1193 by Affreca, wife of John de Courcy. Extensive and well maintained remains, including decorative West Door and two tiers of lancet windows.

Inch Abbey   3 **P6**
Downpatrick, Co Down. Well maintained, beautifully sited ruins of a Cistercian abbey on the bank of the River Quoile. Established in 1180 by John de Courcy in atonement for his destruction of the abbey at Brenagh, which had resisted his advance into Ulster. Fragments remain of the nave and transepts, tower and presbytery, cloister, chapter house and bakery. Note the 13thC chancel windows in the east wall of the choir.

Old Cathedral of St Patrick   3 **M6**
Armagh, Co Armagh. (Church of Ireland.) Stands on the hilltop where St Patrick erected a church in AD445. It is probably the oldest church in Ireland, still in use and contains many fine marble monuments and the colours of famous Irish regiments.

Our Lady of Bethlehem Abbey   3 **N3**
Portglenone, Co Antrim. Begun in 1962 by Patrick Murray, a modern Cistercian monastery built of concrete and brick around a cloister. It has a certain impressive austerity.

Parish church   3 **O5**
Hillsborough, Co Down. The town is built in the classical style, whilst this church is in the 18thC Gothic mode. Planned like a Greek cross, with towers at the end of each transept balancing the great western spire. The interior is full of elegant 18thC plasterwork, including false vaults.

St Anne's Cathedral   3 **P5**
Belfast, Co Antrim. Begun in 1899 and still not finished, as the variety of its styles shows. Sir Thomas Drew designed it in Romanesque style and it is a heavy, pretentious edifice. The floor of the nave contains stones from every part of Ireland. In the west portals stands a 1914–18 war memorial by Charles Nicholson. In the baptistry are mosaics by Gertrude Stein.

St Columb's Cathedral   2 **K3**
Londonderry, Co Londonderry. The square tower and tall, graceful late Georgian spire make this church more like a London parish church of the 16thC than a cathedral. The general style is a pure Gothic of great simplicity, which has come to be called 'Planter's Gothic'. Look out for the Tomkins and Elvin memorial commemorating the first Planters and John Elvin, who became mayor and lived to be 102.

St Patrick's Catholic Cathedral   3 **M6**
Armagh, Co Armagh. It stands on a hill facing the old cathedral. A stately building with two exquisite spires, the foundation stone was laid on St Patrick's Day 1840; it was consecrated and opened in 1873, building having been delayed by the Great Famine.

Castles & ruins

Antrim Round Tower   3 **O4**
Antrim, Co Antrim. Almost perfect example, 93 feet
high with a 50-foot circumference at the base and
walls several feet thick. The entrance door, seven
feet above the ground, is only wide enough to admit
one person at a time. The four windows facing the
cardinal points ensured a good look-out for the
monks who built the tower. 9thC–12thC.

Belfast Castle   3 **P5**
Belfast, Co Antrim. A full-blooded Victorian castle
built in 1870 by Belfast architects. Standing high
above the city, the castle looks like a misplaced
Balmoral. In fact it is a curious mixture of Scottish
Baronial and French Renaissance. In the mortuary
chapel in the grounds there is a marble group of the
Earl of Belfast dying on a sofa and mourned by his
mother. It is life size and sums up the Victorian way
of death.

Belfast Castle

Carrickfergus Castle   3 **P4**
Carrickfergus, Co Antrim. A fine example of a large
Norman stronghold. Begun in 1180 by John de
Courcy, first Anglo-Norman invader of Ulster, it
stands on a rocky headland and its keep and outer
and inner courts are impressive remains of this
enormous fortress. Attacked frequently from the
seige of King John in 1210 to the late 18thC. The
cannons along the outer walls date from the 19thC,
when the castle was still an armoury.

Castle Archdale   2 **J5**
Co Fermanagh, 4 miles W of Irvinestown. Ruins of the
archetypal 17thC Plantation castle built by an
Englishman, John Archdale, between 1615–18. It
stands on the east shore of Lower Lough Erne.

Castle Carra   3 **O2**
Cushendun, Co Antrim. The keep of Castle Carra has
all the essential qualities of a romantic ruin. Remote,
ivy-clad chunks of masonry are scattered on the
slopes of the north east coast, and they have the
required associations with a legendary hero—Sean
the Proud. Here is true picturesque desolation.

Dundrum Castle   3 **P6**
Dundrum, Co Down. Striking remains of a Norman
castle, built in 1177 by John de Courcy. It was
besieged and taken in 1210 by King John and
bombarded by Cromwellian troops in 1652. The tall
keep affords magnificent views of mountains and
sea. *Closed Mon.*

Dunluce Castle   3 **M1**
Portrush, Co Antrim. Picturesque turreted ruin on a
steep, sea-tunnelled crag, three miles west of Giant's
Causeway. Probably built about 1300 by the
Norman, Richard de Burgo. Vacated after the
kitchen and servants fell into the sea in 1639. The
cave below penetrates right through the crag from
the land to the sea.

Greencastle   3 **O8**
Greencastle, Co Down. Substantial ruined royal castle
at the south east point of Northern Ireland.
Completed in 1261 at the same time as Carlingford
Castle on the opposite shore, to control Carlingford
Lough; it was abandoned after bombardment by
Cromwell's army in 1652. The best example in Co
Down of 13thC military architecture, comparable in
plan and size with great Norman towers in England,
and firmly illustrating the Anglo-Norman's
determination to command Irish sea access.

Kilclief Castle   3 **Q6**
Nr Strangford, Co Down. Perhaps the earliest datable
tower house in Ireland, on the seashore two miles
south of Strangford, and a possible model for many
similar ones throughout Ulster. Built in the early
15thC as the residence of a Bishop of Down (later
unfrocked for living with a married woman in the
castle).

Killyleagh Castle   3 **P6**
Killyleagh, Co Down. 17thC house remodelled by Sir
Charles Lanyon in 1850, who gave it a lavish
Tudor-style interior with arcaded gallery and a bold,
Scottish Baronial-style exterior, much welcomed by
Ulster settlers conscious of their Scottish heritage,
with turreted towers and machicolated,
battlemented parapets. The large walled bawn
belongs to the original house.

Maguire's Castle   2 **J6**
Enniskillen, Co Fermanagh. Guards the island town
of Enniskillen on the narrows linking Upper and
Lower Lough Erne. Home of the two world famous
regiments, the Inniskilling Dragoon Guards and the
Royal Inniskilling Fusiliers. Their history, from the
Seige of Derry by way of Waterloo to World War II,
is commemorated in the new museum behind the
picturesque, turreted water gate. The castle is the
former stronghold of the chieftains of Fermanagh.

Monea Castle

Monea Castle   2 **J6**
Monea, Co Fermanagh. A ruined Plantation castle
near the west side of Lower Lough Erne showing
marked Scottish influence. It was the governor of
Enniskillen's residence in the late 17thC.

Navan Fort 3 M6
Co Armagh, 2 miles W of Armagh. Iron Age remains on the site of the long-vanished residence of the kings of Ulster, Eamhain. Legend has it that the palace was founded by Queen Macha (c300BC), and it is mentioned in Ptolemy's 'Geography'.

Struell Wells 3 P6
Downpatrick, Co Down. The site is associated with St Patrick, who is reputed to have come here to bathe from his nearby church at Saul, thus extending Christian auspices to the pagan Irish reverence for holy wells. Drinking Well and Eye Well are still visited for cures on midsummer night. Water still flows through the men's and women's bath houses (17thC).

Tullaghoge Fort 3 M4
Tullaghoge, nr Cookstown, Co Tyrone. A hilltop ring fort. Interesting as the site of the inaugurations of the O'Neills, kings of Ulster, by sub-chieftains from the 11thC onward. The inauguration stone was smashed in 1602 on the orders of Queen Elizabeth's Lord Deputy Mountjoy. The kings were not crowned; instead the chieftains placed a shoe on the O'Neill's foot.

Unusual buildings

Ballycopeland Windmill 3 Q4
Millisle, Co Down. An 18thC corn grinding mill with good machinery, kept in working order.

Belfast City Hall 3 P4
Belfast, Co Antrim. A sumptuous Edwardian Baroque building of 1906 that dominates Donegall Square. Inside it is a classic of the icing-sugar school, slightly improved by some recent murals. The copper-covered dome is visible for miles.

Bishop Gate and the City Wall 2 K3
Londonderry, Co Londonderry. The gate was built in 1789 and takes the form of a triumphal arch to commemorate the epic siege of 1688–89. It is an austere design by Aaron Baker, carved with laurels and martial trophies by Edward Smyth. The city walls were built by the first Protestant settlers from England, who clearly felt the need for complete protection from the native Irish. You can walk along the great stone walls and see the four massive bastions. The city has now spread far beyond its walls.

Crown Liquor Saloon 3 P5
Belfast, Co Antrim. Just opposite the Europa Hotel is this most magnificent, lavish Victorian pub. It is full of polished mahogany, brass and mirrors, and has remained unspoilt. A glass of stout in this sombre, beautiful temple is a delicious experience.

Gray's Printing Press 2 K3
Strabane, Co Tyrone. 18thC printing press where John Dunlap, who later printed the American Declaration of Independence, and James Wilson, grandfather of Woodrow Wilson, are reputed to have been apprenticed. *Closed winter.*

The Mall 3 M6
Armagh, Co Armagh. A well preserved terrace terminating in a classical courthouse, all designed by Francis Johnston in 1809. This is a lighter version of the famous Dublin terraces, with particularly fine fanlights shaped like a sunflower cut in half.

Mussenden Temple 3 M2
Downhill, Co Londonderry. Built on the cliffs by the megalomaniac fourth Earl of Bristol, who was Bishop of Derry from 1768. He built himself Downhill (now ruined) as his home, to be about the

Mussenden Temple, Co. Londonderry

size of Blenheim. This circular temple with its untopped dome was his library, where he sat alone long into the night. *Open summer. Closed Fri.*

The Round Tower 2 J6
Devenish Isle, Lower Lough Erne, Co Fermanagh. The best preserved and best built round tower in Ireland. Once part of the monastery of St Molaise, it is remarkable for its fine-cut ashlar masonry and a rare decorated frieze below the cap. At each point of the compass on the frieze is a carved head, each with a luxuriant moustache. The perfection of the tower is enhanced by the surrounding ruins.

St Columb's Wells 2 K3
Londonderry, Co Londonderry. During the middle years of the 19thC Londonderry became a great centre for those fleeing from the potato famine. Large numbers of Catholic workers from the south came to work in the shirt factories of Londonderry, and they built this maze of small-scale streets next to the sober Georgian area of the Protestants. The houses are one-storeyed and resemble the country cottages the emigrants had left behind. Now the cottages are brightly painted, with Gaelic script over some of the shops.

St Cooey's Wells 3 Q6
Nr Portaferry, Co Down. Three holy wells (eye, skin and intestines) and a small church ruin on a rocky coast, recently refurbished. Awesome isolation.

The 'Saint's Tomb' 3 M3
Bovevagh, Dungiven, Co Londonderry. A tiny stone oratory on a wooded slope above the River Roe, said to date from the 11thC. It is a rare form of dry-stone construction, the side walls projecting strangely beyond the gables. A curious ecclesiastical remnant that retains much mystery.

Wellbrook Beetling Mill 3 M4
Nr Cookstown, Co Tyrone. 18thC water-powered beetling mill restored to working order. Used in the final process of linen manufacture, when the cloth is hammered to give an even finish. *Open summer. Closed Fri.*

Houses & gardens

Ardress House 3 N5
Nr Portadown, Co Armagh. A mid-17thC manor that was extended to create the present house by the architect George Ensor, who married the heiress to the estate. He employed the craftsman Michael Stapleton to carry out the stucco work. The decoration bears his distinctive mark—a vigorous, almost rococo style using natural forms and classical detail. The rooms have recently been completely restored using Stapleton's surviving drawings. *Open summer.*

Baronscourt 2 K4
Co Tyrone, 3½ miles SW of Newtownstewart. One of the grandest of Ireland's neoclassical buildings. An early 18thC house built by George Stewart in 1779;

Baronscourt

replanned by Sir John Soane in 1791–92, who turned the whole design back to front; remodelled by W V Morrison in the mid-19thC and renovated by Sir Albert Richardson in 1947. The house has a long, central block with boldly projecting portico and flanking wings connected by colonnades. To the south east is the charming Agents House. Designed by James Martin in 1741 and remodelled 1781, it's a small, trim brick-built Palladian house, single storeyed with a three-bay front featuring recessed entrance loggia crowned by Tuscan portico. *Not open to the public.*

Caledon House 3 M6
Caledon, Co Tyrone. Handsome Georgian and Regency mansion standing 1¼ miles to the south west of the model village. The main central block was designed by Thomas Cooley in 1779. The encircling complex of colonnades, domed pavilions and entrance portico were added by John Nash in 1812; the second floor was added in 1835. *Private.*

Castlecoole 2 K6
Co Fermanagh, 1½ miles SE of Enniskillen. James Wyatt designed this great house in the late 18thC and it remains exactly as it was—designed and made all at one time. The composition is traditional, a central block flanked by colonnades with small terminal pavilions, and it relates perfectly to its setting among the great trees. The house was built of Portland stone shipped from England at fantastic cost. Inside, the rooms are a triumph of restrained classical decoration, particularly the salon with its black, grey and white plasterwork. The furniture, doors, bookcases and shutters were made on the spot and all the accounts survive. *Open summer.*

Castle Upton 3 O4
Templepatrick, Co Antrim. 17thC house, formerly known as Norton Castle, on the site of 13thC priory of the Knights of St John; redesigned 1783 by Robert Adam, who also reconstructed the Knights' vaulted refectory. *Not open to the public.* In the churchyard is the Upton mausoleum, a triumphal arch with sombre funerary urns also by Adam. *Open all year.*

Castle Ward 3 P6
Co Down, 7 miles NE of Downpatrick. A splendid estate on the shores of Strangford Lough with an unusual house designed in a mixture of Classical and Gothic in the 18thC. Look out for the amazing collection of buildings surrounding this house. There is a Victorian laundry, an 18thC summerhouse and two 15thC castles. The garden temple is an amazing replica of Palladio's Redentore. The whole park should be seen on a slightly misty day, when it is just like a painting by Claude. Castle *open summer,* grounds *all year.*

Clandeboye 3 P4
Crawfordsburn, Co Down. Seat of the Marquis of Dufferin and Ava, it was originally a 17thC house remodelled in 1820 by Sir Richard Morrison. Standing in the wooded grounds with its lakes is a Scottish Baronial-style ornamental tower, designed 1848 by William Burn. *Irregular opening.*

Derrymore House 3 N7
Nr Newry, Co Armagh. A very rare survivor of the small, thatched country houses that were popular with the Irish yeomanry during the 18thC. Probably built for a member of parliament in 1776. By tradition the house was often visited by Lord Castlereagh, and the Act of Union 1880 was drawn up in the Treaty Room. *Open by appointment.*

Florence Court 2 J6
Co Fermanagh, 7 miles SW of Enniskillen. Remarkably elaborate house built in 1751 and given a Palladian dressing by Davis Durcat in 1770, who added pedimented pavilions attached to the main house by handsome arcades crowned by balustrading. It was restored after a fire in 1955, and has some fine rococo decorative work. A wild garden with notable rhododendron glen. The original Irish yews, from which all other cultivated Irish yews descend, were discovered here in 1780. *Open summer. Closed Fri.*

Hezlett House 3 M2
Liffock, Co Londonderry, 4 miles NW of Coleraine. Important 17thC house with unusual cruck/truss roof construction and thatched roof; until mid-18thC, residence of clergy of Dunboe parish. *Open summer.*

Lady Dixon Park 3 P5
Malone, Belfast, Co Antrim. The scene throughout the summer of the greatest International Rose Trials in the British Isles, when about 20,000 roses of all kinds form an extensive display. *Open all year.*

Mount Stewart 3 Q5
Co Down, 5 miles SE of Newtownards. Childhood home of Lord Castlereagh. Begun in 1780, it was completed in 1830 by W V Morrison, who added an Ionic portico and galleried hall. The handsome octagonal banqueting hall, two storeys high with columned porches and balconies, was modelled on the 'Temple of the Winds' in Athens. There is much to be seen in the 78 acres of gardens, which were planned by Edith, Lady Londonderry in 1921; formal layouts such as the sunken Spanish garden, the Tír na n-óg and the Italian gardens are surrounded by woodland. Tender plants and shrubs abound: eucalyptus, palms, bamboos, mimosa trees, lapagerias. See the shamrock garden, laid out in the shape of that most Irish of plants with the Red Hand of Ulster planted at its centre. Topiary is superb, including hunting scenes and Irish harps. *Open summer. Closed Fri.*

Rowallane 3 P5
Nr Saintfield, Co Down, 11 miles SE of Belfast. Renowned for rare and beautiful plants, its 50 acres were planned in 1903 by Hugh Armytage-Moore from rocky farmland. There are the famous Rowallane primulas, viburnams and hypericums here and this is the headquarters of the National Trust in Northern Ireland. *Open summer.*

Springhill

Springhill 3 M4
Nr Moneymore, Co Londonderry. A late 17thC house; once fortified it was exactly the kind of stronghold needed by settlers supporting Cromwell. Today the

fortifications have gone, but the low outbuildings for the servants remain with the laundry, turf shed and brew house. This is a lovely plain Plantation house of the kind found only in Ireland, reputedly occupied by two arguing ghosts. There is also a costume museum. *Open summer. Closed Fri.*

Museums & galleries

Armagh County Museum   **3 M6**
Armagh, Co Armagh. Collections of archaeological and folk material, local history, natural history and paintings by Irish artists. *Closed Sun.*

The Arts Council Gallery   **3 P5**
Bedford St, Belfast, Co Antrim. Recently bombed but under reconstruction. Tel. Belfast 663591 for details.

Ballycastle Museum   **3 O1**
Ballycastle, Co Antrim. Illustrated natural history of the locality together with local glassware and domestic utensils. *Open summer.*

Castle Keep   **2 J6**
Enniskillen, Co Fermanagh. Regimental museum of the Royal Inniskilling Fusiliers. *Closed weekends.*

Fermanagh County Museum   **2 J6**
Castle Barracks, Enniskillen, Co Fermanagh. Interesting exhibition with models and dioramas of life and activities in early Fermanagh, including examples of lake dwellings. *Closed Sun.*

Larne District Historical Centre   **3 P3**
Cross Street, Larne, Co Antrim. Exhibition of turn-of-the-century domestic furniture and utensils, including a country kitchen of c1900 with open peat hearth; milk house of c1920 with plunge churn and butter maker; old time smithy with anvil. *Closed Sun.*

Mullaghbane Folk Museum   **3 N7**
Mullaghbane, Co Armagh. Traditional south Armagh farmhouse. *Open weekends.*

Linen Museum   **3 M3**
Upperlands, Co Londonderry. Original weaving, bleaching and finishing machinery. Owned by the Clark family, landlords here since 1740. *Open to groups by appointment during working hours* (Tel Maghera 42214).

The Planetarium and Hall of Astronomy   **3 M6**
Armagh, Co Armagh. The only planetarium in Britain outside London; has a permanent display of astronomical instruments including a public telescope. It adjoins the Observatory, which has been in use since 1789. *Closed Sun.*

The Sovereign's House   **3 M6**
The Mall, Armagh, Co Armagh. Regimental museum of the Royal Irish Fusiliers. *Closed weekends.*

Transport Museum   **3 P5**
Witham St, Belfast, Co Antrim. Contains a collection of ancient vehicles, including Belfast trams, spanning over 200 years of transport history. *Closed Sun.*

Ulster American Folk Park   **2 K5**
Camphill, Omagh, Co Tyrone. Symbol of the link forged down the centuries between Ulster and the USA. Illustrates bygone rural life in Ulster in pioneer America with numerous reconstructed buildings. Key exhibit is the ancestral home of the Mellon family of Pittsburgh, a humble cottage now restored and open to visitors. In a nearby barn is an exhibition of farm implements. There is a new Folk Centre with a small auditorium for lectures and audio-visual shows. *Open summer.*

Conestoga wagon, Ulster American Folk Park

Ulster Folk and Transport Museum   **3 P4**
Cultra Manor, Holywood, Co Down. The traditional life of Northern Ireland can be sampled here, in the house and 136-acre grounds of Cultra Manor. A water-powered spade mill continues to make spades and other agricultural and domestic implements by the traditional methods; even the workmen are descendants of the original family. A weaver produces damask linen to be spread on a bleach green, which is defended by a traditional stone sentry tower; two centuries ago the sentry was entitled to shoot anyone attempting to steal the linen. A scutch mill shows the original process of turning the flax into linen fibre. Griddle baking and rural cookery are demonstrated in the traditionally furnished cottages. A miniature railway carries visitors around the Transport Museum, which has many interesting examples of early forms of transport. *Open all year.*

Ulster Museum   **3 P5**
Botanic Gardens, Belfast, Co Antrim. Departments of antiquities, art, botany and zoology, geology and technology. It also has a café, a cinema and a shop. The antiquities department has good exhibits of life in Ireland since the arrival of the first human beings in 6,000 BC. The outstanding treasure is priceless jewellery recovered by divers from the wreck of a Spanish Armada galleon at the Giant's Causeway. Part of the museum is housed in an exciting new building. *Open all year. Closed Fri.*

Warrenpoint Museum   **2 O7**
Warrenpoint, Co Down. Small local museum. *Closed winter weekends.*

Wellbrook Beetling Mill   **3 M4**
Co Tyrone, 3 miles SW of Cookstown on Omagh road B4. A water-powered mill operated from 1765 to 1961. Fully restored to working order and now a museum. Beetling is the process of finishing linen with hammers to produce a sheen. *Open summer. Closed Fri.*

Nature trails & reserves

Brandy Pad   **3 O7**
Co Down. This eight-mile route, passing the Diamond Rocks and the Hare's Gap, follows the old smugglers' track right through the Mournes from Bloody Bridge to Hilltown.

Castle Caldwell Nature Reserve   **2 I5**
Co Fermanagh, 5 miles E of Belleek. Mixed commercial woodland and Lough Erne shore, woodland birds and wildfowl. Nature trail and displays. No permit required. Signposted from the main Belleek–Kesh road.

Castle Ward Nature Trail   **3 Q6**
Co Down. Start at Stable Yard car park, 1½ miles W of Strangford on A25. Woodland and Strangford Lough wildlife. One mile. Display and self-guiding panels. *Open summer.*

Giant's Causeway Nature Trail 3 N1
Co Antrim. Off B146, 9 miles E of Portrush. Coastal birds and superb geology. Three miles.

Mourne Coastal Path 3 P7
Co Down. On the Newcastle–Kilkeel road A2. The path follows the shores of Dundrum Bay with the highest peak in the Mourne Mountains, Slieve Donard, towering above. Don't miss the site of St Mary's, Ballaghanery, with its associations with St Donard.

Murlough National Nature Reserve 3 P6
Co Down, 2 miles NW of Newcastle. Two-mile dune walk with botanic and archaeological interest. Illustrated information panels and guided walks.

North Antrim Cliff Path 3 N1
Co Antrim. Eleven-mile-long footpath following the wide arc of bays and stormy headlands from Runkerry to Ballintoy. It passes the cliff-like slopes of the Giant's Causeway, 'discovered' in 1692 by the Bishop of Derry; Dunseverick Castle; and Whitepark Bay. This is a paradise for birdwatchers. A wild, romantic and forbidding stretch of the coast overlooking the North Channel.

Oxford Island Nature Reserve 3 N5
Co Armagh, 4 miles N of Lurgan. New and imaginative ecological trail, hides and exhibition centre featuring geology, botany, ornithology and archaeology.

Portglenone Nature Reserve 3 N3
Co Antrim, ¾ mile S of Portglenone. Mainly commercial woodland, with arboretum and typical woodland birds. Nature trail. No permit necessary. Signposted on main Portglenone–Ballymena road.

Quoile Pondage Nature Reserve 3 P6
Co Down, 2 miles N of Downpatrick. A fresh-water basin formed when a flood-control barrier was built at Castle Island. Its 450 acres run from the island to Quoile Bridge and offer much of interest to the botanist, especially fresh-water vegetation such as alders and willows along the old seashore. In spring great crested grebes and mergansers flock here, and mute swans, moorhens, coots, little grebes, mallards and tufted ducks can also be seen.

Shane's Castle Nature Reserve 3 O4
Nr Antrim, Co Antrim. Woodland birds and wildfowl on adjacent Lough Neagh, RSPB reserve with nature trail and miniature railway. Access from main Antrim–Randalstown road. *Open summer weekends.*

The Ulster Way
A long-distance footpath of 450 miles that encircles all of Ulster. Most of the Way traverses wild moorland and mountainous country, where the route will be marked by a simple track, and the best waymarked areas will be found on the Fermanagh Lakeland Route and the Moyle Way (start at Ballycastle). There are alternative routes, especially in North Antrim and the Mournes, for those who prefer a shorter trek.

Whitepark Bay Nature Trail 3 N1
Co Antrim, 1½ miles W of Ballintoy. One-mile trail demonstrates different vegetation types established on sand and chalk and illustrates geological features.

The shores of Whitepark Bay

Birdwatching

The 300 miles of coastline of Northern Ireland and its islands, five sea loughs, the abundance of fresh water, woodland, moor and mountain offer a unique opportunity to see many species. The lack of industrial pollution and scarcity of large mechanical farms has meant more hedgerow, clean water and more birds.

Bar Mouth 3 M2
Co Londonderry, 3 miles E of Castlerock. A wildlife sanctuary on the shores of the Bann estuary where you can see a wide selection of birds. Observation hide and illustrated information panels.

Castle Caldwell 2 I5
Co Fermanagh. Forest area on the shores of Lower Lough Erne, which is an important breeding site for the common scoter.

Copeland Islands 3 Q4
Off Donaghadee, Co Down. Good observatory. For details write to Dinah Brown, RSPB, Belvoir Park Forest, Belfast BT8 4QT. Tel. Belfast 692547.

Garron Plateau 3 O2
Co Antrim. For 30 miles you can walk without seeing any sign of human habitation. A good area for the lovely golden plover.

Green Island 3 O7
Carlingford Lough, Co Down. A nature reserve under the control of the RSPB. There is a hide from which four species of tern can be watched. Permits from RSPB.

Lough Erne 2 J5
Co Fermanagh. Both parts of the lough are rich in birdlife, particularly attractive heronries. Also great crested grebe, common scoter, dunlin and tern. Flamingoes sometimes nest here.

Lough Neagh 3 N4
Good birdwatching of all kinds, especially where there are beds of tall reeds.

North Antrim Cliffs 3 O2
Co Antrim. This is the best area to see buzzards.

Randalstown Nature Reserve 3 N4
Co Antrim. Two hides run by RSPB give excellent views of water fowl.

Rathlin Island 3 O1
Co Antrim. The cliffs are an important breeding ground for seabirds, especially the razor-bill, guillemot, fulmar and kittiwake. Also to be seen are shag, black guillemot, puffin and eider duck.

Rostrevor Forest Nature Reserve 3 O7
Co Tyrone. Woodland birdlife, especially good for jays.

Sheep Island 3 N1
Nr Ballintoy, Co Antrim. Extensive colonies of razor-bill and kittiwake gulls.

Sperrin Mountains 3 L4
Co Tyrone and Co Londonderry. This mountainous region is a haunt of the peregrine falcon, raven and golden plover.

Strangford Lough 3 Q5
Co Down. A number of wildlife refuges and hides at several sites around the lough. Tern, ringed plover, oystercatchers, redshanks, lapwings, snipes, greylag geese and mute swans are only some of the species. Visitors wanting to discover the best places to visit on the lough should contact the National Trust Warden, Dr R A Brown. Tel. Strangford 636.

Forests

Perhaps the most notable forests are Tollymore and Castlewellan, both in the Mourne Mountains. They are full of fine specimen trees including unusual Californian redwoods and the National Arboretum is at Castlewellan. Tollymore Forest has a wildlife museum. Much of the forestry in Northern Ireland is organised into areas for camping, fishing and recreational use. Among the best parks out of over 50 are: Lough Navar Forest Park, Co Fermanagh; Slieve Gullion Forest Recreation Area, Co Armagh; Glengariff Forest Park and Knocklayd Forest, Ballycastle, Co Antrim.

Castlewellan, Tollymore and Donard   3 O7
Co Down. Three neighbouring forest parks in the Mourne Mountains with good collections of trees; silver firs and magnificent Californian redwoods, which are over 120 feet high.

Lough Navar   2 J5
Lower Lough Erne, Co Fermanagh. Good country park with spectacular views; the forest is mostly conifers. Small caravan site.

Randalstown Forest   3 N4
Nr Randalstown, Co Antrim. To the west of Shane's Castle; fallow and white deer, red squirrels and water birds. Access by permit from Forestry Division of Department of Agriculture.

Seskinore   2 K5
Nr Omagh, Co Tyrone. Beautiful mixed woodland in this small reserve. Look out for the game farm. Small caravan park.

Hills & mountains

Northern Ireland is shaped like a saucer with hills and mountains around the edge. Lough Neagh sits in the middle, the largest lake in the British Isles.

Drumlins
The landscape of Co Down is dominated by many smooth, humpbacked hills called drumlins. They emerged from the melting glaciers of the ice age some 10,000 years ago when wolves, mammoths and the giant Irish deer were the only inhabitants.

Glens of Antrim   3 O3
Co Antrim. A series of wooded valleys that run from the Antrim Mountains down to the sea. Dense foliage, rushing waterfalls and streams are your companions as you walk in these lush vales. At the foot of each glen is a village with a sandy beach—Glenarm, Carnlough, Glenariff, Cushendall, Cushendun and Ballycastle.

Mountains of Fermanagh   2 J6
Co Fermanagh. A range that rises steeply from the shore of Lough Erne and is mainly limestone. The Belmore Plateau, especially the Marble Arch caves, is a Mecca for speleologists. From the high point of Lough Navar Forest there are great views to the mountains of Donegal. Inside these great carboniferous limestone hills are the remains of animals over 320 million years old. Fine fossils can still be collected from the gorges.

Mourne Mountains   3 O7
Co Down. A group of outstandingly beautiful granite mountains that lie just a little way from the sea. Most of the peaks are about 2,000 feet high but one, Slieve Donard, is almost 3,000 feet high. They are excellent for walking as no roads reach the higher regions. Look out for several secret lakes and the Mourne diamonds, semi-precious stones of quartz crystal that can be chipped from the rocks.

Mourne Mountains

Slieve Gullion Mountains   3 N7
Co Armagh. On the border with the Irish Republic. The highest peak, Slieve Gullion (1,893 feet), is mounted by a scenic drive that provides excellent views of northern and southern Ireland. This region is remote and quiet and the people seem to be occupying the last stronghold of a bygone rural life-style.

Sperrin Mountains   3 L4
Co Londonderry and Co Tyrone. An extensive range of sparsely inhabited peaks where the spirit of the Stone Age still walks. You can see the Beamhore circles and alignments high up on the moors between Cookstown and Strabane.

Countryside

Antrim
The north east corner of Ireland, separated at Torr Head from Scotland by only 13 miles of water, has to the west the lush, fertile Bann Valley running down to the shores of Lough Neagh. In the east, the hills rise steeply to a vast plateau of high, rolling moorland, dropping abruptly into the sea in a skyscraper wall of cliffs along the north and east coasts. Here, there is a series of beautiful narrow valleys—the nine Glens of Antrim—cascading down from the hills to the sea between Larne, beside Lough Larne in the south, and Ballycastle in the north. Beyond Fair Head is the Giant's Causeway, a strange terrace of steps some 600 feet high where golden eagles nest.

Armagh
A county of gentle hills that rise in the south some 1,893 feet to the tip of Slieve Gullion. It is a fruit-growing area, especially in the north, and is sometimes called 'The Garden of Ireland'. Flax is also grown, Lurgan and Portadown being the twin centres of the linen industry.

Down
Perhaps the most fertile of Ireland's counties. The north is drumlin country, a blanket of low hillocks, like giant eggs, which are glacial in origin. The Legananny Hills, with 1,755-foot-high Slieve Croob towering amongst them, occupy the centre. To the south are the beautiful granite Mourne Mountains, where Slieve Donard rises to 2,796 feet, their southern feet washed by Carlingford Lough. To the east is the Ards Peninsula, a lush green blanket of land lined with fine resorts that forms a barrier between the almost land-locked Strangford Lough and the Irish Sea.

Fermanagh
Wrapped around the beautiful River Erne and its great chain of lakes, Upper and Lower Lough Erne are dotted with leafy islets while the land on either side sweeps steeply up, rising along the Cavan border to some 2,188 feet in the Cuilcagh Mountains. To the west are limestone hills riddled with caves, bordering the shores of Lough Melvin in the north west and Upper and Lower Lough

Macnean to the south east. It's a county scattered with smoky villages, steep-sided mountains naked of grass and trees, and thick-walled cottages clustering against the rolling hills which surround the 'lakeland of Ulster'.

Londonderry

A wild mountainous county of deep glens and winding river valleys. To the south east is the leafy Faughan valley, a quiet picturesque world, whilst to the south are the Sperrin Mountains, climbing to some 2,240 feet along the borders with Co Tyrone. To the north are surf-washed, curving beaches along the Atlantic coast.

Tyrone

The borders with Co Londonderry are sealed by the Sperrin Mountains, whilst inland lie attractive glens, moorland and flowing river valleys dotted with low, whitewashed farmhouses. Towards the east, the land shelves sharply and runs low along the edge of Lough Neagh. Beautiful Clogher Valley is a richly wooded haven, stretching across the south to Fermanagh.

Rivers & loughs

In this lush, green country of glens and loughs there are many rushing rivers and streams. There is not one major river that outclasses all the others but the capital of the province, Belfast, stands at the mouth of the River Lagan. The best reason for visiting the rivers of Northern Ireland is for the fishing.

Belfast Lough 3 P4

Co Antrim. A good natural inlet for big ships, which has enabled the famous shipyards to flourish here. Four miles wide and twelve miles long, it is a busy, industrialised waterway. It was here that John Paul Jones, the American sea captain, defeated the British ship 'Drake' in 1778.

Carlingford Lough 3 O7

Co Down. Almost on the border but now the smugglers are being replaced by more profitable commerce. Port improvements at Warrenpoint and Newry.

Lough Erne 2 J5

Co Fermanagh. An attractive, wild stretch of water with lots of splendid islands in both the lower and upper loughs. Of special interest is Devenish Island (round tower, ancient abbey, etc.) and White Island—a good boating centre. Enniskillen, Kesh, Bellanaleck, St Huberts (near Perrylin), Killadeas and Carrybridge are your centres to hire a boat, and then you can set off to explore one of the largest areas of navigable water in Europe. The Erne Lakes hold the world record for match coarse fishing. The SHARE centre at Smith's Strand, near Lisnakea, offers holidays for the disabled.

Lough Neagh

Lough Neagh 3 N4

153 square miles of water, this largest lake in the British Isles is fed by ten rivers but only one, the Lower Bann, flows out of it to the sea. Beyond its shallow edges the lake drops sharply to a uniform depth of 40–50 feet. Vast numbers of wild fowl live on the lake; thousands of geese spend the winter here and in late autumn whooper swans rest after a direct 800-mile flight from Iceland. Salmon, eels, pike and trout can be caught in the rivers entering the lake; the lake itself is a commercial fishery.

River Bann 3 N3

Co Antrim and Co Londonderry. Best river for grilse and sea trout, the centre for this river is Coleraine. The Lower Bann flows through Co Londonderry where the fishing is even better; you can catch spring salmon, brown trout and a variety of coarse fish. The Upper Bann has excellent roach and bream.

River Dun 3 O2

Co Antrim. Good for spring salmon and brown trout; the best centre is at Cushendun. Fast flowing with attractive walks.

River Erne 2 K7

Co Fermanagh. Like so many of the rivers of Ulster this one flows well into the neighbouring Republic counties, particularly Donegal. It is a good source of trout (both the sea and brown varieties) and grilse. At Lisnaskea there is also coarse fishing.

River Foyle tributaries 2 K3

Nr Strabane, Co Tyrone. A great many streams with salmon, brown trout and coarse fish flow into the Foyle around Co Londonderry and Co Tyrone.

Strangford Lough 3 Q5

Co Down. One of the loveliest wildlife sanctuaries in the British Isles. A good spot to see herons, migrating geese and all kinds of waders. Seals can often be seen on the islands. Nearby is Castle Ward, one of the most charming buildings in Ulster.

Canals

Northern Ireland is criss-crossed by canals but, sadly, not one of them is navigable for more than a couple of miles, and their appeal is limited to those interested in industrial archaeology, canal history and coarse fishing. It is in a way surprising that so many artificial navigation systems were built in Ulster. Unlike those in England, few of them withstood the wintry blast of railway competition in the 19thC. Canal promoters in Ulster were encouraged by two basic geographical considerations: the vast inland lake known as Lough Neagh, and the relative flatness of the landscape in the north. The result was a web of waterways radiating from Lough Neagh.

Newry Canal was thus the first purely artificial waterway in the British Isles. This ran as a barge canal from Portadown to the port of Newry, on the east coast, and thence by a ship canal for three miles down to the sea. But the barge canal has been closed for many years, and now even the port itself has been transferred to Warrenpoint. There is, however, still plenty of water in the Newry Canal. Things to see include the flight of locks at Terryhoogan (10 miles north of Newry) and the old wharves in Newry itself. Other forgotten canals of Ulster include the Lagan Navigation, the Bann Navigation, the Coalisland Canal, the Tyrone Navigation, and the Ulster Canal. All these are disused, but all offer interest in the many bridges, locks and old pieces of machinery waiting to be unearthed. In this respect at least, the Ulster canals offer rich rewards to the walker.

Archaeological sites

Aghanaglack 2 J6
Between Belcoo and Boho, Co Fermanagh. A late Neolithic long-cairn containing two double-chambered galleries set back-to-back and separated by a common end-stone. Each gallery has a forecourt formed by the extended ends of the cairn.

Annaghmore 3 N7
Nr Crossmaglen, Co Armagh. A well-preserved example of a single-court grave, a type of Neolithic burial cairn characteristic of the northern half of Ireland. The cairn is long, with one end extended into 'horns', forming a forecourt to the entrance; this court is lined with massive upright stones, alternating with drystone walling. The gallery inside is divided by stone jambs into three chambers, and was originally corbel-roofed. Towards the back of the cairn are two later chambers, built back-to-back, with corbelled roofs and portals opening out at the sides.

Ballynoe Stone Circle 3 P6
Nr Downpatrick, Co Down. Outer circle of over 50 standing stones, some over six feet high, surrounds an elliptical inner circle enclosing a Neolithic burial mound.

Stone circles at Beaghmore

Beaghmore 3 M4
Nr Cookstown, Co Tyrone. This fine group of religious monuments, probably dating from the early Bronze Age, was discovered by peat-cutters earlier this century. There are seven stone circles, of which six are grouped in pairs, with alignments of stone uprights running from them, and several burial cairns, some of which are incorporated with the circles.

Boviel 3 M3
Nr Dungiven, Co Londonderry. An example of a Neolithic wedge-grave, so-called from the sloping shape of the chamber, contained in an oval cairn. The chamber is divided by a stone doorway, forming an antechamber, and is lined with stone uprights. Only one of the roof-slabs survives, carried on a single row of corbels. A second row of stones follows the outline of the gallery, and the entrance is stone-faced.

Budore 3 O4
Nr Crumlin, Co Antrim. A well-preserved pair of raths, typical of the many in south Antrim. The majority of these circular enclosures date from the first millenium, but they continued to be built during the Middle Ages. Some of the larger raths may have been forts, but they were more commonly the homesteads of farmers. The south rath at Budore has a single bank and ditch, and is probably the earlier as the ditch is more silted. The other has a double ditch and bank, of which the inner has been levelled off.

Drumena 3 O6
Nr Lough Island Reavy, Co Down. The cashel at Drumena is a good example of these drystone enclosures, and probably held an Iron Age farmstead; the ruins of a more recent farm can be seen on the site today. There is also an Iron Age souterrain, an underground gallery now entered by modern steps, but with its original entrance and opposed chamber still preserved.

Giant's Ring 3 O5
Ballylesson, Newtownbreda, Co Antrim, 2 miles S of Belfast. The large enclosure at Ballylesson is probably a type of henge monument, dating from the later Neolithic period. The surrounding bank, standing 12 feet high, is built of stones, and has a slight depression around the interior; there are now five entrances, but these are probably not all original. Just off-centre is a grave with a single chamber, built of five uprights with a capstone seven feet across; there are also traces of an entrance passage.

Killadeas 2 J5
Nr Lower Lough Erne, Co Fermanagh. The graveyard at Killadeas has three sculptured stones, including one with cup-marks and a second with a small Greek cross. The most interesting is the Bishop's Stone, which probably dates from the 8thC; this shows an ecclesiastic carrying a bell and crozier, and has a grotesque head carved on the narrow edge.

Knockmany 3 L5
Nr Augher, Co Tyrone. A large round cairn containing an unroofed oval chamber; three of the massive uprights have incised decoration, including cup-marks, concentric circles, and twisting motifs. The chamber may have had a small entrance, but no passage; the radial slabs which project into the cairn from the chamber are an unusual feature.

Interior of Knockmany Chambered Cairn

Lough-na-Cranagh 3 O1
Nr Ballycastle, Co Antrim. Lake-dwellings, or crannogs, were constructed on a foundation of brushwood and logs, or boulders and peat, from the Neolithic period until the early Middle Ages. The example at Lough-na-Cranagh is an oval island contained within drystone walling, which rises some six feet above the water.

Navan Fort 3 M6
Nr Armagh, Co Armagh. Navan was the traditional palace of the kings of Ulster for six centuries and an annual assembly place. The large circular hilltop enclosure, with its bank and internal ditch, suggests ritual rather than defensive use. The main earthworks are probably Iron Age in date, and contain a rath and a cairn.

Slieve Gullion 3 N7
Co Armagh, nr Newry, Co Down. The cairn at the summit contains a fine example of an early type of Neolithic passage-grave, built almost completely of horizontal slabs without the more usual massive uprights. The polygonal chamber had a corbelled vault, and the surviving walls are ten feet in height; at the end, opposite the passage, is a recess. The passage still has its flat slab roof, but the entrance end is destroyed. Also on the site is a large Bronze Age round cairn.

Tirnony 3 M3
Nr Maghera, Co Londonderry. An impressive example of a 'dolmen', one of the massive stones left when most of a cairn has been robbed for use in building. The stones formed the entrance and chamber of a Neolithic portal-grave, a single-chambered cairn characterised by a tall built entrance. The grave at Tirnony also has a large pillar in front of one side, suggesting a built forecourt.

White Island 2 J5
Lough Erne, Co Fermanagh. The ruined 12thC church on White Island contains eight sculptured figures, including two bishops carved sometime after the 8thC. They were found built into the church, and were probably deliberately hidden because of their stylistic links with traditional pagan carvings.

Fossil hunting
Visit the local museum. Its fossil collection usually states where individual fossils have been found. When visiting quarries always seek permission to enter if they look privately owned or worked. Be careful of falls of rock.

Much of the land is covered by basalt, which makes up the Giant's Causeway, but other, sedimentary rocks occur in places.

Upper Ordovician and Silurian rocks with trilobites and brachiopods outcrop around Pomeroy, Co Tyrone, and there are Silurian graptolites on the foreshore at Coalpit Bay, Donaghadee, Co Down. Lower Carboniferous limestones with corals, algal reefs and shells are found in the Dungannon area of Co Tyrone. Rhaetic and lias beds with ammonites, belemnites and brachiopods are to be seen on the foreshore at Larne, at Island Magee, Portrush, and Collin Glen, near Belfast. Upper Cretaceous chalk occurs also at Collin Glen and Portrush, and at Island Magee, Lisburn and Ballintoy.

Regional sports

Boating
Upper and Lower Lough Erne constitute a continuous waterway over 50 miles long, in delightful scenery. The total area of water is many times that of the Broads in England. Motor cruisers equipped with depth-sounders may be hired, as well as small sailing boats.

Fishing
There are splendid facilities for coarse, game and sea fishing. Co Fermanagh and Co Tyrone are noted for game and coarse fishing, and lakes and rivers there hold several coarse fishing records. Strangford Lough, Co Down, is noted for gigantic skate of up to 180 lbs. The Giant's Causeway coast, in Co Antrim, attracts deep-sea shark fishermen.

Gaelic football and hurling
Gaelic football may be described as a combination of rugby and soccer, while hurling has been libellously called 'hockey without rules'. Hurling is an interesting game to watch, and a dangerous game to play, as the sticks have broad, thin blades and can be whirled around the head. Both hurling and Gaelic football are generally played on Sundays. Big matches are held in Belfast, but other centres are Irvinestown, Co Fermanagh and Kilkeel, Co Down.

Horse racing
Point-to-point steeplechasing is particularly popular, the main formal race-meetings being at the Maze, Lisburn, Co Antrim, and Downpatrick, Co Down. International showjumping competitions are held at the Royal Ulster Agricultural Showgrounds, Balmoral, Belfast, at the end of *May*.

Motorcycling
A passion with many in Northern Ireland. The Ulster Grand Prix on the Dundrod Circuit, Co Antrim, in *Aug*, and the North-West 200 on a circuit adjoining Coleraine, Co Londonderry, in *May*, are events that attract international riders. Motor-cycle grass track races are frequent events in many areas.

Riding and pony-trekking
There are advanced riding schools at Ashbrooke, Co Fermanagh; Comber and Craigantlet, Co Down. Pony-trekking stables are numerous, mainly in the area surrounding the Mountains of Mourne and the Antrim Mountains.

Road Bowls
A unique Irish sport, also called 'bullets', played exclusively on Sundays around Armagh. Iron balls weighing 28oz are hurled along a road course of several miles. The winner is the player who makes the least throws.

Festivals

There are a number of local festivals and events—contact the local Information Centre for details.

Lammas Fair 3 O1
Ballycastle, Co Antrim. Held for two days every year, this popular fair is one of the best in Ireland. Dating back over 400 years, it is a mass of sideshows and showmen. Lots of stalls sell traditional 'fairings'. *Late Aug.*

The Queen's University Festival 3 P5
Belfast, Co Antrim. Irish excess at its best. In a few weeks they get through about 40 classical, 8 folk song and 7 jazz concerts, 5 operas, 5 plays, 15 films and the very popular Guiness lectures. Top British artists and the cream of Irish talent. *Mid-Nov.*

Special attractions

Belfast Zoological Gardens 3 P4
Bellevue Park, Antrim Road, Newtownabbey, Co Antrim. Now enlarged to 13 acres, its enclosures are mostly open-air, merging with the wooded slopes of Cave Hill. Aquarium, monkey house, bird and reptile collections. Llamas, lions and wolves bred here. *Open all year.*

Causeway Coast Lion Park 3 N2
Benvarden, Co Antrim, 6 miles E of Coleraine. A visit to this extensive safari park makes you feel you could be in Kenya as you drive close to the free-roaming lions, zebras, pumas, tigers, baboons and other exotic species of African wildlife. Also a shop selling African handicrafts and numerous other attractions. *Open summer.*

Drum Manor Forest Park 3 M4
Nr Cookstown, Co Tyrone. This must be the only garden specially created to attract butterflies. It is full of wild plants and shrubs that are frequently covered with the most colourful species of these delicate creatures.

Kilgad Lake Fishery 3 O4
Nr Kells, Co Antrim. Three-acre fly-fishing lake stocked with rainbow trout. *Fee payable. Open summer. Contact Kells 891570.*

Miniature railway 3 O4
Shane's Castle, Lough Neagh, Co Antrim. A steam engine pulls this train along the shores of Lough Neagh. A good diversion for the children visiting Shane's Castle Nature Reserve. *Open summer.*

Western Ireland

2

Donegal
Galway
Leitrim

Mayo
Roscommon
Sligo

The western part of Ireland covers the historic province of Connacht—Galway, Leitrim, Mayo, Roscommon and Sligo—and also includes Co Donegal, a wild, beautiful and largely Irish-speaking world, where traditional crafts still flourish. One of the nine counties forming the province of Ulster, Donegal remains, like Cavan and Monaghan, independent of the six counties that now form Northern Ireland. Donegal has a history dating back to pre-Christian times. The county town of Donegal was once the site of a Viking fortress and later chief stronghold of the O'Donnells. Glencolumbkille, in the heart of the Donegal Gaeltacht, is a gently sloping glen running inland through the hills from Glen Bay. A place where Bonnie Prince Charlie is said to have spent some time, it is rich in portal dolmens, souterrains and Bronze Age cairns. Seven miles south of Fahan, the Grianán of Aileach, a huge circular fort crowning the Greenan Mountains, was the residence of the Ulster kings from as long ago as 1500BC. Of all Donegal's historic sites, the most venerated is the island retreat on Lough Derg, the most celebrated holy place in Ireland; here, according to legend, St Patrick spent 40 days praying and fasting in a cave.

Immediately to the south are the five counties of Connacht, also an Irish-speaking stronghold. A beautiful, wild province with a torn and jagged coastline, where great handfuls of rock claw at boulder-strewn bays and narrow watery inlets of the inhospitable Atlantic. Abutting Donegal to the north is Leitrim, a magnificent lake country boasting some of the best coarse fishing in Ireland. Its county town is Carrick on Shannon, on the site of an ancient ford. Breffini Castle, now a ruin on the banks of the River Bonet near quiet Dromahair village, was the home of Dervorgilla, wife of Tiernan O'Rourke, who eloped with Dermot MacMurrough, King of Leinster, in the 12thC. Outlawed by the neighbouring clans, Dermot sought help from Henry II and the Welsh barons, resulting in the fateful Anglo-Norman invasion of Ireland.

To the west is beautiful Sligo county, W B Yeats's 'Land of Hearts Desire', where he spent his boyhood summers immersed in a poetic mixture of mountain, lake and golden coastal scenery. In Drumcliff churchyard, a tree-shaded spot on rising ground to the south, Yeats is buried. South east of Sligo are the long, narrow waters of Lough Gill with the tiny island of Innisfree, immortalised in Yeats's poem, 'The Lake Isle of Innisfree'. This is an area rich in prehistoric remains; to the north of Lough Gill near Fermoyle is the Stone of Cu, an enormous megalithic tomb crowning a hill. At Carrowmore, west of Sligo town, is the largest group of prehistoric remains in Ireland and at Carrowkeel, north west of Ballinafad, is a late Stone Age passage-

Grave of W B Yeats, Drumcliff, Co Sligo

Harbour at Killybegs, Co Donegal

grave cemetery high up in the Bricklieve Mountains. There are incomparable beauty spots like the Curlew Hills, scene of numerous military encounters, where Red Hugh O'Donnell defeated an English army in 1599 and the Caves of Kesh in Keshcorran Hill, where Cormac MacAirt, celebrated King of Ireland, was born and nurtured by a she-wolf.

To the south east is Roscommon, a green plain rich in island-spattered lakes, with the River Shannon marking its eastern boundary. It was at Roscommon, the county town, that St Coman established a monastery in early Christian times and that the Anglo-Normans built an impressive fortress on the hillside above in the 13thC. The sculptured stone at Castlestrange is one of the finest examples of early Iron Age decorative work in Ireland and the ruined 12thC Cistercian Abbey at Boyle is one of the glories of the county.

To the west is the rolling upland of Mayo. Stretching from Lough Corrib and Killary

Killary Harbour

Harbour in the south to the Mullet Peninsula and Killala Bay in the north, it is a magical mixture of traditional Ireland at its very best and just enough modern leisure facilities. It sports a wide range of scenery from the plains of East Mayo to Achill Island, the largest off the Irish coast, and from the Holy Mountain of Croagh Patrick, an isolated cone-shaped mountain along the shore of Clew Bay in the south to the rugged moorlands of Ennis in the north.

Galway is Ireland's second largest county and perhaps the most breathtaking of them all. Clifden, the principal town of Connemara in the west of the county, lies blanketed in lush green folds of hill on the edge of the Atlantic, in superb scenery dominated by the scarred and crumpled Twelve Bens. Galway city, to the south, spread round the head of a large bay, is the major city of Connacht. At Clonfert, on the banks of the Shannon 13 miles south east of Ballinasloe, is one of the best examples of Irish Romanesque decorative work in the fine portal of the cathedral. It was here that St Brendan established a monastic settlement in AD563. On Inishmore, the largest of the Aran islands, stands one of the most impressive prehistoric monuments in Western Europe, Dun Aengus, a huge stone fortress perched precipitously on top of a 300-foot cliff. Also on the island are remains of the churches built when Aran was the seminary of the early Irish Church.

Scollop thatch
on a house in Co Galway

The coast

Ardara
2 **H4**

Co Donegal. Pop 700. EC Wed. Smoky town no bigger than a village lying scattered along the banks of the River Owentocker as it enters Loughros More Bay. Behind is a wide valley edged by crumpled hills. Ardara is noted for its homespun tweed, embroidery and knitting industries, as well as being a fine centre for fishing. Numerous prehistoric and early Christian remains nearby.

Ballina
1 **F7**

Co Mayo. Pop 6,100. EC Thur. First town to be captured by the French during the 1798 insurrection, it is a bustling market town and small breezy sea port at the head of the broad Moy estuary, and the largest town in the county. To the east are the shadowy crags of the Ox Mountains; to the south west is Lough Conn, a calm mirror beneath the brooding energies of 2,646-foot Mount Nephin. Of interest: remains of 15thC Augustinian friary; Dolmen of the Four Maols, consisting of three standing stones surmounted by a capstone; ruins of 15thC Franciscan Rosserk Abbey, four miles to the north; remains of Kilmoremoy, the Great Church of Moy, established by St Olcan, a disciple of St Patrick. Good centre for game fishing.

Ballintra
2 **I5**

Co Donegal. A stone's throw from the scimitar curves of Donegal Bay, the village lies with an air of carefree idleness in a swell of high green hillocks. The nearby River Blackwater carves its spectacular way through limestone hills, occasionally dropping down through deep caverns or rushing headlong over bright, sunlit cliffs. Of particular interest are the Pullans, a series of caves through which the river runs, and the waterfall by Aghadullagh Old Mill. South of the village is Racoon, the site of a monastery founded by St Patrick in the 5thC; two miles south west is Ard Fothadh, McGonigle's Fort, thought to be the burial place of the 6thC King Hugh MacAinmire.

Ballycastle
1 **E6**

Co Mayo. Raffish little resort full of cheery insouciance, standing in sheltered quiet beside the River Ballinglen, inland from a dune-backed bay.

Beach at Ballycastle

Downpatrick Head, four miles north east, is a sandstone cliff carved into Baroque fantasies by the snarling grey Atlantic. Crowning the cliff are the ruins of St Patrick's Church. This area is an archaeological treasure trove with several promontory forts, burial cairns, Tobas Phadraig—a holy well—and an early cross pillar in the ruins of Kitbride Church.

Ballyconneely
1 **C10**

Co Galway. Tiny village on a crooked finger of land pointing out to sea. To the north is Mannin Bay, with many fine beaches. Of particular interest is Coral Strand, a Baroque reef of *Lithothamnion*, a calcareous seaweed.

Ballycroy
1 **D7**

Co Mayo. Hamlet standing astride the main road between Bangor and Mularanny with the Nephin Beg range to the east. Of interest: remains of 16thC Doona Castle, tucked down a lane to the west where jagged fragments of coast break out into the bay; several prehistoric and early Christian works. Good fishing.

Ballysadare
2 **H7**

Co Sligo. Sea-shanty town scattered in delightful disorder beside the banks of the River Owenmore as it rushes in a series of swoops and sudden dives down a rocky incline into Ballysadare Bay. On the west bank of the river are the remains of a 7thC monastery, including a pre-Romanesque church. In the 12thC, a second priory was built 300 yards downstream; remains include part of the 13thC church. Good angling, especially salmon.

Ballyshannon
2 **I5**

Co Donegal. Pop 2,500. EC Wed. Bustling market town and busy seaport hanging on a steep-sided hill along the north bank of the Erne estuary. A strategic river-crossing, it was here that Red Hugh O'Donnell routed an English force in 1597. A medieval stronghold of the O'Donnells until the defeat of the Gaelic north; fragments of their 15thC castle survive near the market-square. Ballyshannon was the birthplace of William Allingham, the poet, in 1824. Of interest: remains of Assaroe Abbey, a 12thC Cistercian foundation, a mile to the north west; Kilbarron Castle, 3½ miles north west, the remains of 16thC fortress of the once-powerful O'Clery family; two ring forts and a prehistoric pillar stone in Twomilestone and Ardpattan townlands; a prehistoric chamber tomb in nearby Coolberg.

Barna
1 **F11**

Co Galway, 6 miles E of Spiddal. Boulder-strewn landscape of thick-walled, single-storey houses embedded in a patchwork of small fields with ribbons of dry stone walling along the northern shore of Galway Bay. Good sheltered beach, the Silver Strand, running eastward to Salthill.

Belmullet
1 **C6**

Co Mayo. A remote village on the northern shores of Blacksod Bay. It was here that the flagship of Don Alfonso de Leyva was stranded in 1588. The bay itself is good for swimming and fishing; sheltering it from the Atlantic furies to the west is The Mullet, a wild cliff-faced peninsula reached by a narrow neck of land to the north, with Belmullet as its gateway. Tiny islands, breaking out into the Atlantic on the south and west, are rich in prehistoric works. Also of interest are the ruins of a cliff-top promontory fort at Doonamo; early Christian remains at Kilmore Erris; ruins of Cross Abbey, a medieval priory church built within spitting distance of the sea two miles west of Binghamstown. Several fine sandy, dune-backed beaches along the sheltered east coast of the peninsula, including Elly Bay.

Cottage at Belmullet

Beltra 2 H7
Co Sligo. Handful of cottages hugging an inlet on the
south side of Ballysadare Bay. Of interest: Tanrego
House, handsome Georgian mansion 1½ miles to the
north; three historic chamber tombs; the ruins of a
castle.

Bunbeg 2 I2
Co Donegal. Pretty pint-sized fishing harbour in the
shadow of cliffs at the mouth of the River Clady.
Good sandy beach at Magheraclogher Strand, half a
mile from the village. Excursions by boat to Gola and
other islands.

Buncrana 2 K2
Co Donegal. Pop 2,900. Sheltered by a crescent of
crumpled hills and mountains including the
2,019-foot Slieve Snaght, Buncrana is a small port
and holiday resort on the eastern bank of Lough
Swilly. The area is rich in megalithic monuments,
including a Bronze Age burial cairn at Crockcashel
one mile to the north; Kinnagoe Giants Grave, a
chambered tomb four miles to the north east. Also of
interest: 14thC keep, remains of a Norman castle
and stronghold of the O'Dohertys, which was rebuilt
in the 17thC following its burning by the English;
Buncrana Castle, built 1716, to which Wolfe Tone is
said to have been brought following his capture in
1798.

Bundoran 2 H5
Co Donegal. Pop 1,400. EC Thur. Important seaside
resort prettily situated along curving sands on the
southern shore of Donegal Bay. To the north, across
the bay, are the sunlit hills of Donegal, scattered
with huddled villages. By Tullan Strand, a fine
beach 1½ miles long, are fossil-rich cliffs worn into a
variety of shapes, including the Fairy Bridge, a
natural rock arch with a 24-foot span and the Puffing
Hole, which ejects a firework display of water in
particularly rough weather. Tucked in the cliffs west
of the town is the awesome Lion's Paw Cave. Some
excellent sandy beaches with good bathing and
fishing in the River Drowes. Facilities for golf and
tennis.

Burtonport 2 H3
Co Donegal. Small fishing village of whitewashed
houses beached round a narrow granite-walled
harbour in a wild coastline. It is the major herring
fishing centre in west Donegal and more salmon and
lobster are landed here than at any other port in the
British Isles. Good place for boat trips to the offshore
islands including Aran Island (Arranmore) with its
monumental cliffs and intriguing caves.

*Burtonport,
Co Donegal.*

Carna 1 D11
Co Galway, 4 miles W of Kilkieran. Remote fishing
village of huddled houses shivering on the windward
side of a hilly peninsula. Tucked behind it, to the
east, is Lough Skannive, which has two crannogs
(fortified islands). St MacDara's Island, one of
Ireland's most venerated holy places, is 1½ miles out
to sea; of particular interest is the tiny stone-roofed
12thC church. Excellent fishing.

Carraroe 1 D11
Co Galway. Handful of houses ducking for shelter in
a rock-bound peninsula riddled with watery inlets,
peat bogs, and undulating ramparts of dry stone
walling defending tiny continents of cultivation. It
was both home and inspiration to the artist, Charles
Lamb, who spent most of his life here. Good
beaches, including the magnificent Coral Strand.

*Shmffane Pier, near Carraroe,
Co. Galway.*

Carrick 2 H4
Co Donegal. Attractive coastal village situated above
the mouth of the River Glen. To the west is
1,972-foot-high Slieve League, the highest coastal
cliff in Europe. Of interest is One Man's Pass, a
notorious tight-rope ledge with sharp drops either
side. The area is a good centre for fishing, with
several trout lakes nearby.

Carrickart 2 J2
Co Donegal. Village resort at the neck of lush
Rosguill Peninsula. Washed by a triangular inlet
from Mulroy Bay to the north, Carrickart has the
Ards Forest Park and Clonmass Bay to the west and
the hump-backed 1,546-foot-high Salt Mountain to
the south. Many fine beaches.

Cashel 1 D10
Co Galway, 6 miles N of Glinsk. Named after the
remains of a stone fort crowning a mountainous hill
half a mile to the north east, it is a picturesque village
wedged firmly on the edge of a narrow inlet of
Bertraghboy Bay. Good fishing centre.

Clarinbridge 4 G12
Co Galway, 4 miles S of Oranmore. Tiny village
fastened tight near the head of a narrow inlet of
Galway Bay. Famed for its shellfish, with an oyster
festival held annually in *Sep.* Numerous prehistoric
remains in vicinity.

Cleggan 1 C10
Co Galway. Monochrome wall of houses and small
fishing harbour sheltering on the southern shores of
Cleggan Bay. From here you can hire a boat to visit
the offshore islands of Inishbofin and Inishark.
Several fine beaches with safe bathing, as well as a
number of interesting prehistoric sites.

Clifden 1 C10
Co Galway. Pop 1,400. EC Thur. Handsome early
19thC market town and fishing harbour spread
generously around a ridge of land at the end of the
northern fork of Clifden Bay. The hunchbacked land
to the rear of the town runs up to the foot of the
Twelve Bens, a wall of mountains to the east. An
ideal centre for exploring the surrounding

*culpen, connemara,
co·Galway·*

countryside. Of interest: ruins of 19thC Clifden
Castle to the west of the town; cairn beside
Derrygimlagh Bog to the south west, marking the
spot where Alcock and Brown crash-landed
following their historic Atlantic flight in June 1919;
several prehistoric sites. Many good beaches,
including coral strand to the south west. Good sea
fishing. Connemara pony show held annually
mid-Aug.

Costelloe   1 E11
Co Galway. Tiny community marooned at the
mouth of the River Casla as it flows out into Casla
Bay. Famed for its salmon river and lakes.

Creeslough   2 J2
Co Donegal. Holiday village lying within spitting
distance of the narrow inlet of Sheep Haven. To the
south west is the 2,197-foot Muckish Mountain. To
the north east, perched on a low promontory of
sea-washed rock and protected by a deep ditch on
the landward side is 16thC Doe Castle. A
MacSweeney stronghold, it consists of a four-storey
house enclosed in a square, turreted bawn;
shipwrecked sailors from the Spanish armada were
given refuge here in 1589, and this was the foster
home of Red Hugh O'Donnell. Also of interest: the
picturesque Duntally bridge and waterfall to the east
of the village; whitewashed Church of St Michael,
built 1971.

Culdaff   3 L1
Co Donegal. Secluded village cocooned in whispering
calm at the mouth of the River Culdaff. Beside
Culdaff Bay is a small, quiet beach. To the north
west, an 800-foot-high curtain of cliffs sweeps round
from Glengad Head to Malin Head. In Clonca, to the
south, is a ruined 17thC church with a fine carved
pre-Romanesque lintel over the west portal.
Standing in a field to the west is St Buadan's Cross, a
12-foot-high high cross carved with the miracle of
the loaves and fishes on one side and with two men
with arms folded on the reverse. Good beaches and
fishing.

Donegal   2 I4
Co Donegal. Pop 1,750. EC Wed. Thriving market
town and minor seaport wedged in a fold of green
hills. Straddling the mouth of the River Eske at the

Donegal Town, co·Donegal·

north east corner of Donegal Bay, it is an ideal centre
for touring the southern half of Co Donegal. Once
occupied by the Vikings, it was catapulted into
prominence in the Middle Ages when the
O'Donnells, kings of Tir Chonaill, made it the
capital of a powerful kingdom. Following the 'Flight
of the Earls' in September 1607, when most of the
leading Ulster families set sail for exile on the
Continent, the town was 'planted' by the English.
The attractive square, a wide triangular space called
the Diamond, was laid out by Sir Basil Brooke in the
early 17thC. Of interest is 15thC Donegal Castle,
now in ruins. Built on the site of a Viking fortress,
the great square tower was added in 1505 by Red
Hugh O'Donnell and the fine Jacobean house was
built by Sir Basil Brooke in 1610. Also of interest:
ruins of Donegal Abbey, a Franciscan friary built in
1474 on the seashore south of the town and largely
destroyed during an early 17thC battle between
O'Donnell and the English. One of the great literary
works of the 17thC, the "Annals of the Four
Masters", was written here. Seven miles north east is
Barnesmore Gap, a spectacular three-mile cutting
through the Blue Stack Mountains, once the haunt
of highwaymen. Good beaches nearby.

Downings   2 J1
Co Donegal, 3 miles NW of Carrickart. Tiny but
popular resort with excellent views of the Rosguill
Peninsula and out across Sheep Haven, a wide angle
of water carving out into the measureless Atlantic
beyond. There is a classical crescent of beach five
miles to the north lining quiet Tranarossan Bay.

Drumcliff   2 H6
Co Sligo, 3½ miles N of Sligo. Quiet village
straddling the river that drains the waters of Lough
Glencar to the sea at Drumcliff Bay. It was here that
St Columba established a monastery in AD574;
remains include parts of a round tower and a fine,
sculptured 10thC high cross. In the little churchyard
lies the grave of W B Yeats, the great Irish poet, who
died in 1939. From it you can see the huge curling
mass of Ben Bulben, a giant limestone cliff 1,730 feet
high, most westerly peak of the Dartry Mountains.
Lissadell House, the home of Countess Markievicz,
is nearby.

Dunfanaghy   2 J2
Co Donegal. Quiet village and holiday resort on the
western shores of Sheep Haven Bay. Standing to the
north across the narrow inlet of water is Horn Head,
rising 600 feet from the water, its rocky cliffs a nest
of sea birds. West of the resort is McSyne's Gun, a
huge blow-hole into which the tide rushes with an
explosive roar in gale-force weather. To the east are
two other small resorts, Port-na-Blagh and Marble
Hill, each with magnificent long beaches.

Dunkineely   2 H4
Co Donegal. Quiet village guarding the entrance to St
John's Point, a long narrow peninsula poking
cautiously into Donegal Bay. On the western bank of
the bay stand the remains of a fortress of the
MacSwynes of Banagh. Good fishing.

Easky   1 F6
Co Sligo. Flanked by Martello towers built as a
defence against Napoleonic invasion, it is a tiny
fishing village on the banks of a rushing river. Of
interest: numerous ruined castles; cromlech known
as the 'Griddle Stone'; Finn MacCool's Finger, a
huge fissured boulder said to have been split by the
giant MacCool.

Enniscrone   1 F6
Co Sligo. Pop 540. EC Wed. Popular seaside resort
of rolling dunes and low cliffs on eastern shore of
Killala Bay. There is a three-mile crescent of sandy
beach and good surfing. Two miles to the north are
the ruins of Castle Firbis, 15thC–16thC stronghold
of the MacFirbises, famed Gaelic poets and
annalists, a learned family that compiled the "Book
of Lecan" in 1416 (now in the Royal Irish Academy,
Dublin). Duald MacFirbis (1585–1670) was the last
in a long-standing hereditary line of 'Sennachies'
(genealogists). Medicinal baths.

Fahan   2 K2
Co Donegal. Tiny resort, sitting at the tip of a nose of
land to the south of Buncrana. St Columba founded
a monastery here in the 6thC, but all that remains is
an 8thC cross-slab associated with St Mura.
Opposite Fahan, floating in the waters of Lough
Swilly, is Inch Island, connected by bridge to the
mainland. There is also a ferry to Rathmullan.

Falcarragh   2 I2
Co Donegal. On the shores of a narrow inlet, it's a
meandering village on the north west coast. The
Gaeltacht College here is a study centre for students
of the Irish language. Good centre from which to
climb the 2,197-foot Muckish Mountain and
2,466-foot Errigal Mountain.

Galway   1 F11
Co Galway. Pop 36,917. EC Thur. Spread round the
mouth of the River Corrib as it flows out into the
north east corner of Galway Bay, this is the
administrative centre of the county as well as the
southern gateway to beautiful Connemara and the
Aran Islands.

History
A small village and Gaelic stronghold in the early
12thC, transformed into a major town following the
conquest of Connacht by the Anglo-Normans in the
early 13thC. Richard de Burgo built a great fortress
here, around which a fortified town grew. It was
made a royal borough by Richard II in 1396. Despite
continual harassment by the dispossessed but still
powerful de Burgo family and the formidable
O'Flahertties, Galway remained a strategic
stronghold of English power in Connacht for the
next 500 years. Virtually a city-state, it was ruled by
an oligarchy of Anglo-Norman and Welsh mercantile
families, the most powerful of which were the
Lynchs. It was this ruling élite that transformed
Galway from an important medieval town into a
major seaport with a flourishing trade in Spain.
In 1473 the town was destroyed by a disastrous fire
but was rebuilt in the 16thC and 17thC on more
spacious lines, with a grid of orderly streets and
handsome courtyard houses. One of the wealthiest
towns in early 17thC Ireland, its fortunes declined
considerably following the town's backing of the
Royalists during England's Civil War. The town was
captured by the Cromwellians in 1652 and much of it
was destroyed. The citizens chose the losing side
again during the Williamite rebellion of 1691.
Galway's importance as an administrative centre of
the British Government increased during the 18thC

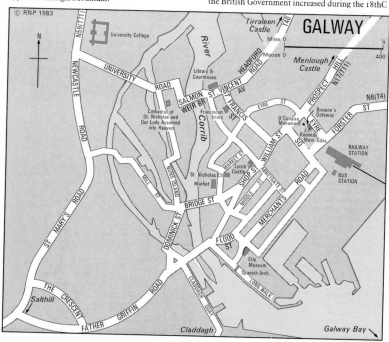

© RNP 1983

and 19thC but with the Great Famine of 1845–47 the town went into further, rapid decline. It was not until this century, particularly after the re-establishment of the state's independence, that Galway began to recover some of its former prosperity and importance.

Galway City

Districts
The heart of the town is Eyre Square, built on a gentle incline. Once an open space where fairs were held in front of the main town gate, it was given to the town in 1710 by the then mayor, Edward Eyre, who had inherited it from his father. Nowadays it contains 17thC Browne's Gateway, re-erected in 1905; the J F Kennedy Memorial Gardens; and the O'Conaire Monument. From here, the main streets of the town spread out in orderly grid, broken only by the winding river and its bridges. The Salmon Weir Bridge, built 1819, is one of the sights of Galway; shoals of salmon can be seen here, leaping upstream to their breeding grounds in Lough Corrib. The Claddagh, a small community on the west bank of the river, was once an Irish haven in a Norman-occupied county. Originally a unique fishing village, it was rebuilt in the 1930s but many traditional customs live on. Salthill, a popular seaside resort, is a suburb lying to the south west of the city.

Cathedrals, abbeys and churches
The most interesting of the churches is St Nicholas' in Lombard Street, its central tower and pyramid-like spire punctuating the centre of the city. Begun by the Anglo-Normans in 1320, it was enlarged in 1486 and again in the 16thC and is the largest medieval church in Ireland. It was here that Columbus is said to have prayed before setting sail for America accompanied by, amongst others, a Galway man named Rice de Culvy. The modern RC Cathedral of St Nicholas and Our Lady Assumed into Heaven was built in 1965. A limestone monolith in the Renaissance style with wall-to-wall carpet of Connemara marble and splendid mosaics in the side chapel, it dominates the skyline from its island site on the River Corrib. Also of interest: Franciscan friary, founded in 1296 by William de Burgo and rebuilt 1836.

Castles & palaces
At the corner of Shop Street and Abbeygate Street is Lynch's Castle, an early 17thC tower house decorated with gargoyles. Now a bank, it is typical of the mansions erected by prosperous Galway merchants of the time. Also of interest: ruined Menlough Castle, two miles north west near Lough Corrib; 13thC Tirraleen Castle, a de Burgo stronghold one mile north on the banks of the river.

Interesting buildings
The city still has a number of 16thC–17thC houses, notably in Market Street, by the north east corner of the churchyard, and in Shop Street, Middle Street and Abbeygate Street. Near the Fish Market, by the site of the old medieval quay at the south west corner of the town, is Spanish Arch; a fragment of the old town wall and gateway built 1594 to protect the quay

The Spanish Arch, Galway City

where Spanish ships unloaded their wines and brandies. Beyond is Spanish Passage, the 16thC promenade of Spanish merchants and their families. Also of interest is the University. Although long celebrated as an educational centre with a fine classical school founded in the 16thC, it was not until the 19thC that Galway achieved a university of its own. It is now a centre for Gaelic studies and was built in 1845 in a Tudor-Gothic style reminiscent of a Cambridge college, on the edge of town. The predilection for historicism characterises much building throughout the 19thC and 20thC: the Court House 1812–15 is of neoclassical design, by Sir Richard Morrison.

Special attractions
The John Fitzgerald Kennedy Memorial Park at Eyre Square is named after the former American President, who addressed the townspeople in June 1963 on being given the freedom of the city. Also of interest: Galway City Museum, depicting life in Galway; 17thC silver sword and Great Mace on exhibition at the Bank of Ireland, Eyre Square. There are several annual festivals in Galway: the Claddagh Festival takes place each *Aug*; the Galway Oyster Festival, in which contestants from various countries compete for the title of 'International Oyster-Opening Champion', is held in *Sep*; the Galway Bay International Sea Angling Festival, also in *Sep*, attracts entrants from all over the world; the Galway Horse Show is held *Jun–Jul*; in autumn there is the Feis Ceoil an Iarthair, a feast of traditional song, dance and story-telling; and of course St Patrick's Week, in *Mar*, is duly festive, with civic parades and cultural events.

Entertainment
Plays are presented in the Irish language all year round, and at the Taibhdhearc na Gaillimhe, Middle Street, a performance of Irish music (*seoda*) takes place three nights a week in *summer*. The Druid Theatre Company at the Fo'castle Theatre also performs mainly during the *summer* months. Galway Leisureland in Salthill on the promenade is excellent for children; there is an 'astroïde', mini-train, trampolines, pitch and putt, even an olympic-size swimming pool. Horse-racing at the Ballybrit Racecourse, two miles from the city, takes place in late *Jul* and in *Sep* and *Oct*; the July meeting makes up the best part of Galway Race Week. Greyhound racing is on offer every week, *Tue and Fri, except Jan*.

Glencolumbkille   2 G4
Co Donegal. Tiny village snared in a trap of rock and sea in a secluded valley at the head of Glen Bay, with the cliffs of Glen Head rising steeply to the north. Interesting folk village nearby, depicting various periods of Irish life. Numerous court cairns and other prehistoric remains from the Bronze Age and beyond surround the village. The Glen of Glencolumbkille was a favourite retreat of St Columba and his disciples.

Ben Bulben
Co Sligo.

Grange 2 H6
Co Sligo. Village straddling the coastal road running
north from Sligo behind the dune-backed beaches
and low-lying hills lining Donegal Bay. Behind it
Ben Bulben curls up like a giant wave about to
break. The flat-topped mountain, a botanist's
paradise, is where the legendary hero of "The
Pursuit of Diarmuid and Grainne" met his death
whilst hunting boar on the lower slopes. Cliffony,
3½ miles further north, is also an attractive village.

Greencastle 3 L1
Co Donegal. Standing guard over the narrow
entrance to Lough Foyle, it's a modest seaside resort
with an excellent bathing beach. Standing on a tiny
outcrop of rock are the overgrown ruins of a great
castle built by Richard de Burgo, the Red Earl of
Ulster, in 1305. In 1316 it fell into the hands of
Edward Bruce; de Burgo recaptured it, only to lose
it finally in 1333 to the O'Dohertys, who held it until
the Inishowen Peninsula was captured by the
English in 1608. Nearby is an early 19thC fort and
martello tower.

Gweesalia 1 D7
Co Mayo, 14 miles SE of Belmullet. Pretty,
Irish-speaking village and sheltered gateway to The
Mullet, a wild, cliff-faced peninsula with
magnificent deep-sea angling around its coast.

Kilcar 2 H4
Co Donegal. Picturesque village lying in crumpled
disorder at the bottom of scarred hills. Thriving
centre of numerous cottage industries, especially
handwoven tweed. To the south is Muckross Head,
a myriad caverns and cliffs cut off at high tide. Small
golden beach at Traloar with the slopes of
Croaghmuckross rising sharply behind.

Kilkieran 1 D11
Co Galway. Handful of houses ducking for shelter
beneath the shadow of hills and the splash of sea
spray. St Kieran passed through here in the 6thC, on
his journey from Clonmacnois to Aran.

Killala 1 F7
Co Mayo. Scene of the French landing in 1798 to
help the insurrection, it is an attractive village and
former port on the west shore of beautiful Killala
Bay. Of interest: remains of early monastery,
including 84-foot-high round tower and large
souterrain; St Patrick's Cross, two miles south east;
remains of 15thC Moyne Abbey, one mile south east;
two ring forts and ruins of 13thC Dominican
Rathfran Friary, two miles north. Good deep-sea
angling with boats for hire.

Killybegs 2 H4
Co Donegal. Pop 1,100. EC Wed. Important fishing
port built round a natural harbour in a narrow inlet
on the north of Donegal Bay. Interesting carved slab
in St Mary's Church commemorating Niall Mor
MacSweeney. Numerous prehistoric remains in
vicinity. Famous for hand-knotted carpets.

Kinvarra 4 F12
Co Galway. Quaint fishing village, once a thriving
town, glued round a narrow inlet to the south east of

Galway Bay. Standing on a rocky pedestal half a mile
to the north east is 16thC Dunguaire Castle. Also of
interest: Doorus House, a fine mansion two miles
north west, where Yeats and others first conceived
the idea of a national theatre.

Leenaun 1 D10
Co Galway. Tiny village at the head of a narrow
estuary, Killary Harbour; the cold mirror of water
reflects the mountains, which rise steeply,
sometimes perpendicularly, on three sides. To the
south west are the Twelve Bens, to the north east the
Partry Mountains: behind, to the south, are the
Maamturk Mountains and to the north west,
immediately behind Killary harbour, the Mweelrea
Mountains climb skyward some 2,688 feet.

Letterfrack 1 C10
Co Galway. Conceived as one of a series of mission
settlements along the Connemara coast by the
Society of Friends in the 19thC, it is an enchanting
village of colour-washed houses and grey, dry stone
walling standing on the edge of Barnaderg Bay.

Kylemore from
Letterfrack, Co Galway.

Letterkenny 2 J3
Co Donegal. Pop 4,950. EC Wed. Set in a
mountain-backed landscape of lush meadows with
the River Swilly curving round to the south before
entering Lough Swilly, it is a cathedral town with
one of the longest main streets in Ireland. It was here
that Wolfe Tone was taken after his capture aboard
the French battleship 'Hoche' in October 1798.
Conwal Cemetery, some distance west of the town,
was the burial place of the legendary O'Donnells.
Three miles west is Scarriffhollis, once an important
ford over the River Swilly, where a powerful
Parliamentarian army under the ruthless Sir Charles
Coote routed an Irish force under Bishop Heber
MacMahon, the last Royalist army in Ulster, in June
1650. Of interest: St Eunan's Cathedral, a
magnificent French Gothic-style monster, begun
1891 by William Hague.

Lettermore 1 D11
Co Galway, 7 miles W of Costelloe. Picturesque
hamlet on Lettermore Island, a raft of boulders and
peat at the mouth of Kilkieran Bay.

Louisburgh 1 D9
Co Mayo. Pop 300. Delightful early 19thC fishing
village at the mouth of the River Bunowen where it
spills out into Clew Bay. Of interest: 15thC Murrisk
Abbey, an Augustinian friary seven miles to the east;
Kilgeever Abbey, ancient church and holy well, one
mile east; prehistoric wedge-grave at Altore, six
miles south; clapper bridge, a primitive stone bridge

Clew Bay, Co Mayo.

at Killeen, five miles south. Sandy beaches and good fishing in Clew Bay, including shark, skate, and cod.

Malin Beg   **2 G4**
Co Donegal. Tiny village huddled in a rocky landscape. Fine sheltering strand to the south east. South west is Pollanamora, a natural bridge.

Malin More   **2 G4**
Co Donegal. Pretty holiday village in a sea of hills with an impressive wall of cliffs rising along the shores of Malin Bay. Many prehistoric remains in area, including a magnificent horned cairn, Cloghanmore, half a mile to the south east. Fine beach, and the waters around Rathlin O'Birne, a tiny island two miles to the south west, are considered to be the best fishing grounds off the Donegal coast.

Millford   **2 J2**
Co Donegal. Pop 750. Angling resort and tourist centre standing modestly on a plateau of land wedged between the head of Mulroy Bay and Lough Fern. Spectacular scenery, notably secluded Bunlin Glen, a quiet shadowy world through which a stream dips and whirls to the Golan Loop and cascades to a second waterfall, the Grey Mare's Tail. To the west are the blue-washed peaks of 1,546-foot Salt Mountain. St Peter's Church, designed 1961 by Corr and McCormick, is an heroic folk building in the form of an elongated hexagon, extended to include a porch and sanctuary, with whitewashed walls and detached bell tower. Numerous prehistoric remains in area include portal dolmens, several chamber tombs and a ring fort.

Mountcharles   **2 I4**
Co Donegal. Colourful line of 18thC and 19thC houses along an undulating ridge of gorse and rock. Birthplace of the writer Seamus MacManus. Sandy beach and good fishing.

Moville   **3 L2**
Co Donegal. Former port of call for transatlantic liners, it is an attractive resort on the western shore of Lough Foyle. Numerous ring forts, souterrains and megalithic tombs in vicinity.

Mularanny   **1 D8**
Co Mayo. Gateway to the Corraun Peninsula with its huge mountain peaks, it is a picturesque place on a narrow isthmus between Clew Bay to the south and a narrow inlet of Blacksod Bay to the north west. Sheltered from the Atlantic by rolling hills, the climate is mild, enabling lovely fuchsias, Mediterranean heather and other rare plants to grow. Good sandy beaches and excellent fishing.

Mullaghmore   **2 H5**
Co Sligo. Popular resort backed by a low hill of gorse and bracken. The harbour was constructed in 1842 by Lord Palmerston. On the highest point of the headland stands Cassiebawn Castle, built in the late 19thC. Fabulous views across an ocean of water to the peaks of Donegal. Good beaches as well as fine boating and fishing.

Newport   **1 E8**
Co Mayo. Fishing village at the north east corner of Clew Bay in the long shadows of the huge Nephin and Nephin Beg mountains. Of interest: parish church designed by Rudolf M Butler in 1914 in a bold Gaelic-Romanesque style; Burrishoole Abbey, 15thC Dominican friary, two miles north west; Carrighahooly Castle, built by the Burke family in the 16thC, where Grace O'Malley withstood a siege.

Oranmore   **4 F11**
Co Galway. Attractive town wrapped in woods and park-plantations round a 17thC castle, at the head of a narrow creek of Galway Bay.

Portacloy   **1 D6**
Co Mayo, 12 miles W of Belderg. Tiny harbour squeezed tight at the end of a narrow bay by high cliffs. To the west is a giant buttress of cliff shooting out of the sea, 829-foot-high Benwee Head. The Stags of Broadhaven are seven precipitous, 300-foot-high rock piers.

Portnoo   **2 H3**
Co Donegal, 7 miles NW of Ardara. Small fishing harbour on the southern shores of Gweebarra Bay. Of interest: Inishkeel, a tiny tidal island with ruined chapel; Narin, fishing village to the east with a good beach; magnificent cliff scenery at Dawros Head.

Portsalon   **2 K1**
Co Donegal. Tiny resort and harbour in a spectacular setting on the edge of Lough Swilly. Two miles to the north are the Seven Arches, spectacular rock-formed tunnels the size of houses. Two miles further north is the Great Arch of Doaghbeg, a huge fragment of rock detached from the great wall of cliffs lining this section of the Fanad Peninsula. Good beaches and fishing.

Raghly   **2 G6**
Co Sligo, 8 miles NW of Sligo. Peaceful fishing village on a peninsula at the mouth of Drumcliff Bay. Of interest: remains of 17thC Ardtermon Castle, once the home of the Gore family; two tidal rock basins, known as the Pigeon Holes.

Rathmelton   **2 K2**
Co Donegal. Attractive angling centre and harbour at the head of a creek of Lough Swilly. Of interest: fine warehouses beside water's edge; Killydonnell Abbey, ruins of a 16thC Franciscan friary, 3½ miles south east.

Rathmullan   **2 K2**
Co Donegal. Attractive resort on the west bank of Lough Swilly, with passenger ferry to Fahan. It was from here that Hugh O'Neill led the 'Flight of the Earls', setting sail with Rory O'Donnell and the leading Ulster families for exile on the Continent in September 1607. The subsequent confiscation of their estates was to change the face of Ulster. Of interest: remains of 15thC Carmelite friary. Good beach and pleasant walks.

Rosapenna   **2 J2**
Co Donegal, 2 miles NW of Carrickart. Pleasant resort with good beach, best known for its golf course. Lovely beach at Tranarossan, off the north west side of the Rosguill Peninsula.

Rosbeg   **2 H3**
Co Donegal, 5 miles NW of Ardara. Small holiday resort with fine beaches, on the northern banks of Loughros More Bay. Dawros Head lies two miles north west.

Rossnowlagh   **2 I5**
Co Donegal, 1 mile N of Coolmore. Tiny seaside resort famed for its beautiful beach and rolling surf. Backdrop of gentle, rolling hills. Good fishing.

Roundstone   **1 C11**
Co Galway. Polychrome wall of houses lining a gently sloping street at the base of the towering

Roundstone Harbour, Connemara

987-foot-high Erristeg Mountain, with a granite-built harbour on the west of Bertaghboy Bay. Built by a Scottish engineer, Alexander Nimmo, early in the 19thC. Dog's Bay and Gorteen Bay both have sparkling white sand.

Sligo 2 **H6**
Co Sligo. Pop 14,100. EC Wed. Lying in sloping, wooded land between two mountains, it's a busy market and manufacturing town and seaport at the mouth of the River Garavogue, which flows from Lough Gill into Sligo Bay. The scene of a 6thC battle between warring Gaelic chiefs and plundered by the Vikings in the early 9thC, it was catapulted into importance in 1245 when Maurice Fitzgerald, the Earl of Kildare, made it his residence. It was he who founded Sligo Abbey for the Dominicans in 1252. Fought over by rival Gaelic clans, the O'Conors and O'Donnells, for many years, the town was captured by Sir Frederick Hamilton during the rebellion of 1641 and fell to Cromwellian forces in 1645. Good centre for touring Co Sligo, with its encircling hills, loughs and long, low, dune-backed coastline; sharp views out to the peaks of Donegal across the bay. Sligo Abbey was burnt in 1414 and rebuilt again only to be severely damaged during the rebellion of 1641. The ruins consist of a nave, a choir and a central tower carried on lofty arches; three sides of the cloisters are intact and have very fine carved capitals with twin colonettes. Also of interest: St John's Church, designed by Richard Castle in the 18thC; the Catholic cathedral, a limestone monolith designed 1870 in the Romanesque style; Venetian-style Town Hall, designed 1866–1870 by William Hayne, a seven-bay Gothic-style palazzo crowned by central turreted tower; the courthouse, 1878. There are numerous historic remains within the vicinity, notably Maeve's Mound, a huge cairn 80 feet high, crowning the 1,078-foot-high Knocknarea to the west of the city; it is a monument to Maeve, the 1stC Queen of Connacht. On a hill at Carrowmore is the largest group of Bronze Age monuments in Ireland. The Sligo County Museum and Art Gallery is also well worth a visit, as is 18thC Hazelwood House, designed by Castle.

Spiddal 1 **E11**
Co Galway. Handful of houses gathered at the mouth of the River Owenboliska on the north shore of Galway Bay. The church of 1904, designed in bold Celtic-Romanesque style by William Scott, is interesting. Good bathing and fishing.

Strandhill 2 **H6**
Co Sligo, 5 miles W of Sligo. Tiny village and seaside resort on Sligo Bay, at the foot of the 1,078-foot-high Knocknarea, a giant cairn-shaped hill as large as a mountain. Two long sandy beaches and good surfing. South west of Knocknarea is a narrow, mile-long glen walled by overgrown, boulder-strewn cliffs.

Teelin 2 **G4**
Co Donegal. On the western edge of Teelin Bay to the south of Carrick, Teelin is a tiny cluster of houses dwarfed by hunchbacked Slieve League to the west. Good place for boat hire. Several prehistoric sites in vicinity. Magnificent cliff scenery.

Tullaghan 2 **H5**
Co Leitrim, 3 miles SW of Bundoran. A colourful line of thick-walled houses on the southern shore of Donegal Bay. The only seaside village in Co Leitrim, it is within easy reach of good salmon fishing rivers and numerous secluded sandy beaches. Magnificent views across the bay to the mountain peaks of Donegal.

Tullycross 1 **C10**
Co Galway, 3 miles N of Letterfrack. A pretty village of thatch-roofed stone cottages transformed in recent years by a rent-a-cottage scheme for holidaymakers. Surrounding landscape is breathtaking.

Westport 1 **E9**
Co Mayo. Pop 3,020. EC Wed. Gracious Georgian town and former port surrounded by trees and mountains on the edge of island-dotted Clew Bay. A planned town, it was designed by James Wyatt in 1780 while he was employed as the architect for the interior design of Westport House by the First Marquess of Sligo. There is a hexagonal market place and delightful boulevard, called the Mall, around which the town was planned. This central street has beautiful Georgian terraced houses and down the middle runs a granite-walled stretch of the River Carrowbeg, under an umbrella of sycamores.

Westport Co Mayo

Gateway to Achill and Connemara, this is also the assembly point for pilgrims climbing the 2,510-foot-high Croagh Patrick on the *last Sun in Jul.* Overshadowing Clew Bay, the peak is Ireland's Holy Mountain. It was on its summit that St Patrick spent 40 days of Lent in AD441, praying that the Christian faith he had brought the Irish would never be lost. Westport House, a handsome Georgian mansion 1½ miles north west of the town, has a 300-acre park, the first in Ireland. Good fishing.

Islands & peninsulas

Achill Island 1 **C8**
Co Mayo. Joined by a bridge across the narrow strait to the mainland, it is the largest island off the Irish coast. Idyllic retreat of intimate calm carpeted with heather-covered hills and crumpled valleys, whilst magnificent cragged peaks, several over 2,000 feet high, hide amongst the clouds. The main centre is the village of Achill Sound, with good boating and bathing. Keel is another attractive village, a cluster of whitewashed cottages at the northern end of the mirrored waters of a broad lough. To the south east are the cliffs of Menawn, a 1,500-foot-high wall of impregnable savagery; to the east are the fan-vaulted caverns of Cathedral Rocks, carved by a relentlessly ferocious sea. The village of Dooagh, a scattered hamlet sitting snugly beside a fine strand, lies 11 miles to the north west. High up on the east slope of Croaghaun sits Corrymore Lodge, where Captain Boycott once lived. The area around the 2,204-foot-high Slievemore peak is rich in prehistoric remains, including the Giant's Grave, a chambered tomb; Keel East Cromlech, a chambered cairn with elliptical court; remains of a megalithic gallery grave on the south slope. Also of interest are the seal caves, carved at the foot of Slievemore as it cascades into the sea. Dug in along the south west are the primitive huts of a 'booley' village, used when the cattle are taken up to the summer pastures.

Achillbeg Island
1 C8

Co Mayo. There are three promontory forts, including the very ambitious Doon Kilmore, built on a finger of land and consisting of an earth enclosure defended by a ditch and stone rampart.

Aran Island
2 H3

Co Donegal. Opposite Burtonport, from which there are regular ferry sailings to Leabgarrow, the main harbour. The west and north shores of rugged cliffs are colonised by sea birds, while the eastern shore has sandy beaches and is the settled area. Of interest to botanists.

Aran Islands
1 D12

Co Galway. Pop 2,150. Adrift in the mouth of Galway Bay are the windswept, treeless Aran Islands: Inishmore, Inishmaan and Inisheer. Their history is as old as the hills. The first inhabitants were the Firbolgs of Meath, who were granted lands to settle, including the Aran Islands which they fortified. It was here that St Enda founded the first of the Irish monasteries cAD490 and it was from here that many of Ireland's saints set out to found their own monastic foundations. The monastery was partially destroyed in 1020, and plundered by the Norsemen in 1081. During the 11thC, the O'Briens took possession of the islands; their claim was challenged by the O'Flahertys, who managed to expel them during the 16thC. By the late 16thC the islands were in the control of the English and were occupied by Cromwellian forces in 1651. After 1691 they were again occupied by the English and a garrison was installed.

Inishmore is the largest island (7,635 acres). Kilronan, the port, is a sprawling village on Killearny Bay. Of interest near the hamlet of Killearny: Doocaher, a promontory fort; Temple Benan, a small stone oratory; several beehive huts and enclosures; remains of a 15thC Franciscan friary; 16thC Arkins Castle, garrisoned by Cromwell's troops in 1651. Near the village of Kilmurry is Temple MacDuagh, an early stone church; St Kieran's Church and well; St Brecan's Church; Dun Aengus, one of the finest stone forts of Western Europe, perched precariously on a high cliff top; Dun Onaght, a circular stone fort; and a dolmen at Cowragh.

Dun Aengus, Inishmore, Aran Islands.

A mile away to the south east is Inishmaan, 2,252 acres, an oval of land three miles long perched securely above a wall of cliffs. Of interest is a small stone oratory, Kilcanonogh, near Carrownlisheen townland, with flat-headed doorway and angular east window; Dun Moher, a stone fort; Dermot and Grainne's Bed, a dolmen with two standing stones; Dun Conor, an oval stone fort; Dunberg, a ring fort; the remains of a clochan. The island is the setting for J M Synge's play, 'Riders to the Sea'.
Further to the south east is Inisheer (1,400 acres). Here there are several stone churches, including a small oratory, Kilgobnet Church, with round-headed east window; St Cavan's Church, complete with nave and chancel; the ruins of a cashel, the Grave of the Seven Daughters; ruins of Furmina Castle, 16thC stronghold of the O'Briens. The islanders, many still speaking Irish, generally wear the traditional rawhide sandals and fish in boats similar to the ancients' coracles, called curachs. They are built of tarred canvas stretched over a framework of laths.

Caher Island
1 C9

Co Mayo. Cobwebbed corner of early Christian Ireland and haunt of wild geese, on the leeward side of Inishturk. Of interest: Templepatrick, a tiny dry stone oratory; Tobermurry, St Mary's holy well; numerous cross-slabs and pillars; remains of an early monastery.

Clare Island
1 C8

Co Mayo. Adrift on the edge of Clew Bay, it is a mountainous island dwarfed by 1,520-foot-high Knockmore. In the lush green centre of the island is Clare Abbey; founded in 1224, remains include fragments of the 13thC buildings and a late 15thC church with exceptionally fine medieval frescoes in the chancel, over which is a dwelling tower. The harbour, on the east coast, is dominated by a 15thC weatherbeaten castle. A monumental three-storey fortress modernised in the 19thC, it was the stronghold of the legendary Grace O'Malley, a much-married 16thC pirate queen whose Amazonian exploits earned her Queen Elizabeth I's grudging respect. Born 1530, the daughter of the Lord of Upper Umhall, the owner of the island, she died in 1600 and is buried in the abbey. Also of interest: Toberfelabride, a holy well; cashel enclosing St Brigid's Bed, a beehive hut; cliff-sited promontory fort to the west of Ooghaniska.

Grace O'Malley's Castle, Co Mayo.

Duvillaun More
1 C7

Co Mayo, 3 miles SW of Inishkea. Tiny island with the remnants of a prehistoric settlement, including ruins of a corbel-roofed oratory and a number of beehive huts.

Fanad Peninsula
2 J1

Co Donegal. Monumental claw of land closing tightly round Mulroy Bay to the west. To the east are the long, broad waters of Lough Swilly. Spectacular cliff scenery.

Gweedore Peninsula
2 I2

Co Donegal. A mainly Irish-speaking peninsula crowned by Bloody Foreland, a ruddy-coloured headland flung out into the Atlantic, it is a wild, shattered landscape. To the east at the end of Dunlewy Lough rise the 2,466-foot-high quartzite peaks of Errigal, the highest mountain in Co Donegal. To the south are the Derryveagh Mountains, a glaciated crescent of peaks that turn pale blue in the bright morning light. At the foot of Errigal beside Dunlewy Lough is Poisoned Glen, a cliff-shadowed corner. Beyond it to the south are the 2,240-foot-high peaks of Slieve Snaght and to the north east is 2,197-foot-high Muckish Mountain.

High Island   1 B10
Co Galway, 7 miles W of Inishbofin. Small island with
remains of early monastery founded by St Fechin of
Fore in AD664.

Inishbofin Island   1 C9
Co Galway. Attractive little island off the
Connemara coast, with a turbulent history. It was
taken by the O'Malleys in 1380 and fortified by
Grace O'Malley in the 16thC for her fleet. In 1652 it
was captured by the Cromwellians, who used it as an
internment camp for priests and monks. The
harbour is guarded by the remains of an impressive
17thC fortress with 24 guns, planned in the shape of
a star. One mile north east of the harbour are the
remains of a 7thC monastery founded by St Colman
and there are various prehistoric remains in the
vicinity. Accessible by boat from Cleggan.

Inishbofin Island

Inishglora Island   1 C6
Co Mayo, 4 miles N of Inishkea. Legendary burial
place of the Children of Lir, this tiny island has the
remains of a monastic settlement founded by St
Brendan in the 6thC, including ruins of St Brendan's
Chapel, St Brendan's Well and several pillar-stones
and cross-slabs.

Inishkea Island   1 C7
Co Mayo. Uninhabited since 1931, it has the remains
of a monastic settlement founded by St Colmcille in
the 6thC. Of interest are a dry stone chapel, three
stone huts and numerous engraved pillar-stones and
cross-slabs. The village, although deserted, is intact.

Inishmurray   2 G5
Co Sligo. Four miles off the coast at the entrance to
Donegal Bay with a precipitous west side but
shelving east shore, it was inhabited until recently by
fishermen. There are extensive well-preserved
remains of a 6thC monastery founded by St Molaise,
which was abandoned in the 9thC. Accessible by
boat from Grange.

Inishowen Peninsula

Inishowen Peninsula   2 L1
Co Donegal. Mainly mountainous region of scarred
and crumpled peaks rising in the centre to the
2,019-foot-high peak of Slieve Snaght. The
peninsula, like the giant shadow of a clenched fist
from the air, is bordered on the east by Lough Foyle
and on the west by Lough Swilly. Malin Head, a
tapering nose of land breaking out from the main
peninsula, is the most northerly point in Ireland.
The main centre is Buncrana, a popular holiday
resort sheltered by hills on three sides. The coastal

scenery to the west and north is spectacular. Of
interest: Hell's Hole, narrow rock-cleft through
which the tide surges; Gap of Mamore, a rocky void
with good views; the Grianán of Aileach, a circular
Bronze Age fort.

Inishturk Island   1 C9
Co Mayo. Seven miles offshore with towering twin
peaks, it has the remains of a church built by St
Columba in the 6thC.

Omey Island   1 C10
Co Galway. A sandy paradise blocking the mouth of
Kingstown Bay, with a tiny medieval church, all that
remains of a 7thC monastic settlement.

Rosguill Peninsula   2 J1
Co Donegal. Largely Irish-speaking peninsula
washed by Sheep Haven Bay to the west and the
narrow waters of Mulroy Bay to the east. The
Atlantic Drive skirts the jagged coastline through
magnificent rock-framed scenery against an awesome
canvas of sky. Bright, windswept roof of land
peopled since the Bronze Age. More recent remains
include ancient Latin cross and Ogham stone.

The Rosses   2 H2
Co Donegal. Lean, hungry landscape of peat bogs
and winding roads, 60,000 acres in extent. It is an
unspoilt district of mountains, rivers and lakes
breaking out in a giant jigsaw of rock and golden
beach on the leeward side of Aran Island. Dungloe,
small fishing harbour at the head of a triangular
inlet, is the main centre. Of interest: Talamto Briste,
a narrow fissure a few yards wide but over a
quarter-mile in length; numerous offshore islands,
including Cruit Island, reached by a bridge.
Burtonport is a good base for boat trips.

Tory Island   2 I1
Co Donegal. A desolate outcrop of cormorants and
lobster fishermen floating seven miles north of
Bloody Foreland. Once the stronghold of the
legendary Fomorian pirates as well as the site of a
monastery founded by St Columba. Remains include
the foundations of two churches, part of a round
tower and an ancient tall cross. Accessible by boat
from Ballyness Bay.

Inland towns & villages

Abbeyknockmoy   4 G11
Co Galway, 5 miles N of Monivea. Hamlet ennobled
by the name of the nearby Cistercian abbey. The
abbey, founded 1189–90, stands on the shores of a
lake. The remains include the church, with nave,
chancel and a transept with two chapels; some
particularly fine medieval frescoes on the north wall
of the chancel. The domestic buildings of the east
wing are also well preserved and there are remains of
the refectory.

Ahascragh   4 H11
Co Galway. Disorderly village lying scattered in the
valley of the River Suck. Of interest nearby:
Castlegar House; Clonbrock House, c1790; Eglish

St Cuan's Well, Ahascragh

Abbey, remains of a Carmelite friary founded late 14thC; St Cuan's Well, a national monument that includes a 17thC gravestone; the prehistoric remains of Lisfineel, Poundfort.

Ardrahan   **4 G12**
Co Galway, 5 miles SE of Kilcolgan. Tiny community beside the main Galway–Limerick road with remains of a 13thC stone keep, built by the Anglo-Norman invaders of Connacht. Remains of a round tower in the churchyard; numerous ring forts in the vicinity.

Athenry   **4 G11**
Co Galway. Pop 1,250. Small market town squashed up defensively behind the remains of its medieval town wall. A strategic centre for the Norman conquest of Ireland and one of the principal towns in the south of Co Galway, it was founded c1235 when the castle was built and Dominican friary established. The town was walled with the profits of the sale of arms taken from the Irish dead following a murderous battle in 1316 between Edward Bruce and the powerful Anglo-Normans of Connacht and Meath. The town was stormed and sacked three times during the 16thC. Much of the town wall remains, including the gate tower at the entrance to the town and five projecting towers. The remains of the 13thC castle, built in the north east corner of the town, consist of an aggressive three-storey keep with gable ends; the main hall, on the first floor, is entered via a magnificent early Gothic portal. To the south are the remains of the friary. Also of interest: Protestant parish church, 1464; 15thC cross depicting crucifixion one side and Virgin and Child the other, in the market place; remains of 15thC Derrydonnell Castle, one of a number of castles of interest in the area.

Athenry Castle

Athleague   **4 I10**
Co Roscommon. Tight-laced, austere village on the banks of the River Suck. Of interest is the ruined 13thC castle divided by a trench down the middle, the result of claims by rival nobles that were never settled. In the demesne of Castlestrange, 1½ miles north west, is Castlestrange Stone, an example of Iron Age decorative work.

Aughrim   **4 H11**
Co Galway. Huddled, solitary village surrounded by hills and mountains, which merge far away into the distant sky. It was here, on a ridge overlooking the village, that a powerful Jacobite army was defeated in June 1691, following a series of blunders, by the Williamites. The battle settled the war between the Jacobites and Williamites and changed the course of Irish history.

Balla   **1 F9**
Co Mayo. Tiny village squeezed in a corner of the site of a 7thC monastery. The monastery, established by St Mochua, was enclosed by a circular wall; remains include fragments of ecclesiastical building, the Tobas Mhuire (the Blessed Well) and ruins of a round tower. Good centre for brown trout fishing.

Ballaghaderreen   **4 H8**
Co Roscommon. Handsome market town near the head of the Lung River, enriched by some dignified Georgian houses. The Gothic-Revival cathedral is full of cramped pretensions. Nearby to the north east is inky-blue Lough Gara.

Ballinafad   **2 H8**
Co Sligo. Small tranquil town at the south west corner of Lough Arrow. Behind it, the Curlew and Bricklieve mountains reach skywards. Of interest is 16thC Curlieus Castle, modelled on a 13thC fortification with a square central block with massive projecting corner towers; Carrowkeel, a group of passage graves high up on a slope of the Bricklieve Mountains; remains of the 16thC Dominican Abbey of Ballindoon on the east bank of Lough Arrow; remains of tiny pre-Romanesque church founded by St Patrick in nearby Aghanagh to the north.

Ballinamore   **2 J7**
Co Leitrim. Pop 800. Friendly, unpretentious village lying in a landscape of little hills and lakes. Good angling centre. Three miles south west are the ruins of Fenagh Abbey, founded by St Columba.

Ballinasloe   **4 I11**
Co Galway. Pop 6,000. EC Wed. Bustling agricultural centre, which was once host to Europe's largest horsefair. Today its magnificent October fair is the largest livestock fair in Ireland. Once a tiny settlement, it was transformed in the early 18thC by the Trench family into a handsome Georgian town of mellow local limestone. Laid out in orderly fashion around the banks of the River Suck, a tributary of the River Shannon, it has many fine buildings, including St Michael's, the Catholic parish church designed 1852–58 by J J McCarthy with some spirited revisions by Pugin. There are many gracious 18thC houses; Garbally, a splendid Georgian mansion designed 1819–24 by Joseph Michael Gandy, is now St Joseph's College, a diocesan school. Also of interest: the mental hospital of 1838, with bold but austere entrance facade; 19thC Ivy Castle; remains of St Mary's Priory in Clontuskert, four miles south east, founded by St Baodan in the 9thC.

Ballinrobe   **1 F10**
Co Mayo. Pop 1,300. EC Mon. Lively market town, its buildings clustered around the River Robe on the edge of the lush green plains of Ellerton, which are bounded on the west by Loughs Mask and Corra with the blue-washed crags of the Partry Mountains beyond. Of interest nearby are the ruins of 15thC Lough Mask Castle, four miles to the south west; Lough Mask House, home of Captain Charles Boycott in the 19thC. On Inishmaine, an island in Lough Mask, are the remains of a 13thC monastery. To the south east of Lough Mask are the ruins of Aghagower Castle, a 15thC three-storey tower house. Excellent fishing.

Ballintober   **1 E9**
Co Mayo, 1 mile NW of Lough Carra. Small village huddled beside the 13thC abbey, now restored, from which it takes its name. The abbey comprises a cruciform church with nave transepts and choir. Down the eastern side of Lough Carra, some nine miles away, is the shell of Moore Hall; once an elegant Georgian house, it was the birthplace of George Moore, the novelist, in 1852.

Ballintober 4 H9
Co Roscommon, 8 miles SW of Tulsk. Cheery village seated quietly beside the ruins of a huge 13thC castle, with a twin-towered gatehouse and polygonal corner towers.

Ballybofey 2 J4
Co Donegal. Pop 2,200. Two towns in one: Ballybofey, a small market town beside the banks of the River Finn, is connected to Stranorlar on the opposite bank by a four-arched bridge. The surrounding scenery is spectacular, particularly the Finn Valley and the galloping landscape climbing up through the Barnesmore Gap towards the distant purple peaks of the Blue Stack Mountains. In the Protestant churchyard of Ballybofey is the grave of Isaac Butt, founder of the Irish Home Rule movement. Good centre for fishing.

Ballyhaunis 4 G9
Co Mayo. Pop 1,100. Handsome market town dwarfed by a giant landscape of tiny lakes. Of interest: remains of 17thC Augustinian friary, on the site of its 14thC predecessor; remains of Dominican friary on the banks of Urlaur Lough; numerous prehistoric remains, including the six-foot-high Bracklaghboy Ogham stone standing on a circular mound in the village of Lisvaun.

Ballyliffin 2 K1
Co Donegal, 6 miles NW of Carndonagh. Smiling secluded resort on the edge of a peninsula of dunes. To the west is the two-mile-long Pollan Strand, a giant sandy scimitar. On the tip of Doagh Isle, a craggy silhouette of land, stand the ruins of 16thC Carrickbrahey Castle and the remnants of a 16thC–17thC bawn. Several prehistoric remains in the area, including Clochtogle, a chamber tomb, two miles to the south west in Cloontagh.

Ballymote 2 H7
Co Sligo. Village-scale town full of cobwebbed corners as old as the hills. On the edge of town to the north are the bare bones of a Franciscan friary where the 14thC "Book of Ballymote", a famous literary codex, was written. To the west of Ballymote are the ivy-clad ruins of a massive, square-planned, curtain-walled fortress built by Richard de Burgo, Earl of Ulster, in 1300. In 1338 it fell into the hands of the O'Conors and then the MacDermots and the MacDonaghs, whose headquarters it was for nearly two centuries until captured by the O'Donnells in 1598. They surrendered to the English in 1603 and in 1652 it was taken by the Cromwellians. In the grounds of Temple House, three miles north west of Ballymote, are the remains of Teach an Teampla, an early 14thC house of the Knights of St John. There are many ring forts in the vicinity. The Slopes of Keshcorran, a 1,182-foot-high peak to the north east, is a world of mythology including Tobar Chormaic (Cormac's Well).

Bellacorick 1 D7
Co Mayo. Tiny island of conviviality drowning in a swell of lush green as the winding Owenmore Valley pours itself out in a rolling wave around the River Oweniny. To the east is Lough Dahybaun; to the south west are the knotted slopes of the 2,369-foot-high Slieve Car mountains. To the north is a turf-fired power station. Of interest is the musical bridge where, by running large stones along the parapet, musical notes can be produced.

Boyle 2 H8
Co Roscommon. Pop 1,750. EC Wed. Wedged between two loughs, and with the crumpled Curlew Hills to the north, this handsome market town stands on the banks of the River Boyle. To the north of the town, spreadeagled along the river banks, are

River Boyle

the well-preserved remains of a Cistercian abbey. Founded in 1161, it has a fine early 13thC cruciform church, one of the best transitional buildings of Romanesque and Gothic Ireland. It was desecrated by the Anglo-Normans in the 13thC and severely damaged by Cromwellian soldiers in 1659. The River Boyle, which winds its way between Lough Gara in the south west and the wooded, island-filled Lough Key in the north east, is crossed at Boyle by a handsome Palladian bridge. To the north lies Lough Arrow, a shining strip of water punctuated by islands. Also of interest: Trinity Abbey, the ruins of a 13thC Premonstratensian priory built on Trinity Island in Lough Key; Rockingham House, a John Nash transformation of 1810, on the southern shores of the lough; rectangular ring fort at Ardsoreen; the ruined medieval church of Asselyn on the southern shores of Lough Key; the Drumanone Portal Grave, a handsome dolmen two miles to the west of Asselyn; numerous crannogs in Lough Gara. Good touring centre. Lough Key Forest Park is two miles north east.

Carndonagh 2 L1
Co Donegal. Pop 1,150. Thriving market town sheltering in a crescent of hills on the Inishowen Peninsula. Two miles northward is hammer-headed Trawbreaga Bay. The Catholic parish church, a Romanesque granite mountain built in 1945, is an Italianate wedding cake full of marzipan charm. The real wonder of the town is the Donagh Cross. Re-erected beside the Buncrana road at the southern entrance to the town, it dates from the 7thC and is considered to be one of the major examples of early Christian art in Ireland. One side has a figure with outstretched hands encircled by four other figures while a cross is formed by a lacework of ribbon; on the reverse is another figure with decorative lacework. Beside the cross are two small carved pillars, probably of the 9thC. In the graveyard of the nearby Church of Ireland church is a third cross-pillar, known as the Marigold Stone, with the crucifixion on one side and a marigold, flanked by two figures, on the other. Numerous prehistoric remains in the area.

Carrick on Shannon 2 I8
Co Leitrim. Pop 1,900. EC Wed. Small county town on a bend of the River Shannon, which is navigable to a point just above here. Given its charter by James I, it soon became a Protestant stronghold. What vestiges of history remain are cramped in a few elusive corners. Of interest: town gaol, early 19thC courthouse and Protestant church of 1827. Good angling and boating centre with trout, pike and perch in abundance in the River Shannon and nearby loughs.

Castlebar 1 E8
Co Mayo. Pop 6,000. EC Thur. County town of Mayo, it is a bustling market centre around a tree-lined mall. Established by Sir John Bingham at

he beginning of the 17thC, the town had a turbulent early history culminating in the ignominious flight of ts English garrison in August 1798 under the onslaught of a less powerful French force led by General Humbert; the event became known as the 'Castlebar Races'. Good leisure centre with tennis, golf and magnificent coarse fishing in the loughs to he west of the town.

Castleblakeney 4 H11
Co Galway. Attractive village made famous by the hospitality of the O'Malleys, whose 14thC festivities once lasted nine months.

Castlerea 4 H9
Co Roscommon. Pop 1,750. Small market town laid out along the lush green banks of the River Suck. The surgeon and archaeologist Sir William Wilde, father of Oscar Wilde, was born here. Of interest: Clonalis House, former home of O'Conor Don; rebuilt in the 19thC, it has a fine library, as well as a good collection of portraits and furniture and the Harp of Carolan, the last of the Irish bards.

Churchill 2 J3
Co Donegal, 10 miles W of Letterkenny. Small angling centre isolated in an idyllic landscape to the south east of Gartan Lough. Sealed amongst the hills to the west is the celebrated birthplace of St Columba in AD521.

Claregalway 4 F11
Co Galway. Small, neat village beside the River Clare. Dominating the river crossing is the 15thC de Burgo castle, a huge square fortress that figured prominently in Cromwellian wars. To the west of the castle are the remains of a 13thC Franciscan friary with handsome bell tower and tiny chapel. Also of interest: 17thC bawn known as Cregboyne Fort in Cahervoley, a square enclosure protected by six-foot walls with two projecting round towers, foundations of rectangular house and remains of gateway; numerous ring forts in vicinity.

Claremorris 1 F9
Co Mayo. Pop 1,700. Railway junction and small market town as intriguing as a timetable. In Lisduff townland, some eight miles south east, is a gallery grave and remains of a ring fort.

Clonbur 1 E10
Co Galway, 4 miles W of Cong. Village of thick-walled houses tucked snugly between Lough Corrib and Lough Mask. The surrounding landscape is awash with streams and woods. A majestic ridge, Mount Gable, where the forces of the Fir Bolg assembled before engaging the Tuatha dé Danann on the Plain of Moytura, is nearby. Of interest: Ross Hill Abbey, including early Christian remains; Ballykine Castle; glittering Lough Corrib, encased in the foothills of Mount Gable.

Clonmany 2 K1
Co Donegal. Picturesque village lying amongst rolling hills. Several prehistoric sites nearby, including a chamber tomb in Meendoran to the south east.

Collooney 2 H7
Co Sligo, 2 miles S of Ballysadare. Diminutive town woven along the banks of the River Owenmore. Joining forces with the River Unshin as it winds its way from Lough Arrow, the Owenmore slices its way north through Collooney Gap, an opening chiselled between the Ox Mountains and Slieve Daeane that has been of strategic importance since the Middle Ages. Red Hugh O'Donnell laid siege to the castle here in 1599, resulting in the Battle of Curlieu, and in 1798 a small force of militia

attempted to block the advance of General Humbert's French force at the Gap. Of interest: Markree Castle, once a modest Georgian house but transformed by Francis Johnston 1802–4 into an extravagant castellated mansion; Church of the Assumption, a Gothic-Revival design of 1843; Annaghmore demesne, handsome house with fine gardens; the Bishop's Stone, a pillar-stone at Killeran, three miles north east.

Cong 1 E10
Co Mayo. Pop 250. Tiny border village on a neck of land between Lough Mask and Lough Corrib, with the undulating lush green of the Plain of Moytura to the east; to the west, the crumpled peaks and hills of Joyce's country block out the sky. On the edge of the village are the remains of a 12thC Augustinian abbey built on the site of an early 6thC monastic foundation. Ruins include some fine carved portals in the Transitional style and part of the cloisters rebuilt in the 19thC. Beside the abbey is Ashford Castle, a late 19thC castellated extravaganza once the home of the Guinness family. The porous limestone belt through which the streams connecting Loughs Mask and Long run has produced a cavernous subterranean world rich in mythology. A channel was dug in the land between the lakes in 1840, to extend navigation, but it would not hold water due to the porous nature of the rock. Of particular interest is Kelly's Cave, a natural cave used as a Bronze Age burial place. There are numerous ancient monuments in the vicinity, including a great stone ring fort near Glebe townland; Caher Mayo, another stone ring fort sited near the hamlet of Cross; and Ballymacgibbon passage grave to the east of Cong. One mile to the north west are the ruins of 15thC Aghalahard Castle. Good holiday centre with excellent walks and fine fishing and shooting.

Ashford Castle, Cong

Coolaney 2 H7
Co Sligo. Picturesque village cradled in a lush green valley in the foothills of the Ox Mountains. Interesting bridge spanning the Owenbeg River. Good perch and trout fishing.

Corrofin 4 G11
Co Galway, 7 miles S of Tuam. Sandwiched between Lough Atedawn and Lough Inchiquin, it's a picturesque village sunning itself beside the River Clare against a backdrop of wooded hills. Of interest: remains of a de Burgo castle and Rathmore, a huge ring fort 1½ miles north east.

Crossmolina 1 E7
Co Mayo. Small market town on the banks of the River Deel near the head of Lough Conn. To the south, cascading down in leaps and bounds to the steely blue waters of Lough Conn, is battered 2,646-foot Nephin Mountain. In the glens beyond are numerous lakes. South east of the town are the ruins of 15thC Errew Abbey, built for the

Augustinians; the long rectangular church is 13thC, with fine trefoil windows. Nearby is a small rectangular oratory built on the site of a 6thC monastic foundation. Close to a farmhouse some three miles to the west is a long cairn with three court graves. Good fishing on the River Deel.

Dromahair 2 I6
Co Leitrim. Pop 180. EC Wed. Quiet village astride the River Bonet, before it flows into Lough Gill a short distance to the west. This was once the stronghold of the powerful O'Rourkes. Of their fortress, Breffni Castle, which adjoins the 17thC Old Hall, only portions of the banqueting hall and ancient prison remain. On the river bank opposite stand the well preserved remains of Creevelea Abbey, a Franciscan friary; founded in 1508, it was the last of the pre-Reformation churches to be built in Ireland. Of interest nearby: O'Rourke's Table, a fern and moss covered outcrop of rock with fabulous views from the top to Lough Gill and Yeats's country; numerous prehistoric tombs in vicinity; Parkes Castle, one of the finest examples of 16thC Plantation style in Ireland, on the north east shores of Lough Gill.

Dromore West 2 G6
Co Sligo, 5 miles SE of Easky. Tiny village draped in picturesque disarray down the wooded banks of the Dunneill River in the Ox Mountains.

Drumshanbo 2 I7
Co Leitrim. Pop 570. EC Wed. Eleven miles north of Carrick on Shannon, it stands on the southern shore of Lough Allen. A thriving market town as well as a magnificent centre for coarse fishing with over twenty lakes within a five-mile radius. Lough Allen, the third largest of the River Shannon lakes, is famed for having the best pike in northern Europe. Dominating the eastern shore is Slieve Anieran, at 1,922 feet the highest of the Iron Mountains range.

Drumsna 2 I8
Co Leitrim, 3 miles SE of Carrick on Shannon. A village on a loop of the River Shannon, once an important trading station along the river with its own courthouse and jail, now in ruins. For a while it was also the home of Anthony Trollope, the writer. Of interest: Doon of Drumsna, half-mile-long prehistoric earthworks consisting of huge ditch and ramparts.

Dunmore 4 G10
Co Galway. Small market town one mile east of a great Norman castle, begun in 1249. Repeatedly burned by the O'Connors, the present castle was built in the early 14thC. Remains consist of a monumental four-storey tower block, surrounded by a motte and part of the curtain wall. The Augustinian Hermits friary in the centre of town was

Dunmore Castle

founded in 1425 by Walter de Bermingham; remains include a fine 15thC west portal, nave, chancel and central tower.

Elphin 4 I8
Co Roscommon. Once an important ecclesiastical centre where St Patrick established a bishopric in the 5thC, with its own cathedral. Burnt by the Anglo-Normans in 1235 and settled by Augustinian and Franciscan monks in the Middle Ages. Now a quiet market village, with nothing left of its pious past but dusty memories. It was here that Oliver Goldsmith was educated.

Fintown 2 I3
Co Donegal. Tiny village on a promontory of rock and gorse at the north east end of narrow Lough Finn. Of interest: Salmon Leap, ten miles east at Cloghan Lodge; Glebe House, where Isaac Butt, founder of the Irish Home Rule Party, was born.

Frenchpark 4 H8
Co Roscommon. Small village eight miles south west of Boyle. Of interest: rectory where Douglas Hyde, founder of the Gaelic League and first President of Ireland, was born in 1860; French Park, early 18thC mansion, now derelict, designed by Richard Castle; ruins of Cloonshanville Abbey, a Dominican foundation established in 1385, standing not far from the village; Rathcroghan, remains of the ancient palace of the Kings of Connacht crowning a hill six miles to the south east.

Glenties 2 I4
Co Donegal. Pop 750. EC Wed. Thriving little town, neat and tidy like a dug-over garden. Busy craft centre situated at the mouth of two glens, a desert island of woodland in a sea of hills and rock. The Rivers Owenea and Stracashel, which meet here, are good for angling as are the nearby lakes. Numerous prehistoric tombs in vicinity.

Gort 4 G12
Co Galway. Pop 1,000. Attractive market town with one long main street winding up and over a low hill. In the centre is a triangular market place lined by a colourful wall of houses. The surrounding countryside is rich in prehistoric as well as literary associations. Of interest: Kilmacduagh Church and round tower, part of a monastery founded in the 6thC, three miles south west; Thoor Ballylee, four miles north east, a 16thC tower house and home of William Butler Yeats from 1921–29; Lough Cultra Castle, castellated mansion built 1811 to a design by John Nash; prehistoric Nostaig Fort with souterrain and two wedge-shaped graves, three miles north east; ruins of 13thC Kiltartan Castle.

Headford 1 F10
Co Galway. Pop 650. Angling resort and small market town within spitting distance of the east bank of Lough Corrib, one of the largest lakes in Ireland. Of interest: remains of 14thC–15thC Ross Abbey, a Franciscan friary 1½ miles north west; Castle Hacket, handsome Georgian mansion rebuilt 1822 following a fire; 552-foot-high Knockma, a holy mountain of a hill, said to be the burial place of Maeve, the legendary Queen of Connacht.

Jamestown 4 I8
Co Leitrim, 2 miles SE of Carrick on Shannon. Former walled town built in 1622 to control a crossing over the River Shannon, now a quiet village with one remaining gateway and a lot of memories.

Keshcarrigan 2 J8
Co Leitrim. Picturesque village snuggling among the lakes and hills north of Carrick on Shannon. On the banks of Lough Scur, to the north west of the village, stand the remains of a 16thC castle.

Kinlough   **2 I5**
Co Leitrim. Attractive village of thick-walled cottages
at the head of Lough Melvin. Three miles from good
beaches and a magnificent angling centre. The long,
narrow waters of Lough Melvin, good for salmon
and trout fishing, are studded with wooded islets.
On one towards the west end of the lough stand the
ruins of 15thC Rossclogher Castle, where a captain
in the Spanish armada sought refuge in 1588 when
three galleons were wrecked off the coast. On the
nearby banks of the lough stand the ruins of
Rossclogher Abbey.

Lifford   **2 K3**
Co Donegal. Pop 1,150. EC Wed. Once a stronghold
of the O'Donnells, it is now an administrative centre
of Co Donegal. A quiet town on the west bank of the
River Foyle, it is the twin town of Strabane on the
east bank. Of interest: the courthouse, handsome
classical building designed 1746 by Michael
Priestley; Port Hall, three miles north east,
handsome classical house with shallow projecting
pedimented central section, built 1746 by Priestley;
Church of St Patrick, one mile north west at
Murlough, modern cruciform-plan building
designed 1963 by Corr and McCormick.

Loughrea   **4 H12**
Co Galway. Pop 3,100. EC Wed. Flourishing market
town lying along the northern shore of a beautiful
lake. Founded originally as a stronghold by Richard
de Burgo in 1300, the town that grew up became an
important administrative centre for Connacht. Of
interest: ruins of Carmelite friary and castle of 1300;
Catholic cathedral, 1897–1903, dull exterior but
interior enriched by fine 20thC stained glass;
Clonfert Museum, interesting historical and folkloric
exhibition arranged in surviving gatehouse of the
town; Turoe Stone, 1stC pillar-stone at Bullaun.
Good trout fishing in Lough Rea and surrounding
rivers such as River Craughwell, which occasionally
has salmon.

Maam   **1 E10**
Co Galway. Hamlet buried in a beautiful valley in
the mountains. Good angling centre with sea trout,
brown trout and salmon. At Maumeen, four miles
south west, is St Patrick's Bed and the curative
waters of St Patrick's Well, a place of pilgrimage on
the *last Sun in Jul.*

Maan valley, Connemara, Co Galway

Manorhamilton   **2 I6**
Co Leitrim. Pop 850. EC Wed. Border village
founded in the 17thC by Sir Frederick Hamilton, a
Scotsman who had been given land confiscated from
the Irish. It lies in a saddle of land formed by the
junction of five fertile valleys, hidden in a
spectacular limestone landscape of steep hillsides,
narrow ravines, loughs, waterfalls and secluded
glens. On a hillside overlooking the village stand the
ruins of Hamilton's castle, built 1638. Many
prehistoric remains in the surrounding area.

Monivea   **4 G11**
Co Galway. Model village laid out in the 1750s by a
reforming landlord, Robert French, after he

succeeded to the estate in 1744. It was designed to
house textile workers. At the end of the main street
is the medieval demesne, at the other a charter
school, now used as a garage. Also of interest: nearby
Killaclogher Castle and Clonstrusk Castle, both late
medieval.

Oughterard   **1 E10**
Co Galway. Pop 650. One of Ireland's leading
angling resorts, with first class trout and salmon
fishing. Built on the north western shores of Lough
Corrib, it makes a charming gateway to Connemara.
Of interest: Aughnanure Castle, 15thC O'Flaherty
stronghold; Ross Castle, 17thC fortified mansion,
five miles south east; Inchagoill Island, the largest
island on Lough Corrib, containing numerous early
Christian remains.

Pettigoe   **2 J5**
Co Donegal. The gateway to Lough Derg, the annual
scene of Ireland's greatest pilgrimage, it is a
pint-sized village lying between gentle hills.

Pontoon   **1 F8**
Co Mayo. Tiny angling resort sealed amongst
mountains and rolling hills on the edge of Lough
Cullin. Immediately northward, separated by a
pontoon bridge from which the village takes its
name, are the mirror-cold waters of Lough Conn.
Both loughs are renowned for their white trout,
known as gillaroo, as well as being amply stocked
with brown trout.

Portumna   **4 I12**
Co Galway. Thriving market town set on the
northern bank of Lough Derg, loveliest of the River
Shannon lakes. Of interest: Portumna Castle, begun
1609, an amalgam of Jacobean and Renaissance
features including a handsome entrance gate by
Adams; destroyed by fire in 1826, it is now being
restored. In the grounds are the remains of 15thC
Dominican friary. Three miles north east is well
preserved Derryhivenry Castle, built 1653.

Raphoe   **2 K3**
Co Donegal. Small cathedral town of genteel
Georgian houses hidden among high hills and
hedgerows. Site of a 6thC monastery founded by St
Columba and transformed into a cathedral by the
9thC. Present day Raphoe is post-Reformation, with
17thC Plantation plan, complete with triangular
'diamond', Gothic cathedral of early 18thC with
monumental tower and ruins of 17thC bishop's
palace, a monumental fortress standing on a
towering hill. On another hilltop 2½ miles to the east
at Beltany is a fine stone circle, consisting of 64
standing stones. Half a mile north is a holy well and
early cross-slabs.

Recess   **1 D10**
Co Galway. Beautifully situated village. Of interest
nearby: beautiful Inagh Valley and Lough sealed
amongst a sky-reaching wall of mountains;
Kylemore Valley, an enchanting valley of lakes
threaded by the salmon- and trout-filled River
Dauros. Towering above them is a great
perpendicular wall of rock, the Dorruagh
Mountains. Squeezed at its feet beside the waters of
the lough is Kylemore Abbey, a delightful
castellated Gothic fantasy smelling of vampires,
framed by shadowy woods. The castle, built
1864–68, is now a convent for the Benedictine nuns
of Ypres. Visitors welcome.

Roscommon   **4 I10**
Co Roscommon. Pop 1,340. EC Thur. County town
of Co Roscommon, it is an old wool town sliding
gently down the southern slopes of a wide hill. Its
name is derived from St Comman who founded a
monastery here in AD746. Nothing now survives of

this monastery, which was pillaged by the Vikings in the early 9thC and burnt by Munster forces in 1135. At the foot of the town lie the ruins of a Dominican priory. Founded by Felim O'Connor, King of Connacht, in 1257 and rebuilt 1453, the long, narrow church has a beautiful window over the west entrance. Of particular interest is the tomb effigy of the founder, buried here in 1265. Crowning a hillside to the north of the town are the ruins of a late 13thC fortress built by the Anglo-Normans, destroyed by Gaelic forces and rebuilt in 1280. A Royalist stronghold in the 17thC, it was surrendered to the Cromwellians, who partly dismantled it in 1652. A large, quadrangular castle, remains include fine twin-towered gatehouse. Also of interest: handsome courthouse with tower and dome designed by Sir Richard Morrison in 1736; ruined wedge-shaped gallery grave at Scregg, eight miles south east.

Strokestown   4 I9
Co Roscommon. Spacious early 19thC market village planned by Maurice Mahon in 1800 with two streets intersecting at right angles, the wider one a handsome tree-lined street terminating at the east end in a spacious demesne. The elegant mansion was a transformation by Richard Castle in 1735 of an early 17thC house. Good centre for coarse fishing; many crannogs are to be found in the surrounding lakes.

Swinford   1 F8
Co Mayo. Quiet market town built along a tributary of the River Moy. Good fishing on the nearby Callowlakes, between Swinford and Foxford, or further north in Loughs Conn and Cullen.

Tobercurry   2 G7
Co Sligo. Attractive market town sheltering in the shadow of the Ox Mountains to the north west. Of interest: ruins of 15thC Banada Abbey, an Augustinian priory four miles to the south west beside the River Moy.

Tuam   4 G10
Co Galway. Pop 3,800. EC Thur. Small market and manufacturing town, which began life as an important religious settlement when St Jarlath built a monastery and school here. By the early 12thC

Tuam Cross

Tuam had become part of Connacht as Turlough O'Connor, High King of Ireland, began to expand his territorial ambitions. He built St Mary's, the Protestant cathedral, in 1130. Originally a small nave and chancel building; only the chancel, a magnificent example of Irish Romanesque architecture, survives. It was incorporated in the present Gothic-Revival structure, designed 1861–63 by Sir Thomas Deane, with some magnificent High Victorian details. The Catholic cathedral, another Gothic-style building, was designed 1827–37 by Dominic Madden; in contrast to the Protestant building, it's more Hammer-horrors Gothic than Hollywood stylishness. Matching the quality of the Romanesque chancel of St Mary's is the Tuam Cross, a 12thC decorated cross standing in Market Square. Also of interest: Farrell's Gate Mill, a 17thC working corn mill with related exhibition; 11thC round tower and 16thC church at Kilbennan, 2½ miles south west; Millbrook House, where the astronomer John Bermingham (1816–1874) lived, nine miles north west. There are numerous prehistoric remains, particularly ring forts, in the vicinity. Standing on the banks of a small lake seven miles south east are the ruins of the 12thC Abbey of Knockmoy, a Cistercian foundation.

Tulsk   4 I9
Co Roscommon. Some cobwebbed remains, including a double-arched portal with central pillar and a motte with baileys, are all that is left of what was once an important centre in the Middle Ages. O'Conor Roe built a formidable fortress here in 1406 and a Dominican abbey was founded in 1443.

Turlough Round Tower

Turlough   1 F8
Co Mayo, 3 miles NE of Castlebar. Attractive village with well-preserved round tower and ruined 17thC church.

Regional features

Autograph Tree   4 G12
Gort, Co Galway. Sole reminder of Coole Park, once the home of Lady Gregory and centre of the Irish Literary Revival. The house was destroyed in 1941 but the tree, with the initials of George Bernard Shaw, Sean O'Casey, Augustus John and W B Yeats, remains.

Bloody Foreland   2 H2
Co Donegal. Sensational sunsets drench the rocks in red and orange light, hence the name.

Donegal Tweed
Known the world over, this material is often produced by part-time hill farmers, who weave the wool into the subtle mixtures of colour for which it is justly famed. The firm of Magge & Co in Donegal town welcome visitors for conducted tours on weekdays and there are many other centres throughout the county.

The Gaeltacht

The name of several areas in Ireland where Irish is the spoken language. As a part of state policy, the Gaeltacht Commission was set up in 1925 to study conditions in these Irish-speaking areas; realising that the survival of the language depended on the survival of such areas, the social, cultural and linguistic traditions of the Gaeltacht areas have been protected. These Gaeltacht communities, some large, some small, are bilingual, the second language being English.

In *Co Mayo*, the Gaeltacht communities are found in the north west part of the county, on the Mullet Peninsula, parts of Achill Island and Curraun. *Co Donegal* has the largest Irish-speaking population in Ireland, with numerous centres including Rosguill, Glenver and Dooey. The main Gaeltacht centres, however, are found along the west coast and include places such as Gweedore, with an all-Irish theatre, Gortahork and Falcarragh in the north; Loughanure and Fintown in the centre; and Glencolumbkille, Carrick, Teelin and Kilcar in the south. The islands of Tory and Arran are also Irish-speaking.

Co Galway's Gaeltacht area covers a great part of Connemara. Called Car-chonnachta, it includes the Aran Islands and a small area north of Lough Corrib from Barna on the coast of Galway Bay to Costelloe and up along the Atlantic to Carna. The northern boundary runs from Maam Cross to Gowla. This was the literary and intellectual centre of the Gaeltacht movement in the early 20thC and it was here that the foundations were laid for the Gaelic League, as well as for the Irish Literary Renaissance. There are numerous Gaelic colleges throughout the area, many offering summer courses between *Jun* and *Aug*. Students cover many aspects of Irish culture, including music, speech and drama.

Glencar Waterfall   2 H6

Co Sligo, 7 miles N of Sligo at Glencar Lake. Two spectacular waterfalls, the upper one dropping 50 feet.

Knock   4 G9

Co Mayo, 7 miles NE of Claremorris. The scene of an apparition of the Blessed Virgin Mary, St Joseph and St John in the village church in 1879. Catapulted into the world spotlight following a series of miraculous cures after the apparitions, it is now one of the world's major Marian shrines, with over 750,000 pilgrims visiting the shrine annually. In 1977 a cavernous basilica was built, with an ambulatory carried on 40 stone pillars (quarried from every part of Ireland) and seating for 20,000 pilgrims.

Peat

For a long time peat was the only fuel available in rural areas. Traditionally cut by hand, machinery is now used in many areas for cutting the peat briquettes, used for domestic as well as industrial and horticultural uses. In many parts of the Atlantic Coast, peat is still cut in the traditional way with a long-handled turf-spade called a slane, consisting of

Cutting peat in Co Galway

a narrow, straight-edged steel blade with a wing at right angles. The wing is designed to facilitate the cutting of the turf at a single stroke. Turf is cut during the dry months of April and May, either vertically (for thin upland bogs) or horizontally (for deep lowland bogs). Left to dry in piles on the roadside or beside cuttings in the bog, the peat is still carted away by donkey-cart in many parts of Connemara. Barges from Rossaveal ferry to the Aran Islands with cargoes of turf, as the islands have no natural resources.

Seven Arches   2 J2

Nr Carrowkeel, Co Donegal. These incredible rock-formed tunnels are up to 300 feet long and between 15–30 feet wide.

Valley of Diamonds   1 F6

Enniscrone & Easky, Co Sligo. The glittering of abundant shells in the sunlight gave rise to the name. Many varieties can be found, as can rare fossils at the back of Enniscrone Pier.

Wild Flowers   1 D12

Aran Islands, Co Galway. Due to the warm climate many unusual flowers and plants flourish here, among them wild orchids, gentians, maidenhair fern and wild garlic.

Famous people

Charles Boycott (1832–1897)   1 F10
Lough Mask House, Ballinrobe, Co Mayo. Home for a time of this notorious land agent, whose behaviour towards his tenants in the face of Land League agitation gave birth to the verb 'boycott'.

Robert O'Hara Burke (1820–1861)   4 H12
St Cleran's, Co Galway, 4 miles NW of Loughrea. Imposing villa-style house built 1810 by Sir Richard Morrison. Birthplace of Robert O'Hara Burke, the famous explorer whose statue stands in Melbourne, Australia; he was the first person to cross Australia from south to north. He died attempting the return journey. *Private.*

Michael Davitt (1846–1906)   1 F8
Strade, Co Mayo. Birthplace of the influential Fenian leader and founder of the Irish Land League. A memorial chapel dedicated to his memory adjoins the abbey ruins.

Lady Gregory (1852–1932)   4 G12
Coole Park, Co Galway, 2½ miles NE of Gort. The house is in ruins, but the yew walk, garden, woods and autographed copper-beech tree are well kept. Lady Gregory, whose home it was from 1880, was one of the founder members of the Abbey Theatre. One of Yeats's closest friends and literary allies, she immersed herself in Irish traditional life and literature and her house became the centre of literary life of the period.

George Moore (1853–1933)   1 E9
Moore Hall, Co Mayo, 9 miles SE of Ballintober. Picturesque ruin standing on the eastern banks of Lough Carra; birthplace and home of the famous Anglo-Irish novelist, dramatist and short-story writer. A founder member of the Irish National Theatre, he began his career as a student of painting in Paris, but abandoned France in 1882. Returning to England, he set about revitalising the Victorian novel, publishing in 1886 his 'A Drama in Muslin', which presents contemporary Irish life.

Patrick Pearse (1879–1916)   1 D11
Pearse's Cottage, Rosmuck, Co Galway, 2½ miles E of Derryrush. This three-roomed cottage was the summer home of the patriot, Patrick Pearse. Poet and author, his sources of inspiration were the

people and places around Rosmuck. He was the Commandant-General of the Irish Republican Army during the Easter Rising of 1916 and was executed along with 14 other leaders of the rebellion.

William Butler Yeats (1865–1939) **4 G12**
Thoor Ballylee, Co Galway, 4 miles NE of Gort.
Home of the poet. Born in Dublin, the eldest son of J B Yeats and brother of Jack Yeats, both renowned painters, Yeats began studying art but abandoned the profession for literature at 21. A nationalist, he applied himself, amongst other things, to the establishment of an Irish national theatre; this was finally achieved when the Abbey Theatre, Dublin

Thoor Ballylee, Gort

was acquired in 1904 and the Irish National Theatre Company created. His own work was concerned primarily with Irish traditional and nationalist themes. From 1922–28 he served as a senator of the Irish Free State. In 1923 he was awarded the Nobel Prize for Literature. He bought this 16thC tower house in 1917 and restored it, living there until 1929. Once more in a ruinous state, it was restored by the Bord Fáilte in 1965 and now has an exhibition of Yeats's work. *Open summer.*

Cathedrals, abbeys & churches

Annaghdown Priory **1 F11**
Annaghdown, Co Galway, 3 miles NW of Cloonboo.
St Brendan, who died here in AD577, founded the original monastery and nunnery. An extensive complex scattered along the shores of a lake, the ruins include a 15thC cathedral into which was incorporated some magnificent 13thC stonework in the Transitional style, such as a beautiful east window complete with weird dragon heads, and a dignified portal. To the north of the cathedral are the remains of an 11thC church. Down a lane to the south are the remains of the 12thC priory, and there are remains of the 15thC fortified monastic quarters along the edge of the cloister. To the south west of the cathedral stand the ruins of a 15thC castle.

Ballindoon Friary **2 H7**
Co Sligo, 4 miles NE of Ballinafad. Built along the banks of Lough Arrow, this Dominican friary was established in 1507. Of particular interest is the church, which has a central tower and belfry.

Ballintober Abbey **1 E9**
Ballintober, Co Mayo, 1 mile NW of Lough Carra.
Built on the site of an earlier monastery, this

Augustinian abbey was founded in 1216 by Cathal O'Connor, King of Connacht. Recently restored, the dark, proud cruciform church gives a memorable picture of a typical 13thC, west of Ireland monastic foundation. The influence of Cistercian architecture is particularly strong, especially in the plan, which has east chapels in the transepts. The chancel has fine ribbed vaulting with elaborately carved capitals and there is a 13thC chapter with an elaborate portal; the cloisters were added in the 15thC. Part of the monastery was burnt in 1265 and rebuilt. Although the monastery was dissolved in 1542 the monks regained possession in 1635, following a petition to the Pope; in 1653 it was partially destroyed by Cromwellian soldiers. It was restored in the 19thC and again in 1966. One of the few churches to hold Mass continually for over 700 years.

Boyle Abbey **2 H8**
Boyle, Co Roscommon. One of the major influences on Irish architecture was the introduction of continental monastic orders to early 12thC Ireland; chief amongst these were the Cistercians. Their first Irish foundation was at Mellifont in 1142. Soon daughter foundations were set up, including the one here at Boyle, which was begun in 1161. One of the best-preserved abbeys of the period, the chancel and transepts with their side-chapels belong to the early period of its foundation. The three lancet windows in the east wall belong to the 13thC. There were several changes in style as well as scale before the consecration of the church in 1218, as shown by the round arches on the south side of the nave and the tall arches of the crossing. The carvings of foliage and animals on the capitals at the west end of the nave are particularly fine. Little remains of the cloister; the surrounding buildings were added in the 16thC and 17thC. It was here that Donnchadh Mór Daly, medieval Ireland's most prominent religious poet, was buried in 1244.

Burrishoole Abbey **1 E8**
Co Mayo, 1 mile NW of Newport. Dominican friary built by Richard de Burgo in 1469 on the edge of a coastal inlet. The domestic buildings have gone and only part of the cloister—the eastern wall—remains, but the church, consisting of a nave and chancel with a southern transept, is well preserved. There is a short stocky tower, rather Cistercian in its severity, and an interesting two-light ogee-headed window, characteristic of the period.

Claregalway Friary **4 F11**
Claregalway, Co Galway. Richly endowed Franciscan friary founded by John de Cogan in 1240. Remains consist of a nave and chancel church and fragments of the cloister. Of particular interest are the widely spaced lancet windows of the choir and the early 14thC triple sedilia. An aisle, with four pointed-arch bays, was added to the north of the nave in the 14thC. The handsome tower was added in the 15thC.

Clonfert Cathedral **4 I11**
Clonfert, Co Galway. Beside a tiny village is the site of an ecclesiastical settlement founded originally by St Brendan the Navigator in the mid-6thC. Ransacked twice by the Norsemen in the 9thC and destroyed several times by fire, it was the 12thC transformation into an Augustinian priory to which it owes its considerable architectural fame. Remains include a small, stone-built cathedral of 1140–80 with an austere entry facade enriched by an ornamental portal, jammed beneath an applied triangular pediment of moulded stone work. This Romanesque jewel, with its six receding orders and grotesque capitals, is the wonder of 12thC Irish architecture. Originally a single cell church with

Portal of Clonfert Cathedral

antae at each gable end, it was transformed in the early 13thC by the addition of a chancel. Fine east windows and decorated chancel arch, added in the 15thC, as were the bell tower and the transepts, of which only the south transept remains.

Clontuskert Abbey 4 I12

Laurencetown, Co Galway. Ruins of an Augustinian abbey founded in the early 9thC to the north west of the village. One of the richest monasteries of 13thC Ireland, it was destroyed by fire in 1413 and by the mid-15thC had been completely rebuilt. Of particular interest is the remarkable moulded portal built in the west wall of the priory church; the stone surrounds are enriched by carvings, including a pelican, a mermaid and two deer, whilst crowning the door is a carved panel decorated with figures, including that of St Michael with scales for judging souls.

Cong Abbey 1 E10

Cong, Co Mayo. Built on the site of an earlier 6thC monastic foundation, the present Augustinian abbey was begun in 1128 by Turlough O'Connor, King of Connacht. Little remains of the church except a magnificent carved Romanesque doorway of the early 13thC. The fine 13thC cloisters were rebuilt in the 19thC. Of particular interest are the three handsome Transitional-style portals of the east range. Highly decorated doorways articulating the passage from cloister to surrounding buildings were traditional in western monasteries; the entrance to the Chapter House, as seen here, was generally singled out for special treatment.

Detail of doorway, cloister, Cong Abbey, Co Mayo

Fenagh Churches 2 J8

Fenagh, Co Leitrim, 2½ miles SW of Ballinamore. Site of a monastery established by St Callin, the remains consist of two churches: the south church has an aisle-less plan with handsome west portal and fine 14thC east window; the 15thC north church has an intriguing corridor or aisle along the south side. The west end of both churches has a first-floor gallery raised above a barrel-vaulted ground storey.

Inishmaine Abbey 1 E10

Inishmaine Island, Co Mayo, 4 miles SW of Ballinrobe. This Augustinian monastery, built on an island in Lough Mask, was founded by St Cormac in the 7thC. It was partially destroyed in 1227 when Hugh O'Connor had it burned. Of particular interest are the 13thC church remains, consisting of a nave and chancel. There is an interesting square-headed entrance portal, probably taken from an earlier church; fine east window with mouldings of fantastic beasts; elaborate foliage and animal carvings on the capitals of the chancel arch.

Ross Abbey 1 F10

Co Galway, 1½ miles NW of Headford. Franciscan friary founded by Sir Raymond de Burgo in 1351. One of the best-preserved friaries in Ireland; remains are mostly 15thC and include nave and chancel church with tower added in 1498. North of the church are two cloisters, one including an arcade.

Rosserk Abbey 1 F7

Co Mayo, 5 miles SE of Killala. One of a series of magnificent Franciscan friaries built during the Renaissance of Gaelic Ireland in the 15thC. This is the best-preserved Franciscan friary in Ireland, consisting of gable-ended buttresses glued tightly round a square cloister. Established in 1460, the remains include the domestic buildings—dormitory, refectory and kitchen, raised above a vaulted ground storey; a single-aisled church with handsome portal, highly crafted east window, and projecting chapel on the south side; tall, narrow, battlemented belfry tower, a characteristic feature of such friaries, with the various stages articulated by string courses.

St MacDara's Church 1 C11

St MacDara's Island, Co Galway, 2 miles E of Mweenish Island. Built c12thC on the eastern shore of a tiny island, it was part of a monastery founded originally in the 6thC by St MacDara. Most churches of the period were small, often no more than 20 feet in length, and invariably rectangular in plan. Measuring 20 × 13 feet, it is a gable-roofed structure built of carefully hewn blocks of stone, larger in the lower courses and smaller higher up. Of particular interest is the way the stone roof and walls project out beyond the gable ends as if in imitation of wooden barge boards. East of the church is the saint's bed as well as fragments of three pilgrimage stations with early Christian decorated cross-slabs.

church, St MacDara's Island

St Michael's 2 J2

Creeslough, Co Donegal. Contoured like a fragment of the mountains beyond, it is a bold, white, rough-cast monolith sparkling against a background of gorse, rock and blue-washed peaks. The crisply sculpted forms of the chapel with detached steel-frame bell tower seem to grow out of the plain overlooking a narrow inlet of Sheep Haven Bay.

Castles & ruins

Ballintober Castle 4 H9
Ballintober, Co Roscommon. As muscle-bound as its syllables sound, this huge 13thC castle is square in plan with a central courtyard and polygonal corner towers. The gatehouse in the east wall has flanking towers and additional defence was provided by an encircling water-filled moat. Following the Norman invasion, the castle became the stronghold of the O'Connors of Connacht, who held it until the 18thC.

Ballymote Castle 2 H7
Ballymote, Co Sligo. Built 1300 by Richard de Burgo, 'Red' Earl of Ulster, it was one of the most formidable castles in Connacht. Many of the castles built by the Normans in the west of Ireland were square or rectangular in plan without any keep-like this one. The ivy-clad ruins consist of a huge, square enclosure protected by a ten-foot-thick curtain wall with projecting angle towers. In the north wall is a double-towered entrance gate. The original encircling moat was filled in and the castle's fortifications rendered harmless in the late 17thC.

Curlieus Castle 2 H8
Ballinafad, Co Sligo. Modelled on a 13thC plan, it's a dumpy, thick-walled square keep dwarfed by monumental corner towers, curved on the outside angle and flat on the inside. The castle, built in 1590 to guard the pass through the Curlew Hills, was garrisoned by a constable and ten men.

Dunguaire Castle 4 F12
Kinvara, Co Galway. One of the best-preserved tower houses in Ireland. Typical fortified chieftain's dwelling of the 16thC, it consists of a six-sided bawn perched on a low outcrop of rock on the edge of Kinvara Bay. Restored to the period; medieval banquets are held here nightly in *summer*.

Tower House, Dunguaire, Co Galway, 16^{m}c.

Parkes Castle 2 H6
Lough Gill, Co Leitrim. Built in 1659 at Newton, on the shore of Lough Gill, on land confiscated from the O'Rourkes. Classic example of an early Planters' castle, it is a rectangular-plan, three-storey-high tower house forming one side of a five-sided bawn. Two round flanking towers protect the corners of the bawn. A through passage in the ground floor of the house gives access to the walled enclosure beyond.

Houses & gardens

Ashford Castle 1 E10
Cong, Co Mayo. Now a hotel and recently enlarged, it is a magnificent castellated mansion built in 1870 to incorporate an old tower house as well as a French chateau-style house. The architect was J F Fuller, and the client was Lord Ardilaun, a member of the famous Guinness family.

Buncrana Castle 2 K2
Buncrana, Co Donegal. Full of decaying majesty, a handsome nine-bay, two-storey house raised above a basement storey. Built by Sir John Vaughan in 1716, it has a fine panelled interior. *Open all year.*

Interior of Clonalis House

Clonalis House 4 H9
Castlerea, Co Roscommon. Nineteenth-century house, of interest as the home of the O'Connor Don, descendant of the O'Connors, former Kings of Connacht. Fine Sheraton furniture, Victorian costumes, rare glass and china together with a unique collection of Gaelic manuscripts and documents. *Open summer.*

Coole Park 4 G12
Co Galway, 2½ miles NE of Gort. Although the house is ruined, the garden is still worth seeing; 'autograph tree' bears the initials, among others, of George Bernard Shaw, Augustus John and John Masefield. Coole Lake is a short walk from the house, with the swans that Yeats loved so much. *Open daily during daylight hours.*

Glenveagh Castle 2 I2
Glenveagh, Co Donegal. A lochside setting with magnificent lawns, palms, cordilines, azaleas and eucryphias. There is a terrace walk with sculpture, Italian garden, a lovely herbaceous border and a spectacular flight of 67 steps flanked by massed rhododendrons. The castellated late 19thC mansion is *not open to the public.*

Hazelwood House 2 H6
Calry, Co Sligo. Handsome, stone-built Palladian house designed by Richard Castle in 1731. Consists of a central block with flanking pavilions and now owned by an Italian industrial company. *Private.*

Lissadell House 2 H6
Co Sligo, 8 miles NW of Sligo. Refined neoclassical house designed by Francis Goodwin in 1834 for Sir Robert Gore-Booth. High rooms washed with light from tall windows, with a marvellous galleried entrance hall lit by rooflights. It was frequented by Yeats, who knew the brilliant Gore-Booth sisters—Eva, a talented poet, and Constance, a leader in the Rising of 1916. *Open summer.*

Lough Cultra Castle 4 G12
Co Galway, 4 miles S of Gort. Castellated house designed by John Nash in 1811 for Viscount Gort and supervised by two assistants, the brothers John and George Pain. Based on Nash's English-style Gothic houses, it consists of the characteristic towers linked by castellated blocks. Stands in superb site on the lake shore. *Not open to the public.*

St Cleran's 4 G12
Co Galway, 1¾ miles E of Craughwell. Handsome villa-style house designed in 1810 by Sir Richard Morrison. Robert O'Hara Burke, the first man to cross Australia from south to north, was born here in 1820. Until recently it was owned by John Huston, the film director, who had it restored by architect Michael Scott. *Not open to the public.*

Westport House 1 E9
Westport, Co Mayo. Handsome Palladian-style

mansion designed 1730–34 by Richard Castle in grey limestone. Marvellous barrel-vaulted entrance hall opening onto a rooflit stairwell. The dining room, with its brilliant decorative stucco work, is by James Wyatt. Fine collection of Waterford glass and Irish silver. Zoo park, the first of its kind in Ireland. *Open summer*.

Museums & galleries

Donegal Museum   2 I5
Franciscan friary, Rossnowlagh, Co Donegal. A museum of archaeology, folklife, history, military memorabilia and numismatics. *Open all year*.

Folk Village Museum   2 G4
Glencolumbkille, Co Donegal. Three cottages from 1700–1900, complete with authentic furniture, illustrating Irish peasant life. *Open all year*.

Mill Museum   4 G10
Shop Street, Tuam, Co Galway. Working corn mill and equipment, with related exhibition. *Open all year*.

St Brendan's Catholic Church   4 H12
Loughrea, Co Galway. Although neither a museum nor a gallery, the interior of this cathedral richly illustrates the development of ecclesiastical arts and crafts from 1903–57, in particular the stained glass windows.

Sligo County Museum & Art Gallery   2 H6
Stephen Street, Sligo, Co Sligo. Exhibits of local and national interest from pre-Christian times to the Anglo-Irish War of 1919–21. There is also a collection of W B Yeats memorabilia, including his Nobel medal. *Open all year*.

Nature trails & reserves

Coole Park   4 G12
Co Galway, 2½ miles N of Gort. Delightful grounds surrounding the site of Lady Gregory's home, now in ruins. Coole Lake is a short distance from the house, with the swans that Yeats loved so much. Picnic areas and forest walks. There is a nature trail (leaflet available) through the park.

Dooney Rock   2 H6
Co Sligo, 4 miles from Sligo. Lying on the southern shore of Lough Gill, this rock is mentioned by Yeats in his poem 'The Fiddler of Dooney'. Scenic nature trail with viewing points, lakeside and forest walks. Leaflet available.

Lough Key Forest Park   2 I8
Co Roscommon, 2 miles E of Boyle. Situated in one of Ireland's most delightful forests; there is a forest walk and nature trail with a viewing tower and deer compound. Wonderful rhododendrons and pleasant bog gardens. Facilities for boating, fishing, cruising and swimming. Also caravan and camping areas, shop, restaurant. A booklet giving details of nature trail is available.

Portumna Forest Park   4 I12
Portumna, Co Galway. Over 1,000 acres of land teeming with animals and birds, including fallow and red deer. Viewing stands, nature trail (leaflet available), forest walks, and picnic sites.

Tourmakeady Demesne   1 E9
Tourmakeady, Co Mayo. Spectacular setting for this park on the western shore of Lough Mask. Delightful forest walks, including one passing a beautiful waterfall. Nature trail (leaflet available). Picnic facilities.

Birdwatching

The lowland areas, especially bog land, offer woodpigeon, pheasants and rooks, and also in lesser quantity, redshank and dunlin. Around the Twelve Bens region, ravens, merlin, golden plover and, if you're lucky, choughs, kestrels and long-eared owls can be sighted.
The coast has a varied collection of birds, especially in the winter months: curlews, turnstones, redshank, ringed plover and even snow buntings. Brent geese can be seen near Tawin Island and red-breasted mergansers in Lough Atalia. Look out, too, for shelduck, black guillemots and barnacle geese, and on the North Mayo coast colonies of auks and kittiwakes. Malin Head and Horn Head in Co Donegal are good centres.

Lough Corrib, Co Galway

The loughs also provide much interest—widgeon, shoveler, white-fronted geese, Bewick's and whooper swans, tufted ducks and coots. Great crested grebe breed on Lough Corrib, whilst little grebes, herons and pochard can be found on the smaller western lakes.
Barnacle geese winter on the Inishkea Islands and at Lissadell in Co Sligo. Inishglova has large colonies of storm petrels and Illanmaster in Co Mayo is noted for its puffins.

Forest parks

There are a large number of forest parks in this area, several of which have been described in the 'Nature trails & reserves' section. One of the most magnificent is **Ards Forest Park**, two miles north of Creeslough in Co Donegal, which offers wonderful walks and picnic spots along Sheep Haven Bay, as well as birdwatching and swimming facilities. For further details on all parks, contact the Forest and Wildlife Service, 22 Upper Merrion Street, Dublin 2 (Tel Dublin 789211).

Hills & mountains

Blue Stack Mountains   2 I4
Co Donegal. It is the scarred and crumpled peaks of these mountains, a deep blue like the famed Blue Ridge Mountains of Virginia, that makes the sweeping view across Donegal Bay from the south so memorable. A chain of peaks drawn in a crescent north of Lough Eske, the highest is Blue Stack at 2,219 feet; Lavagh More, to the west, is 2,211 feet and Binmore, north east of Blue Stack, is 2,118 feet.

Maamturk Mountains   1 D10
Co Galway. To the north east of the Twelve Bens, divided by a broad green valley and the scimitar-shaped waters of Lough Inagh. Beyond the mountain wall is Joyce's country.

Partry Mountains   1 E9
Co Galway. Baroque ridge of rock clawing at green
handfuls of the Erriff valley to the north west, whilst
to the south its foothills are edged by the wide waters
of Lough Mask. Lying at its feet to the south is
Lough Nafooey. The main peaks here are Devil's
Mothers, 2,131 feet; to the west and the 2,039-foot
Knocklaur to the east; to the north is Benwel, 2,239
feet, and 2,207-foot Maumtrasna is the last peak, a
little to the north east.

The Twelve Bens   1 D10
Ballynahinch, Co Galway. The lush green
lough-filled landscape of Connemara is shadowed by
the purple peaks of the Twelve Bens, a giant star-fish
of lichen-covered rock erupting in a series of
quartzite pinnacles that glint in the summer's sun.

The highest peak is
Benbaun, 2,395 feet; to
the south are
Benglenisky, 1,710 feet;
Benlettery, 1,904 feet;
Bengower, 2,184 feet.
To the north is
Benbrack, 1,922 feet; to
the west is Bencullagh,
2,084 feet, and
Muckanaght, 2,153
feet; to the south east,
cascading down to the
glassy waters of
Derryclare lough, are
Bencorr, 2,336 feet,
Bencollaghduff, 2,290   *The Twelve Bens*
feet, and Derryclare, 2,220 feet. To the east lurches
Bencorrbeg, 1,908 feet, its feet clawing out towards
the banks of Lough Inagh.

Countryside

Donegal
The most northerly county in Ireland, it's a wild,
beautiful landscape of shadow-washed mountains.
The lush green valleys are scattered with lakes and
smoky villages. The lovely Rosguill peninsula,
wedged between the bays of Sheep Haven and
Mulroy is encircled by the Atlantic Drive, one of
Ireland's finest scenic drives. To the east, Malin
Head at the tip of the Inishowen peninsula is the
most northerly point in Ireland. Just north east of
Donegal is the Barnesmore Gap, squeezing tightly
through a rock-strewn pass in the Blue Stack
Mountains. To the south, washed by the waters of
Donegal Bay, is a world of fine golden beaches and
quiet coves protected by a wall of cliffs.

Galway
One of Ireland's most spectacular counties. It is
divided by Lough Corrib and Lough Mask and
stretches from the boulder-strewn Irish-speaking
world of Connemara between the lakes and the
Atlantic in the west to a level plain of bog and
farmland running across the banks of the River
Shannon and Lough Derg in the east. Thirty miles
offshore are the legendary Aran Isles rising from the
heaving sea, their folklore and culture immortalised
in the writings of J M Synge and rich in early
Christian and prehistoric remains.

Leitrim
A spectacular lake district and rolling blanket of land
touching the eastern edge of Co Sligo and stretching
50 miles from Co Longford in the south to the sea at
Tullaghan in the north west. The county is split in
two by a vast ocean of water, Lough Allen, the first
of the River Shannon's great lakes. To the east is a

scarred and crumpled landscape of mountains rising
in the north, beyond Glencar, to 2,000-foot-high
peaks. To the south, the myriad lakes are sealed
among gentle rolling hills.

Mayo
On the western coast, Mayo boasts some of Ireland's
most spectacular coastal scenery of rugged
headlands, huge cliffs, islands and long curving
sandy beaches backed by great walls of rock. Inland
there are extensive high plains.

Roscommon
A lush green blanket of river meadow and bogland,
filled with island-dotted lakes such as Lough Key.
Low hills relieve the flatness; the River Shannon
encloses the eastern boundary.

Sligo
A county of mountains, lakes and beautiful coastal
scenery, with many tiny fishing harbours. Some of
the most spectacular views in Ireland across the
sun-bright sea. Rising out of the rolling landscape
are huge limestone ridges like Ben Bulben. To the
east are the long, narrow waters of Lough Gill, with
the tiny island of Innisfree near the south eastern
shore, and Lough Arrow, riddled with tiny leafy
islands and encircled by hills. A beautiful county full
of prehistoric remains.

Rivers & loughs

Ballynahinch Lough   1 D10
Co Galway. Calm blue lake washing the scarred and
crumpled feet of the 1,900-foot Benlettery peak, one
of the Twelve Bens. It is one of a series of lakes
partially encircling the cone-like mountains, their
quartzite peaks glinting jewel-like on a clear blue
day. On a lush green island in the lake stand the
melancholy ruins of an ancient castle keep. In a
commanding position on the south bank of the lough
stands the much altered 18thC Ballynahinch Castle,
now a hotel; it was originally the home of Richard
Martin, one of the founders of the RSPCA in 1824.

Lough Derg   2 J4
Co Donegal. Solitary lake formed by the River
Shannon sealed among rolling hills and moorland.
Station Island, half a mile from the shore, is the
scene of an annual pilgrimage dating from the
mid-12thC. It was here that St Patrick is supposed to
have spent 40 days of prayer and fasting in a cave.
The legend, circulated throughout Christendom in
the Middle Ages, brought pilgrims in their
thousands from all over Europe. The remains of a
monastery established by one of St Patrick's
disciples are on Saints Island, to the north west.

Lough Gill   2 H6
Co Sligo. Three miles south east of the city of Sligo,
it is a spectacularly beautiful area—a five-mile
stretch of water enclosed on three sides by wooded
mountain slopes. Rich in pike, salmon and trout, a
short stretch of tree-lined river connects the lake to
the sea. On the south bank of the river is Cairns Hill,
with two cashels and cairns and a stone circle. On the
north bank is a fine Palladian house, Hazelwood,
designed 1731 by Richard Castle. Numerous wooded
islands fill the lough, including Yeats' magical isle of
Innisfree, celebrated in his beautiful poem 'The
Lake Isle of Innisfree'; Cottage Island, with ruins of
a church; and Church Island, where there are
remains of a 6thC church reputed to have been
founded by St Coman.

Lough Key   2 I8
Co Roscommon. Virgilian scene of calm, luminous
skies, unruffled waters and wooded islets with

blue-washed mountain peaks beyond. It was in the hamlet of Cootehall, to the east of the lough, that the Annals of Lough Cé, now in Trinity College Library, Dublin, were compiled. On one of the islands in the lake stand the foliage-covered ruins of Trinity Abbey.

River Shannon
Stocked with salmon, pike, perch, trout and bream, its wildflower-rich banks are a home of grebes, cormorants, curlew, herons and snipe. This is the most beautiful by far of Ireland's rivers; over 200 miles long from source to sea, it rises in the foothills of Cuilcagh Mountain in Co Fermanagh and flows through the length of the country to Limerick and the sea in the south west. Co Leitrim is almost split in two by Lough Allen, the first of the River Shannon's great lakes. The Shannon winds its way south from Lough Allen and narrows to bend past a series of lakes beside the town of Carrick on Shannon. It winds south east through Lough Boderg, down along the borders of Longford and Roscommon and through the island-studded waters of Lough Ree, the second largest of the Shannon lakes. Its course continues past Athlone on the southern tip of the lough and then down, in two giant doglegs, to Lough Derg, the largest of the Shannon lakes. Bending in a great sweep south west the river opens out in a great funnel of water past Limerick and on into the Atlantic beyond. Good river for fishing, with abundance of pike, bream, rudd and perch. Carrick on Shannon, which is Ireland's major centre for coarse fishing, has a large marina with four companies hiring river cruisers.

Archaeological sites

Carrowkeel Passage-Grave Cemetery   2 H8
Co Sligo, 2 miles NW of Ballinafad. Part of an ancient village site built in the Bricklieve Mountains during the late Stone Age between 2,500–2,000BC these passage-graves are predominantly round mounds. Characteristic of the Irish passage-grave, their plans consist of a long passage opening into a central chamber, around the sides of which are smaller chambers. Some 300 feet below, on a terrace of land to the north east of the mountain, is the site of the village. Remains consist of the foundations of about 50 round huts.

Carrowmore Megalithic Cemetery   2 H6
Co Sligo, 3 miles S of Sligo. The largest megalithic cemetery in Ireland, consisting of numerous passage-graves and dolmens.

Castlestrange Decorated Stone   4 I10
Co Roscommon, 1½ miles NW of Athleague. A magnificent example of the Celtic La Tène style, it is an egg-shaped granite boulder engraved with

Castlestrange Decorated Stone

marvellous flowing spirals. It is one of three outstanding Iron Age cult stones found in Ireland, conceived as phallic symbols and dating from 300BC; this one is symbolic of the female element.

Creevykeel Court Cairn   2 H5
Co Sligo, 6 miles SW of Bundoran. One of the finest court cairns in western Europe. Built in the late Stone Age about 2500BC, it consists of a wedge-shaped mound with a central open court. Several passage-graves were added at a later date.

Grianán of Aileach

Grianán of Aileach   2 K2
Co Donegal, 7 miles S of Fahan. Remarkable concentric fort dating from about the 7thC BC and crowning the top of the 803-foot-high Greenan Mountain. It is 77 feet in diameter with a 17-foot-high terraced walls over 13 feet thick at the base. A long, lintelled entrance gives access to the fort. It later became the royal residence of the O'Neills, kings of Ulster. It was partly destroyed in 1101 by Murrough O'Brien, King of Munster, in revenge for the destruction of his own fort at Kincora, Co Clare by the O'Neills.

Inishglora Island   1 C6
Co Mayo, 7 miles NE of Inishkea North. Remains of a monastery, founded by St Brendan the Navigator in the 6thC, consisting of three chapels, including St Brendan's oratory, a tiny rectangle with square-headed east window and flat-headed entrance portal. There are also remains of several beehive huts, fragments of the monastic wall, a holy well and numerous early cross-slabs and pillars.

Inishkea North   1 C7
Co Mayo. This uninhabited island supported a thriving monastic community during the early Christian period. Of particular interest is the Bailey Mór, a giant mound 60 feet high and 500 feet in diameter, on which were found several beehive huts and square-planned houses built of dry stone walling. There are nine ancient cross-slabs and pillars. To the north is another mound, Bailey Dóighte, with a flanking mound, Bailey Beag, to the south.

Inishmurray Island   2 G5
Co Sligo. Remarkable remains of early Christian monastery founded in the 6thC by St Molaise. Considered to be the finest and most characteristic example of such a complex, it is surrounded by a 13-foot-high stone wall with five entrances giving access to the central area. Divided into four enclosures, the central area contains a largish church with antae and flat-headed portal; a smaller, more primitive stone-roofed church with one door and round-headed window; a small beehive hut, numerous cross-slabs and pillar-stones.

Rathcroghan   4 H8
Co Roscommon, 6 miles SE of Frenchpark. Pagan palace and pre-Christian capital of Connacht. It was

here that the kings of Connacht, who reigned at Tara, were inaugurated; consisting of numerous earthworks and enclosures, the site covers some two square miles. Of interest is Roilig na Ri (Cemetery of the Kings), which consists of a seven-foot-high red sandstone pillar standing at the centre of a ring fort. It is said to mark the burial place of King Dathi, the last pre-Christian king of Ireland.

The Turoe Stone   **4 H11**
Bullaun, Co Galway, 3 miles N of Loughrea.
Remarkable granite pillar stone three feet high. A phallic pillar of AD1stC Celtic Ireland, the lower part is decorated with incised rings and the rounded top is carved in curvilinear relief work. It is one of the finest examples in Ireland of La Tène-style decorative work.

Regional sport

Fox hunting
The famous 'Galway Blazers' are based at Craughwell, eight miles west of Loughrea, and there are hunts all over the Galway district. Horses can be hired from local stables. The East Galway Hunt is also a major pack in the area.

Rock climbing
The rugged terrain of western Ireland offers some excellent rock climbing districts. The Derryveagh Mountains in the north west are a particularly exciting area; many steep climbs can be found above Lough Barra. The area around Glenveagh provides granite routes and Maumtrasna in Co Galway offers some less steep climbs on sandstone. Slievemore Achill in Co Mayo also has routes of varying degrees of difficulty.

Sailing
Donegal Bay is popular for sailing and there are several clubs offering facilities to visitors, such as the one at Rosses Point. Inland sailing is available at Portumna on Lough Derg, which has a modern marina. Loughrea is a popular centre for sailing on the nearby lake and regattas are held here every season.

Sea angling
Clew Bay in Co Mayo provides some of the finest sea angling grounds in Europe. Many record catches have been made in the area. Westport also has excellent facilities and Newport to the north is another important centre. Among the fish to be caught in the Clew Bay area are bream, tope, skate, wrasse, mackerel and shark.

Surfing
Ireland's geographical position ensures that the Atlantic breakers reaching its shores compare favourably with those to be found in the great surfing resorts of the world. Waves are an average of 3–12 feet. Easky in Co Sligo is a popular centre; strong winds here give good conditions. Rossnowlagh, Co Donegal, is another popular spot, where surfboards can also be hired. The Irish National Surfing Championships are held here annually in *Sep.*

Festivals

An Tostal   **2 I7**
Drumshanbo, Co Leitrim. A truly Irish festival in *Jun*, featuring singing, dancing and performances by local groups of 'Wren-Boys'.

Ballina Salmon Festival   **1 F7**
Ballina, Co Mayo. There are lots of attractions for all ages and selection of the Queen of the May, although the festival is in *Jul.*

Ballinasloe Angling Week   **4 I11**
Ballinasloe, Co Galway. One of Ireland's biggest coarse fishing competitions held in *May* on the River Suck. Also the great **October Fair**, a very large livestock show, is held here.

Claremorris Ham Fair & Festival   **1 F9**
Claremorris, Co Mayo. The All-Ireland Pony Jumping Competition and agricultural show is held annually here in *Aug.*

Festival of the Shannon
Drumshanbo, Co Leitrim. A fortnight's jamboree in *Jul* with lots of attractions, including the Queen of Shannon beauty competition.

Galway Oyster Festival   **4 G12**
Clarinbridge, Co Galway. A celebration of the famous Galway oyster, with oyster-opening championship. Annually in *Sep.*

Westport Horse Show   **1 E9**
Westport, Co Mayo. One of the best in the country, it is a three-day event held in *Jun.*

Wild Rose Festival   **2 I6**
Manorhamilton, Co Leitrim. Lasting for a week towards the end of *Aug*, the main attraction is the selection of the 'Wild Rose Colleen', with several other events during the week.

Special attractions

Adventureland Astoria   **2 H5**
Bundoran, Co Donegal. Indoor entertainments for children *10–6 daily.*

Children's Playground Complex   **1 F6**
Enniscrone, Co Sligo. Lots of amusements for children here. *Open summer.*

Connemara Marble Factory   **1 F11**
Moycullen, Co Galway. Demonstrations of cutting, grinding and polishing the marble quarried nearby.

Creeslough Adventure Sports   **2 J2**
Creeslough, Co Donegal. Weekend and longer courses available for outside activities such as canoeing, orienteering and surfing. Tel. Creeslough 43.

Donegal Carpets   **2 H4**
Killybegs, Co Donegal. Visitors can see the making of Killybegs hand-knotted carpets, rugs and wall hangings at the factory. Tel. Killybegs 21.

Dunguaire Castle   **4 F12**
Kinvarra, Co Galway. Medieval banquets are held every night during *May to Sep* with true Irish entertainments and music. Reservations necessary via tourist office.

Galway Leisureland   **1 F11**
Salthill, Galway City, Co Galway. Luxury entertainment for all ages including trampolines, 'astroglide', mini-cars and train, plus an olympic-size indoor swimming pool.

Lough Gill Cruises   **2 H6**
Co Sligo. A motor cruiser around the lake makes a 2½-hour trip, including a ½-hour stop to eat.

Pony trekking
This is very popular in Connemara, Co Galway, and is available at various places in the region, with or without supervision. Among them are Errislannan Manor Riding Stables, Clifden, The Angler's Return, Ballinafad and Canrower Pony Stud, Oughterard.

Westport House   **1 E9**
Westport, Co Mayo. Zoo park in the grounds of this beautiful house of the Marquess of Sligo. *Open summer.*

Eastern Ireland

3

Carlow   **Louth**
Cavan   **Meath**
Dublin   **Monaghan**
Kildare   **Offaly**
Kilkenny   **Westmeath**
Laois   **Wexford**
Longford   **Wicklow**

Leinster, the most fertile and richest of Ireland's provinces, was a fine prey to Norse and Anglo-Norman invader alike. The heart of the district is Georgian Dublin, a gently undulating blanket of spacious streets spread generously in a broad saddle of land along the River Liffey. Sheltered on the south by the Wicklow Hills, it is washed to the east by Dublin Bay, a great crescent of coast riddled with holiday resorts sweeping from the rocky Hill of Howth in the north to the wind-blown headland of Dalkey in the south. Eighth-century naval base of the plundering Vikings and later an Anglo-Norman stronghold where Henry II held court in 1172, Dublin supported the Royalist cause against Cromwell and sided with the Jacobites in the Williamite wars. It was here that the struggle for Irish parliamentary independence finally succeeded and that the Gaelic League was established in 1893, intent on the restoration of the Irish language. The Irish literary renaissance blossomed here with the foundation of the Abbey Theatre. Wrapped in the mysteries of nightfall Dublin can, in the gathering dusk, take on the character of Swift's age, or that of William Butler Yeats, Lady Gregory and John Millington Synge, founders of the Abbey Theatre. In the evening it's a genial city, even after the pubs are closed. So different from the hungover mornings, blatant with modernity, a silent

Georgian houses, Merrion Square, Dublin

white-faced sea of people passing by, a far cry from the cheerful host out singing in the streets till three.

To the north west lies Meath, a mystical county spread generously with heavy grasslands and low, wooded hills enclosing winding river valleys like that of the Boyne. A treasure trove of Stone Age tombs such as at Newgrange, Knowth and Dowth, part of the legendary burial place of the pre-Christian kings of Ireland. It was at Tara, six miles south of Navan, that the prehistoric priest-kings had their seat; in the 6thC Tara had become the most powerful of the five ancient kingdoms of Ireland and the high kings of Ireland had their residence here. It was also not far from here at Kells, in a quiet, wooded part of the River Blackwater valley, that St Columba established a monastery in the 6thC; one of the world's greatest examples of illuminated art, 'The Book of Kells', was produced here in the 9thC. The full might of Anglo-Norman power can also be seen here in Trim Castle, Ireland's largest medieval fortress.

To the north east of Meath is Louth, a small strip of picturesque seaboard wedged between the Boyne and the mountains of Armagh, beyond Dundalk to the north. To the north east is the wild and rugged Cooley Peninsula, a mountainous, heather-covered paradise rising steeply from the sea with only the icy waters of Carlingford Lough between it and the famed Mountains of Mourne, a measureless mirage beyond. Louth is pre-eminent in the epic tales of ancient Ireland; it was at the foot of Slieve Foye on the southern shore of Carlingford Lough that St Patrick is said to have landed on his return from exile and where, later, the Norsemen established a settlement. It was at Ardee, strategically important even in pre-Christian Ireland, that the legendary four-day hand-to-hand combat took place in which Cuchulainn finally slew his friend Ferdia. At Mellifont the Cistercians built their first and greatest Irish abbey, along the banks of the River Matlock in 1142.

To the north west of Louth lies Monaghan, another of Ulster's independent counties. A celebrated coarse fishing centre, Monaghan is a county of low hills, like basking whales, and little lakes. Once dominated by the powerful MacMahon clan, it now has a shy air, and is overshadowed by the mountains of Armagh to the north.

To the south west of Monaghan lies Cavan, a wild district of mountain and bog endowed with a chain of lakes in the south. An angler's paradise, it is one of the nine counties of Ulster but opted out of the new political division of Northern Ireland and is in the Republic. Along the borders with Co Leitrim and Co Fermanagh bulges the shadow-creased 2,188-foot-high Cuilcagh Mountain, on the southern slopes of which the River Shannon has its source.

On the borders of Lough Ree to the north west, is Longford, a quiet county of farmland and brown bog. Bounded on the west by the River Shannon and walled in by the majestic Angna Mountains to the north, it's a delightful centre for fishing and river cruising. At Pallas, not far from the trout-fishing centre of Ballymahon, Oliver Goldsmith

River Barrow, Co Carlow

was born. On the south western edge of Granard are the remains of a large moat, said to have been the royal residence of Cairbre, eldest son of Niall the Great. Four miles north of Granard is Lough Gowna, a trout-filled lake and source of the River Erne.

Westmeath, to the east, is an attractive lake-filled county of lush grazing land, encircled by low hills and bounded by Lough Ree and the River Shannon in the west. In the north east is a gently undulating ridge of limestone hills. It was at Athlone, astride the River Shannon, that Brian Boru, High King of Ireland, convened a great hosting in 1001. A little to the north, around Lissoy, is the poet Oliver Goldsmith's country; this was Goldsmith's boyhood home, which he reincarnated as "Sweet Auburn! Loveliest village of the plain" in his poem, 'The Deserted Village'.

Offaly, to the south, is wedged in an angle stretching from the River Shannon across the Bog of Allen to the heathery Slieve Bloom mountain range in the south east. Largely bog and level plain, Offaly is nevertheless full of hidden treasures. It was at Clonmacnois, on the banks of the River Shannon four miles north of Shannonbridge, that St Ciaran founded a monastery in AD548; it was to become one of Ireland's most celebrated holy places and the last High King, Rory O'Conor, was buried here in 1198.

Bordering Dublin to the west lies the vast central plain of Kildare, an ocean of grassland and lush pasture ruffled by gently rolling hills. To the south west is the Bog of Allen and the border to the east is lined by the foothills of the Wicklow Mountains, from whose glens the Irish clans poured in raiding parties to harass the Anglo-Normans. This is the famous centre of the Irish horse-breeding industry, and the Curragh Plain, a celebrated 18thC meeting place for sportsmen, is the course for all the Irish classics including the famed Irish Derby. Kildare is also resplendent with magnificent houses, a testimony to 18thC elegance, such as Castletown, a monumental Palladian-style mansion built 1722 for William Conolly, the Speaker of the Irish House of Commons, and Carton House, a grand Georgian design of 1740 near Maynooth.

South is Laois, a flat and boggy land walled in by the Slieve Bloom Mountains in the north west and by a belt of hills to the south east. The Rock of Danamase, four miles east of Portlaoise, the county town, is crowned with the ruins of a castle; this was once the fortress of Dermot MacMurrough, 12thC king of Leinster and instigator of the Anglo-Norman invasion of Ireland.

To the south east is rural Carlow, a small farming county with the River Barrow to the west, a large plain of fertile limestone in the centre and the River Slaney winding along the east. A stronghold of the Anglo-Normans, Carlow was frequently besieged or burnt, being a strategic point on the border of the English Pale.

Kilkenny, to the south west of Carlow, was a stronghold of the Butlers, Lords of Ormonde. It's an undulating blanket of limestone edged with gently sloping hills, such as the Slieveardagh; the river valleys of the Nore and Barrow wind gently through an idyllic countryside. Rich in fine monastic foundations such as Jerpoint Abbey, a Cistercian establishment begun in 1158, the county is full of history. In Kilkenny itself you will find a collage of medieval fragments spreadeagled along the banks of the Nore, where many 14thC parliaments were held including that of 1366, which passed the infamous Statute of Kilkenny banning fraternisation between the Anglo-Normans and the native Irish.

The south eastern corner of the country is occupied by Wexford, a county of lush pasture and long, sweeping sandy beaches, of low hills and snaking river valleys. It has a fertile plain of rich farmland irrigated by the River Slaney, bordered to the north by the rolling foothills of the Wicklow Mountains and to the west by the Blackstairs Mountains and the River Barrow. It was the Vikings who first established Wexford as a settlement in the 9thC, only to be besieged and finally driven out by the Anglo-Normans in 1169. It was the pikemen of Wexford who fought so heroically against overwhelming odds during the Rising of 1798. It's a land of old-world towns, like picturesque Enniscorthy lining steeply sloping ground

Enniscorthy, Co Wexford

on either side of the River Slaney, or New Ross, a winding nest of streets crowning a hill overlooking the river Barrow. There are picturesque fishing villages like Duncannon, glued to a rocky headland at the mouth of an estuary. Rosslare, a popular seaside resort, is the terminus for the car ferries from Fishguard and Le Havre.

Wicklow, north of Wexford and south of Dublin, is called the 'Garden of Ireland'. Just a moment away from the drawing rooms of Georgian Dublin are the lights and shadows of wooded Glencree, where the playwright John Millington Synge roamed with his beloved Molly Allgood; he immortalised the area in his poem, 'To The Oaks Of Glencree'. Wicklow has a low, sandy coast with fine resorts topping rocky headlands, as at Bray, whilst inland it's a mysterious, shadow-filled granite landscape of towering mountain peaks penetrated by deep glens and long, winding, wooded valleys. At Glendalough, a once-famous monastic school to which scholars flocked in their thousands from all over Europe, St Kevin lived and died in the 6thC and 7thC, a hermit in search of solitude. Palladius, the first Christian missionary to Ireland is said to have landed at Arklow in AD430. Wicklow is also rich with stately homes; Powerscourt Demesne is a 14,000-acre estate with beautiful gardens, celebrated waterfall and fine herds of deer. At Avondale, a mile north of Rathdrum, there are marvellous wooded gardens; Charles Stewart Parnell lived here. The nearby River Avonmore runs south to the famous Meeting of the Waters, of which Thomas Moore wrote, "There is not in this wide world a valley so sweet/As that vale in whose bosom the bright waters meet".

The Coast

Ardamine 8 O15
Co Wexford. Tiny village nestled in a secluded cove.
Handsome church designed by George Edmund
Street, architect of the London Law Courts.

Arklow 5 O14
Co Wicklow. Pop 6,950. EC Wed. Bustling resort
wedged between the mouth of the River Avoca and
the undulating foothills of the Wicklow Mountains.
Once known only as a boat building, shipping and
fishing centre, today it is one of the major holiday
resorts of the east coast. It was here that Palladius,
the first Christian missionary to Ireland, landed in
430. Here also St Patrick is thought to have landed,
two years later, when he returned from a period of
monastic apprenticeship at Auxerre on the banks of
the River Yonne in France, having dedicated his life
to the conversion of the pagan Gaels. An important
Norse settlement, Arklow became an Anglo-Norman
town in the 12thC. It was here that a decisive battle
was fought between the rebels and the British forces
of General Needham in 1798.

arklow, church.

Of interest: remains of 13thC Dominican friary; St
Saviour's Church, Hollywood Gothic of 1900 with
fine stained glass by Harry Clarke; Maritime
Museum in St Mary's Road, with collection
illustrating the maritime history of the port. Good
fishing from the pier, shore and sea, particularly for
skate, ray and occasionally conger. The Rivers Ahare
and Ennercilly abound in small brown trout.

Arthurstown 8 M17
Co Wexford. Pint-sized village stranded on the
eastern shore of Waterford harbour.

Balbriggan 5 O10
Co Dublin. Minor seaside resort and hosiery
manufacturing town on the edge of a gently curving
bay with long, sheltered beaches flanking a quiet
valley, through which the River Delvin flows. At
Fournocks, five miles west, is an important
prehistoric site. Good game fishing on the River
Delvin and shore and deep-sea fishing for conger,
cod, pollack, ray and dogfish.

Ballyhack 8 L17
Co Wexford, 1/2 mile NW of Arthurstown. Handful of
gable-ended two-storey houses with narrow front
gardens, wrapped round a tiny granite harbour at the
end of a winding lane. The town is enclosed by a
tight fold of rolling green hills.

Ballymoney 5 O14
Co Wexford. Minute holiday resort, worth a visit.
Sandy beach.

Blackrock 5 O11
Co Dublin, 2 1/2 miles NW of Dun Laoghaire.
Once-fashionable 18thC watering place, which still
boasts one or two architectural splendours. See the
remains of the Villa Frascati, the home of Lord
Edward Fitzgerald from 1793–99.

Black Rock 3 N8
Co Louth. Popular resort by the mouth of the River
Fane on the eastern shore of Dundalk Bay. Of
interest: remains of early Christian monastery with
round tower and sculptured high cross at
Dromiskin, five miles south; ruins of Rossmakea
Abbey, a medieval foundation on the banks of the
River Fane; Castlebellingham, a magnificent 18thC
castle, now a hotel, eight miles south.

Blackwater 8 N16
Co Wexford. Small seaside town, spring-cleaned tidy
and quiet, standing on the northern end of Wexford
Bay, which is famous for its swans.

Bray 5 O12
Co Wicklow. Pop 14,470. EC Wed. One of Ireland's
largest seaside resorts, it consists of a colourful,
undulating wall of the bay windows of guest houses
lining a mile-long sandy beach, which curves gently
south to Bray Head, a 791-foot-high shadow of rock
and heather jutting out into Killiney Bay, where it
rises steeply from the dark water. To the west are the
rolling hills and heather-clad slopes of the Wicklow
Mountains and the Glen of the Dargle, a thickly
wooded valley through which the winding River
Dargle cascades. A massive cantilever of rock,
Lover's Leap, juts out romantically high above the
valley. Good sailing and fishing and a magnificent
cliff walk round the foot of Bray Head to Greystones,
five miles south.

Carlingford 3 O7
Co Louth. Tiny town tucked neatly up by the foot of
the 1,935-foot-high Slieve Foye Mountain on the
southern shore of Carlingford Lough. To the north
are sharp views out across the icy waters to the
surging peaks of the Mountains of Mourne. Once a
Norse base for raiding parties, it later became an
Anglo-Norman stronghold, with the remains of
King John's Castle, a massive D-shaped 13thC castle
glaring belligerently across the harbour from a rocky
pedestal of land. There are several 15thC and 16thC
houses of interest, including Taaffe's Castle and The
Mint; the latter is a 15thC tower house with
projecting turret over the door. The Tholsel is one of
the old town gates, with a room above where the
elders of the town used to meet. At Ballymascanlon,
at the western corner of the peninsula, is the Proleek
Dolmen, with two three-foot-high support stones
surmounted by a 46-ton capstone. Good sea fishing
in Carlingford Lough. Annual Carlingford Festival,
Jun–Jul.

King John's Castle, Carlingford

Clogher 5 O9
Co Louth. Picturesque fishing village beside a sandy
beach on the southern side of Clogher Head, a
205-foot-high wall of rock steaming into the Irish Sea
like a giant tug in a swell.

Courtown 8 O15
Co Wexford. Pop 290. 19thC village and popular holiday resort curled round a small harbour built in 1830. Two miles of sandy beach. Good angling in the sea and the River Ounavarragh.

Curracloe 8 N16
Co Wexford, 4 miles SW of Blackwater. Bubbling with old-world charm this resort consists of whitewashed houses resting peacefully along the edge of a six-mile stretch of golden beach.

Dalkey 5 O11
Co Dublin. Attractive village twined round the edge of a hill rising steeply out of the sea to the north of Killiney Bay. The village has two tiny fishing harbours, Coliemore and Bullock, and elegant rows of terraced houses step sedately up the steep hillside behind. In the High Street are two 15thC fortified houses, remnants of Dalkey's medieval past as a flourishing port. Of particular interest is Archbold's Castle, a three-storey granite tower with machicolated parapet. Offshore is Dalkey Island.

Drogheda 5 N9
Co Louth. Pop 19,760. EC Thur. Thriving market town and seaport on a wide bend in the River Boyne. Fortified by the Vikings in AD911, it was walled by the Anglo-Normans in the 13thC; St Laurence's Gate, a barbican flanked by two tall battlemented round towers, still stands. An Augustinian friary was founded in the 13thC; remains include a 15thC tower house with a pointed arch spanning narrow Abbey Lane. Richard II held court here in 1394 and the town has been the venue for several parliaments, including that of 1494 which passed the notorious Poynings Law. Also of interest: remains of a Dominican friary founded in 1224; St Peter's Roman Catholic Church, rebuilt 1740–53 with handsome tower and spire by Francis Johnston; the Tholsel, classical-style building with cupola, designed by Francis Johnston in 1770; the fine Court House and Market Hall, also by Johnston; the Boyne Viaduct, magnificent feat of 19thC engineering by John McNeill carrying the Dublin/Belfast line across the River Boyne; Millmount, legendary Iron Age burial ground south of the town used later as an Anglo-Norman motte; several fine 18thC houses, including Singleton House. In the Millmount House Museum there is an exhibition illustrating the history of the town. Good fishing on the Rivers Nanny, Dee and Boyne.

Dublin 5 O11
Co Dublin. Pop 660,332. EC Wed, Sat. Capital of the Republic and Ireland's principal sea port, it's a medium-sized city, more at home as a quiet backwater than in the role of the international metropolis it is struggling to be. Its grand 18thC vistas are now diluted by dreary new architecture as banal as anything anywhere; a townscape of vast horizontals is relieved here and there by a handsome cupola or factory chimney but, despite its venerable literary ancestry, Dublin is a cultural cul-de-sac. Spreadeagled around the mouth of the River Liffey at the head of Dublin Bay, it's a city of broad, spacious streets and handsome squares laced together by the Grand Canal, a thin line of inky water circling the heart of the city. The long, crypt-like backstreets are sporadically enlivened by a street-corner raucousness and occasional, delightfully bizarre flashes of colour gleaming in the Guinness-drenched sunshine. A salt-aired vigour is wafted in along the River Liffey, its banks lined with brown-walled wharves, and the spacious main streets have a freshness and lightness that make this one of the most exhilarating of European cities.

History
The ford over the River Liffey has been important since Celtic times, and there was a thriving Christian community here from the 5thC, following their conversion by St Patrick in AD448. In AD840 the marauding Vikings landed here, built a fortress on the high ground and established a settlement along the banks of the estuary. Originally a base for their numerous raiding sorties, it soon became a flourishing trading port as well, but Viking dominance was severely curtailed following a defeat by Brian Boru at the Battle of Clontarf in 1014.

River Liffey, Dublin

Converted to Christianity, the Vikings were finally driven out by the Anglo-Normans under Strongbow, who took Dublin by storm, executing the Viking leader, Hasculf. In 1172 Henry II, having established his feudal rights over the invading force, received the submission of the Irish chieftains on the site of College Green. He granted the city by charter to the men of Bristol, from whence the Anglo-Normans had originally come.
The city and surrounding area, established as the seat of English government and protected by an enclosing wall and strategic castles, was known as The Pale. Frequently attacked during the 12thC and 13thC by the Irish clans based in the Wicklow Mountains, it was assaulted unsuccessfully by Edward Bruce in 1316. The city witnessed the crowning of Lambert Simnel, pretender to the English throne, in Christ Church in 1486. Unmoved by the rebellion of 'Silken' Thomas Fitzgerald in 1534, the inhabitants remained loyal to the English crown, supporting King Charles during the Civil Wars. Captured by the Parliamentarians in 1647, the city underwent a great architectural expansion following the Restoration of Charles II. During the Williamite wars Dublin was a Jacobite stronghold. It was here that James II held his last parliament in 1689.
By the end of the 17thC, Dublin was already a flourishing commercial centre; public street lighting had been introduced in 1697 and during the following century the city was transformed into one of the handsomest of Georgian cities. The 'Wide Streets Commission' was established in 1757 and in 1773 the Paving Board was formed. New, elegantly spacious streets and squares were planned and palatial town houses built. In 1783 the Irish Parliament was granted a short-lived autonomy but there was growing political unrest, which erupted in the uprising of 1798. Lord Edward Fitzgerald died of wounds sustained resisting arrest and in 1800 the detested Act of Union was established and the fortunes of the city began to wane.
With government now in London, few of the noblemen required their fine mansions and many

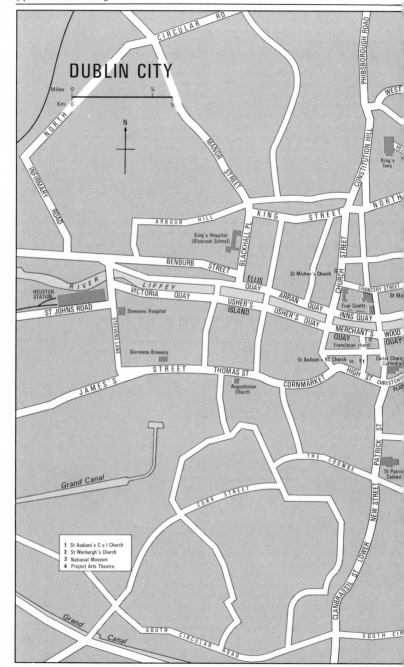

DUBLIN CITY

Miles 0 ¼
Km 0 ½

N

CIRCULAR RD

PHIBSBOROUGH ROAD

WEST

NORTH

INFIRMARY ROAD

MANOR STREET

CONSTITUTION HILL

King's Inns

HE

ARBOUR HILL

KING STREET

NORTH

King's Hospital (Bluecoat School)

BLACKHALL PL

BENBURB STREET

ELLIS QUAY

St Michan's Church

CHURCH STREET

CHANCERY STREET

St Ma

RIVER LIFFEY

VICTORIA QUAY

ARRAN QUAY

Four Courts

HEUSTON STATION

ST JOHNS ROAD

USHER'S ISLAND

USHER'S QUAY

INNS QUAY

WOOD QUAY

Steevens Hospital

MERCHANT'S QUAY

STEEVENS LANE

Franciscan church

Christ Church Cathedral

Guinness Brewery

St Audoen's RC Church

1

STREET

THOMAS ST

HIGH ST

CHRISTCHI

JAMES'S

Augustinian Church

CORNMARKET

PLA

PATRICK ST

THE COOMBE

St Patri Cathed

Grand Canal

CORK STREET

NEW STREET

1 St Audoen's C o I Church
2 St Werburgh's Church
3 National Museum
4 Project Arts Theatre

CLANBRASSIL ST LOWER

Grand Canal

SOUTH CIRCULAR ROAD

SOUTH CIT

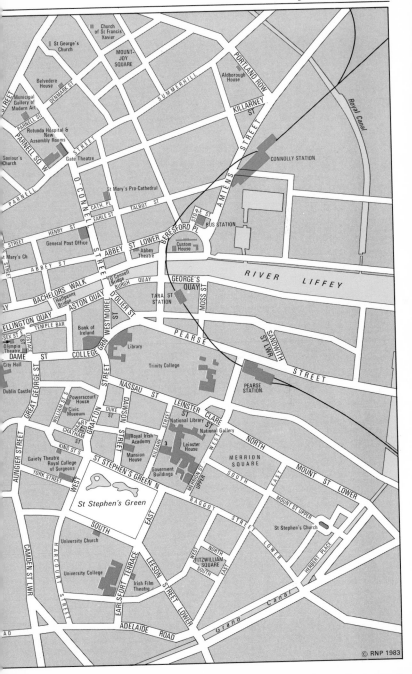

St George's Church
Church of St Francis Xavier
MOUNT-JOY SQUARE
PORTLAND ROW
Aldborough House
KILLARNEY ST
Belvedere House
DENMARK ST
Municipal Gallery of Modern Art
PARNELL SQ
Rotunda Hospital & New Assembly Rooms
Saviour's Church
PARNELL SQ W
Gate Theatre
CONNOLLY STATION
AMIENS STREET
SUMMERHILL
Royal Canal
PARNELL
O'CONNELL STREET
St Mary's Pro-Cathedral
CATH. PL
EARLE ST
TALBOT ST
HENRY ST
General Post Office
St Mary's Ch
ABBEY ST LOWER
BERESFORD PL
STORE ST
BUS STATION
ABBEY ST
Abbey Theatre
Custom House
BACHELORS WALK
O'Connell Bridge
Halfpenny Bridge
BURGH QUAY
GEORGE'S QUAY
RIVER LIFFEY
ASTON QUAY
D'OLIER ST
WESTMORELAND ST
MOSS ST
ELLINGTON QUAY
TEMPLE BAR
TARA ST STATION
SEX ST
FLEET ST
Bank of Ireland
PEARSE
SANDWITH ST LWR
Olympia Theatre
DAME ST
COLLEGE GRN
Library
City Hall
Trinity College
STREET
Dublin Castle
NASSAU ST
PEARSE STATION
GREAT GEORGE ST
WILLIAM ST
Powerscourt House
Civic Museum
DAWSON STREET
GRAFTON STREET
DUKE ST
LEINSTER ST
CLARE ST
National Library
National Gallery
AUNGIER STREET
CHATHAM ST
KING ST S
Royal Irish Academy
3
KILDARE STREET
Leinster House
NORTH
MERRION SQUARE
MOUNT ST LOWER
Gaiety Theatre
Royal College of Surgeons
YORK STREET
WEST
Mansion House
Government Buildings
MERRION ST UPPER
SOUTH
EAST
MOUNT ST UPPER
ST STEPHEN'S GREEN N
BAGGOT STREET
St Stephen's Church
St Stephen's Green
SOUTH
EAST
HERBERT PLACE
CAMDEN ST LWR
HARCOURT STREET
University Church
EARLSFORT TERRACE
LEESON STREET LOWER
NORTH
FITZWILLIAM SQUARE
SOUTH
EAST
University College
Irish Film Theatre
A D
ADELAIDE ROAD
Grand Canal

© RNP 1983

returned to their country estates or left for London. Bitterness increased; in 1803 the Lord Chief Justice was assassinated and Robert Emmet, the leader of an abortive insurrection, was hanged. The newspaper 'The Nation' was established by Charles Gavan Duffy in 1842, the heyday of the Repeal Movement. In 1841 Daniel O'Connell was elected Lord Mayor; only three years later he was interned in Richmond Gaol for campaigning for the repeal of the Union and the restoration of Grattan's 'Irish Parliament'. In 1873 the first great Home Rule Conference was held. In 1879 the Land League was formed, whose leaders, including Parnell and Davitt, were imprisoned for their pains. In 1882 the new Chief Secretary, Lord Frederick Cavendish, and his Under-Secretary were assassinated in Phoenix Park by the Invincibles, a new terrorist organisation. As the campaign for Home Rule gathered momentum, the Gaelic League, which started the Irish literary renaissance, was established by Douglas Hyde and Eóin MacNeill in 1893. Conceived as a means of reviving interest in the Irish language and traditional Irish life, the Gaelic League was also responsible for a remarkable literary revival resulting in the formation of the Abbey Theatre in 1904 where plays by J M Synge, Sean O'Casey and W B Yeats, amongst others, were performed.

Custom House, Dublin, in the late 18thC

In 1905 the Sinn Fein movement was formed, in 1909 the Irish Transport and General Workers Union was set up under the leadership of James Connolly, and in 1913 there was a massive strike, paralysing the city. In 1914 the Irish Volunteers came into being, largely to combat the Ulster Volunteers. These latter were raised by Edward Carson in January 1913 to defend the right of Ulster to remain united with Great Britain. In 1916 the Irish Volunteers siezed the Post Office in Lower O'Connell Street as their headquarters and the Easter Rising had begun. It was quickly crushed, but so brutally that public conscience, clearly appalled, overwhelmingly elected Sinn Fein at the general election of December 1918 with de Valera as the new president. Whilst the Dublin faction were openly in support of the guerilla bands operating across the country, the Ulster Unionists set up their own provisional government, and the ambushes and assassinations which characterised the Anglo-Irish War, featuring the notorious Black and Tans, began in bloody earnest. The war ended in the truce of July 1921. Despite the ratification of the Irish Free State in January 1922, a large and dissatisfied faction of leaders in the Irish movement took up arms against their former comrades and seized the Four Courts, which they held for two months. The subsequent shelling ordered by the new Dublin Government destroyed much of O'Connell Street but by the 1930s most of the public buildings had been restored.

Districts

Dublin is compact and quite small for a capital city, and its city centre extends for only a mile or so along O'Connell Street and Grafton Street on either side of the Liffey. The river flows from west to east across the city and is crossed by ten road bridges, two rail- and one foot-bridge. Although no longer the focal point of the city, the O'Connell Bridge is a good central landmark from which to find one's bearings. The city centre, a busy area with cramped, bustling streets, is circled by the north and south circular roads. To the west is the 2,000-acre Phoenix Park and to the east is Dublin Bay. The harbour was begun in 1714 with the embanking of the River Liffey and the construction of the first of the three great sea-walls, the North Wall quay. To the south east is Ballsbridge, an attractive residential area with many small parks and mansion-like houses; the city's diplomatic quarter, it is lined with elegant terraces but ruined by such bizarre blemishes as the American Embassy of 1963–64—a dumpy, circular grille of cement and glass more at home as a fast food restaurant than as anything more dignified. Half a mile beyond lies Sandymount, a seaside community on the sandy shore of the bay. The northern part of the city is mostly quiet, well-to-do residential areas like Clontarf, and the outer suburbs to the south, like Terenure and Rathfarnham, are suburban red-brick with little of interest to the visitor. The hilly promontory of Howth, eight miles to the north on the coast, is a prosperous resort with a castle and lighthouse, and to the south the city runs into Dun Laoghaire (pronounced 'Dunleary'), which is the terminal for ferries from Holyhead and Heysham.

Streets

Walking south down the centre of Dublin, one comes first to O'Connell Street, now a bawdy honky-tonk strip alive with cinemas, ice-cream parlours and big stores. A long, spacious street, once the haunt of fashionable Dublin society, it was planned on a grand scale in 1784; all that is left of its classical heyday is Francis Johnston's handsome façade of the General Post Office. Westmoreland Street, the continuation to the south of O'Connell Bridge, was laid out as a shopping street in 1800, with elegant pilastered ground storeys. Walking south past Trinity College on the left we come to Grafton Street; originally a country lane and later a fashionable 18thC residential street, it is now a chic and expensive shopping area. Harcourt Street, running ahead after St Stephen's Green Park, is a once-fashionable late 18thC residential street, built on a gentle curve; now a flourishing commercial centre with numerous hotels. Heading east from St Audoen's Church is High Street, the major artery of Medieval Dublin; it has remains of two of the Norse town's parish churches. Skirting the famous Christchurch Cathedral ahead is Christchurch Place, also a centre of the Norse and Medieval city. Past Edward Street and Cork Hill, with City Hall and the castle, we come to Dame Street; widened in 1785–86, it is the main commercial and insurance centre of Dublin, and home of the handsome Commercial Buildings of 1796–99, by Edward Parkes. Past College Green and Trinity College, we come to Dawson Street, a fashionable residential district of early 18thC Dublin with some fine houses, including the Mansion House of 1705 and Academy House of 1770.

Cathedrals, abbeys & churches

Dublin is filled with religious edifices, many worth a visit. **Christchurch Cathedral**, in Christchurch Place was heavily restored by George Edmund Street between 1871–78. A church was originally founded here by Dunan, Bishop of Dublin, in 1038; the

thedral itself was founded by Strongbow in 1173
and is, with St Patrick's, one of the best examples in
eland of early Gothic architecture. It has an
nusual 12thC crypt running the length of the
aurch and an ambulatory with three chapels
tached; the aisled six-bay nave was completed in
234 and the choir which, with the transepts, is
 transitional in style, was completed in 1250 and
rgely reconstructed by Street in the 19thC. The
elfry was built in 1330.

t Patrick's
runstone
ublin

t Patrick's Cathedral in Patrick Street is over 340
eet in length, the longest cathedral in Ireland. Like
Christchurch, it is a fine example of Early English
rchitecture, with a cruciform plan, simpler in
etail, and marvellously spacious. The National
Cathedral of the Church of Ireland, it was built
etween 1220–54 and was restored in the 19thC.
There are several interesting tombs including that of
onathan Swift, who was Dean here for 32 years. In
he south transept is a door with a hole in it where
he Earls of Ormond and Kildare finally shook hands
n 1491, after years of conflict.
St Audoen's, in the High Street, is Dublin's only
urviving medieval church, with a portal of 1190.
The bell tower, restored in the 19thC, has three
5thC bells. Confusingly enough, in the same street
we find St Audoen's RC Church. Designed by
Patrick Byrne in 1841–47, it has a monumental,
liff-like exterior with a huge Corinthian portico
dded by Stephen Ashlin in 1898; wonderful
neoclassical interior with a barrel-vaulted roof, lit by
unettes cut into the roof above a bold cornice. St
Mary's Abbey in Meetinghouse Lane is a Cistercian
oundation, established in 1139; remains include a
ine vaulted Chapter House of 1190. Another very
arly site is that of St Michan's Church in Church
Street; founded in 1095 and largely rebuilt in 1685, it
s a rectangular church with a gallery, west tower,
crypt with mummified bodies and fine 18thC organ
said to have been played by Handel. St Werburgh's
Church in Werburgh Street was originally the site of
an Anglo-Norman foundation, but the present
church was built 1715–19 and rebuilt following a fire
between 1759–68; lovely interior by John Smith,
with fine carved pulpit by Richard Stewart.
The 19thC has also left a fine ecclesiastical legacy.
The Augustinian Church in Thomas Street is one of
he finest Gothic Revival buildings in Dublin; it was
designed by E W Pugin and G C Ashlin in 1862 and
has a mountainous exterior with lofty side aisles to
he nave and 160-foot-high tower crowned by a
spire. St Saviour's in Dominick Street was
designed by J J McCarthy, a disciple of Pugin, in
1858; it's an extravagant French-style Gothic edifice
with bold west door under a triangular hood

crowned by a large rose window. St Stephen's in
Mount Street Crescent is a handsome neoclassical
church with Erechtheon-inspired Greek-style
portico; the belfry tower is modelled on the
monument of Lysicrates, Athens. Terminating the
view up Upper Mount Street, from Merrion Square,
it was designed by John Bowden in 1824.
Other sights worth mentioning include the
University Church on St Stephen's Green South, a
neo-Byzantine marble monolith and St Mary's
Pro-Cathedral in Cathedral Street, a Greek
Doric-style building modelled on the Church of St
Philippe, Rue St Honoré, Paris; built 1815–25 by
John Sweetman, it has a domed interior and
monumental hexastyle portico. St Mary's in Mary
Street is a handsome galleried church designed by
Thomas Burgh in 1627; associated with many
famous people, it was here that Wolfe Tone was
baptised in 1763 and Sean O'Casey in 1880. St
George's in Temple Street is a neoclassical church,
acting as a handsome focal point for three city
streets; designed by Francis Johnston in 1802, it has
a bold portico and 200-foot-high steeple modelled on
St Martin-in-the-Fields, London. Known as Adam
and Eve's, the Franciscan Church in Merchant's
Quay was designed 1830 by Patrick Byrne with a
severe neoclassical façade articulated by pilasters and
a plain belfry tower to one side crowned by a tiny
Greek temple. The Church of St Francis Xavier in
Upper Gardiner Street was designed by Joseph
Keane in 1832, and has a Latin cross plan and
elegant Ionic portico. Finally, St Anne's Church in
Dawson Street, designed by Isaac Wells in 1720, has
a galleried interior and curved apse; the
Romanesque-style façade was added by Sir Thomas
Deane in 1868.

Interesting buildings

Many of the most intriguing sights in Dublin lie
along the central north/south axis of the city. At the
north of the city centre is Great Denmark Street,
where you will find Belvedere House. A handsome
five-bay town house with a projecting Tuscan-style
porch in the centre of a rusticated ground storey, it
was designed by Michael Stapleton in 1785 and
became a Jesuit school in 1841. James Joyce was one
of its pupils. At the south end of the street is Parnell
Square, with the Municipal Art Gallery and the
Rotunda Hospital, a complex of buildings including
Ireland's first maternity hospital. The Doric façade,
linked by curving colonnades to flanking pavilions,
was designed by Richard Castle in 1751. The
Rotunda, a lofty 80-foot-diameter hall, was designed
in 1755 by George Ensor to provide financial support
for the hospital. To the north east are the New
Assembly Rooms. Designed by Richard Johnston
1784–86, they were also intended to provide
additional support for the hospital.
Continuing south from the square, past the Gate
Theatre, is O'Connell Street, with the General Post
Office on the right. Designed by Francis Johnston
and completed in 1818, it has a two-storey astylar
façade raised above a rusticated ground storey; a
lofty Ionic portico, with fluted columns and statuary
crowning the pediment, straddles the pavement in
front. Shortly before O'Connell Street reaches the
river, Abbey Street runs off to the east. Here stands
the famous Abbey Theatre, a banal, contemporary-
style building on the site of the historic theatre of
Yeats, Synge and O'Casey, which was destroyed by
fire in 1951. The new theatre, designed by Michael
Scott, was opened in 1966. At the far end of the
street, on the river, stands the Custom House. The
masterpiece of James Gandon, who designed it in
1781, it has a magnificent long riverside frontage
with projecting ends articulated by a recessed loggia,

Customs House, Dublin 1781

whilst a high central block is punctuated by a bold pedimented portico and the whole Baroque complex is crowned with a slender dome on a columned drum.

Further west at Aston Quay is the **Halfpenny Bridge**, so called because of the toll pedestrians once had to pay to cross the bridge; it is an elegantly spidery structure, springing across the River Liffey in one single cast-iron arch. At nearby College Green is the 1729 **Bank of Ireland**, designed by Sir Edward Lovett Pearce. It was originally the old Parliament House, the first of a series of great public buildings erected in 18thC Dublin, and has a monumental Ionic colonnaded front façade to which curved wings were later added. To the west at the end of Dame Street is Cork Hill, where we find **City Hall** and **Dublin Castle**. City Hall in Lord Edward Street was originally designed as the Royal Exchange by Thomas Cooley between 1769–79, and remodelled in the 19thC; it is a square-plan building with a handsome Corinthian portico and walls articulated by a giant order of Corinthian pilasters. The castle was originally built 1204–28 as part of Dublin's defensive system. The Record or Wardrobe Tower is the principal remnant of the 13thC Anglo-Norman fortress and has 16-foot-thick walls. The 15thC Bermingham Tower was once the state prison, where Red Hugh O'Donnell was interned in the 16thC. In Lower Castle Yard is the Gothic Revival-style Royal Chapel, designed by Francis Johnston 1807–14. Also of interest; the State Apartments, formerly the residence of the English viceroys, and the Heraldic Museum.

Returning to College Green, the famous **Trinity College** dominates the intersection. Of the original Elizabethan college, founded in 1592, the only remains are the Royal Arms beside the Library. The cruciform complex wrapped round quadrangles and gardens has an impressive 300-foot Palladian façade designed by Henry Keene and John Sanderford in 1759, with a pedimented central section with engaged columns standing on high plinths and flanked by projecting end pavilions articulated by

New Museum, Trinity College, Dublin 1854

Corinthian pilasters. Sir William Chambers designed the chapel and theatre; Richard Castle designed the Printing House, a miniature temple, and the handsome 18thC Dining Hall. The Great Library, a long, red-brick building, was designed by Thomas Burgh in 1712. The Museum, a Venetian-style building, was built by Deane and Woodward in 1853. On the south east is the New Library, designed by Ahrends, Burton and Koralek, 1961–67, a handsomely austere building of boldly articulated blockwork volumes oversailing glazed entrances and oriels. The library's great treasures include the 8thC Book of Kells, the Book of Durrow, the Book of Armagh and the Liber Hymnorum. To the south west of the college on South William Street stands **Powerscourt House**, a classical-style mansion designed by Robert Mack, 1771–74, and consisting of a huge cliff-like frontage crowned by a blind attic storey. South east is St Stephen's Green; on the west side stands the **Royal College of Surgeons**, an essay in laid-back classicism with spacious proportions by Edward Park, 1806–27. Heading off St Stephen's Green North is Dawson Street, with the **Mansion House**, 1705, on the right. It has been the official residence of the Lord Mayor of Dublin since 1715. The stucco façade was a remodelling in the 19thC to accommodate the Round Room. To the east in Kildare Street is **Leinster House**. Originally a handsome town mansion designed by Richard Castle for the Earl of Kildare in 1745, it has been the Parliament House since 1922. Behind it in Upper Merrion Street are the **Government Buildings**. Designed by Sir Aston Webb and Sir Thomas Deane, they were begun in 1904 and represent an heroic Edwardian reinterpretation of the grand Georgian masterpieces built along the river front in the 18thC, with end sections with recessed columns and a central columned entrance flanked by tall, narrow, pedimented pavilions.

Four Courts, Dublin

To the north of the river on Inns Quay is the **Four Courts**. Almost completely destroyed in 1922, it was later rebuilt. Designed by James Gandon in 1785, it has a 450-foot river frontage and a square central block with circular hall crowned by a shallow dome carried on a high columned drum. The central block, with a great Corinthian portico, is connected to flanking wings by rusticated arcaded screen walls punctuated centrally by triumphal arches. West of the Four Courts in Blackhall Place is **King's Hospital**, also called Blue Coat School. Founded in 1669, it is a handsome Palladian-style complex designed by Thomas Ivory, 1780. It is owned by the Law Society. North of the Four Courts are the **King's Inns**, in Bolton Street. Designed by James Gandon in 1795, there is a central block with columned recess on the first floor crowned by an octagonal, columned cupola and flanked by pedimented pavilions and side-wings added at a later date; handsome dining hall and fine library. North west of the Four Courts is **Broadstone Railway**

Station, a boldly austere Graeco-Egyptian-style building designed by John Skipton Mulvany in 1850. Terminus of the old Midland Great Western line to Galway and Sligo, it's a daringly plain building with a projecting central section tapering, with the entrance portal, like an Egyptian temple pylon.

Broadstone Station
Dublin 1850

To the north east of the city centre in Portland Row is **Aldborough House**; thought to have been designed by Sir William Chambers in 1796, it is one of the grandest of Dublin's Georgian town houses. Further out, in the Marino district, is the **Marino Casino**, a miniature Palladian-style masterpiece designed by Sir William Chambers in 1762. Built as a little pleasure-house beside Lord Charlemont's country residence for the enormous sum of £60,000, it's a remarkably compact building planned in a Greek cross and articulated by both free-standing columns and pilasters with rusticated main walls. The circular hall inside, ringed by columns, is crowned by a coffered dome. The graceful urns crowning the attic storey are chimneys.
To the west of the city on the south bank of the river is **Heuston Station**. Originally Kingsbridge Station, it's a pompous palazzo-style building with flanking cupolas by Sancton Wood, 1845–61; the great iron and glass passenger shed is by the engineer, Sir John Macneill. A large, airy structure of great distinction. South of the station in Steeven's Lane is **Steeven's Hospital**; one of the oldest public hospitals in Ireland, it was designed round an arcaded courtyard by Thomas Burgh in 1720. To the west, in the Kilmainham district, is the **Royal Hospital**, consisting of a two-storey quadrangle with elegant tower and spire. It's a gentle Dutch-style classical building designed by Sir William Robinson in 1680–87.

Parks, gardens & squares
Phoenix Park, covering over 1,760 acres, is the best-known park in Ireland. Enclosed by an 8-mile-long stone wall, the park was laid out in the mid-18thC and was the scene of the Phoenix Park murders in 1882, when the Chief Secretary and Under-Secretary for Ireland were assassinated. The park includes a number of buildings, the most important of which is Aras an Uachtarain; a private house built in 1751, it later became the house of the President of Ireland when Dr Douglas Hyde moved there in 1938. Other buildings are the houses of the Pope's ambassador and the American ambassador; St Mary's Hospital with handsome chapel by Thomas Cooley of 1771; the Magazine Fort of 1734. There is a racecourse at the north end, the people's gardens by the main entrance on Parkgate Street, and a zoo. The **National Botanic Gardens** in Glasnevin provide 50 acres of magnificent gardens with a fabulous collection of plants, shrubs and trees, established in 1790. Many of the plants come from tropical Africa and South America.
In the heart of the city, **St Stephen's Green** was originally an open common enclosed in 1663. The earliest as well as the largest of Dublin's squares, it is encircled by magnificent 18thC and 19thC buildings, in particular no 85 by Richard Castle in 1739; no 86 by Robert West in 1765; on the west side, nos 119–20 by Richard Castle and the Royal College of Surgeons by Edward Pike in 1806. The Green itself, opened to the general public in 1877, has a kind of duck-pond landscape more in keeping with the bizarre University Church opposite than the elegant Georgian buildings still remaining. To the south east is **Fitzwilliam Square**, the Harley Street of Dublin. It is the smallest and handsomest of the city's Georgian squares and was laid out in 1825. It was here that W B Yeats lived at no 42 between 1928–32; fine brick-fronted town houses with elegant entrance portals. **Merrion Square**, to the north, is a large Georgian square lined with elegant, brick-fronted town houses; it was planned by James Ensor in 1762. On the west side is 18thC Leinster House, now Parliament House, with the 19thC National Gallery to the north. Daniel O'Connell lived at no 58, the parents of Oscar Wilde at no 21 and W B Yeats at no 52 from 1922–28. **College Green**, at the junction of Grafton Street, Dame Street and Westmoreland Street, is the last remnant of medieval Hoggen Green. Focal point of the city, it has Trinity College to the east and the Bank of Ireland to the north. In the north part of the city is **Parnell Square**. Second oldest of Dublin's great Georgian squares, it was begun in the mid-18thC; on the east side is Charlemont House, now the Municipal Gallery of Modern Art, a fine town mansion by Sir William Chambers, 1762. **Mountjoy Square**, a handsome but sadly decayed square, was laid out in 1818; no 50 is the headquarters of the Irish Georgian Society. **St Anne's Park**, to the north east in Dollymount, is a large park covering over 270 acres and wooded with evergreen, oak, pine, beech, chestnut and lime. There is a lovely rose garden, opened in 1975. Formerly the house of the Guinness family.

Museums & galleries
The **National Museum** in Kildare Street houses a fabulous collection of national antiquities including Bronze Age gold ornaments. The **Dublin Civic Museum** in South William Street has a permanent exhibition about the City of Dublin. The **National Gallery**, in Merrion Square West, was opened in 1864 and has a fine collection of old masters including drawings, watercolours and miniatures; Irish works include paintings by the celebrated Jack B Yeats, who died in 1957. There is an Art Reference Library. The **National Library** in Kildare Street offers over half a million books as well as an extensive collection of maps, prints and manuscripts and an invaluable collection of Irish newspapers.

Library, Trinity College, Dublin
1961-67

Trinity College Library, in College Green, is the oldest and most famous of the city's libraries, and has over a million books plus a magnificent collection of early illuminated manuscripts, including the famous Book of Kells.

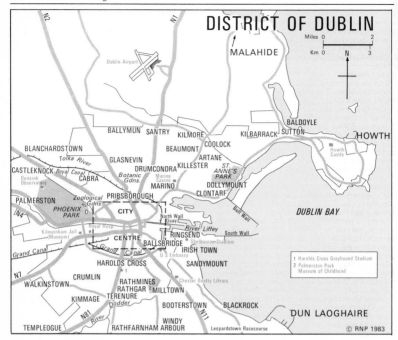

The **Museum of Childhood**, in Palmerston Park, Rathmines, has a charming private collection of antique dolls and toys. The **Royal Irish Academy** is in Dawson Street. Established 1852 in an 18thC house designed by James Ensor, it has a priceless

Gate of Kilmainham Jail, Dublin

collection of early Irish manuscripts, including the Book of Ballymote and the Book of the Dun Cow. The **Municipal Gallery of Modern Art** in Parnell Square was established in 1908. It has a fine collection of European and Irish artists, including a group of paintings from the famous Lane Collection featuring Renoir, Manet, Boudin, Corot and others. The **Chester Beatty Library and Gallery of Oriental Art** in Shrewsbury Road houses one of the finest collections of oriental manuscripts and miniatures in the world. The **Kilmainham Jail Historical Museum**, celebrated in Irish history, was built in 1796 when it housed its first political prisoners. The countless patriots imprisoned here until 1924 include Emmet and his United Irishmen colleagues, the Fenians, the Invincibles, and the Irish Volunteers of the Easter Rising. Abandoned in 1924, it was restored from 1960 as a national monument and historical museum. It was opened by Eamon de Valera, Easter 1966.

Special attractions

Bewley's Café in Grafton Street is a bustling place with bent-wood chairs and tiered cake racks on each table, from which you help yourself. A nostalgic journey into Dublin's past; good coffee. The **Guinness Brewery** in St James's Gate was established in 1759 and is now the largest exporting brewery in the world. Children under 12 not admitted. The **Zoological Gardens** are in Phoenix Park. Famed for the breeding of lions and other large cats, the zoo has attractive gardens encircling two natural lakes, filled with pelicans, flamingoes, ducks and geese. The **Dunsink Observatory**, to the north of Phoenix Park, was established in 1783 and is one of the oldest observatories in the world. There are two major racecourses on the edge of the city, in Phoenix Park and at Leopardstown, although the Irish classics are run at the Curragh. One of Ireland's leading spectator sports is greyhound racing. The chief venues are at the Shelbourne Park Stadium, Ringsend on *Mon, Wed & Sat* and at Harold's Cross Stadium on *Tue, Thur & Fri.*

Entertainment

There are a number of fine theatres, including the celebrated **Abbey Theatre** in Lower Abbey Street, which is the National Theatre, performing works by Synge, O'Casey, Shaw, etc; the **Peacock Theatre** in the same street; the **Gaiety Theatre**, South King Street; the **Eblana Theatre**, Stone Street; the **Project Arts Centre**, a more avant-garde theatre in East Essex Street; the **Gate Theatre**, Parnell Square and the **Olympia Theatre**, Dame Street, which are more commercial in content. Numerous cinemas, including the **Irish Film Theatre** in Earlsfort Terrace.

Live jazz or traditional Irish music abound in the city's numerous pubs. There is a veritable warren of pubs of all sizes, 600 in all. Of interest are: **Doheny and Nesbitt** in Lower Baggot Street, with its early Victorian aura; **Neary's**, in Chatham Street, a plush, spacious place with marble counter; **Davy Byrne's** at 21 Duke Street, a Cheerful Charlie of a place with a glorious red façade, mentioned in James Joyce's 'Ulysses', since when it has not looked back; **The Brazen Head** in Lower Bridge Street, a pint-sized pub with bags of atmosphere, said to be the oldest in Dublin; **James Toner's** in Lower Baggot Street, a delightfully old-world pub with engraved mirrors and partitioned bar; and **McDaids** at no 3 Harry Street, a high-ceilinged hole once the haunt of Dublin literary luminaries such as Patrick Kavanagh and Brendan Behan.

Shopping

Mainly centred round Grafton Street and O'Connell Street. The former is the smartest; a world of well-heeled young ladies in natty attire, it is the Bond Street of Dublin with high-style *haute couture*, Waterford Crystal and Donegal Tweed. O'Connell Street is a more earthy sort of place, a kind of New Oxford Street alight with neon and bright with beefburgers and cheaper stores. The surrounding side-streets and arcades abound in antiques, lace and Celtic crafts.

Duncannon   8 M17

Co Wexford, 2 miles S of Arthurstown. Relaxing seaside resort with fine sandy beach.

Dundalk   5 N8

Co Louth. Pop 21,670. EC Thur. Busy seaport and market town at the head of Dundalk Bay. Legendary prehistoric fortress, guarding a gap in the mountains to the north, and early Celtic stronghold; a powerful Norse fleet was captured here in AD929. Taken by the Anglo-Normans in 1177, it was made a borough by King John in 1220. It was captured by Edward Bruce in 1316 and he was killed in the defence of it in 1318. A frontier town of the English Pale, the Jacobite army withdrew in 1690 leaving the town to its fate in the hands of the Williamites.

Of interest: St Nicholas Parish Church, remnants of 13thC building remodelled in 1689 and again by Francis Johnston in the early 19thC; St Patrick's Catholic Church of 1848, a carbon copy of King's College Chapel, Cambridge; Seatown Castle, really the tower of a Franciscan friary of 1240; 19thC Seatown Windmill, at seven storeys high one of the largest windmills in Ireland; the Court House of 1813–18 and 19thC Town Hall, once the Corn Exchange. 1½ miles to the west is Castletown Castle, a four-storey tower house built 1472–79. Good

Court House, Dundalk

fishing for sea trout, brown trout and salmon on the Rivers Fane and Glyde.

Dun Laoghaire   5 O11

Co Dublin. Pop 98,380. EC Wed. Major ferry port from Holyhead as well as Dublin's largest suburb and seaside resort; known as Kingstown from 1821–1920, in commemoration of a visit here by George IV, the resort is named after Laoghaire, a 5thC Irish king who built a fortress here. It has a magnificent promenade—tree-lined Marine Parade, a mile-long wall of gaily coloured buildings gently indented round Scotsman's Bay to the south east and bulging out to the north west by the giant granite artificial harbour, built by John Rennie in 1817–21 for the mailboat service. Punctuating the junction between sweeping concave and convex curves are the tall, thin towered spires of two churches. East Pier is another popular mile-long promenade, complete with summertime band concerts. To the west, across Marine Parade, are Pavilion Gardens with the handsome Gothic Revival town hall, resplendent in multicoloured brickwork, opposite. Ireland's principal yachting centre, it has two particularly splendid yacht clubs designed by J S Mulvany: the Royal St George, 1832, and the Royal Irish, 1846. There is also a splendid granite-built neoclassical railway station. In Sandy Cove, the birthplace of Sir Roger Casement, on a tiny peninsula of land to the east of Scotsman's Bay, there is James Joyce's Tower, once temporary residence and now museum of the author housed in a Martello tower, built 1806, and Geragh, a white rendered international-style house of 1937 by Michael Scott. There is a National Maritime Museum at the Mariner's Church, Haigh Terrace. Monkston Church, one mile to the west, is a marvellous turreted Gothic Revival church with fine plaster vault designed 1830 by John Semple.

Dun Laoghaire

Sandycove

Good beaches and bathing at Seapoint and Sandycove; pier and rock fishing; Summer Festival *late Jun*, Glencullen Festival *early Jul* and Arts Week *early Sep*.

Fethard 8 M17
Co Wexford. Secluded village on the eastern side of the Hook Peninsula, surrounded by sandy beaches. On the peninsula is the Hook Lighthouse; one of the four oldest lighthouses in the world, the tower is 13thC and a light has been kept burning here since the 4thC.

Giles Quay 3 O8
Co Louth, 4 miles S of Carlingford. Handful of houses battened down along the southern side of the Cooley Peninsula overlooking Dundalk Bay.

Greenore 3 O8
Co Louth. Tiny village on a narrow triangle of land on the edge of a three-mile-long shingle beach beside the entrance to Carlingford Lough.

Greystones 5 O12
Co Wicklow. Pop 4,520. EC Wed. Attractive seaside resort surrounded by woods on the Wicklow coast. Delgany, 1½ miles south west, is a picturesque village hidden amongst the trees. South are the tiny resorts of Kilcoole and Newcastle.

Howth 5 O11
Co Dublin. EC Thur. Picturesque fishing village and resort anchored on the northern shore of the Nose of Howth, a strip of land exploding in the centre in a giant carbuncle of rock, the 560-foot Hill of Howth. The peninsula encloses the northern side of Dublin Bay. One mile north of the harbour is the tiny islet, Ireland's Eye, a favourite picnic spot. Of interest: ruins of Howth Abbey; Howth Castle, a 17thC baronial mansion on earlier foundations with fabulous gardens. Good deep-sea fishing and safe bathing at Claremount Strand and Balscadden Beach.

Killiney 5 O11
Co Dublin, 2½ miles S of Dalkey. Charming little resort of white stuccoed and stone villas set in woodlands running up the eastern slopes of Killiney Hill. The hill rises steeply from the water's edge on the northern shores of beautiful crescent-shaped Killiney Bay. Good bathing from Killiney Beach and White Rock.

Kilmore Quay 8 N17
Co Wexford. Quiet fishing village of thatched cottages with a tiny harbour. The three islands known as the Saltee Islands, a birdwatcher's paradise, can be reached by boat from the harbour. To the west is Bannow, a 12thC Norman town buried in a shifting avalanche of sand in the 17thC, with only the ruins of St Mary's Church standing ghost-like above hills of earth and sand.

Laytown and Bettystown 5 O9
Co Meath. Pop 1,880. EC Thur. These twin resorts stand at either end of a ten-mile-long stretch of sandy beach, Laytown to the south, Bettystown to the north. The beach is famed for the Annual Strand Races when one day each year in either June, July or August depending on the tides, the beach becomes a race course. Of interest: The Maiden Tower, dating from the 17thC, is a beacon for ships entering Drogheda on the River Boyne; Gormanston Castle, built in 1786 four miles south of Laytown, stands on the site of a 14thC castle.

Loughshinny 5 O10
Co Dublin, 2½ miles S of Skerries. Tiny fishing village sheltering on the edge of lovely little bay. Two miles south west is the Holy Well and Oratory of St Mobhi, a 7thC saint.

Malahide 5 O10
Co Dublin. Pop 3,830. EC Wed. Small seaside resort on the southern side of a narrow estuary. To the south west stands battlemented Malahide Castle. Seat of the Talbot family from 1185–1976, twin towers were added in suitably medieval style in 1765. Now in public ownership, it displays a large part of the National Portrait Collection. The oldest part is a keep-like tower dating from the 14thC. Nearby is Emsworth, a handsome pedimented villa with a two-storey recessed central section flanked by one-storey pavilions, designed by James Gandon in 1790.

Malahide Castle

Omeath 3 O7
Co Louth, 6 miles NW of Carlingford. Tiny but popular holiday resort towards the head of Carlingford Lough. You can hire a 'jaunting car' from the strand to the Cavalry Shrine. Omeath Gala Week annually *late Aug*.

Portmarnock 5 O11
Co Dublin, 5 miles NW of Howth. Popular little resort on the edge of Velvet Strand, a three-mile stretch of magnificent sandy beach, with a famous championship golf course. Two miles west is the 12thC–14thC church of St Doulagh; built on the site of the saint's 7thC anchorite cell, it has a high pitched stone roof and 14thC tower.

Rosslare 8 N17
Co Wexford. Pop 590. EC Thur. Pretty resort south east of Wexford on the edge of a six-mile scimitar of sand and shingle. Five miles south is Rosslare Harbour, terminus of car ferries from Fishguard, Cherbourg and Le Havre. Of interest: 18-hole championship golf course; Lady's Island, site of an early Christian monastery in a narrow sea inlet called Lady's Lake four miles south, with remains of an Augustinian priory and 12thC Norman castle. Seven miles north west is Johnstown Castle, 19thC Gothic Revival mansion, now an agricultural college, with fine landscaped gardens. Good sea fishing.

Rush   5 O10
Co Dublin. Weatherbeaten fishing village with a sea of white-faced Dublin day-trippers. At Lusk, four miles west, is a five-storey round tower, sole survivor of a monastery founded originally in the 6thC.

Skerries   5 O10
Co Dublin. Pop 3,040. EC Thur. Popular seaside resort with dry, bracing climate that smacks you in the face. Has all the fun of the sea plus barnacled, fishing-village spirit. Three interesting offshore islands, Shenick, Colt and St Patrick's. Five miles out to sea the Rockabill Lighthouse crowns an isolated acropolis of rock. Three miles south are the 13thC ruins of Baldongan Castle, an Anglo-Norman fortress and scene of a massacre by Cromwellian troops in 1642. Excellent beaches and good, safe bathing. Pier and rock fishing for pollack, mackerel and flatfish.

Wexford   8 N16
Co Wexford. Pop 14,740. EC Thur. A tight knot of winding, narrow streets tied to a long quay along the southern bank of the River Slaney as it opens out into Wexford harbour. Named 'Waesfjord' (the harbour of mud flats) by the Vikings, who established it originally as a base for raiding parties in the 9thC, it soon developed into an important trading post. Captured by the Anglo-Normans in 1169, it became a major English stronghold protected by a huge encircling wall with five fortified gateways and four massive fortresses. Later a Confederate stronghold, it was captured by Cromwell in 1649, who brutally massacred the inhabitants. During the uprising of 1798 it was held by Irish insurgents, following the withdrawal of the English garrison. Of the old town gates only the Westgate Tower, a square battlemented structure, remains. At the north west edge of the town are the ruins of Selskar Abbey, a late 12thC priory; remains include 14thC tower and 15thC nave. At the east end of the town are fragments of 14thC St Patrick's Church. In the town centre are the remains of St Mary's Church, a priory of the Knights Hospitallers. Also of interest: the twin Gothic Revival churches of the Assumption and of the Immaculate Conception, designed 1851–58 by Robert Pierce; no 29 South Main Street, a house where Cromwell stayed in 1649; Maritime Museum, situated in a converted lightship along the quay, has an interesting exhibition of Wexford's seafaring past; Wexford Wildfowl Reserve, situated three miles away on the north shores of Wexford harbour, where white-fronted geese from Greenland winter. Good fishing in the estuary for sea trout, mullet, bass and flounder and in the River Slaney for salmon and brown trout. The Wexford Festival, world-famous opera festival, takes place annually in *late Oct*.

Wicklow   5 O13
Co Wicklow. Pop 3,900. EC Thur. Cheery seaside resort on the lower slopes of Ballyguile Hill at the southern end of a long crescent of bay. A compact nest of salt-aired narrow streets, it was originally a 9thC Norse settlement called Wykinglo, hence the name. Used as a Viking maritime base. Following the Anglo-Norman invasion, granted by Strongbow to Maurice Fitzgerald, who built Black Castle in 1176; it is now a ruin standing on a rocky pedestal east of the town. Considerably strengthened in 1375, the town was frequently attacked by the Irish. Also of interest: remains of a Franciscan friary founded in 1279; 18thC Church of Ireland with square tower and dome incorporating a handsome Romanesque portal; Mount Usher Gardens, four miles north at Ashford; Devil's Glen, a deep, shadowy gorge covered in trees and shrubs five miles north west.

The River Vartry winds its way along a boulder-strewn path tumbling headlong over a 100-foot cliff to the Devil's Punch Bowl, a deep basin in the rock below. Miles of sand and shingle beach with safe bathing. At Brittas Bay, six miles south, there is a three-mile stretch of sandy beach backed by hilly dunes. Good sea fishing for flounder, coalfish and occasionally bass, whilst inland the River Vartry abounds in brown and sea trout.

Islands & peninsulas

Cooley Peninsula   3 O8
Co Louth. Broken nose of land projecting between Dundalk Bay and Carlingford Lough. Sixty square miles, it's a fabulous tract of land sealed amongst mountains with magnificent views out across the lough to the Mountains of Mourne, galloping away in layers of blue to beyond the horizon.

Dalkey Island   5 O11
Off Dalkey, Co Dublin. Largest of a group of islands. Remains of St Begnet's Church, including characteristic lintelled portal and antae at both gable ends, and an early 19thC Martello tower.

Lambay Island   5 O10
Off Rush, Co Dublin. Porphyry outcrop 418 feet high and 617 acres in extent. Scene of the first Viking raid in AD795; remains of curious defence-works, 1551. Now a bird sanctuary, owned by Lord Revelstoke.

Lambay Island

St Patrick's, Shenick & Colt Islands   5 O10
Off Skerries, Co Dublin. Three interesting little islands nestling close to the shore. St Patrick's, locally called 'Church Island', has the ruins of a church said to have been built by St Patrick on his way to Tara; on Shenick, which can be reached on foot at low tide, stands a well preserved Martello tower.

Saltee Islands   8 N17
Off Kilmore Quay, Co Wexford. A group of three islands surrounded by dangerous reefs, once a terror to navigators. During the Wexford insurrection, two of the rebel leaders were caught hiding on Great Saltee and taken to Wexford to be beheaded. Now the most famous bird sanctuary in Ireland, with a population in late spring and summer of over three million birds.

Inland towns & villages

Abbeyleix   5 K13
Co Laois. Pop 1,030. C Wed. Built two miles north east of the site of a now-vanished late 12thC monastery, from which it takes its name. A quiet

Abbeyleix House

town, it was planned in the mid-18thC by Viscount de Vesci and has attractive tree-lined streets, handsome Market House and a church with fine front and spire by John Semple. Nearby is Abbeyleix House and gardens.

Aghavannagh 5 N13
Co Wicklow, 6 miles NW of Aughrim. Remote mountain hamlet hemmed in by mountains in a wild and desolate valley. Reached by the Military Road, which swoops up and over the hills, the youth hostel was once one of the blockhouses built in a chain to guard the road. In the late 19thC it was used by Parnell as a shooting box and in the early 20thC by John Redman, leader of the Irish Party at Westminster, as a residence.

Annamoe 5 O13
Co Wicklow. Attractive village cloaked in woods in a picturesque spot on the banks of the River Annamoe. It was here that 18thC writer Laurence Sterne, author of 'Tristram Shandy', fell into the churning mill race and miraculously escaped unhurt. The mill is now a ruin.

Ardagh 4 J9
Co Longford, 5 miles SE of Longford. Picturesque cuckoo-clock hamlet built as a model estate village for the Featherstone family in 1863. Goldsmith mistook Ardagh House for a country inn and used the incident in 'She Stoops to Conquer'.

Ardee 5 N8
Co Louth. Pop 3,090. EC Thur. Bustling market town on the banks of the River Dee. Of importance in pre-Christian times, it was here Cuchulainn slew his friend Ferdia after an epic four-day hand-to-hand combat. Ardee was also an important medieval border town of the Pale. Of interest: Ardee Castle, now the Court House, rebuilt in the 15thC round a 13thC keep; 13thC Hatch's Castle with unusual rounded corners; St Mary's Protestant Church incorporating parts of a medieval Carmelite friary; Smarmore Castle, a square 14thC keep four miles south. Good salmon, trout and pike fishing on the River Dee.

Athboy 5 M10
Co Meath. Pop 700. EC Wed. Once a walled stronghold of the Pale, it's now a quiet agricultural town in wooded country along the banks of the River Athboy. One mile east is the Hill of Ward, site of the ancient palace of Tlachtga. Three miles north are the 15thC ruins of Rathmore Castle and church.

Athlone 4 I11
Co Westmeath. Pop 9,820. EC Thur. Busy market town straddling the River Shannon below its exit to the south of Lough Ree. It was occupied by the Anglo-Normans, who built a huge fortress here on the west bank of the River Shannon in 1210–13, a multifaceted castle, now much altered. Of strategic importance during the Elizabethan wars, Athlone was also the setting for a spirited Jacobite defence following their defeat at the Boyne in 1690. Attacked by a Williamite army of 10,000 men, which was repelled, the town finally fell following a ten-day artillery bombardment in 1691. Of interest: remaining portions of the old town walls; ruins of a Franciscan friary of 1241; 18thC Court Devenish Castle; Waterston House, ruins of a handsome classical mansion designed by Richard Castle, five miles north east; octagonal spired dovecote in the gardens. Good coarse fishing on the River Shannon and surrounding loughs. Annual events: All-Ireland Amateur Drama Festival held each *Apr* and The Meadow, two-day horse and pony show held each *Aug*.

Athy 5 M13
Co Kildare. Pop 4,270. EC Thur. Originally a 13thC Anglo-Norman settlement built to control a crossing over the River Barrow, it is now an important market centre and has spread, in leaps and bounds, either side of a junction of the Grand Canal with the River Barrow. Of interest: ruins of Woodstock Castle, 13thC fortress with huge 15thC rectangular tower; Whites Castle, built 1507 to defend the bridge across the river, rebuilt in 1575 with a monumental rectangular tower with square angle turrets; modern Dominican church, built 1963–65 and considered a showpiece of modern Irish architecture, with austere pentagonal plan and rather jarring roof. At Ardscull, four miles north east, there is a 35-foot-high 12thC motte where Edward Bruce defeated an English army in 1315.

Aughrim

Aughrim 8 N14
Co Wicklow. Handful of black-and-white houses in a tranquil setting at the junction of several mountain valleys. The Ow Valley, down which a winding river runs, clambers north west for 10 miles to the foot of the 3,039-foot-high Lugnaquilla Mountain.

Bailieborough 5 L8
Co Cavan. Large village on a spacious main street in the heart of the tumbling hills and crumpled valleys of the quiet lake district of south east Cavan. Some good early 19thC buildings, including the Court House and Market House. Good coarse fishing on the nearby lakes.

Ballybay 5 M7
Co Monaghan. Pop 750. C Thur. Frontier town sheltering among low-lying hills beside the shores of Lough Major. Good coarse fishing on the surrounding lakes and rivers.

Ballyconnell 2 K7
Co Cavan. Celebrated coarse fishing centre, lying along the foot of the rolling Slieve Rushen Hills

eside the River Woodford. Numerous prehistoric
remains in vicinity, including interesting cairnstones
t nearby Ballyheady. Good coarse fishing on the
rivers Woodford and Blackwater.

Ballyjamesduff 5 L8
Co Cavan. Picturesque place built down the side of a
hill to the south of Lough Nadreegeel. Has
delightfully wide streets and no-nonsense granite
market house of 1813. Catapulted to fame by the
popular ballad 'Come Back Paddy Reilly to
Ballyjamesduff' by Percy French. Of interest:
Crosserlough Folk Museum, showing period kitchen
and farm implements.

Ballymahon 4 J10
Co Longford. Pop 700. EC Wed. Small town winding
along a picturesque stretch of the River Inny in the
heart of Goldsmith country. Fine five-arched bridge
leapfrogs across the river. Oliver Goldsmith, the
18thC dramatist, novelist and poet, was born at
Pallas, three miles east. The village of Lissoy, five
miles south west in Co Westmeath, was the "Sweet
Auburn" of Goldsmith's poem, 'The Deserted
Village'. At Abbeyshrule, on the banks of the River
Inny, are the ruins of a 13thC Cistercian abbey.

Baltinglass 8 M13
Co Wicklow. Pop 1,350. EC Wed. Small town on the
banks of the River Slaney, overshadowed by the
1,258-foot-high Baltinglass Hill, which rises steeply
to the east, and the 1,023-foot-high Tinoran Hill to
the west. In the 12thC a Cistercian monastery was
established here by Dermot MacMurrough, a sister
foundation of Mellifont; its remains include south
arcade of choir and nave and parts of the cloister and
the decorative stonework is a synthesis of Cistercian
and Irish Romanesque carving. The Castleruddery
Transport Museum has an interesting collection of
trams and trolley buses. Good trout fishing on the
River Slaney.

Banagher 4 I12
Co Offaly. Pop 1,050. EC Thur. Pretty houses in an
orderly row along the east bank of the River
Shannon. The novelist Anthony Trollope was
stationed here as Post Office surveyor in 1841. There
is a fine house in the High Street with bow-fronted
porch and door crowned by a curved pediment, and
a long, handsome bridge, built 1843. Also of
interest: 13thC Cloghan Castle, two miles south;
Clohony Castle, four miles east, a Tudor fortress
remarkably well preserved; Garry Castle, a huge
MacCoghlan stronghold two miles south east. Trout
fishing on the River Shannon beside the town and on
the River Brosna.

Belturbet 2 K7
Co Cavan. Pop 1,090. C Tue. Attractive, quiet
market town on the east bank of the River Erne,
flanked by the jig-saw winding waters of Lough
Oughter and Upper Lough Erne. By Milltown, 4½
miles south west, are the ruins of 14thC Drumlane
Church and Round Tower, built on the site of a 6thC
abbey. Good trout and coarse fishing on the nearby
lakes and rivers.

Birr 4 J12
Co Offaly. Pop 3,320. C Thur. Attractively situated
in the west of the county near the meeting of the
Rivers Camcor and Brosna, it's a handsomely
planned town laid out in the 18thC and 19thC with
spacious malls and a small square. The Protestant
church, with fine Gothic interior, was designed by
John Johnston in 1810. There is an Ionic temple,
now used as a school house, designed 1828 by Lord
Rosse as a memorial to his son. Birr Castle, rebuilt in
the 17thC on the site of an earlier fortress, was
remodelled by John Johnston in the early 19thC; in

Birr Castle

the lovely grounds are the remains of a gigantic
telescope, designed by the third Earl of Rosse, which
was the largest in the world for over 80 years. Good
trout fishing in the River Brosna. 'Birr Vintage
Week' held annually in Aug.

Blacklion 2 J6
Co Cavan, ½ mile S of Belcoo. Tiny village wedged
between the ice-cold waters of Upper and Lower
Lough MacNean in the rolling foothills west of the
2,188-foot-high Cuilcagh Mountain. Popular
pot-holing district. There are also numerous
prehistoric cairns and ring forts. To the south is
Shannon Pot, source of the River Shannon,
overshadowed by a wall of mountains.

Blessington 5 N12
Co Wicklow. Pop 1,170. EC Wed. Attractive late
17thC village lining a wide tree-lined street. During
the era of horse-drawn mail coaches, it was a staging
post on the Dublin–Carlow run. To the east is a
huge, man-made lake. Nearby is Russborough
House, a handsome Palladian mansion. Good trout
fishing on the lake.

Borris 8 M15
Co Carlow. Picturesque Georgian town on a shoulder
of land in the shadow of the Blackstairs Mountains
and Brandon Hill. Of interest: beautiful demesne of
Borris House; remains of the monastery of St
Mullins, nine miles south. Good trout and salmon
fishing on the River Barrow to the south.

Borris-in-Ossory 4 J13
Co Laois. One-horse town consisting of a single long
main street lined by a meandering wall of houses.
Once a strategic gateway to Munster, the highway
was guarded by the now-ruined Fitzpatrick
stronghold. At Aghaboe, a little to the south east, are
the remains of an Augustinian priory, founded in the
6thC and largely rebuilt in 1346. Nearby are the
ruins of a Dominican friary, built in 1382, consisting
of a long nave and south chapel.

Bunclody 8 M15
Co Wexford, 7 miles NW of Ferns. Pop 1,540. EC
Thur. Picturesque huddle of houses on the River

Slaney, which winds its way through the rolling foothills of Mount Leinster along the boundary of Co Wexford. The Blackstairs mountain range forms a curtain here between the counties of Wexford and Carlow. The River Slaney, which is one of Ireland's best salmon rivers, is also excellent for trout fishing.

Callan 8 K15
*Co Kilkenny, 10 miles SW of Kilkenny. Pop 2,050.
EC Thur.* Busy market town on a fertile plain west of Kilkenny. Granted its charter by William Marshall in 1271, it was a flourishing walled town in the Middle Ages. An Augustinian friary was established here in 1462. Interesting remains include long rectangular church crowned by a central tower and · with a handsome sedilia in the choir and the Parish Church of St Mary's, which was built originally in 1460 on the site of an early 13thC church.

Augustinian friary, Callan

Famous residents include Robert Furton, designer of the world's first steamship, who was born here in 1765; the famous Fenian novelist and poet, John Locke, was born here in 1847. In Westcourt, on the edge of the town, is a recently restored 18thC farmstead where Edmund Ignatius Rice, founder of the Irish Christian Brothers, was born in 1762. Good trout fishing on the River Kings.

Carlow 5 M14
Co Carlow. Pop 9,600. EC Thur. Thriving market and manufacturing centre scattered along the east bank of the River Barrow, once a strategic Anglo-Norman stronghold. A motte-and-bailey castle was first built here in 1180 to control the river crossing. It was replaced by a stone fortress, built shortly after the town was given its charter in 1208; planned as a huge rectangular keep with drum towers at the corners, it was considered one of the finest Norman castles in Leinster but was largely demolished in the early 19thC by attempts to dynamite parts of the castle to make room for building a lunatic asylum. Once a walled town standing on the edge of the Pale, Carlow was beset by bitter struggles for possession, frequently changing hands during the Cromwellian Wars, and was the scene of a bloody battle in 1798 when over 690 Irish insurgents were killed in hand-to-hand fighting in the winding streets. Also of interest: handsome courthouse designed 1830 by William Morrison; Catholic cathedral, a Gothic Revival essay of 1833 with 151-foot-high lantern tower; Browne's Hill Dolmen, two miles east, with largest capstone in Ireland, if not Europe, 5 feet thick, 20 feet square and weighing about 100 tons; Oak Park, handsome 19thC house with Ionic portico, two miles north east; Killeshin Church, three miles west, with remains of fine Romanesque chapel and portal.

Carrickmacross 3 M8
Co Monaghan. Pop 2,100. C Wed. Granted to the Earl of Essex, who built a castle here, by Elizabeth I. It consists of a spacious main street flanked by multicoloured buildings. Attractive town celebrated for its hand-made lace, an industry flourishing here since 1820. Of interest: Mannan Castle, a huge hilltop motte and bailey of the early 13thC. Inniskeen Folk Museum, seven miles north east; Inniskeen Round Tower, remains of a monastery founded in the 6thC.

Castleblayney 3 M7
Co Monaghan. Quiet town spread down a ridge of land along the north western corner of picturesque Lough Muckno, the largest of the Monaghan lakes. Good trout fishing on Loughs Muckno and Ross and excellent coarse fishing on numerous other nearby lakes.

Castlecomer 5 L14
Co Kilkenny. Pop 1,890. EC Wed. Little town on the site of an Anglo-Norman castle destroyed in 1200, from which it takes its name. It lies cradled in a wooded valley amongst the hills of northern Kilkenny. Planted by English colonists in the early 17thC, the town was planned and landscaped in an elegant Italianate manner in 1637 and has a handsome, tree-lined central boulevard. Captured by the confederate Catholics in 1641, it was also attacked and set on fire during the uprising of 1798. Once the centre of the country's largest coalfield, it's now a quiet country backwater. Good trout fishing on the River Dinan.

Castledermot 5 M13
Co Kildare. Originally an Anglo-Norman settlement where Hugh de Lacy built a fortress in the 12thC, it is now a small peat town. Interesting remains include a 10thC round tower, two 9thC or 10thC granite crosses and the ruins of a Franciscan friary. Three miles north west is Kilkea Castle; built originally in 1180, it was restored in 1849 and is now a luxury hotel and health farm.

Castlepollard 5 K9
Co Westmeath. Pop 690. EC Thur. Angling centre in the low hills to the north east of Lough Derravaragh. Of interest: Tullynally Castle and gardens 1½ miles north west, a 17thC garrison house Gothicised by Francis Johnston 1804–6, with a flamboyant forest of towers and turrets.

Cavan 5 K8
Co Cavan. Pop 3,270. C Mon. County town with pretentious neo-Renaissance cathedral in a sea of green hills on the edge of spectacular lake district to the north west. Of interest: pedimented Court House with Doric porch, the Royal Arms and Protestant church, all early 19thC buildings by John Bowden, a Dublin architect; belfry tower, sole survivor of 14thC Franciscan friary; Clough Oughter, 14thC circular keep built on an island in Lough Oughter five miles north west. Cavan International Song Contest held annually in *mid-Apr.* Good trout and coarse fishing on nearby rivers and lakes.

Celbridge 5 N11
Co Kildare, 4½ miles SW of Lucan. Picturesque village with large 18thC mills, on the banks of the River Liffey. This was the early 18thC home of Esther Vanhomrigh, who became involved with the author Jonathan Swift and is immortalised in his poem, "Cadenus and Vanessa". At the eastern end of the village is Castletown, the finest 18thC house in Ireland. Also of interest: Oakley Park, 1720; Conolly's Folly, an 18thC monument to William Conolly, 1¾ miles to the west.

Clara 4 J11

Co Offaly. Originally a Quaker settlement, now a market and manufacturing town by the River Brosna. Handsome Protestant church of 1770. Good trout fishing on the river.

Clonard 5 L11

Co Meath, 9 miles W of Innfield. Tiny village on the site of the great monastic school founded by St Finian in the 6thC and an Augustinian foundation established in 1175. No trace remains of either. It was here that the last major battle of the 1798 rebellion was fought.

Clondra 4 J9

Co Longford, 5 miles W of Longford. Delightful village with an old stone harbour on the Royal Canal. There is a Teach Cheoil or Irish Music House, where traditional Irish music, song and dance are performed. Its twin village, Tarmonbarry on the banks of the River Shannon, is an overnight stop for cruisers.

Clones 5 L7

Co Monaghan. Pop 2,160. C Tue. Important agricultural centre on the Fermanagh border. Site of an early Christian monastery founded in AD549; remains include a 75-foot-high round tower from a later abbey and a 15-foot-high Celtic cross standing in the main square. Also of interest: St Tighearnach's Grave, an early Christian sarcophagus; Tiredigan Court Cairn, an early Bronze Age courtyard on a steep slope. Two miles east is Aughnakillagh, where James Connolly (one of the leaders of the 1916 rising) was born in 1870.

Cootehill 3 L7

Co Cavan, 10 miles NW of Shercock. Pop 1,410. Prosperous town lying on a terrace of land between the Rivers Annagh and Dromore. The town was founded in the 17thC by the Cootes, on land confiscated from the O'Reillys. To the north of the town is Bellamont Forest; one of the finest Palladian houses in Ireland, it was built for Thomas Coote 1729–30. Fine double court cairn at Cohaw, three miles to the south east.

Daingean 5 K11

Co Offaly. Located on the Grand Canal, it was originally named Philipstown after Philip II of Spain, consort of 'Bloody Mary'. Originally the county town, it never grew and by 1833 this role passed to Tullamore. The Court House is by James Gandon.

Droichead Nua 5 M12

Co Kildare. Pop 6,440. EC Tue. Built along the banks of the River Liffey around an early 19thC British Cavalry barracks; now a thriving industrial centre. At Great Connell, 1½ miles south east, are the remains of an Augustinian abbey founded in 1202; once one of the most important Anglo-Irish monasteries, it was suppressed in 1541.

Duleek 5 N9

Co Meath. Pop 660. EC Wed. Handful of houses spilled in a shallow saucer of land in the winding River Nanny valley. The site of a 5thC monastic establishment, the village was frequently plundered between AD830 and 1149. Hugh de Lacy founded an Augustinian priory here in 1182; fragments remain near the river, and in the cemetery above the village is the 80-foot belfry. Standing in the village is the Dowdall Cross, a decorated wayside cross erected in 1601. It was across the bridge to the south east of the village that the Jacobite army retreated in 1690. Duleek House is a handsome Georgian stone mansion designed 1750 by Richard Castle with a tall, narrow pedimented central section and pedimented

Duleek Priory

door with side lights and Palladian window above. Donore, a little village four miles north, is near the site of the Battle of the Boyne in July 1690, when James II lost the crown of England to William III. Three miles south is Athcarne Castle, a monumental Elizabethan mansion.

Durrow 8 K14

Co Laois. Attractive village encircling a large green along the banks of the River Erkina with the woods of Castle Durrow for shelter. Designed by William Flower, its first owner, in 1713–32, the castle is a handsome Renaissance-style house with a two-storey façade articulated by giant pilasters and an attic storey in the large hipped roof above a bold cornice.

Edenderry 5 L11

Co Offaly. Pop 2,950. C Mon. Handsome Georgian market town entrenched in low-lying country amongst the ruined border castles on the edge of the Pale. On a hilltop south of the town are the ruins of Blundell's Castle. The 2nd Marquess of Downshire, who acquired the Edenderry property through marriage in the late 18thC, built much of the town including the elegant Corn Market of 1826, which was also used as the Court House. Recently burnt, it was reconstructed as the Father Paul Murphy Memorial Hall. Two miles north are the ruins of 13thC Carrickoris Castle and medieval church. Two miles west lie the ruins of Monasteroris Monastery; founded in 1325, remains consist of ruined church and dovecot. A Celtic cross in the graveyard marks the burial place of two leaders of the 1798 uprising who were hanged at Edenderry. Nearby is Kinnafad Castle, a de Bermingham stronghold. Trout fishing on the River Boyne.

Edgeworthstown 4 J9

Co Longford. Pop 540. EC Wed. Neat little market village east of Longford. Of interest: Georgian

Edgeworthstown

Edgeworthstown House, to the east of the village, built for the author and inventor, Richard Lovell Edgeworth, in the late 18thC and now a nursing home; Maria Edgeworth Museum, with mementos of the famous novelist, 1767–1849, and her family, who settled in the village in 1583.

Enniscorthy   8 N15
Co Wexford. Pop 6,640. EC Thur. A tight knot of steeply winding streets on a ridge of land along the River Slaney. Thriving market town in the heart of the lush agricultural lands of Wexford, it was an important Anglo-Norman stronghold where a four-storey castle-keep was built in the 13thC; rebuilt in the late 16thC, it was captured by Cromwell in 1649, used as a prison during the rising of 1798, as a residence in the 19thC and since 1963 it has been a folk museum. Overlooking the town on the east bank of the river is the 398-foot-high Vinegar Hill, with the shell of the windmill where the 1798 rebels made a last stand before the onslaught of General Lake and his 13,000 men. Of interest: St Aidan's Cathedral, a Gothic Revival building designed by Pugin in 1843.

Enniskerry   5 O12
Co Wicklow. Pop 770. EC Wed. Tudor-style estate village of the 19thC arranged picturesquely around a square by the gates of the celebrated Powerscourt Demesne, in 14,000 acres of beautiful countryside with glens and mountains. The 47 acres of gardens at Powerscourt include a 400-foot-high waterfall, the highest in Ireland; there are also fine herds of deer in the park. North of the village is The Scalp, a narrow boulder-strewn gap in the hills through which the main Enniskerry–Dublin road barely squeezes.

Enniskerry
Co Wicklow

Ferns   8 N15
Co Wexford. Pop 700. EC Thur. Once an important 6thC religious settlement, it was plundered by the Norsemen in AD930 and became Dermot MacMurrough's royal capital of Leinster in the 12thC. Portions of MacMurrough's abbey survive, including the tower with square lower stage crowned by a round section. Nearby are the ruins of 16thC St Peter's Church. The castle, a large rectangular keep with round corner towers, was built by William Marshall in the early 13thC.

Freshford   8 K14
Co Kilkenny. Handful of houses pressed together round a handsome tree-lined square. The Protestant parish church, built 1730, incorporates the 12thC Romanesque portal of an earlier monastic church. The deep entrance, articulated by three orders, is covered by a moulded hood.

Glaslough   3 M6
Co Monaghan, 5 miles NE of Monaghan. Picturesque village tucked in beside the gates of Castle Leslie along the banks of a lough of the same name. The Italianate Glaslough House, with its fabulous gardens which run along the shores of the lake, is *not open to the public*.

Glenealy   5 O13
Co Wicklow. Tiny village hidden in a wooded valley at the foot of Carrick Mountain, five miles south west of Wicklow. Of interest: the Agricultural Museum, with collection of old farm machinery dating back to the early 19thC. Nearby is the Ballymanus Forest walk.

Gorey   8 O14
Co Wexford. Quiet market town nestling in the shadows of the south east slopes of the Wicklow Mountains. The Loreto Convent and the Church of St Michael were designed by Pugin. To the western end of Gorey is the 418-foot-high Gorey Hill, where the rebels of 1798 camped before marching on Arklow. To the north east is the 833-foot-high Tara Hill, crowned by a cairn.

Gowna   2 K8
Co Cavan. Picturesque village tucked up in a wooded corner of the shores of Lough Gowna. Source of the River Erne, the lake is excellent for coarse fishing.

Gowran   8 L15
Co Kilkenny. Sleepy village rich in memories. Of strategic importance in pre-Norman Ireland, it commanded an ancient path through the bogs and forests of the Leinster-Ossory marches. The royal residence of the Kings of Ossory was here. Captured by Strongbow during the Anglo-Norman invasion, the village later fell to Edward Bruce in 1317. Of interest: 13thC parish church with aisled nave and chancel, to which a huge square central tower was added in the 14thC; ruins of Ballyshawnmore Castle, a Butler fortress. Horse racing at Gowran Park Racecourse.

Graiguenamanagh   8 L15
Co Kilkenny, 8 miles E of Thomastown. Pop 1,300. EC Wed. Picturesque market town on the lush green banks of the River Barrow near the border with Co Carlow. To the south is the 1,694-foot-high Brandon Hill, crowned by a prehistoric cairn and stone circle, whilst on the east bank, half a mile south east of the town, is Tinnahinch Castle, a former Butler fortress. The river itself is spanned by a seven-arched 18thC bridge. Throughout the town, propping up cobwebbed corners or encased in modern construction are the extensive remains of Duiske Abbey, considered to have been one of the finest Cistercian foundations in Ireland. Good coarse fishing on the River Barrow and exhilarating walks amongst the scarred and crumpled slopes of the Blackstairs Mountains.

Granard   4 K9
Co Longford. Pop 1,050. EC Thur. Small market town and angling centre near the border with Co Cavan. It was sacked by Edward Bruce in 1315. The Motte of Granard, to the south west of the town, is the largest in Ireland and is said to have been a royal residence of Niall the Great's eldest son, Cairbre; it was fortified by the Anglo-Normans in 1200. Also of interest: Abbey Laragh, remains of a Cistercian abbey founded in 1214; prehistoric earthworks known as Black Pigs Race. Five miles north west is Lough Gowna, with ruins of a church with late Romanesque windows. To the east are Loughs Sheelin and Kinale. Good trout fishing, with coarse fishing on Lough Gowna.

Hacketstown   8 N14
Co Carlow. Tiny village sealed in the rolling foothills of the Wicklow Mountains; it was the site of two bloody engagements between the yeomanry and Irish insurgents in 1798. Two miles south is Clonmore, site of a 6thC monastery founded by St Maedhoc.

nistioge 8 L15

Co Kilkenny, 5 miles SW of Thomastown. Pop 180. EC Wed. Sunlit village surrounding a tree-lined quare on the wooded banks of the River Nore. There is a handsome 18thC ten-arched bridge. It was ere that the King of Ossory defeated the Norsemen f Dublin in AD962 and the Anglo-Normans stablished an Augustinian priory in 1210, parts of vhich are now incorporated into the Protestant arish church. There is an arboretum at Woodstock 'ark, one mile from the village. Good salmon and rout fishing on the River Nore.

nnfield 5 M11

Co Meath. Small, spick-and-span village close to the Royal Canal. Also called Enfield. Good fishing for erch, pike, tench and bream.

johnstown 5 M11

Co Kildare, 1 mile NE of Naas. Attractive village vith handsome early 19thC mansion, Palmerston House, at one end; it is the seat of the Earl of Mayo.

Kells 8 L15

Co Kilkenny. Pop 2,390. EC Wed. The site of a 6thC nonastic settlement established by St Columba, it's a quiet, unassuming town basking in the glory of its pious past. In the wooded valley of the River Blackwater, it was raided frequently by both Vikings and Irish from he 10thC to 11thC; it vas in this monastery hat the famous 9thC lluminated manuscript, The Book of Kells, was vritten. Remains of the nonastery include west gable of the church, dating from the 15thC, 10thC round tower and numerous high crosses. Of interest: St Columba's House, 10thC oratory with steep, stone roof; Catholic church and Court House, both by Francis Johnston, the latter with a pedimented gable end, two storeys in height with central door and flanking windows set in blind arches; the

High cross, Kells

Taylour column, a monument crowning a hill to the west, built in 1791 in the form of a lighthouse. Excellent brown trout fishing in nearby rivers.

Kilbeggan 4 K12

Co Westmeath. Pop 640. EC Wed. Attractive little market town sitting sedately on the banks of the River Brosna. It was given its charter in the 17thC, and has an elegant 18thC due, due partly to prosperity brought in by a branch of the Grand Canal, with handsome limestone Court House and Market Hall. To the south, near Tullamore is the 10thC Durrow High Cross, on the site of a 6thC monastery. Three miles north east is Newforest, fine Georgian mansion of 1757. Good trout fishing on the River Brosna.

Kilcullin 5 M12

Co Kildare, 8 miles SW of Naas. Little town cocooned in silence on a picturesque stretch of the River Liffey. Of interest: remains of c5thC monastery with three 9thC stone crosses and part of a round tower at Old Kilcullin, to the south west; remains of a 12thC Romanesque church.

Kildare 5 M12

Co Kildare. Pop 3,140. EC Wed. An important ecclesiastical town in the Middle Ages and now horse breeding and training centre of Ireland, it's a bustling market town on the western edge of the Curragh Plain. St Brigid established a monastery here in the 5thC; frequently raided by the Vikings from the 9thC–13thC, its site is marked by St Brigid's Cathedral, a 13thC Anglo-Norman church heavily restored in the 19thC. Nearby is a 100-foot-high round tower and plain granite cross. Also of interest: National Stud and Irish Horse Museum, one mile east of the town, with lovely Japanese Gardens designed in the early 20thC. Annual Irish Sweeps Derby in *Jun*. Good coarse fishing on the Grand Canal at Rathangan.

Kilkenny 8 L15

Co Kilkenny. Pop 13,300. EC Thur. Handsome market town in a lush expanse of farmland, mingling medieval passages and lanes with elegant Georgian terraces on both banks of the River Nore. Ancient capital of the Kings of Ossory and an important ecclesiastical and civil centre from the 6thC, it was here that Strongbow built a monumental fortress on a low cliff above the river to the east of the town in 1172. The site of numerous parliaments from the early 13thC onwards, Kilkenny was at the height of her fame and prosperity in the 14thC when the notorious Statutes of Kilkenny were passed, forbidding the fraternisation of the Anglo-Normans with the native Irish. Ravaged by the Black Death, 1348–49, it was besieged by Sir James Fitzmaurice in 1568, designated a city by James I in 1609, and from 1642–48 was the seat of the confederate parliament, an assembly of Irish and Anglo-Norman Catholics. Replaced by a Royalist garrison in 1648, the city fell to Cromwell after a five-day siege in 1650. The castle, a grey stone cliff of a building with massive drum towers on the site of Strongbow's fortress, was largely rebuilt in 1826–35 by William Robertson. The main entrance in the west wall is a handsome classical portal of 1684. St Canice's Cathedral, one of the finest 13thC cathedrals in Ireland, was built on the site of an earlier church founded by St Canice in the 6thC. St Francis' Abbey contains a ruined chancel from a once-extensive 13thC Franciscan friary. In Abbey Street is Black Friar's Church, a restored Catholic church composed of the nave and south transept of a 13thC Dominican church. In Lower John Street are the remains of St John's Priory, an Augustinian priory founded in the 13thC and consisting of a choir with handsome mullioned windows. Also of interest: 13thC parish church and hall behind the Tholsel; the Tholsel, old exchange and town hall built in 1761 and consisting of a handsome assembly hall raised above an open arcaded ground storey; Rothe House, a characteristic merchant's house of the Tudor period, built in 1594; Shee's Almshouses, hospital for the poor built in Rose Inn Street in 1594; Black Freren Gate, one of the original gates to the city; Green's Bridge, handsome Palladian essay of 1765; Kells Priory, ruins of a 12thC Augustinian priory on a gentle sloping bank of the River King nine miles south; Dunmore Cave, a labyrinth of caverns carved out of the limestone seven miles north, where 1,000 citizens hiding from

Kilkenny, Tholsel

Viking raiders were caught and massacred in AD928. Magnificent centre for Gaelic football and hurling. Good salmon and trout fishing on the River Nore. Good horse racing at nearby Gowran Park. The Kilkenny Arts week, with exhibitions, concerts and fringe events, is held annually in *late Aug*.

Kingscourt 3 M8
Co Cavan. Well planned stone estate village of largely 19thC houses on a single main street, begun in the late 18thC by Mervyn Pratt, a local landlord. The Pratt family home, Cabra Castle, now a hotel, is a monumental castellated mansion.

Kinnegad 5 L10
Co Westmeath. Pop 360. Pretty border village with a handsome altar in the Catholic church, said to have been carved by Willie Pearse. Pearse was executed, along with his brother Patrick, following the Rising of 1916.

Kinnitty

Kinnitty 4 J12
Co Offaly. Delightful handful of houses huddled in picturesque disarray at the foot of the Slieve Bloom Mountains. In a fold in the nearby hills is Forelacka Glen, echoing with the sound of a bubbling tree-shaded mountain stream. Four miles south west is Seir Kieran, the site of a 5thC monastery founded by St Ciaran. Castle Bernard, on the outskirts of Kinnitty, was designed by the Pain brothers in 1833.

Lanesborough 4 I9
Co Longford. Angling centre on the River Shannon at the northern corner of Lough Ree. A nine-arched bridge links the town to Ballyclare in Co Roscommon. On an island in Lough Ree are the remains of Inchleraun monastery, founded in the 6thC by St Diarmuid. There is a small rectangular church with antae and flat-headed doorway; beside it on the northern side is Teampall Mór, a larger 13thC church with two lancet windows to the east. There are several Ogham stones.

Laragh 5 O13
Co Wicklow, 6 miles NW of Rathdrum. Quiet crossroads village huddled at the junction of several lush green glens and winding mountain roads. The 19thC Military Road winds through Glenmacnass and then runs southward over the hills into the valley of Glenmalure, where the ruins of a military block house stand guard beside Drumgoff. Glenmalure was the hideout of Irish resistance leaders in the late 16thC. It was here that Flach MacHugh O'Bryne defeated a British army in 1580 and that Red Hugh O'Donnell sought refuge following his escape from Dublin Castle in 1592. The glen is enclosed by a wall of mountains, the 3,039-foot-high Lugnaquilla, the highest mountain in Ireland, amongst them.

Leighlinbridge 8 L14
Co Carlow, 8 miles NW of Muine Bheag. Tiny village tucked into the Barrow Valley. On the banks of the river stand the gaunt ruins of Black Castle; originally a 12thC Anglo-Norman fortress built to control the river crossing, the present remains are 16thC. To the

south is Dinn Righ or 'Hill of the Kings', a 60-foot mound 135 feet in diameter, which was the ancient seat of the Kings of Leinster. At Agha, three miles east, are the ruins of 12thC church with antae at the gable ends. Two miles west is Oldleighlin, the site of a 7thC monastic foundation; remains include 13thC cathedral enlarged in the early 16thC.

St Mel's Cathedral, Longford

Longford 4 J9
Co Longford. Pop 3,870. C Thur. Pleasant county town laid out round wide, spacious streets along the south bank of the River Camlin. At the centre of the town is St Mel's, handsome classical-style Catholic cathedral begun by J B Keane in 1840 and completed by G C Ashlin in 1893; it has a wide Ionic portico with richly sculptured pediment above, and the front bay of the church is crowned by an elegant four-stage octagonal bell tower capped by a little dome. Also of interest: Renaissance-style Court House; Carriglass Manor, a Tudor-Revival mansion of 1837, three miles north east with classical stables and entrance arch by James Gandon. Good fishing on the Rivers Shannon and Camlin.

Louth 5 N8
Co Louth. Tiny village on the site of an early 6thC monastery established by St Mochta, a disciple of St Patrick. Of interest: St Mochta's House, a small 10thC–11thC church with high pitched stone roof; 14thC fragments of Lough Abbey, a Dominican foundation.

Lucan 5 N11
Co Dublin. Once-popular spa beside an Isambard Brunel bridge across the River Liffey. Of interest: ruins of 16thC Sarsfield House; Luttrelstown Castle, a castellated mansion designed 1800 by Sir Richard Morrison; Lucan House, handsome Palladian mansion of 1776.

Maynooth 5 N11
Co Kildare, 3½ miles SE of Kilcock. Neat, orderly university town, bubbling with old-world charm beside the Royal Canal. St Patrick's College, considered to be one of the greatest Catholic seminaries in the world, was established here in 1795. Also of interest: remains of 12thC Maynooth Castle, with well preserved gatehouse, monumental keep and great hall; Carton House, an imposing mansion designed by Richard Castle in 1740, to the east of the town.

Moate 4 J11
Co Westmeath. Pop 1,380. EC Wed. Named after the Mota Ghrainne Oige, a large rath or motte to the south west, Moate is an important market and cattle town with a long, wide main street lined by an undulating wall of colourful houses. Also of interest:

9thC Twyford Cross, a sculptured high cross at Bealin, three miles west; 13thC Donore Castle, two miles west. Numerous prehistoric remains in vicinity.

Monaghan 3 L6
Co Monaghan. Pop 5,250. C Thur. Busy county town and shoe manufacturing centre, it was given its charter by James I in 1613. Site of an early Christian monastery and 15thC Franciscan friary, it has a number of handsome 18thC and 19thC buildings including a small, elegant ashlar-faced Market House of 1791–92 complete with pediment; pedimented Court House of 1829; aloofly classical St Macartan's College, built 1840; St Macartan's Cathedral, Gothic-Revival building glaring across the town from rising ground to the south, designed 1861–92 by J J McCarthy. One mile south is Rossmore Forest Park. Good coarse and game fishing on nearby lakes.

Monasterevin 5 L12
Co Kildare. Handsome 18thC canal town with fine merchants' houses and well built warehouses round a spacious square. Of interest: Charter School, a large hipped-roof building three storeys high with austere pediment, built along the canal in 1740; 18thC Moore Abbey, huge castellated mansion with pointed windows, now a hospital; 676-foot Hill of Allen, eight miles north east, the site of a prehistoric tumulus is now occupied by a 19thC folly. The town was also one of the three royal residences in Leinster. The Curragh, a 5,000-acre plain, is wedged between here and Newbridge.

Mountmellick 5 K12
Co Laois. Sober as Sunday, it was originally a Quaker settlement established in 1677 and has neat 18thC houses lining the principal streets. It is almost encircled by the River Owenass.

Mountrath 8 K13
Co Laois. Quiet 17thC market town tucked unassumingly in at the foot of the Slieve Bloom Mountains, beside a tributary of the River Nore. Two miles east is Clonenagh Church, on the site of a celebrated monastic school founded in AD548 by St Fintan. A curiosity is St Fintan's Well embedded in the trunk of a large sycamore. Of interest: Roundwood House, 18thC Palladian villa three miles south west; 19thC Ballyfin House, handsome classical house designed by Sir Richard Morrison, five miles north east. Good walks and nature trails through Monicknew Woods seven miles north. Excellent game and coarse fishing on the nearby rivers.

Muine Bheag 5 M14
Co Carlow. Little market town sitting discreetly on the banks of the River Barrow, the 18thC creation of Walter Bagenal of Dunleckny Manor, who created it with grand architectural pretensions and named it 'Versailles'. The diversion of the old coach route in the 19thC thwarted his ambitious plans and left it a quiet backwater struggling under the name of Bagenalstown until the 20thC. Of interest: Greek-Revival courthouse; ruins of 14thC Ballymoon Castle, two miles east, with square, walled courtyard with projecting towers and entrance gate; fragments of Ballylonghan Castle, a 13thC fortress with twin-towered gatehouse, three miles south east.

Mullingar 5 K10
Co Westmeath. Pop 6,790. C Wed. Bustling market town amidst rich pastureland in the heart of the ancient Kingdom of Meath. Encircling it is a ring of lakes, with Lough Ennell to the south, Loughs Owel

and Iron to the north west, Lough Derravaragh to the north and tiny Loughs Drin and Dritan to the north east. Dominating the town are the 140-foot-high twin towers of the Renaissance-style Cathedral of Christ the King, built 1936 in a kind of marzipan classicism. Good 18thC Town Hall and Court House. Uisneach Hill, 12 miles west, was the ancient seat of the High Kings in pre-Christian Ireland.

Multyfarnham 5 K10
Co Westmeath, 7 miles N of Mullingar. Neat little village with remains of a 14thC Franciscan friary church. Wilson's Hospital, 1½ miles to the south west, is an 18thC Palladian complex.

Naas 5 M12
Co Kildare. Market centre and county town, it was once one of the residences of the kings of Leinster. Prosperous during the Middle Ages, it was fortified by the Anglo-Normans in 1316 and burnt by Edward Bruce a few years later. Of interest: Catholic parish church of SS Mary and David, a handsome Gothic-style building by Thomas Cobden, 1827; Jigginstown House, one mile south west, a palatial brick building of early 17thC; Furness House, built 1731, probably to the designs of Francis Bindon. Behind the house stands the gallaun, or standing stone, of Forenaughts. At nearby Punchestown is a 23-foot-high standing stone, one of the finest in Ireland. Popular racecourses at Naas and Punchestown, three miles to the south east.

Navan 5 M9
Co Meath. Pop 4,600. EC Thur. Prosperous market town at the confluence of the Rivers Boyne and Blackwater. Walled by the Anglo-Normans, and once a strategic outpost of the Pale, the town fell on hard times following the wars of 1641. Of interest: motte of an Anglo-Norman castle built on rising ground to the south of the River Blackwater; ruins of Athlumney Castle, a 15thC tower house with 17thC Tudor addition on the east bank of the River Boyne; Bective Abbey, five miles south, extensive ruins of a 12thC Cistercian foundation with well preserved cloisters; Rathaldron Castle, 15thC quadrangular tower with addition of 19thC castellated mansion; ruins of Dunmoe Castle, impressive 16thC fortress in 13thC style; Tara, six miles south, once residence of the high kings of Ireland and cultural and religious capital of the country.

Newbliss 3 L7
Co Monaghan, 5 miles E of Clones. Picturesque village resting on a quiet terrace of land beside a winding river in a rolling blanket of woodland.

New Ross 8 L16
Co Wexford. Pop 5,150. EC Wed. Winding narrow lanes, tall gabled houses and steep cobbled paths flanked by terraces of cottages clamber up the side of a steep hill along the River Barrow. Centre of one of the richest agricultural areas in Ireland and a thriving industrial town, it is also an important inland port, 20 miles from the sea and connected

Tintern Abbey, New Ross

with Dublin and the interior by the Grand Canal as well as the River Barrow. An important Anglo-Norman settlement, granted numerous royal charters, it was a commercial rival to Wexford in the late Middle Ages. One of the oldest towns in the county, it was severely damaged during the Cromwellian wars when it finally fell to the Parliamentarians in 1649. During the uprising of 1798, much of the town was destroyed by fire. Of interest: ruins of St Mary's Abbey, founded in the 13thC; the Tholsel, the municipal offices erected 1749 and rebuilt 1806 with handsome clock tower and cupola; 12thC Dunbrody Abbey, a picturesque ruin with graceful cruciform church eight miles south; ruins of 13thC Tintern Abbey, twelve miles south and named after its famous Welsh counterpart; John F Kennedy Park and arboretum on the slopes of Slieve Coilte. Good fishing for bass and mullet from Pink Rock, three miles south.

Oldcastle 5 L9
Co Meath. Pop 760. EC Wed. Neat little town, in Victorian Sunday best, three miles north west of the Loughcrew Hills. The hills rise to 904 feet at Slieve na Caillagh, the highest of the three principal peaks. Dug in around their summits is a remarkable group of neolithic chambered cairns, considered to be one of the finest archaeological sites in Ireland.

Portarlington 5 L12
Co Laois. Pop 3,110. C Mon. Handsome town of crisp, neat 18thC houses, many set back-to-front facing the River Barrow, an influence of Huguenot immigrants. The town was established by the Earl of Galway in 1667. There is a plain, but dignified market house of 1800 with hipped roof and arcaded ground storey. Ireland's first peat-fired electric power station, opened in 1950, is north of the town. The ruins of Lea Castle, a 13thC Fitzgerald castle, square in plan with three-quarter round towers at the angles, stands 2½ miles north east; it was burnt by Edward Bruce in 1315, sheltered Silken Thomas following the rebellion of 1535 and was finally destroyed by the Parliamentarians in 1650. Good trout fishing on the River Barrow.

Portlaoise 5 K13
Co Laois. Pop 3,900. C Mon. Originally called Maryborough, it was fortified by the English settlers during the reign of Philip and Mary as part of a plan to subdue the local chiefs. Named Portlaoise following Irish independence, it has a number of fine buildings. The Court House, with fine staircase and boldly rusticated and pilastered façade, was designed by Sir Richard Morrison in the early 19thC. The gaol, designed by the Pain brothers in 1830 on a radiating plan, has a castellated gatehouse. The Protestant church has an obelisk spire crowning the tower designed by James Gandon. Also of interest: the Rock of Danamase, 150-foot-high rock, 3½ miles west, crowned by the impressive ruins of an 8thC fortress with keeps and courtyards plundered by the Vikings in AD844. Eight miles south east is the Timahoe Round Tower, built 11thC, the only remnant of a 7thC monastery founded by St Mochua. A veteran and vintage car rally is held annually in *Jul*.

Rock of Danamase, Portlaoise

Prosperous 5 M11
Co Kildare. Once a busy 18thC canal village with a prosperous cotton industry, hence the name. Of interest: Landenstown House, simple but dignified house of 1740 with central block with projecting pavilions and pedimented centre attached to low, flanking wings by arches; 18thC Killybegs, handsome brick-built Georgian house. Fine coarse fishing centre with a ten-mile stretch of the Grand Canal stocked with bream, perch, pike, eel and rudd. Freshwater Angling Gala Week in *mid-May*.

Rathdowney 7 K14
Co Laois. Diminutive market town celebrated by the thirsty for its beer. A renowned 18thC antiquary, Ledwich, was curate here for a time, and Thomas Prior, a philanthropist and founder of the Royal Dublin Society, was born here in 1679. Several castles of interest in the vicinity, including Kilbreedy, Gort-na-Clay and Culahill, a principal stronghold of the Fitzpatricks built in 1425.

Rathdrum 5 O13
Co Wicklow. Pop 1,140. EC Wed. Little town huddled high up on the western side of the beautiful Avonmore Valley. The winding River Avonmore, with its small brown trout, flows through the lovely Vale of Clara, a lush green valley between high hills. Also of interest: Avondale House, 1½ miles south, the birthplace of Charles Stewart Parnell.

Rathvilly 5 M13
Co Carlow. Pretty village embedded in a garden of flowers. Beside the village is a 600-foot-high motte with commanding views. Nearby are several examples of grooved pillar-stones, including Williamstown Gallán or the Six Fingers, two miles to the south east.

Robertstown 5 M11
Co Kildare. Handsome 18thC village built on a bend in the Grand Canal. Recently restored waterfront has whitewashed vernacular buildings nicely contrasted with the grand, pedimented Canal Hotel, which offers candlelight banquets in *summer*. Grand Canal Festa held here during weekends in *Jul and Aug*.

Roundwood 5 O13
Co Wicklow, 6 miles SW of Mt Kennedy. Handful of houses sealed amongst the mountains 780 feet above sea level to the east of Lough Dan.

Shercock 3 M8
Co Cavan. Picturesque village on rising ground south east of Lough Sillan. Annual Water Sports Regatta on Lough Sillan in *Aug*.

Slane 5 N9
Co Meath. Pop 420. EC Thur. Gentle Georgian village centred on a handsome diamond-shaped square in the lovely Boyne Valley. A mile to the north is 500-foot-high Slane Hill, where St Patrick is said to have lit the Paschal Fire in AD433 in celebration of the triumph of Christianity over paganism in 5thC Ireland. Nearby are the remains of a 16thC church, marking the site of an earlier church and monastic school founded by the saint. Beside the parish church is a cobwebbed Gothic ruin, the Hermitage of St Erc, named after the first Bishop of Slane. Slane Castle, beside the river to the west, is one of the finest Gothic Revival castles in Ireland; designed by James Wyatt in 1785 with contributions by Chambers, Gandon and Francis Johnston among others, the mansion incorporated an earlier castle and has a magnificent circular Gothic library, as well as grounds landscaped by Capability Brown. Only the restaurant is open to the public. Downstream to the east is an area known as Brugh na Bóinne, a famous neolithic site where some of the finest

xamples of passage graves in Ireland are to be ound. Good fishing for salmon and sea trout in the lane Estate Fishery.

tradbally 5 L13
Co Laois. Small 18thC village. Of interest: tradbally Steam Museum; remains of prehistoric ill fort at Boley Hill; Brockley Park, handsome nansion designed by Davis Ducart in 1768, to the orth east; ruins of 12thC Killeshin Church, once art of a monastery founded in the early 6thC, with a ovely Hiberno-Romanesque portal.

Round tower and church tower, Swords

Swords 5 O10
Co Dublin. On the site of a mid-6thC monastic foundation established by St Columba, the village stands near the banks of the estuary of the River Ward. Of interest: 13thC Archbishop's Castle; 75-foot-high round tower, last remains, with a square tower, of the early monastery.

Thomastown 8 L15
Co Kilkenny. Pop 1,270. EC Thur. Once a strategic stronghold of the Anglo-Normans, who built a notte-and-bailey castle here in the 13thC, it's now a ousy market town traversed by winding streets on he banks of the River Nore, which was navigable until the river silted up in the early 19thC. Of nterest: ruins of fine 13thC three-aisled church with chancel; surviving motte of 13thC castle; ruins of Grianán Castle on the bank of the River Nore to the outh east; 13thC round tower at Tullaherin, two niles north; Dysert Castle, 18thC house of Bishop George Berkeley, world-famous philosopher and

philanthropist, after whom the city and university of Berkeley, California were named; Jerpoint Abbey, magnificent Cistercian monastery to the south west. Good salmon and trout fishing on the River Nore.

Trim 5 M10
Co Meath. Pop 1,700. EC Thur. Charming market town on a bend in the River Boyne. Standing at the heart of a lush, green plain, it is one of the oldest ecclesiastical centres in Ireland, with a see established here in the 5thC. Built round an ancient ford across the River Boyne, Trim was granted along with the county to Hugh de Lacy, following the Anglo-Norman invasion. The castle, an awesome ruin with huge 70-foot-high keep, was begun in 1173. The largest Anglo-Norman fortress to be built in 13thC Ireland, it was here that Richard II imprisoned Lord Gloucester and Henry of Lancaster, later Henry IV. Walled in 1359, the town was the venue for several 15thC parliaments. Occupied by 'Silken' Thomas Fitzgerald during his brief rebellion in the 16thC against Henry VIII and later garrisoned by Confederates in 1642, the town fell to Cromwell, who massacred many of its inhabitants in 1649. The remnants of the medieval town walls include Sheep Gate with 15-foot-high arch. Nearby Yellow Steeple, a 125-foot-high ruin, is a gangling skeleton buttressed by fragments of the 13thC Augustinian abbey to which it belonged; used as a watch tower in the 17thC, it was partially destroyed in 1649 to prevent it falling into Cromwellian hands. There are a number of fine 18thC houses, a Town Gaol of 1800 with austere rusticated façade. Across the river stand the remains of Talbot Castle, a fortified house of 1415, and 15thC Nangle Castle. At Newtown Trim, to the south east, are the ruins of a medieval cathedral and priory of the early 13thC. Two miles south is the village of Laracor where the author of 'Gulliver's Travels', Jonathan Swift, was rector from 1700–13. Eight miles south west is Donore Castle, a 40-foot-high tower house built in 1429.

Tullamore

Tullamore 4 K11
Co Offaly. Pop 6,800. C Mon. Prosperous market and manufacturing centre, it was originally a small village, transformed during the late 18thC into a handsome Georgian town. Created by the Burys, Earls of Charleville, it was originally the terminus of the Grand Canal and has some fine remnants of canal architecture, including the Presbytery, Canal Harbour, built originally by the Grand Canal Company as a hotel. There is an 18thC market house with pedimented façade and arcaded ground storey, now blocked up, and handsome cupola crowning the roof. The Court House, with Ionic portico, was built 1835 by J B Keane, and Francis Johnston, the architect of nearby Charleville Castle, a baronial-style mansion of 1801, designed the Gothic-Revival Protestant church in 1818. Also of interest: ruins of 16thC church at Tihelly, one mile north west,

including interesting high cross; ruins of Sragh Castle, an Elizabethan fortress on the north bank of the canal; to the north, remains of Durrow Abbey, including 10thC high cross and St Columba's Well, founded by St Columba in the 6thC. It was here that the celebrated Book of Durrow, now in Trinity College, Dublin, was written in the 7thC. At Lynally, four miles south west, are the remains of a monastery founded in AD580. At Rahan, seven miles west, are the remains of a 6thC monastic foundation including the ruins of three small Romanesque churches. Good trout fishing on the Rivers Silver and Clodragh. Coarse fishing on the Grand Canal.

Tullow   8 M14
Co Carlow. Pop 1,840. EC Wed. Pleasant agricultural centre with a fine market square, on the banks of the River Slaney. It was the site of an Anglo-Norman castle and 13thC Augustinian friary, of which little remains. In the square stands a statue of Father John Murphy, leader of the 1798 uprising, who was hanged at Tullow. Of interest: Rathgall, ancient stone fortress crowning a high hill three miles to the east, consisting of a complex of four ramparts, of which the outer one is 1,000 feet in diameter; holed stone at Ardristan; dolmen at Tobinstown. Fine salmon and trout fishing in the River Slaney.

Tyrellspass   5 K11
Co Westmeath. Neat little village, scene of a defeat of an Elizabethan army by an Irish force in 1597; some interesting houses.

Urlingford   4 J14
Co Kilkenny. Marooned in a flat, boggy landscape under a giant canvas of sky. Of interest: ruins of Urlingford Castle, a former Butler fortress; simple nave and chancel church; Foulkstown House, handsome Georgian mansion two miles north west; large dolmen and ancient rath at nearby Borrismore; remains of twelve castles in vicinity.

Virginia   5 L9
Co Cavan. Pop 580. EC Tue. Attractive town in picturesque landscape on the wooded northern shore of Lough Ramor. Eight miles south are the Loughcrew Hills, rich in megalithic tombs. Three miles north east is Cuilcagh Lough, site of the house where Swift began to write 'Gulliver's Travels'. Five miles west is Killinkere, birthplace of General Sheridan, hero of the American Civil War. Excellent angling centre with four rivers and ten lakes within a five-mile radius.

Woodenbridge   8 O14
Co Wicklow, 5 miles NW of Arklow. Charming jumble of houses wedged on terraces cut out of thickly wooded land at the junction of the Avoca, Arklow and Aughrim valleys. South west of the village is the 1,987-foot-high Croghan Kinsella Mountain, at the head of the Golden Mines River. Source of material for the goldsmiths of ancient Ireland, a nugget was found here in 1796, precipitating a gold rush that uncovered 2,600 ounces of gold in a matter of months.

Regional features

Crystal
Cavan Crystal Ltd. in Dublin Road, Cavan, has tours on weekdays; the adjoining shop sells seconds and discontinued lines at good reductions. *Open all year.*
Visitors are also welcome at Simon Pearce Glass, Bennettsbridge, Co Kilkenny, where you can watch glass-blowing. *Open all year.*

The Gaeltacht
This is the name given to several areas in Ireland where the Irish language and cultural tradition are strenuously upheld and officially encouraged. The colony in Co Meath was established between 1935–40 by the Land Commission. Centred around Rathcairn, Kilbride, Gibbstown and Clonfill, a strong, flourishing community has grown from the 120 migrant families that originally settled here. There is a community centre at Rathcairn providing social evenings, complete with traditional entertainment.

Horses
The main breeding and training centres are in Co Kildare, with the Curragh racecourse near Kildare and Goff's bloodstock sales at Kill. More information from The Irish Horse Board, St Maelruan's, Tallaght, Co Dublin. Tel. 510122.

Lace-making
This is still a flourishing home craft, producing such specialities as a fine cotton Irish crochet known as Limerick and Carrickmacross lace. St Louis Convent, Carrickmacross, Co Monaghan, has kept this tradition going over the years and welcomes visitors.

Musical instruments
Irish harps are made both here and in Limerick, and you can watch them being made at Marley Park craft courtyard, Rathfarnham, Dublin 14, along with many other Irish crafts.

Tweed
The wool textile industry originated around the sheep rearing areas of Donegal, Mayo, Galway, Kerry and Wicklow but many of the weavers are now working in the Dublin area, making scarves, lightweight dress fabrics, bedspreads and hats.

Famous people

Brendan Behan (1923–1964)   5 O11
Dublin, Co Dublin. Home of the writer; a house painter by trade and one-time member of the IRA (which led to a period of imprisonment), he was the author of 'The Quare Fellow', 1956. In 1958 he wrote the autobiographical 'Borstal Boy' and 'The Hostage', his last full-length play.

George Berkeley (1685–1753)   8 L15
Dysert Castle, Thomastown, Co Kilkenny. Birthplace of the philosopher, after whom the city and University of California campus of Berkeley in the United States are named. Educated at Kilkenny and Trinity College, Dublin, he was appointed Dean of Derry in 1724 and Bishop of Cloyne in 1734. His works include 'Essay towards a New Theory of Vision', 'Principles of Human Knowledge' and the dialogues of 'Siris' and 'Alciphon'.

Michael Dwyer (1771–1826)   8 N13
Dwyer-MacAllister Cottage, Derrynamuck, Co Wicklow. Situated in the south of the Glen of Imail, the cottage commemorates the famous rebel, Michael Dwyer, leader of the Wicklow uprising in

Dwyer - MacAllister
Cottage, Derrynamuck. co. wicklow

1798, who was trapped here with four colleagues by British forces. Thanks to the heroism of his friend Sam MacAllister, who drew the fire upon himself and was killed, Dwyer managed to escape. The two-roomed cottage has rope chairs, a settle bed, a roasting spit and cooking utensils.

Oliver Goldsmith (1730–1774)   **4 J10**
Lissoy, Co Westmeath, 5 miles SW of Ballymahon, Co Longford. Lissoy was the "Sweet Auburn" of Goldsmith's poem, 'The Deserted Village'. His father was rector here from 1730 until his death in 1747. Parts of the rectory still remain, as well as other places mentioned in the poet's work. Dramatist, novelist and poet, Goldsmith graduated from Trinity College in 1749, leaving to study medicine at Edinburgh and Leyden. Following extensive European travels he arrived in London, destitute, in 1756. A friend of Samuel Johnson, his most celebrated works are the play 'She Stoops to Conquer', the poem, 'The Deserted Village' and the novel 'The Vicar of Wakefield'.

James Joyce (1882–1941)   **5 O11**
James Joyce Tower, Nr Dun Laoghaire, Co Dublin. Situated in Sandycove, to the east of Scotsman's Bay, the museum contains a fascinating collection of the writer's memorabilia and is housed in a Martello tower built 1806 as part of a coastal defensive system against possible invasion from France. Once the temporary residence of the author, it is featured in the opening pages of 'Ulysses'. Born in Dublin, Joyce was educated at two Jesuit schools and at University College, Dublin. Dissatisfied with the narrowness and bigotry of Irish Catholicism, he left Ireland for good in 1904 and lived the remainder of his life in Europe at Trieste, Paris and Zurich. Living in comparative poverty, he supported himself by teaching English. His first work 'Chamber Music', a collection of verse, was published in 1907. It was shortly followed by 'Portrait of the Artist as a Young Man' and in 1914 by a brilliant collection of short stories, 'The Dubliners'. His most famous work 'Ulysses', a richly comic description of a day in the life of a middle-class Dubliner, was published in 1922. 'Finnegans Wake', the most complex and avant-garde of all his works, was published in 1939. James Joyce Museum *open May–Sep.*

Thomas Moore (1779–1852)   **5 O13**
Vale of Avoca, Co Wicklow. It was by the confluence of the Rivers Avonmore and Avonbeg that Thomas Moore composed his famous poem 'The Meeting of the Waters', in which he wrote "There is not in this wide world a valley so sweet/As that vale in whose bosom the bright waters meet". Nearby is Tom Moore's tree, where the poet is said to have spent many hours composing songs and poems. Born in Dublin, the son of a grocer, he was a musician as well as a poet; with the publication of 'Irish Melodies' in 1807 he became the leading lyricist in Ireland. Later in life he wrote several biographies, including those of Byron, Sheridan and Lord Edward Fitzgerald.

Sean O'Casey (1880–1964)   **5 O11**
Dublin, Co Dublin. Birthplace of this famous playwright. O'Casey had no formal education due to a combination of an eye disease, contracted in childhood, and his widowed mother's poverty. Working as a labourer for many years, his first play was 'The Shadow of a Gunman', first performed at the Abbey Theatre in 1923. This was soon followed by 'Juno and the Paycock', his masterpiece, in 1924 and 'Ploughs and the Stars' in 1926. That same year he left for England and in 1928, after the Abbey Theatre rejected one of his new plays, decided not to return to Ireland.

Avondale House, Co Wicklow

Charles Stewart Parnell (1846–1891)   **5 O13**
Avondale house, nr Rathdrum, Co Wicklow. The birthplace of this great Irish leader. The house now belongs to the Forest and Wildlife Service and is used as a Forestry School. It was built in 1779 for Samuel Hayes and many of the trees he planted still stand today on the 550-acre estate. The son of a country gentleman, Parnell became one of the great leaders of Irish democracy. Founder, with Michael Davitt, of the Land League in 1877, he campaigned vigorously for agrarian reforms such as peasant proprietorship as well as for Home Rule. When he was cited in a divorce case in 1890, the Home Rule Party which he had created voted against his continued leadership because of the scandal. A year later, he was dead. Avondale House *open May–Sep.*

George Bernard Shaw (1856–1950)   **5 O11**
Torca Cottage, Torca Road, Dalkey, Co Dublin. Home of the playwright from 1866–74, the cottage stands on Dalkey Hill, with magnificent views across the bay to Dublin. Born in Dublin, Shaw left for London in 1876, where he worked as a music and drama critic. A member of the Fabian Society, he began writing for the stage in the 1890s. The leading playwright of his time, his first success was 'John Bull's Other Island' followed by a series of plays, including 'Pygmalion'. In 1925 he was awarded the Nobel Prize for Literature.

Richard Brinsley Sheridan (1751–1816)   **5 O11**
Upper Dorset Street, Dublin, Co Dublin. Birthplace of this famous playwright, who later moved to London. Author of three magnificent comedies 'The Rivals', 'The School for Scandal' and 'The Critic', Sheridan was elected as Member of Parliament for Stafford in 1780 and devoted himself to public affairs; he was implacably opposed to the Union of 1800.

John Millington Synge (1879–1909)   **5 O11**
Glencree, Co Wicklow. Beautiful place beloved of this dramatist. Born in Rathfarnham, the northern entrance to the Wicklow Mountains four miles south west of Dublin, Synge was educated at Trinity College, Dublin; he soon left for Paris, where he met Yeats and, persuaded by him, published a memorable description of Irish life in 'The Aran Islands' in 1907. That same year his masterpiece, 'The Playboy of the Western World', was staged. Two years later, in the lights and shadows of wooded Glencree he roamed with his beloved Molly Allgood and wrote 'To the Oaks of Glencree'. Not long after he was dead, aged 37.

Oscar Wilde (1854–1900)   **5 O11**
Dublin, Co Dublin. Birthplace of this renowned playwright, poet and wit. Wilde was educated at Portora Royal School, Trinity College, Dublin and Magdalen College, Oxford. He left Dublin for London in 1879 and published his successful novel, 'The Picture of Dorian Gray' in 1891. His masterpiece, 'The Importance of Being Earnest' was published in 1895. Tried on a charge of homosexuality, he was imprisoned for two years. On his release he left for France, where he wrote 'The Ballad of Reading Gaol'.

Cathedrals, abbeys & churches

Clonmacnois   4 I11
Co Offaly, 9 miles NW of Cloghan. One of Ireland's
most celebrated holy places, the monastery was
founded by St Ciaran in AD548 on the banks of the
River Shannon. It became one of the major
scholastic centres of Europe, famed for the quality of
its illuminated manuscripts, such as the 11thC
Annals of Tighernach and the 12thC Book of the
Dun Cow, as well as for its high level of
craftsmanship. It was repeatedly plundered by the
Vikings from the early 9thC to 1012 and was burnt
by the Normans in 1179; it was finally ransacked for
its valuables by the English in 1552 and the buildings
became deserted. Remains include the cathedral, the
largest building on the site; much altered in the
10thC, 11thC and 12thC, it has antae, a Romanesque
west door and a chancel, divided in the 15thC with
three vaulted chapels. To the east is Temple Ciaran,
ruins of a tiny 10thC church. To the north, near the
enclosing wall, is Temple Connor, a restored 11thC
church. To the north west of this, built in a break in
the enclosing wall, is Temple Finghin, the ruins of a
12thC nave and chancel church with a low round
tower attached to the chancel, which acted as a
belfry. To the west is a larger round tower, built
AD964 and restored in 1134. From the graveyard a
narrow causeway leads eastward to the Nun's
Church, a fine Romanesque church with nave and
chancel and handsome decorative portal and chancel
arch, built in 1157. To the north of the car park is an
Anglo-Norman castle built in the early 13thC,
remains consisting of a gateway, courtyard and
tower. There are three carved high crosses and over
200 monumental slabs.

Clonmacnois

Coolbanagher Church   5 M12
Nr Portarlington, Co Laois. Handsome Protestant
parish church designed by James Gandon with west
tower and spire. Inside is a magnificent carved font.
To the south east is an elegant mausoleum also
designed by Gandon, with round arch at the base
and incised bands articulating the main façade,
which is crowned by a shallow pediment and urn.

Duiske Abbey   8 L15
Graiguenamanagh, Co Kilkenny. Cistercian abbey
founded by William Marshall in 1207 on the banks
of the River Barrow. The extensive ruins are largely
swamped by modern buildings. The Abbey Church,
now accommodated in the Catholic church, has a
choir, transepts and nave and the Baptistery has a
gorgeous 13thC portal in the Transitional style. The
Chapter House and many domestic buildings to the
south are embedded in new buildings. Inside the
church is an interesting effigy of a 13thC armoured
knight and the east window is particularly fine.

Durrow Abbey   4 K11
Nr Tullamore, Co Offaly. Founded by St Columba in
AD553, the earliest object to be found here was the
beautiful 7thC illuminated manuscript, the Book of
Durrow, now in the library of Trinity College,

Durrow Abbey

Dublin. The monastery, frequently plundered, was
taken over by the Augustinians in the 12thC. The
church was transformed into a parish church in the
mid-16thC. Abandoned in 1582, it was restored for
use in the 18thC and again in the 19thC. To the west
is a fine 10thC high cross decorated with biblical
scenes, the principal faces depicting David killing
the lion, Christ in glory with David and the sacrifice
of Isaac. On the reverse side is a scene of the soldiers
guarding the tomb of Christ, the scourging at the
pillar and the Crucifixion.

Fore Abbey   5 L9
Co Westmeath, 3 miles NE of Castlepollard. Site of
Christian monastery established by Saint Feichin in
AD640. Pillaged and burned from the 9thC to the
13thC, remains include a primitive 10thC
rectangular church, St Feichin's, with antae and
inscribed lintel over the door. In 1200 a Benedictine
priory was established here. Extensive remains
include portions of 15thC cloister, fortified west
tower and part of the town walls, together with two
town gates that were built to protect the priory and
settlement in 1436. In the village is the old jail,
incorporated in the remains of a medieval tower.
Also of interest is a large motte to the east on the Ben
of Fore.

Glendalough   5 N13
Co Wicklow, 9 miles NW of Rathdrum. A rolling
landscape of wild, lush green walled in by
cloud-covered peaks and lit by bright shafts of light.
It was here, in the 'valley of the two lakes', that St
Kevin founded a monastery that grew into one of
Europe's most celebrated centres of learning.
Students flocked to it from every civilised country in
Europe. From the tiny hamlet built around the
shores of the upper lake, it expanded into a
flourishing monastic city in the 11thC with a huge
walled enclosure. Plundered by the Danes in the
9thC and 10thC, it was severely damaged by fire in

St. Kevin's Church, Glendalough

1163. Appropriated by the Anglo-Normans, who united it with the see of Dublin in 1214, it was sacked by the Dublin English in 1398 and rapidly fell into decay. Restoration took place in the late 19thC and then again in the early 20thC. Apart from St Kevin who died in AD618, the most illustrious name connected with Glendalough is that of St Laurence O'Toole. Appointed Abbot of Glendalough in 1153, he became Archbishop of Dublin in 1163 and was canonised in 1226. The most important remains at Glendalough are those grouped round the shores of the lower lake and by the entrance to the valley in the east. The Gateway, the main entrance to the monastery, consisting of two round-headed arches and a large stone carved with a cross, is the only surviving example of its period in Ireland. To the west is a well preserved 103-foot-high round tower, and to the south is the cathedral; the largest church in Glendalough, it dates from the 11thC and consists of a nave, chancel and sacristy. Beyond it is St Kevin's Church; also known as St Kevin's Kitchen, it's a nave and chancel church of the 11thC–12thC, has a stone roof, a small round tower with a conical roof over the western gable end, and a small chamber above the nave. To the east is Trinity Church, an 11thC–12thC nave and chancel church with a round-headed portal. Further east across the river is St Saviour's Priory; founded by St Laurence O'Toole in 1162, it has the finest Romanesque decorative work to be found in Glendalough, especially on the chancel arch and east window. To the west, around the head of Upper Lake and along the southern shore is St Kevin's Bed, a tiny cave carved in the cliff-face some 25 feet above the lake; St Kevin's Cell, foundations of a small beehive hut; Reefert Church, 11thC nave and chancel church with flat-headed entrance portal, round-headed windows and projecting corbels at the corners to hold the rafters. There are numerous stone crosses throughout the site and on the eastern shore of the Upper Lake is the Caher, a Bronze Age or Early Iron Age fort with the foundations of many stone huts.

the cloister, Jerpoint

Jerpoint Abbey   8 L15
Co Kilkenny, 1½ miles SW of Thomastown. A sheer wall of stone layered like elaborate traceried work, it stands on a dog leg in the road surrounded by lush, green, rolling farmland. One of the finest Cistercian monastic ruins in Ireland, it was founded by the King of Ossory for the Benedictines in 1158 and was taken over by the Cistercians in 1180. Affiliated to Fountains Abbey, Yorkshire in the early 13thC, it is the archetypal Cistercian monastery with huge three-aisled church engulfing the north side of a quadrangle. To the south were the cellars, lay dormitory, monks' dormitory, kitchen, chapter house, sacristy and other ancillary buildings, grouped round three sides of a handsome cloister arcade of the 15thC. The cloister, recently restored, has some remarkably rich figure sculpture and the church itself has some fine sculptured tombs.

Kells Priory   8 L15
Co Kilkenny, 6 miles W of Thomastown. Striking group of medieval buildings dating from the 14thC and 15thC. Founded for the Augustinians by Geoffrey de Marisco in 1193. Remains consist of a nave and chancel church crowned by a square, central tower; a west aisle; a chapel tucked in the southern angle by the tower; and a second tower, thought to have been the prior's residence, punctuating the north west angle of the church. To the south are remains of once-extensive domestic buildings, including a five-acre fortified enclosure.

Killoughternane Church   8 M15
Co Carlow, 4 miles NE of Borris. Small, rectangular church of the early 12thC with antae at each gable end. There is a round-headed east window and square, baptismal font.

Mellifont Abbey   5 N9
Co Louth, 6 miles NW of Drogheda. Apart from the suppression of the monasteries in the 16thC, the most profound effect on Irish monasticism and architecture was the introduction of new Continental monastic orders in the 12thC. The major influence was that of the Cistercians, followed by the Augustinians and the Benedictines. Mellifont was the first, and greatest, Cistercian house in Ireland. Established by St Malachy O'Morgair, Archbishop of Armagh in 1142, for monks from Clairvaux, it was burned in the 14thC and rebuilt up to the 15thC. Interesting remains include the impressive Lavabo, a two-storey octagonal washing place or fountain house of the 13thC; the Gate House, a massive, square 50-foot-high tower; parts of the early 13thC cloister.

Monasterboice   5 N9
Co Louth, 5 miles NW of Drogheda. Remains of a late 5thC monastic settlement founded by St Buithe. The importance of the monastery is that it contains the 10thC cross of Muiredach, one of the most perfect of Ireland's high crosses. Nearly 18 feet high, the cross is adorned with beautiful decorated panels, depicting biblical scenes. Also of interest, the 21½-foot-high West Cross and the 16-foot-high North Cross, although the carvings are far less elaborate. There are two simple rectangular stone churches, South Church and North Church, of the 10thC–11thC and a 110-foot-high round tower.

Moone High Cross and Church   8 M13
Co Kildare, 8 miles E of Athy. Marking the site of an early Christian monastery, this is one of the finest high crosses in Ireland and dates from the 9thC. It is 17 feet high, decorated with flat, stylised figures; it has 51 sculptured panels illustrating biblical scenes. The church, which was built in the 13thC, has antae at the gable ends.

Moone High Cross

Round tower   5 O10
Lusk, Co Dublin. Five-storey 9thC round tower with
original conical roof. Part of a monastery founded by
St MacCulin in the early 6thC. Attached to the tower
is a square tower built in the 16thC. At each corner
are three additional round towers.

St Brigid's Cathedral   5 M12
Kildare, Co Kildare. Built on the site of an early 5thC
monastery by Ralph of Bristol in 1223, it retains only
a portion from this period, including the south
transept and part of the tower. Partially restored in
the 13thC, it has some fine medieval tombs,
including a stone slab with a carving of the
Crucifixion on which is an inscription granting
indulgence. In 1875 it was restored by G E Street.
An aisle-less, cruciform building, it has an embattled
parapet carried from buttress to buttress by arches.
In the churchyard are a high cross and round tower.

St Canice's Cathedral   8 L15
Kilkenny, Co Kilkenny. Remarkably consistent in
style and highly symmetrical in plan, it's one of the
finest 13thC churches in Ireland, consisting of a
cruciform plan with five-bay aisled nave with
combined chancel and choir flanked by chapels.
Begun in 1251 by Bishop Hugh de Mapilton it was
completed in 1280. The massive square central tower
was added in the 14thC. An unusual feature is the
gallery under the west window. To the south is a
round tower belonging to the earlier church. Also of
interest: fine 16thC and 17thC tomb stones.

St Columba's Monastery   5 M9
Kells, Co Meath. Founded in the 6thC, and
refounded in AD804 for monks fleeing from Viking
raiders around Iona. Remains include five 10thC
high crosses; a 100-foot-high round tower built in
the early 11thC, with five windows piercing the top
stage. St Columba's Church, a high stone-roofed
oratory with vaulted floor, is remarkably similar to
St Kevin's Church, Glendalough.

St Mary's Church   8 L16
New Ross, Co Wexford. Founded by William
Marshall between 1207–20, it was one of the largest
medieval parish churches in Ireland. Remains
include chancel, two transepts and fine lancet
windows in the east gable end.

St Mullins   8 M15
Co Carlow, 9 miles S of Borris. Burial place of the
Kings of South Leinster, the monastery was founded
by St Moling in the late 7thC. Plundered by the
Vikings in the mid-10thC and burnt in 1138,
remains include a medieval nave and chancel church,
the lower stage of a round tower, small oratory, a
granite high cross and a medieval domestic building
with interesting diamond-shaped east window.

Timahoe Round Tower   8 K13

Nr Portlaoise, Co Laois.
The only remnant of a
7thC monastery, it's 96 feet
high and is unique in
having a fine double
Romanesque portal, some
17 feet above ground level.
The third floor has a
Romanesque window.
Nearby are the ruins of a
15thC church, later
transformed into a
castle.

Timahoe Round Tower

Castles & ruins

Ferns Castle   8 N15
Ferns, Co Wexford. Classic example of an early type
of castle peculiar to Ireland is this rectangular keep
with round towers at the angles but without a central
courtyard. Built in the early 13thC and some 80 feet
by 30 feet, it was originally three storeys in height.
Along the upper walls some graceful 13thC
trefoil-headed windows still stand. Of particular
interest is the remarkable vaulted circular chapel on
the first floor of the south east tower.

Kilkenny Castle   8 L15
Kilkenny, Co Kilkenny. Grey stone cliff of wall
perched on a high pedestal of rock on a bend in the
River Nore, articulated by giant round towers and
battlemented parapets. On the site of a motte
constructed by Strongbow in 1172 and rebuilt in
stone in 1204, the castle, although frequently
reconstructed, retains its original quadrilateral plan.
The present building occupies three sides of the
original plan and was largely rebuilt by William
Robertson in 1826–35. From 1391–1935 it was the
chief residence of the Butler family. Now in state
care, it has a fine classical west portal built 1684;
interesting collection of paintings; formal gardens
and extensive parklands.

Swords Castle   5 O10
Swords, Co Dublin. Built as an episcopal manor in
1200, it consists of a huge, five-sided courtyard
entered via a fortified gate-house. Beyond it stands a
14thC chapel and to the north is a tower at one time
the residence of the constable of the castle.

Trim Castle, Co Meath.

Trim Castle   5 M10
Trim, Co Meath. The largest Anglo-Norman fortress
in Ireland, Trim Castle was begun in 1172 by Hugh
de Lacy and later remodelled and extended by
Richard Pippard in 1220. Standing on a bank of the
River Boyne, it dominates the town with its
monumental 70-foot-high keep. The keep, which is
square in plan, has a smaller, rectangular tower
projecting from the centre of each side. Its walls are
11 feet thick, and inside is a great hall and small
chapel. The 500-yard-long curtain wall is reinforced
by ten D-shaped towers and a moat that could be
flooded from the River Boyne. On one side is a
barbican projecting from a round tower, which
originally spanned the water-filled moat. On the west
side is a square gateway.

Unusual buildings

Carlow Court House   8 M14
Carlow, Co Carlow. Handsome classical-style
courthouse with graceful Ionic portico, designed by
William Vitruvius Morrison 1828–30.

Conolly's Folly   5 N11
Castletown, Celbridge, Co Kildare. Designed 1740 by
Richard Castle, it's a monumental obelisk-crowned
triumphal arch built by William Conolly's widow.
Like numerous other follies of the period, it was
erected to provide relief work.

Dundalk Court House   3 N8
Dundalk, Co Louth. Magnificently austere Greek
Doric-style courthouse with each part—portico, hall
and two court rooms—clearly articulated as separate
elements yet marvellously welded as a whole by the
stark simplicity of the granite walls, stripped of any
decorative distractions. Designed 1813–18 by
Edward Parke and John Bowden.

St Patrick's College   5 N11
Maynooth, Co Kildare. Magnificent complex of
19thC buildings set around two quadrangles, one
built in 1795 and the other in 1845 in the Gothic style
by A W Pugin. The centre-piece is the College
Chapel, designed by J J McCarthy in 1875, with
lofty spire proportioned to control the whole
complex like an Italian campanile. It is the major
Catholic seminary in Ireland and was founded in
1795, for the education of priests forced to abandon a
Continental education by the European wars. There
is a fine collection of illuminated manuscripts and
other exhibits in the College museum.

Seatown Windmill   5 N8
Dundalk, Co Louth. Unfortunately without its sails
since 1870, it is seven storeys high and was one of
Ireland's largest working windmills up until 1855.

Wilson's Hospital   5 K10
Multyfarnham, Co Westmeath. Designed by John
Pentland in 1760, it is a Protestant boys' school
consisting of a pedimented main block with central
court, ground storey arcading and curved links to
flanking pavilions in the best Palladian tradition.
Briefly the headquarters of the Franco-Irish army in
1798.

Wonderful Barn   5 N11
Leixlip, Nr Celbridge, Co Kildare. Built for Speaker
Conolly's widow in 1743, it's a huge, six-stage
conical structure of brick and stone, with five storeys
consisting of a domed room each with projecting
ground-storey porches placed on axis with gable
ends. Goods were winched up through a central
opening in the floors. There is a stone staircase
wrapped in a corkscrew around the outside of the
barn.

Wonderful Barn

Houses & gardens

Abbeyleix House   8 K13
Abbeyleix, Co Laois. A square three-storey block
with balustraded parapet, large hipped roof with
attic storey and a pedimented central section with
bold cornice encircling the building. Refaced in the
19thC, it was designed by James Wyatt and built by
Sir William Chambers for the first Viscount de Vesci
between 1773–74. The house is *not open*, but the
beautiful terrace gardens, laid out by Emma, wife of
the third Viscount de Vesci in the early 19thC, are.
There is a large pond surrounded by azaleas, a
pinetum, and delightful area known as the
Wilderness—a carpet of bluebells beneath ancient
oak trees. *Open summer afternoons.*

Birr Castle Demesne   4 J12
Birr, Co Offaly. A beautiful garden belonging to the
Earl and Countess of Rosse, delightful in spring with
many shrubs, particularly magnolias, and ablaze
with russet tints in autumn. There are tall box
hedges in the formal gardens and a huge disused
telescope used by the 3rd Earl, an astronomer, to
map the Milky Way. *Open all year.*

Carton House   5 N11
Nr Maynooth, Co Kildare. Inspired remodelling and
enlargement of a Dutch-style manor house by
Richard Castle in 1739–45, it consists of a
monumental main block with pedimented central
section and projecting wings with curving
colonnades linking low pavilions; remodelled in the
19thC by Sir Richard Morrison, who transformed
the back into a front. Handsome landscaped
gardens, including balustraded bridge and curious
Shell House, lined with sea shells. *Irregular opening.*

Interior of Castletown

Castletown   5 N11
Celbridge, Co Kildare. The finest 18thC house in
Ireland, it was built between 1719–32 for William
Conolly (1662–1729), one-time speaker of the Irish
House of Commons, and remained in the possession
of the Conolly family until 1965. Designed by the
Italian architect Alessandro Galilei in association
with Sir Edward Lovett Pearce, it's a handsome
Renaissance-style palazzo with high central block
linked on either side by a low, curving colonnade to
flanking pavilions. It became the prototypical
Georgian mansion from which less grand, but
nevertheless impressive, copies were made. The
interiors, completed under the direction of Thomas
Conolly, the speaker's grand-nephew, include a
magnificent entrance hall; handsome great staircase
by Vierpyl with decorative stucco work by the
Francini brothers between 1759–60; Pompeian-style
long gallery enriched by Venetian chandeliers; fine
18thC print room and Irish furniture of the period.
In the grounds, which include half-mile avenue of

limes leading up to the house, is Conolly's Folly or obelisk. The house is now the headquarters of the Irish Georgian Society. *Open summer.*

Geragh 5 O11
Nr Dun Laoghaire, Co Dublin. One of the finest examples of modern architecture in Ireland, it is a handsome white rendered house tucked in a corner of Sandycove to the east of Scotsmans Bay. Designed by Michael Scott in 1937, it has a plain, almost box-like entrance and service wing with the principal rooms curving out to the bay in delightful streamlined elegance as they step down in two terraces. *Not open to the public.*

Howth Castle Gardens 5 O11
Howth, Co Dublin. Famous for the glorious rhododendrons, which cover the side of a hill. There is also a large dolmen known as Aideen's Grave and the ruins of 16thC Corr Castle. *Open all year.*

Japanese Gardens 5 M12
National Stud, Kildare, Co Kildare. Laid out in 1906 by Eida, the Japanese landscape gardener, these are beautiful miniature gardens representing in symbolic manner the life of man from the cradle to the grave. *Open summer.*

Jigginstown House 5 M12
Naas, Co Kildare. Ruins of a monumental brick mansion surmounting a vaulted, stone-faced basement. Designed by Thomas Wentworth for the Earl of Strafford in 1636, with an impressive 380-foot-long frontage. It was begun as a summer residence where the earl could entertain Charles I, but the monarch never came and Strafford was executed in 1639. His house, which would have been the largest residence ever built in Ireland, soon fell into picturesque decay. *Open all year.*

Johnstown Castle Gardens 8 N17
Rosslare, Co Wexford. Splendid trees, two great lakes and terraced walks. There is a good heather collection, formal and walled gardens. *Open all year.*

Kilruddery 5 O12
Bray, Co Wicklow. The seat of the Earl of Meath, there is a mainly 17thC garden in the French manner, with 10-foot-high hedging known as The Angles, statuary, fountains and a miniature amphitheatre. On the east side is a natural rock garden. *Open by appointment only.*

Drawing room, Lucan House

Lucan House 5 N11
Lucan, Co Dublin. Designed in 1776 by an amateur architect, the Rt Hon Agmondisham Vesey, with advice from Chambers. The principal rooms were decorated by James Wyatt and Michael Stapleton. Now the residence of the Italian Ambassador, the house has a high central section complete with engaged Ionic columns and pediment. *Not open to the public.*

Mount Kennedy 5 O12
Nr Greystones, Co Wicklow. Designed by the brilliant English architect James Wyatt in 1772, it is a magnificent neoclassical building, two storeys in height with the ground floor articulated by a low, pedimented portico and the upper floor differentiated by a plain string course and a large semicircular ancient Roman window, placed symmetrically above the entrance. The remaining windows are austerely plain. *Not open to the public.*

Mount Usher 8 O13
Ashford, Co Wicklow. A beautiful garden created around the River Vartry, offering some of the most exotic and tender plants; it is of enormous interest to any plantsman and should not be missed. *Open summer.*

Powerscourt gardens, Enniskerry

Powerscourt 5 O12
Enniskerry, Co Wicklow. A series of stepped terraces built in the 1740s lead eventually to a pool, flanked by winged horses of Fame and Victory. There is a grand arboretum, including a 200-foot Sitka spruce, a collection of monkey-puzzles and a towering eucalyptus. The fine 18thC mansion was sadly destroyed by fire in 1974. The 14,000 acres of woodlands and gardens include a magnificent 400-foot waterfall, the highest in Ireland, tumbling headlong over a skyscraper of cliff. The gutted ruins of the house are reached by a mile-long avenue. *Open summer.*

Rothe House 8 L15
Kilkenny, Co Kilkenny. Magnificent example of the wealthy merchant's houses to be found in the more affluent towns of 16thC Ireland. It has a three-storey stone façade with a central gable crowned by a chimney. There is a boldly moulded string course, an asymmetrical first floor with off-centre oriel window, an arcaded ground storey with half basement to one side and a central vaulted passageway leading to an enclosed courtyard beyond. There are two more courtyard houses. *Irregular opening.*

Russborough House 5 N12
Blessington, Co Wicklow. Designed by Richard Castle in 1742, it is one of the finest Palladian mansions in Ireland. A remarkably handsome complex, it consists of a large central block linked to low flanking pavilions by curving colonnades. A characteristic feature of Castle's work is the

superimposed portico. Also here is the world-famous Beit Art Collection with works by Franz Hals, Jan Vermeer, Velasquez, Gainsborough, Goya and others. There is also an outstanding collection of Irish silver from the late 17thC to early 19thC. *Irregular opening.*

Stradbally Hall   5 **L13**
Stradbally, Co Laois. Lovely 18thC gardens with fabulous herbaceous border and over 90 species of perennials. *Open summer.*

Tullynally Castle Gardens   5 **K9**
Castlepollard, Co Westmeath. This seat of the earls of Longford is a multi-turreted family home, one of the largest and most romantic in Ireland. Part of the house and the lovely gardens are *open summer.*

Museums & galleries

Agricultural Museum   5 **O13**
Glenealy, Co Wicklow. Old farm implements and machinery. *Open weekdays.*

Ballintore Museum   5 **M13**
Nr Athy, Co Kildare. The old meeting house of a once-flourishing Quaker settlement; the public library also has a museum, with much of interest. *Irregular opening.*

Castleruddery Transport Museum   8 **M13**
Donard, Baltinglass, Co Wicklow. Trams, trollies and buses. *Open summer.*

Derragara Museum   2 **K7**
Butlersbridge, Co Cavan. A full-size replica of an 18thC mud-and-wattle homestead plus old household paraphernalia. *Open all year.*

Inniskeen Folk Museum   3 **N8**
Co Monaghan, 7 miles NE of Carrickmacross. Local history, folk life and a section on Patrick Kavanagh, the poet. *Open all year.*

Irish Horse Museum and National Stud   5 **M12**
Nr Kildare, Co Kildare. The museum is in the grounds of the stud farm and traces the evolution of the horse in Ireland. *Open summer.*

Russborough House   5 **N12**
Nr Blessington, Co Wicklow. Georgian setting for the famous Beit Art Collection and also Irish Silver (1680–1820). Collection of miniature steam trains in basement. *Irregular opening.*

Stradbally Steam Museum   8 **L13**
Stradbally, Co Laois. The first museum of its kind in Ireland, it was set up by the Irish Steam Preservation Society to illustrate the social history of steam; includes amongst other things motor cars, fire engines and steam trains. *Open all year.* Annual rally first weekend in *Aug.*

Transport Museum   5 **N9**
Rathgory, Dunleer, Co Louth. Vintage cars, fire-tenders and old motor bikes. *Open summer.*

Nature trails & reserves

Avondale Forest Park   8 **O13**
Co Wicklow, 1 mile S of Rathdrum. Planned walks, nature trails and picnic area in the grounds of Avondale House, the birthplace of Parnell. The house itself is open weekday afternoons in *summer.* Booklet available at the park.

Bellevue   5 **O12**
Co Wicklow, 5 miles S of Bray. Picnic area, forest walks and nature trail. Leaflet available at the site.

Cruagh and Tibradden   5 **O11**
Co Dublin, 5 miles S of Rathfarnham. Two areas both offering forest walks, nature trails and picnic facilities. From Cruagh there is a wilderness trek to the Military Road via Featherbed Mountain, and from Tibradden there are paths to Cruagh Wood and Military Road. Leaflets are available at both forests.

Devil's Glen   8 **O13**
Co Wicklow, 2½ miles W of Ashford. A tight gash in rocky country with the River Vartry flowing through the middle. There are picnic facilities, forest walks, a waterfall and a nature trail (leaflet available), and this is the home of the beautiful Mount Usher Gardens, 20 acres of rare trees and shrubs inspired by Edward Walpole in 1860.

Dun A' Ri Forest Park   3 **M8**
Co Cavan, 1 mile N of Kingscourt. Now managed by the Dept of Fisheries and Forests, the park covers 560 acres around the River Cabra. A wishing well, ice house and Cromwell's bridge are interesting additions to an already beautiful forest park, where deer can still be seen. There are also planned walks, a picnic place and a nature trail (booklet available at the park).

Glendalough   5 **N13**
Co Wicklow, 1 mile W of Laragh. Amidst one of the most extensive complexes of monastic ruins in Ireland, there is a nature trail (leaflet available), forest walks and a picnic place. Boat trips to St Kevin's Bed.

Glendalough
Co Wicklow

Killykeen Forest Park   2 **K8**
Co Cavan, 8 miles W of Cavan. On the shores of the River Erne and Lough Oughter; there are many pleasant forest walks, picnic areas, a marina for boats, swimming facilities, fishing, a shop, restaurant and a nature trail (booklet available).

Monicknew Woods   4 **K12**
Co Laois, 7 miles N of Mountrath. Forest walks, picnic area, viewing points and a scenic route over the Slieve Bloom nature trail. Leaflet available.

Ravensdale   3 **N7**
Co Louth, 4 miles N of Dundalk. Picnic area, forest walks and a nature trail (leaflet on site).

Rossmore Forest Park   3 **L7**
Co Monaghan, 1 mile S of Monaghan. A lakeside park with wonderful views, walks, nature trails and picnic sites. Fishing facilities. Booklet including nature trail notes available.

Townley Hall   5 **N9**
Co Louth, 4 miles W of Drogheda. A Georgian mansion by Francis Johnston 1794, at the site of the Battle of the Boyne. It was Johnston's only classical house, and is now the agricultural research centre for Trinity College. In the extensive grounds there are pleasant walks, picnic sites and a nature trail (leaflet available at the house). Also nearby are an intriguing passage grave and neolithic dwelling site.

Birdwatching

Lambay Island   5 O10
Off Rush, Co Dublin. Bird sanctuary four miles in circumference with 400-foot cliffs, owned by Lord Revelstoke. Boats from Rogerstown, near Rush. Contact the Steward, Lambay Island, Rush, for permission to visit.

Saltee Islands   8 N17
Off Kilmore Quay, Co Wexford. The most famous bird sanctuary in Ireland, with a population in late spring and summer of over three million birds. Boats from Kilmore Quay.

Wicklow Mountains   8 N13
Co Wicklow. Irish heron can be spotted on the Rivers Glencree and Glencullen, and ravens can be seen in Powerscourt Demesne.

Forests

There are numerous forest parks in this part of the country. A full list can be obtained from the Forest and Wildlife Service, 22 Upper Merrion Street, Dublin 2 (Dublin 789211). See also the listings under 'Nature trails'.

Glen of the Dargle   5 O12
Nr Bray, Co Wicklow. A narrow path leads through a densely wooded glen, passing the Lovers' Leap—a massive rocky promontory.

The John F Kennedy Park   8 L16
Dunganstown, Co Wexford. A 410-acre park, over half of which is an arboretum. There are picnic facilities, viewing points and a café.

Hills & mountains

Croghan Valley   8 O14
Co Wicklow, 5 miles SW of Arklow. Idyllic world of leafy glens, meandering streams and rivers dotted with tiny villages with melodic names like Shillelagh or Tinahelly. The 2,000-foot-high Croghan Mountain was the scene of an 18thC gold-rush.

Glencree   5 O12
Co Wicklow. A beautiful, rugged valley, winding in a series of corkscrew curves for seven miles from its base in the shadows of the 1,659-foot-high Great Sugar Loaf Mountain to the foot of Glendoo Mountain in the north west; through it runs the River Glencree.

Glen of the Downs   5 O12
Co Wicklow. Beautiful wooded ravine two miles west of Greystones, winding between the Great and Little Sugar Loaf Mountains. The Bellvue Forest nature trail is situated here.

Slieve Bloom Mountains   4 J13
Co Offaly. Straddling the borders of Co Offaly and Co Laois, the scarred and crumpled range riddled with lush green glens rises in the north east 1,590 feet to the top of Clarnahinch Mountain. At its feet

Slieve Bloom Mountains

the River Owenass runs eastwards to Mountmellick. In the south, beyond Kinnitty, the range climbs higher still to the 1,733-foot-high Arderin. It is here that the Rivers Barrow and Nore begin, amidst the quiet contentment of the Moniknew Woods, the Barrow Valley and Forelacka Glen. A little to the east is Leap Castle, remains of the 16thC O'Carroll stronghold.

The Vale of Avoca   8 O14
Co Wicklow. Immortalised by Thomas Moore, the delightful winding vale where the Rivers Avonmore and Avonbeg converge at 'The Meeting of the Waters' lies two miles north of the village of Avoca. Best seen in spring, when bright shafts of light and blossom abound. Two miles away crowning an 800-foot hill overlooking Avoca stands the Motte Stone, a glacial boulder said to be the 'hurling-stone' of Finn McCool. South of Avoca is Ballymoyle Hill, with fine forest walks and spectacular views.

Sugarloaf Mountain, Co Wicklow

The Wicklow Mountains   5 N13
Co Wicklow. The Wicklow Mountains, running a few miles inland from Dun Laoghaire in the north east to Aghavannagh in the south, are full of mysterious glens and long, winding, heather-covered valleys. Best seen from the 19thC Military Road built to prevent a recurrence of the troubles of 1798. The northern entrance point is Rathfarnham, four miles south of Dublin. Crowning Montpellier Hill, four miles south, is an old stone building used in the early 18thC as a Hell Fire Club. Not far away is Glencree, the first of the major mountain passes in Wicklow. Nearby beauty spots include Glendhu, Pine Forest and Glenasmole. There are numerous nature trails, and on Djouce Mountain red and sika deer, hares, foxes and badgers can still be seen. To the south are the mountain tarns of Upper and Lower Lough Bray, deep in the shadows of the 2,475-foot-high Kippure Mountain. Not far away is the source of the River Liffey, a tiny stream of bog water. Further south still is Sally Gap, with the icy mountain waters of Loughs Tay and Dan to the south east. The road winds southwards to Glenmacnass, a wooded valley entombed by a towering wall of mountains washed at one end by a frothing waterfall. To the west is lovely Glendalough with Laragh, its gateway, to the east at the foot of Glenmacnass. From here the Military Road runs south east to Rathdrum, a tiny town perched high on a shelf of land on the western slopes of the Avonmore Valley.

Countryside

Carlow

One of the smallest counties in eastern Ireland. To the east the county is hilly; the southern limits of the Wicklow Mountains reach down into the north east corner and below them lie the gentler Blackstairs Mountains. The county is bordered in the west by the River Barrow—one of Ireland's many excellent angling rivers.

Cavan
A county of extremes, stretching from the Iron Mountains in the west soaring to 2,188 feet on Cuilcagh, to Kingscourt in the east, wallowing in undulating agricultural land. The county is dotted with lakes, including Lough Gowna, which protrudes over the border from Co Longford. The River Erne, flowing northward from Lough Gowna, breaks out into a succession of smaller lakes before reaching Lower Lough Erne, which stretches across Cavan's northern border into Co Fermanagh. The numerous lakes afford spectacular scenery.

Dublin
Dublin is washed to the north and west by the lush green plains of Meath and the coast is dotted by oases of leisure resorts and sandy beaches. To the south of Dublin city the hum of the metropolis gives way to tranquility in the Dublin mountains, a line of giant hills galloping away into the measureless horizon of the Wicklow Mountains beyond, with beautiful pine forests, glens and lakes. Straddling the border, the Kippure Mountain claws its way skyward, its 2,475-foot-high peak peeping out occasionally from behind the clouds. The River Liffey cuts the county and the city in two, running out from Wicklow through Kildare to Dublin city.

Kildare
Kildare is renowned throughout the world as a sporting and racing area. It consists mainly of open grasslands and arable land, although there are traces of the boglands that have played a large part in Ireland's past, notably the Bog of Allen, one end of which spills over from Co Offaly. The huge tracts of grasslands bear witness to Kildare's role as a horse-breeding county—the undulating nature of the land is ideal for the racing and training of horses; the famous Curragh racecourse lies at the heart of Kildare. The River Liffey and the Grand Canal flow through the county, which is predominantly flat; what hills there are, such as the Hill of Allen and the Chair of Kildare, stand up like sentries guarding the surrounding land.

The Curragh racecourse, Co Kildare

Kilkenny
The Rivers Barrow and Nore flow here, the latter cutting through the limestone plain that underlies most of the county. To the north west lie the Slieveardagh and Booley Hills, gentle ripples in the lush green landscape; crops such as sugar beet are grown in profusion.

Laois
A small, square-shaped county situated in the west of the ancient province of Leinster. The Slieve Bloom Mountains rise lonely in the north west, the only high point in this mostly flat county. The Rock of Danamase, near Portlaoise, is the only other exception—a 200-foot-high limestone hill surmounted by the ruins of long fought-over fortifications. Laois also lies on Ireland's central limestone plain, an area of rich, undulating farmland, relieved by many streams and areas of woodland. The Slieve Bloom Mountains, which are more like gently rounded hills, rise to only 1,734 feet at their highest point; they are a mixture of sandstone and limestone, heavily forested with larch and conifers. Large areas of Laois are administered by the Forestry Division, and its verdant woodlands are perhaps its most appealing feature.

Longford
A small inland county bordered in the west by the River Shannon and a pattern of lakes, including Lough Ree. In the north east is a range of low hills; Carn Clonhugh, their chief, reaches only 916 feet. Between the hills and the river lies a patchwork quilt of agricultural land.

Louth
The smallest county in Ireland, a neat blanket of low-lying farmland crossed by toyland rivers and trimmed with sandy beaches. To the north, the Cooley Peninsula extends a rocky arm into the Irish Sea. One of the most scenic areas on the eastern coast, the peninsula has long been associated with Irish legends; its harsh mountainous areas are rich with ruins. It is also a birdwatcher's paradise.

River Boyne, Co Meath

Meath
Once the seat of the High Kings of Ireland, Meath still retains something of its royal past. The land is extremely fertile, particularly the valley of the River Boyne, and lives up to the traditional image of Ireland as a country of rolling green hills. At the coast, the limestone crumbles into a string of sandy beaches.

Monaghan
Towering over neighbouring Cavan, Monaghan is a sea of hills, most around the 1,000-foot mark. An angler's paradise, the county is dotted with fish-filled lakes.

Offaly
A sprawling county in the centre of the country, edged by the Slieve Bloom Mountains in the south eastern corner. For the most part, the county is made up of a vast limestone plain and the Bog of Allen, a good source of turf for burning during winter months. Today the boglands are undergoing extensive development—after the peat has been removed, the soil left behind makes extremely fertile agricultural land. Ireland is a major exporter of peat. The River Shannon forms part of Co Offaly's western border and the River Brosna flows to meet it, cutting across the north western corner of the county from Clara to Banagher.

Westmeath
A land-locked county punctuated by large loughs set amidst lovely scenery. Lough Ree borders the county to the west. Mullingar, a busy market town, sits at the centre of the lake district, surrounded by fertile land used primarily for raising cattle. The principal jewels of the lake district are Lough Ennell, Lough Owel and Lower Derravaragh, which with its fringe of trees has an air of mystery and is one of the most picturesque spots in the county.

Wexford
Wexford faces south east across St George's Channel towards North Wales, with the Irish Sea to the north and the Celtic Sea to the south. It is a low-lying county with fertile coastal plains, and is crossed by the River Slaney on its north–south path to Wexford town and the sea. In the west the Blackstairs Mountains straddle the border with Co Carlow, and the southern tip of the Wicklow Mountains forms the border with Co Wicklow to the north.

Wicklow
A county of contrasts: to the east are low-lying coastal areas, numerous beaches and several large resorts, but the main feature of the county is the Wicklow Mountain range. Formed mainly of granite, covered in many places by a layer of peat, the mountains are gashed by deep valleys, hidden glens and gorges. The peaks themselves are generally rather rounded in outline and covered with heather and bracken, and offer excellent walking country. There are many small lakes set high in the mountains, which rise to 3,039 feet at the peak of Lugnaquilla, and much of the county is carpeted with forests.

Rivers & loughs

District of the Waters   5 K10
Nr Mullingar, Co Westmeath. Old name for the lake district encircling Mullingar. Ten miles north east is beautiful Lough Lene; three miles south west is Lough Ennell, the largest of the lakes, with handsome Belvedere House, an 18thC mansion standing on the east shore; to the north west is Lough Owel, with remains of an early monastic settlement on an island in the lake; beyond it lie the narrow waters of Lough Iron. Good trout fishing, and coarse fishing for pike and perch.

Lough Oughter   2 K8
Co Cavan. Large labyrinth of narrow waters filled with islands and carved by a jagged line of limestone hills. The River Erne runs through it from Lough Gowna in the south to Upper Lough Erne, a more open stretch of water by Enniskillen in the far north.

Lough Oughter

River Boyne
The River Boyne winds its way north east from the Bog of Allen, just north of Edenberry, sidestepping through Trim in two great curves and on through Co Louth, past the famous abbeys of Monasterboice and Mellifont to the site of the famous Battle of the Boyne at the mouth of the River Mattock. Straddling the mouth of the river, to the east, is the historic town of Drogheda. The course of the river is enmeshed with that of Irish history, from the legendary Hill of Tara, seat of Ireland's High Kings, just south of Navan in Co Meath to prehistoric Newgrange, Knowth and Dowth, a few miles downstream from Slane in the north.

River Liffey
A great curving scimitar of water, it links the counties of Dublin and Kildare. Spanned by handsome bridges, it curves west from the Pollaphuca Reservoir on the edge of the Wicklow Mountains, skirts north of Kilcullen and passes along the east of Droichead Nua. It then winds north east under the Grand Canal, through Celbridge curving eastward, through Lucan and on through the heart of Dublin to Dublin Bay beyond.

Canals

Grand Canal
Early in the 18thC many people had discussed the idea of opening up the centre of the country, and in 1751 the Irish Parliament established a corporation for promoting and carrying on the inland navigation of Ireland. Although dissolved in 1787, it had already achieved miracles with work started on the River Shannon in 1755, on the Grand Canal in 1756 and the Rivers Barrow and Boyne in 1759.

Grand Canal, Dublin

The Grand Canal was one of two principal arteries to be built across Ireland. The first was the Lagan Navigation, built 1756–94 linking Belfast with Lough Neagh; the Grand Canal was the second. Designed to link Dublin with the Shannon, work began on the Grand Canal in 1756 but by 1768 only 20 miles had been completed and, because of prohibitive costs, work was abandoned. A company was formed to continue the work and in 1773 they invited John Smeaten and William Jessop to act as consultants. They conceived a less ambitious scheme and by 1805 work was completed. Its major offshoot was the River Barrow, which was part river navigation and part canal, but there were other, smaller branches as well. From its junction with the River Barrow at Athy in Co Kildare, it runs north along the edge of the Bog of Allen and through Robertstown, a picturesque 18thC canal village, where it joins the main route. It then curves eastwards to Clondalkin, just west of Dublin, and then on into the city through the southern suburbs into the River Liffey at Hanover Quay. From Robertstown in Co Kildare, the main canal runs across to the River Shannon and then up to Ballinasloe, the western terminus of the canal in Co Galway.

Royal Canal
The canal mania that seized the English imagination in the 18thC roused little interest in Ireland, primarily because it was not so much private as public funds that financed the Irish canals. The one major exception was the Royal Canal, running from Dublin to the Upper Shannon. In 1789 a private company was formed to promote the canal. Costs soon became prohibitive, however, and despite a large government grant of £96,850 and with over £1,000,000 spent on its construction, the canal was far from complete. In 1813 the Directors-General of

nland Navigation took over. The canal was finally completed in 1817 and the New Royal Canal Company took over the management of its affairs. It starts at a junction with the River Shannon just north of Lough Ree in Co Longford and runs south, turning east just north of Ballymahon, through the heart of Goldsmith country. Passing along the southern edge of Mullingar, the county and market town of Westmeath, it then skirts south of Maynooth and on through the northern suburbs of Dublin. Curving round the outside of the North Circular Road, it crosses through Croke Park and turns southwards to join the River Liffey by North Wall Quay. Once a thriving business concern, by the late 1830s it carried over 88,334 tons of cargo and 46,450 passengers a year.

Archaeological sites

Baltinglass Hill   8 M13
Baltinglass, Co Wicklow. Crowning the 1,258 foot-high hill are the remains of two late Stone Age passage graves, one with five recesses off a central chamber and two spiral decorated stones. The remains of a large defensive stone wall belong to the Iron Age fortification system of Rathcoran, once a great hill fort.

Browne's Hill Dolmen, Carlow

Brugh na Bóinne   5 N9
Nr Slane, Co Meath. Sited along the north bank of the River Boyne, the Brugh na Bóinne (the Palace of the Boyne) is a six-square-mile cemetery, once the legendary burial place of the pre-Christian kings of Ireland. There are 15 passage graves in the area, of which the principal ones are those at Newgrange, Knowth and Dowth.

Dowth   5 N9
Nr Slane, Co Meath. A 50-foot-high mound, 280 feet in diameter, it contains two prehistoric tombs dating from 2500BC. Around the base of the mound are a number of decorated stones. The round burial chambers in both tombs are reached by passages. At the entrance to one is an Early Christian souterrain.

Dowth Mound

Fournocks Hill   5 O10
Nr Balbriggan, Co Dublin. Fine cruciform passage grave c1800BC; large pear-shaped main chamber with decorated stone uprights and lintels, one engraved with a human face. On higher ground nearby is a rock-cut trench used as a crematorium.

Hill of Knockaulin   5 M12
Nr Kilcullen, Co Kildare. This 600-foot-high hill was an early seat of the kings of Leinster; there are remains of a 20-acre circular hill-fort, Dun Aillinne, which crowned the summit, ringed by a huge earth bank and ditch.

Hill of Tailte   5 M9
Nr Kells, Co Meath. Crowning the Hill of Tailte at Teltown, six miles south east of Kells, is the site of an ancient palace, one of the four royal residences built by King Tuathal in prehistoric Ireland. This was the site of ancient assemblies and games, which took place each August.

Knowth   5 N9
Nr Slane, Co Meath. A 40-foot-high mound, 220 feet in diameter and containing two huge passage graves, one with a corbelled roof, the other flat. Surrounding the base of the larger mound is a series of decorated kerbstones. During the late 12thC the Anglo-Normans used the mound as a motte.

Loughcrew Hills   5 L9
Nr Oldcastle, Co Meath. One of Ireland's most remarkable groups of passage graves, consisting of over 30 tombs built on the two principal peaks of the Loughcrew Hills. The largest are found on Carnbane West, one with a diameter of over 180 feet; one of them, Cairn K, has five chambers and a standing stone inside. On the 904-foot-high Slieve na Calliagh, Cairn T is a most interesting classic example of a passage grave; it is 115 feet in diameter and has a number of side chambers off the principal chamber. Inside the tombs are several carved stones, similar to those at Newgrange, decorated with concentric circles, arcs, zigzags and flower-motifs.

Carved stone, Loughcrew Hills

Newgrange   5 N9
Nr Slane, Co Meath. Dating from 2500BC, this is one of the finest passage graves to be found in Western Europe, a heart-shaped mound 40 feet high and nearly 300 feet in diameter. Surrounding the base are massive kerbstones, many decorated in geometric patterns. Unique to Newgrange is the decorative triple spiral carved on the stone marking the entrance. The tomb itself consists of a 62-foot-long passage, many of its stones decorated with zigzags and spirals, leading to a cruciform chamber built of unmortared stone. Beside the car park is a small exhibition centre with drawings, photographs and plaster casts.

Punchestown Standing Stone   5 **M12**
Nr Naas, Co Kildare. One of the finest examples of
its kind in Ireland, it's a tall, tapering, granite stone,
23 feet high and weighing 9 tons. It was found in
1931 to have a Bronze Age burial chamber at its
base.

Hill of Tara

Tara   5 **M10**
Co Meath, 6 miles S of Navan. A 512-foot-high hill
standing on wild meadowland, it represents Irish
folklore at its most heroic. It was here that the
famous chase that was to cover the length and
breadth of Ireland began, when Finn was deserted
by his beloved Grainne for Diairmaid. Of religious
and political importance for over 2,000 years, this
low, grassy hill, was the seat of the High Kings in
pre-Christian Ireland. With the introduction of
Christianity in the 5thC, Tara lost its religious
importance and in 1022 it was finally abandoned as a
seat of the High King by Mael Schechlainn. All that
remains are simple earthworks and a world of
memories. One of the most prominent remains is the
1800BC Mound of the Hostages, a passage grave
consisting of a narrow passage giving access to a
small chamber; it stands to the northern side of an
Iron Age hill fort. In the centre of the enclosure are
two linked ring forts, the one to the west is Cormac's
House, to the east is the Royal Seat. Outside the
main enclosure to the north is the Banqueting Hall, a
long hollow edged by banks.

Regional sport

Canoeing
Several rivers in the area offer excellent canoeing,
especially the Liffey, Slaney, Boyne, Nore and
Barrow. The River Liffey is among the best canoeing
rivers in Europe, and the annual Liffey Canoe
Descent attracts competitors from many countries.
The River Barrow is navigable for almost its entire
length and the upper and middle reaches of the River
Slaney offer exciting white-water canoeing. This is a
magnificent area for canoe-camping, all year round.

Golf
Some of the best 18-hole courses in the country are
to be found in and around Dublin, and at Skerries,
Co Dublin, there are 30 courses. Visitors can usually
play Mon–Fri, and some clubs allow free play in the
off-season.

Hill walking
The centre for trekkers is the Wicklow Mountains
area, with miles and miles of beautiful open country,
criss-crossed by lush glen valleys. There are
magnificent views to be had and in many areas you
can walk for hours without meeting a soul. The land
can be boggy in parts and there are few tracks, so
maps and compasses are advisable.
Rock climbing on granite for various levels at
Glendalough.

Sea fishing
Large number of competitions, mostly *Feb–Nov*.
Among the many centres are Skerries, Greystones,
Wexford, Dun Laoghaire and Howth. Fish available
include conger, polack, flounder, whiting and
mackerel.

Festivals

Dublin Horse Show   5 **O11**
Ballsbridge, Co Dublin. One of the major Irish events
with over 2,000 horses entered; a week long, with
jumping events every day, including Grand Prix,
Nations Cup and Aga Khan trophy. *Aug.*

National Steam Traction Rally   5 **L13**
Stradbally, Co Laois. A very popular family occasion
with traction engines and lots of steam. *Early Aug.*

Wexford Opera Festival   8 **N16**
Held in the charming 19thC Theatre Royal,
Wexford, it has become renowned for its
productions of the lesser-known operas of the 18thC
and 19thC. Recitals, concerts and chamber music are
also performed during the festival weeks. *Annually
Oct–Nov.*

Special attractions

The Curragh   5 **M12**
Nr Kildare, Co Kildare. A vast 5,000-acre plain, it's
the headquarters of the Irish horse-racing world with
35 racing stables as well as the famous Curragh
Racecourse. Renowned for its Irish Sweeps Derby
held each *Jun*, other classics include the Irish St
Leger, the Irish Oaks, and the 1,000 and 2,000
Guineas.

Dunmore Cave   8 **L14**
*Co Kilkenny, 7 miles from Kilkenny on Castlecomer
Road.* A natural limestone cavern, which was sacked
by the Vikings in AD928; 1,000 sheltering people
died in the raid. Guided tours *daily*, lighting and
viewing galleries.

Dunmore Cave

Falconry   5 **M11**
Robertstown, Co Kildare. Guided tours of the largest
Irish falconry *daily*, followed by a horse-drawn barge
trip and an 18thC candlelit banquet at the old Grand
Canal Hotel *in summer.*

Fonntrai   5 **O11**
Culturlann na h Éireann, Monkstown, Co Dublin. A
show of Irish entertainment presented twice weekly
in *summer* by Comhaltas Cheoltóiri Éireann.
Musicians talk and demonstrate instruments once a
week here also.

Woodenbridge Trout Farm   5 **O14**
Nr Arklow, Co Wicklow. Fish-your-own with
equipment supplied free. Children welcome. Charge
only for fish caught in well stocked lake.

Southern Ireland

4

Clare	**Limerick**
Cork	**Tipperary**
Kerry	**Waterford**

This region covers the whole of the ancient kingdom of Munster, the largest province in Ireland, and includes also Co Clare, part of the kingdom of Connacht until the 4thC. Waterford was originally a Norse stronghold and was the first area to be occupied by the Anglo-Normans in the 12thC.

Clare, which sprawls across a large triangular peninsula on the north of the River Shannon, is rich and fertile along the estuary but further north it becomes more barren. The hills gallop north west to the rugged coast, where 700-foot, bone-white cliffs such as the skyscraper Cliffs of Moher rise vertically above the wild seas. Nearby is The Burren, a vast limestone moonscape, unique in Europe and a haven for botanists and archaeologists; it is littered with prehistoric sites and has inspired passionate reactions from such writers as Shaw and Yeats. From Black Head in the north to Loop Head in the south at the mouth of the estuary of the Shannon,

gort, co clare.

Ireland's greatest river, there is a magnificent coastline of cathedral-like caverns, scimitars of sandy beach and formidable walls of cliffs. To the east, the Slieve Bernagh and Slieve Aughty Mountains corkscrew skywards above Lough Derg and the Shannon, whilst inland the lowland region is covered with a complex network of lakes. Twelve miles south east of Ennis are the space age comforts of Shannon Airport, the first customs-free airport in the world, and within easy reach are 150 ancient churches, 190 castles and over 2,300 stone or earthen forts. The haunt of anglers for the mayfly season on Lough Derg, Co Clare also has its romantic side: Ellen Hanley, the 'Colleen Bawn' is buried at Killimer, six miles east of Kilrush. Her tragic drowning at the hands of a jealous husband was immortalised by Gerald Griffin in his novel, 'The Collegians'. At Spanish Point, two miles east of the little resort of Milltown Malbay, the bodies of Spanish seamen were washed ashore following the wreck of six of their Armada ships in 1588.

Tipperary is bordered to the north east by Lough Derg, the largest and lowest of the Shannon lakes, and stretches in a trapezium of land to the south east across the Golden Vale, erupting along the borders with Co Waterford in the sky-reaching peaks of the Galtee and Knockmealdown Mountains. The rich plain of the Golden Vale occupies the middle of the county and through it the River Suir flows from the northern borders with Co Laois, bypasses the Galty Mountains to the east and then runs out along the borders of Co Waterford to Waterford Harbour and the sea beyond. Clonmel, the county town, was originally a Danish settlement, walled in the 14thC by the Anglo-Normans. It was here that an Italian pedlar, Charles Bianconi, started Ireland's first transport service in 1815. Cashel is one of Ireland's great historic sites; a remarkable complex of ruins crown a huge limestone rock standing 200 feet above the surrounding plain. This was the seat of Munster kings from the 4thC; remains include Cormac's Chapel, a unique example of Irish early Romanesque building.

Limerick, part of the rich plain of the Golden Vale which runs north west of the Galty Mountains, is a low undulating area of fertile land bordering the southern bank of the River Shannon from Limerick city in the north, where the Shannon becomes tidal, to halfway down the estuary. To the south, the boundary with Co Cork is sealed by rolling, green hills. It's a quiet, rural place, its tranquil charm belying its turbulent past when Brian Boru attacked Limerick city, then a Danish settlement, or when it was captured by the Anglo-Normans in the 12thC only to be recovered by the O'Briens in 1194. Limerick was a commercial rival to Galway in the 17thC and the Irish army returned here following their defeat at the Battle of the Boyne in 1690, resulting in the famous siege of Limerick of 1690–91.

vernacular buildings
Fringe Co Limerick

Kerry, which straddles an armful of peninsulas poking out into the Atlantic between Bantry Bay in the south and the Shannon estuary in the north, is covered in a magnificent gnarled and crumpled mountainscape except to the north, where a lush green plain runs inland some way from the Shannon estuary, past Listowel with its decorative pubs to Ballyheige Bay on the Atlantic. From Tralee, encircled by moors and bogland, the Dingle Peninsula runs out to the west, a heaving mountain mass with roads pinned tightly on steep passes beside the rocky coast and cliffs. There is beautiful Dingle itself, a light-hearted place on a steep hill with magnificent views out to sea or over gorse-covered mountainside. To the south west, behind the wall of mountains, lies little Gallarus Oratory, the best preserved of Ireland's early Christian buildings. A mile west of Ardfert is a little earthen fort, where Sir Roger Casement was arrested in 1916 having landed from a German submarine with a cache of arms for the Easter Rising. South across Dingle Bay is the second of Kerry's giant promontories, the broad Iveragh Peninsula, where some of Ireland's finest mountain scenery can be admired from the famous 'Ring of Kerry' road. At the entrance to the peninsula is Killarney, the heart of a beautiful, wooded lake district abounding in salmon and trout. South, across Kenmare River, is the Beara Peninsula, which it shares with Cork.

Cork, the largest of Ireland's counties, is separated from Kerry in the west by a great wall of mountains, the Caha, Derrynasaggart and Boggeragh Mountains. The refuge of fugitives throughout the ages, it's a lovely undulating stretch of limestone with picturesque river valleys walled by long ridges of sandstone. Beautiful rocky coastal landscape runs east from Bantry Bay via a series of deep, island-strewn bays like Roaring Water Bay, past Kinsale, with its English aura, and the huddled fishing harbours and spacious holiday resorts lining Cork harbour to Youghal, one of the county's major holiday centres, on the mouth of the River Blackwater at the edge of Youghal Bay. Cork is the home of the famous Blarney Stone, set in the wall below Blarney Castle five miles north of Cork; according to tradition, kissing the stone imparts the 'gift of the gab'. At Youghal, Sir Walter Raleigh is said to have smoked the first tobacco and grown the first potatoes in Ireland. It's a remarkably beautiful county with shadowy lakes and quiet river valleys sealed amongst mountains. The coast is rich in resorts like Kinsale, Clonakilty, or Bantry at the head of a beautiful bay. Inland there are quiet oases like Bandon or Macroom or spectacular Gougane Barra, encircled on three sides by spruce, pine, ash and birch crowding the mountainside whilst in the saucer of land below, the River Lee rises, flowing out north through the mountain gap.

Waterford was the first county to be occupied by the Anglo-Normans and Waterford city was the site of a massive Viking fortress from the mid-9thC until 1170 when the Anglo-Normans, under Strongbow, took the city. It is a mainly mountainous county; particularly prominent are the Comeragh and Knockmealdown Mountains, the former riddled with shadow-filled lake corries, with the attractive River Suir winding north and east. To the west beyond Knockmealdown Mountains is the River Blackwater, snaking east from Co Kerry. The remainder of the county is strewn with green hills, crumpled valleys and, at the coast, long bays curving away in great crescents of sand, rugged headlands and huge walls of cliff. It was at Waterford city that Henry II landed to take possession of Ireland in 1171, and it was here that Perkin Warbeck, pretender to the English throne, was repulsed in 1497. Lismore, the salmon and fishing resort of the River Blackwater, was one of the renowned universities of early Christian Europe and at the height of its fame in the 8thC it was a huge monastic city with over 20 monastic schools. The handsome Round Tower at Ardmore marks the site of another early Christian settlement founded by St Declan, a bishop of Munster. It was here that the remnants of the confederate army hid in 1642, only to be found by the English who promptly hanged 117 of the 154-man force.

The Coast

Anascaul   **6 C17**
Co Kerry. Handful of houses crouched in the shadow
of scarred and crumpled mountain peaks. The banks
of the streams are rich in royal fern in the spring, and
orchids and Irish-green spurge abound. Of interest:
South Pole Inn, named after Tom Crean
(1877–1938), a former landlord and member of the
British Navy who, as a member of the Scott
expedition to the South Pole, discovered the bodies
of the explorer and his companions following their
tragic return journey; ruins of Minard castle, three
miles south west; several Ogham stones and crosses.

Annestown   **8 K17**
Co Waterford. Popular seaside resort on a shallow
plinth of land behind a good sandy beach.

Ardmore   **7 J18**
Co Waterford. Pop 240. Tiny holiday resort lying on
a long, sandy beach and renowned for the remains of
its 7thC monastic foundation established by St
Declan, and its round tower.

Ballybunion, Co Kerry

Ballybunion   **6 D15**
Co Kerry. Pop 1,290. Popular holiday resort on a
dramatic coastline of cave-riddled cliffs on the shores
of a bay warmed by the Gulf Stream. Dividing the
golden strand in front of the town is a promontory
with the remains of late 16thC Ballybunion Castle, a
Fitzmaurice stronghold. Also of interest: Lick
Castle, a clifftop Fitzgerald fortress visited by the
poet Tennyson in 1842; 92-foot-high Rattoo Tower
of the early 13thC—one of the best preserved round
towers in Ireland, standing beside the ruins of
Rattoo Abbey at Ballyduff, five miles south east.
Good beaches, safe bathing, angling and a golf
course considered to be one of the best in the world.

Ballycotton   **7 I19**
Co Cork. Pop 390. Fishing village perched on a cliff
top above Ballycotton Bay, 26 miles south east of
Cork City. At its feet is the small sheltered harbour,
a colourful sight in summer with its waters packed
tight with a forest of masts.

Ballydehob   **6 E20**
Co Cork. Former copper-mining centre, now a
hamlet, snared in a trap of rock and crumpled hills at
the head of a narrow inlet of Roaring Water Bay. To
the south west is Rossbrin Castle, a 14thC
O'Mahoney stronghold.

Ballyheige   **6 C16**
Co Kerry. Colourful wall of boldly painted houses
behind a long sandy promenade sheltered from the
north by Kerry Head. To the north of the village
stands the gaunt skeleton of Ballyheige Castle, an
early 19thC design by Sir Richard Morrison, burnt
by the Republicans in 1922. Four miles north is
Ballingarry Castle, small, mid-17thC fortress.

Ballylickey   **6 E19**
Co Cork, 4 miles N of Bantry. Little hamlet on the
edge of a narrow creek of Bantry Bay. Magnificent
waterfalls and wooded glens to the north.

Ballylongford   **6 E15**
Co Kerry. Tiny village at the head of a narrow creek
of the Shannon estuary, surrounded by fertile
farmland. To the north are the remains of
Lislaughtin Abbey, a 15thC Franciscan friary;
roofless ruin haunted by gulls and the howl of wind,
it has a lovely carved sedilia. To the north, standing
on a terrace of land abutting the Shannon estuary,
are the ruins of the 15thC–16thC Carrigafoyle Castle,
an O'Connor stronghold partially destroyed by the
Cromwellians in 1649.

Ballyvaughan   **1 F12**
Co Clare. Neat little fishing harbour on the southern
shore of Galway Bay. Shelved on a terrace of land on
the north east edge of the Burren, it is reached by a
corkscrew road dropping sharply in a series of
zigzags through a thickly wooded valley. Of interest:
Corcomroe Abbey, a 12thC Cistercian foundation,
six miles east of the village; Gleninagh Castle, a
four-storey L-shaped tower house built in the 16thC;
Newton Castle, a 16thC tower house, five storeys in
height and consisting of a square ground storey with
a round tower above; Aillwee Cave, magnificent
high-roofed cavern with a fan vault of stalagmites
and stalactites, two miles south east.

Baltimore   **6 E20**
Co Cork. Handful of houses clinging tightly together
on the edge of a narrow strip of land beside a tiny
harbour. On a pedestal of rock high above the
harbour are the ruins of a 15thC O'Driscoll castle.
Sheltering the bay is hump-backed Sherkin Island,
with the remains of a Franciscan abbey and medieval
castle. Further south is Cape Clear Island, an
Irish-speaking world with ruins of another
O'Driscoll castle to the north west. To the south is
famous Fastnet Rock, a solitary outcrop complete
with lighthouse.

Baltimore

Bantry   **6 E19**
Co Cork. Pop 2,530. EC Wed. Wedge of streets and
roofs jammed tightly between green hills at the head
of Bantry Bay, the most beautiful of Irish bays. The
large harbour is now used by oil tankers unloading at
the terminal on Whiddy Island. A sub-tropical
paradise of exotic plants washed by the Gulf Stream,
the bay was twice invaded by French fleets, in 1689
to help James II and in 1796 when General Hoche's
expeditionary force was fought off by storms. Of
interest: Bantry House, elegant Georgian house and
former home of the Earls of Bantry; Falls of
Donemarc on the River Mealagh, two miles north
west.

Bunmahon   **8 K17**
Co Waterford, 3 miles W of Annestown. Tiny fishing
village washed up on a quiet sandy beach backed by
cliffs at the edge of a narrow inlet.

Caherdaniel   6 B19
Co Kerry. Attractive village sitting colourfully at the
head of Derrynane Bay. Of interest: Derrynane
House, home of Daniel O'Connell, and Derrynane
National Historic Park; Ogham stone beside the
Derrynane road; rock-hewn St Crohane's
Hermitage.

Cahirciveen   6 B18
*Co Kerry, 9 miles N of Waterville. Pop 1,550. EC
Thur.* Capital of the Iveragh peninsula with
close-packed houses jammed tight at the head of
Valentia Harbour, in the shadows north of Bentee
Mountain along the banks of the River Fertha. Of
interest: prehistoric hill fort, Leacanabuaill Fort,
standing on an outcrop of rock three miles north
west; ruins of 15thC Ballycarbery Castle, 2½ miles
north west with nearby prehistoric Cahergal, a stone
fort; ruins of Carhan House, one mile east, where
Daniel O'Connell was born in 1775. One mile to the
west is the Weather Observatory, Valentia, one of
Western Europe's major weather stations. Good
salmon and trout fishing on the nearby Dereen,
Carhan and Fertha rivers. Good beaches three miles
away at White Strand and Cooncrome.

Camp   6 C17
Co Kerry, 7 miles SW of Tralee. Handful of houses
fastened to clumps of rock and gorse on the west of
the Slieve Mish Mountains at the mouth of Glen
Fao near Tralee Bay. High up on the mountain
slopes above stand the remains of a large stone
promontory fort with panoramic views of the Dingle
Peninsula.

Carrigaholt   6 D15
Co Clare. Little seaside village on the north bank of
the Shannon estuary. South east of the pier is a
slender, five-storey tower house standing on one
corner of a bawn; built by the MacMahons in the
15thC, it was captured from them in 1599 by the
Earl of Thomond following a four-day siege.

Castlecove   6 C19
Co Kerry, 7 miles E of Caherdaniel. Tiny resort neatly
and tidily laid out along a fine sandy beach at the
head of a narrow inlet of the beautiful Kenmare
River. Staigue Fort, 2½ miles west, is an early Iron
Age stronghold.

Castlegregory   6 C16
Co Kerry. Informal community lounging on a narrow
isthmus dividing the waters of Tralee and Brandon
Bays. To the west is picturesque Lough Gill, filled
with bass, trout and tope. To the south is a
formidable rampart of peaks up to 2,713 feet high.
North of Rough Point, at the tip of the peninsula are
the Seven Hogs, of which the largest, Illauntannig,
has the remains of an early monastery consisting of
two oratories, three beehive huts and an enclosing
wall.

Castletownbere   6 C19
Co Cork. Pop 800. Small town huddled on a platform
of land sheltered by Bear Island to the south east
with the wall of the Slieve Miskish Mountains to the
north west. Two miles to the west is Dunboy Castle,
17thC stronghold of the O'Sullivan Bere, standing in
parkland beside a narrow inlet of the sea. Allihies, to
the south west, was a busy copper-mining centre in
the 19thC. Numerous prehistoric and early Christian
remains in vicinity including an Ogham stone at
Eyeries to the north, the largest of its kind in
Ireland, standing 17½ feet high.

Castletownshend   6 E20
Co Cork. Dreamy village in a sheltered haven on the
west bank of a narrow, winding creek. Standing
offshore are the 'stags', three crumpled towers of

rock. At the water's edge beside the village is Bryans'
Fort, built 1650 by Col Richard Townshend, a
Planter. To the north east is Knockdrum Fort, a
prehistoric stone fort.

Cloghane   6 B16
Co Kerry, 7 miles NE of Dingle. Small holiday village
on a balcony of land at the south west corner of
Brandon Bay in the shadow of the Brandon
Mountains. Good beaches; curachs for hire.
Mackerel and flatfish angling in the sea; salmon and
trout fishing in the River Owenmore.

Clonakilty   7 G20
Co Cork. Pop 2,430. EC Wed. Small, neat market
town built around a square with a tall spired church,
laid out by the 1st Earl of Cork in 1614. At the head
of a winding inlet of Clonakilty Bay, it is the centre
of a rolling blanket of fertile farmland. Woodfield,
3½ miles west, was the birth place of Michael Collins
(1890–1922), the Irish resistance leader. Of interest:
Emmet Square, walled by elegant Georgian town
houses with a luxurious garden in the centre;
Catholic church, Gothic Revival building of 1880
with a distinct French flavour. Near the Court
House is a late 19thC water pump nicknamed locally
the 'Wheel of Fortune'. Good fishing and bathing
from fine sandy beaches. Galley Head is a good place
for watching sea birds, particularly manx
shearwaters, gannets, kittiwakes and fulmars.

Cobh   7 H19
Co Cork. Pop 6,000. C Wed. Margate and Ramsgate
rolled into one, it was the port of call for transatlantic
liners, and stands on Great Island in Cork harbour.
A series of widening terraces step up a steep wooded
ridge of land crowned by a lofty French Gothic-style
cathedral, St Colman's, designed by Pugin and
Ashlin in 1868 with a towering spire. It was from
Cobh's land-locked harbour that the notorious
'coffin ships' set sail, filled with penniless emigrants.
Three miles north is 16thC Belvelly Castle and an
early 19thC Martello tower. Cobh museum has an
interesting maritime exhibition, including relics of
the Lusitania disaster. Good bathing and sea fishing.

cobh, co cork.

Cork   7 I18
Co Cork. Pop 139,092. EC Wed. An important sea
port, commercial and manufacturing centre, and
cathedral city with both Catholic and Protestant
bishops. It is the second largest city in the Irish
Republic. An undulating carpet of streets, buildings
and bridges laid out around two winding channels of
the River Lee, Cork spread slowly at first across the
valley floor and then, in leaps and bounds, up and
over the surrounding hills. It's a landscape of
horizontals, with grey, crypt-like streets of
warehouses set alight by the occasional bright wall of
terraces. A busy shopping centre, its principal
streets lined with friendly stores, the city is also in
the heart of breathtaking pastoral land. The coastline
sports golden beaches and cheery-peopled holiday
resorts within a stone's throw of the city centre.

History

Originally the site of a monastery founded by St
Finbarr in the 6thC–7thC on the south bank of the
River Lee. Frequently raided by the Vikings
throughout the 9thC who, eventually tiring of such
activities, switched to trade and established a
settlement at the marshy mouth of the river valley in
AD917: the beginnings of Cork city proper.
Diarmuid MacCarthy, Lord of Desmond, seized the
city from the Danes in the early 12thC and then
submitted to Henry II in 1172. Settled by the
Anglo-Normans from 1177, the city was under
constant attack from the Gaelic clans. Franciscan
and Dominican friaries were established in the early
13thC. The town received its charter from Henry III
in 1241 and in 1284 new city walls were built. In the
early 14thC an Augustinian friary was founded and
in 1378 the city was burned by the Irish.

Grand Parade, Cork

Gradually the Anglo-Normans, cut off from the
more secure crown lands, 'went native' and although
English laws were ostensibly in force, the city was
remarkably independent. The edicts of the
prosperous merchants carried most weight at this
period; they sided with Perkin Warbeck in his claim
to the English throne in 1491 and after the defeat of
his cause the mayor and leading citizens were
executed at Tyburn and the city's charter annulled.
Cork was the headquarters of the English army
during the Desmond rebellion of 1590–1600 and
during the English Civil War it joined forces with the
Royalists, although it offered no resistance to
Cromwell when he walked into the town in 1649.
Backing the Jacobite cause, the city finally fell to the
Williamite army following a five-day siege in 1690,
after which the town's fortifications were
dismantled. It was from here that Patrick Sarsfield
and the bulk of the Jacobite army set sail for France
in 1691.
The 18thC was a prosperous period for the city; its
glass industry became famous, and many handsome
houses were built. By the 19thC, Cork's rebellious
spirit was roused once more and it became the centre
of the Fenian movement. In this century, the city
played a prominent role in the Anglo-Irish War of
1919–21; much of the town centre was burned by the
notorious 'Black and Tans'. Lord Mayor
MacCurtain, an ardent member of the Sinn Fein,
was assassinated by a gang connected with the
British forces and his successor, Terence
MacSwiney, died on hunger strike in Brixton gaol.

Districts

The main business and shopping centre of the city
occupies an island wedged between two branches of
the River Lee. The river quays have some interesting
Georgian houses, particularly Bachelor's Quay, and
at this prow of the island stands the handsome
Custom House surrounded by busy quays lined with
ships. Running across the middle of the island are
North and South Main Street, the main
thoroughfares of the old city; the old city walls once
circled this area. The modern main artery is St
Patrick's Street, made in 1789 by covering in a
channel of the river. To the west of the island is
Mardyke Parade, once a fashionable promenade
admired by Thackeray. The main shopping area is
Grand Parade, planned in the 18thC, and the
business centre is the South Mall. Most of the
eastern part of the island was burned in the war of
1920 and it presents a stark contrast to the 18thC
houses opposite and those surrounding the National
Monument to the south of the island.

Cathedrals, abbeys & churches

There are three interesting churches on the central
island. **Christ Church** in South Main Street was
designed by Coltsman in 1702; built on the site of a
late 13thC Norman church, the interior was later
remodelled by George Pain, who also added the
handsome west front in 1825. The **Church of St
Peter and St Paul**, off Paul Street, is a brilliant
Gothic Revival essay by E W Pugin. **Holy Trinity
Church**, on Friar Matthew Quay, was designed in
1832 by George Pain and has a handsome lantern
spire.
In the northern part of the city in Sunday's Well
stands **St Vincent's**, a Gothic Revival parish church
by John Benson. In Shandon is **St Anne's Church**,
famed for its bells, which was immortalised by
Father Prout in the doggerel 'The Bells of Shandon';
it was built 1722–26 with a sandstone and limestone
facing on the bell tower. Visitors can ring the bells
for a small fee. **St Mary's Pro-Cathedral**, also in
Shandon, is a red-brick monolith of 1808; the
interior was remodelled by George Pain in 1820
following a fire. To the east, in Lower Glanimire
Road, is **St Patrick's**, a handsome classical design of
1836.
The southern area of the city also has its
ecclesiastical riches. The **Honan Chapel** in
Donovan's Road is a heavy Irish-Romanesque
Revival pastiche on the 12thC Cormac's Chapel at
Cashel, built in 1915. **St Marie's of the Isle** in
Sharman Crawford Street is an 1850 convent in red
sandstone with white limestone dressings. **St
Finbarre's Cathedral**, at the junction of Dean Street
and Bishop Street, is in encrusted French Gothic
style, with triple portals for the west front and a
240-foot spire; it was designed by William Burgess in
1867–79. The **Red Abbey Tower** in Abbey Street,
the last relic of medieval Cork, was part of the
Augustinian friary established here in the early
14thC. **St Finbarr's South**, usually known as South
Chapel, is an elegant Georgian church of 1766.

*St. Fin Barre's Protestant church,
Cork / W. Burges 1867*

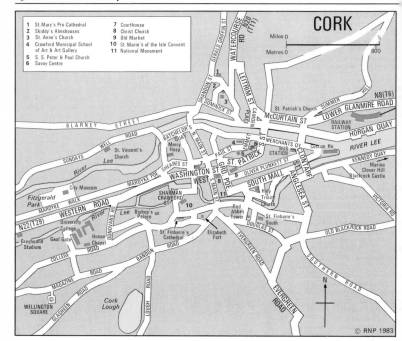

```
1  St. Mary's Pro-Cathedral        7   Courthouse
2  Skiddy's Almshouses             8   Christ Church
3  St. Anne's Church               9   Old Market
4  Crawford Municipal School      10   St. Marie's of the Isle Convent
   of Art & Art Gallery           11   National Monument
5  S. S. Peter & Paul Church
6  Savoy Centre
```

CORK

Miles 0 ½
Metres 0 800

© RNP 1983

Castles & Palaces
Bishop's Palace, in Bishop Street, is an interesting
18thC building surrounded by verdant woods.
Elizabeth Fort, near Barrack Street, was built in the
16thC and converted into a prison in 1838. On the
south side of the River Lee, 3½ miles to the east,
stands **Blackrock Castle**, a Gothic Revival mansion
designed by James and George Pain in 1830, on the
banks of Cork harbour.
Interesting buildings
In Shandon, **Skiddy's Almshouses** form a fine
18thC complex with Italianate arcades and two
figures of orphans on the gateway. Also of interest in
the northern part of the city: handsome red-brick
houses in **Camden Place**.
On the central island, off Patrick Street, is the **Old
Market**; built 1786, it is the last remnant of Cork's
18thC high-style architecture. The **Court House**,
Washington Street, is a fine building by James and
George Pain with handsome Corinthian portico.
Mercy Hospital, at the western end of the island,
was designed by Davis Ducart 1765–68 and was
formerly the Mayoralty House. Also of interest:
bow-fronted houses at nos 46–47 **Grand Parade**,
with slate-hung façades; 18thC houses in **Sheares
Street**; **Opera House** on Lavitt's Quay, designed by
Michael Scott in 1965 to replace an earlier building
razed by fire in 1955.
The **County Gaol**, to the south west, was
demolished to make way for the expanding
University College, but the handsome Doric-style
entrance gate, designed by the brothers Pain in 1823,
has been preserved. Also of interest: **Wellington
Square**, small 19thC complex of houses.
Parks & gardens
There are many pleasant walks through parks and

gardens, including the **Marina**, a riverside walk to
Blackrock; public park and arboretum at **Clover
Hill**, Blackrock; the **Lough**, beside Lough Road, a
large lake with interesting wildlife including feral
geese; **Fitzgeralds Park**, along the banks of the River
Lee at the south west end of Mardyke Walk.
Museums & galleries
Together with the **Crawford Municipal School of
Art** in Emmet Place is the Art Gallery, which
exhibits Rodin bronzes, and sculptures and
paintings, especially by local artists. The **Cork
Public Museum** in Fitzgerald Park was opened in
1945 and contains a collection of objects of local
interest, many of which serve to illustrate the history
and archaeology of the city; for example, exhibits of
Cork glass and lace and locally printed books.
Special attractions
River cruises from the city centre quay tour the
River Lee and Cork harbour by modern launch.
There is greyhound racing at the Western Road
track three evenings a week, and numerous sports
facilities include more than twenty tennis clubs,
three 18-hole golf courses and three swimming pools
in the suburbs.
The **Cork Craftsman's Guild**, Savoy Centre, Patrick
Street, is open to the public, who can watch
woodwork, pottery and other local crafts in progress.
There is another centre on the Cork/Macroom road.
Entertainment
Regular lunchtime concerts *May–Jun* and evening
concerts *Oct–Jun*, either *Wed or Fri*. Annual Cork
Choral Festival early *May* and Film Festival early
Jun. Band concerts *Weds and Suns*, *Jul–Aug* in
Fitzgerald Park. Six cinemas, three theatres and one
concert hall. Traditional Irish evenings are held at
the Entertainment Centre in *summer*.

Crookhaven   6 D20
Co Cork. Tiny fishing village on a narrow finger of
land sheltering a safe anchorage. Good bathing and
popular centre for yachtsmen. Two miles south is
Barley Cove with fine sandy beaches. Mizen Head, a
700-foot sheer wall of rock, is the most south-
westerly tip of Ireland.

Crosshaven   7 I19
Co Cork. Pop 1,230. Popular seaside resort tucked
onto a sheltered ledge of land at the mouth of the
River Owenboy as it pours out past secluded coves
and narrow inlets into Cork harbour. Former
fortress town guarding the approaches to Cork:
remnants of the past include Aghmatra Castle, a
Desmond stronghold to the west of the village with a
commanding view across the harbour; Dun Ui
Mheachair, late 18thC harbour fortification. Good
fishing, sailing and fine beaches at Church Bay,
Myrtleville and Robert's Cove.

Dingle   6 B17
Co Kerry. Pop 1,400. EC Thur. A troupe of winding
streets dancing down a steep slope of rock and gorse
on the north side of Dingle harbour, enclosed to east
and west by large hills, with the Brandon Mountains
blocking the north. It was a prosperous port in the
Middle Ages with a flourishing trade with Spain. To
the west is Ventry Harbour, a tiny fishing village at
the head of a crescent of bay. Further west is Slea
Head, a great mountain of hills tumbling headlong
into the sea. Adrift in the Atlantic to the south west
are the Blasket Islands, fortresses of rock with a
curtain of cliffs rising 961 feet along the northern
coast of the Great Blasket, uninhabited since 1953.
On Inishtooskert, the furthest north, are the remains
of St Brendan's oratory. Many prehistoric early
Christian remains in vicinity of Dingle.

Dingle

Doolin   1 E13
Co Clare, 5 miles SW of Lisdoonvarna. Handful of
houses thrown around a small fishing harbour on the
edge of a sandy bay. South is a great, undulating wall
of rock, the Cliffs of Moher. Nearby is Doonafore
Castle, unusual for having a circular tower, instead
of the traditional square tower, in a bawn. The
village is famous for its wealth of Irish folk music.

Dungarvan   7 J17
Co Waterford. Pop 5,580. EC Thur. Bustling market
town full of barnacled charm beside a sheltered
harbour at the mouth of the River Colligan. A major
Anglo-Norman port and stronghold, it was besieged
countless times during the English Civil War, finally
surrendering to Cromwell in 1649. Dungarvan
Castle, with massive circular keep, was built
originally in the late 12thC and stands on the banks
of the river east of the town. Five miles south is
Ring, an Irish-speaking village. Nearby is
Ballynagaul, a tiny hamlet with a little sheltered
harbour. Helvick Head, a sweeping curve of rock

230 feet high, curves round Dungarvan harbour like
a giant harbour wall. Many fine beaches and good
deep sea angling and river fishing.

Dunmore East   8 L17
Co Waterford. Patchwork of terraces stitched in long,
meandering lines up a steep ridge of land above a
picturesque port at the mouth of Waterford harbour.
Good fishing and sailing with many pleasantly
sheltered coves and beaches.

Fenit   6 C16
Co Kerry. Sea-sprayed port on the shores of Tralee
Bay, it is the harbour from which St Brendan is said
to have set sail for America. Overgrown Fenit Castle,
a round fortress, stands on an island guarding the
entrance to Barrow Bay, two miles to the east. Good
fishing and bathing.

Foynes   6 F15
Co Limerick. Pop 630. EC Thur. Small seaport on the
south shore of the Shannon estuary, once the
terminus for transatlantic seaplanes. It was from
here that a blockade runner sailed with uniforms for
the Confederates during the American Civil War. Sir
Stephen de Vere, 19thC philanthropist who
campaigned with Charlotte O'Brien for legislation to
eliminate the notorious coffin ships carrying
penniless emigrants to North America, was buried in
the Catholic church here in 1904. On a hill
overlooking the village is a giant limestone cross, a
memorial to Stephen Edmund Spring-Rice
(1814–1865), poet and writer.

Glandore   6 F20
Co Cork. Attractive coastal village at the head of the
narrow waters of Glandore harbour. Blocking the
mouth of the harbour, half-submerged, are the little
islands of Adam and Eve. Drombeg stone circle, 1¾
miles to the east, dates from about 150BC and ¾ mile
south east is Kilfinnan Castle, now a hotel, with
commanding views of the harbour. Good bathing
and fishing in Lakes Ballinlough and Shepperton.

Glenbeigh   6 C17
Co Kerry. Pop 270. EC Mon. Quiet paradise nestled
in the shelter of the 1,621-foot Seefin Mountain
where the River Behy pours out into Dingle Bay. A
winding glen runs inland to a fantastic amphitheatre
of crumpled mountains called the Glenbeigh
Horseshoe. There's a four-mile stretch of golden
dune-backed beach one mile away at Rossbeigh.
Good rock fishing for mackerel, conger, dog fish and
pollack, and salmon and trout are caught in the
River Caragh and Lough Coomasaharn. Nearby,
framed by broom and heather-covered hills, is
Wynne's Folly, a castellated mansion in Hammer
Horror style, built 1867.

Glengarriff   6 D19
Co Cork. Pop 250. Secluded village lying in a
luxuriantly vegetated glen around an inlet at the
head of Bantry Bay. Surrounded by lofty hills and
mountains, the area is famous for its natural beauty
and pleasant climate. The islet-studded waters are
guarded to the south by Garinish Island, which has
been transformed into a sub-tropical Italianate
garden. Good fishing and bathing.

Glin   6 E15
Co Limerick. Attractive village on the bank of the
Shannon estuary. On the edge of the village is the
ruined keep of the 13thC Castle of Glin: seat of the
Knight of Glin since the early Middle Ages, a new
castle was built in 1770 to the west of the village; it
was remodelled in the early 19thC by the addition of
battlements, Gothic-Revival wing and three
pepper-potted Gothic lodges. Its white-painted
façades have a delightful, Alice-in-Wonderland
quality.

Goleen　　　　　　　　　　　　　　**6 D20**
Co Cork. Pint-sized village lying on rolling land
along the edge of Spanish Cove.

Inch　　　　　　　　　　　　　　**6 C17**
Co Kerry. Sheltered seaside resort and gateway to
Inch Peninsula, a long plank of land framed by sand
dunes, at the head of Dingle Bay. The Slieve Mish
Mountains and MacGillycuddy's Reeks tower on
either side. Safe bathing and good fishing.

Kells　　　　　　　　　　　　　　**6 C18**
Co Kerry, 7 miles SW of Glenbeigh. Handful of
houses on a terrace of land on the southern side of
Dingle Bay. Good bathing at Kells and Foileye Bays.

Kenmare　　　　　　　　　　　　**6 D18**
Co Kerry. Pop 900. EC Thur. Neat town on gently
rising ground in an amphitheatre of the Kerry Hills,
situated at the head of the River Kenmare.
Established in 1670 by Sir William Petty, an English
settler, it comprises a monochrome wall of houses
drawn spaciously round two parallel streets and a
small square with clear views out to surrounding
hills and water. Of interest: Druids circle, 15
prehistoric standing stones ¾ mile to the south west;
Dunkerron Castle, late 16thC O'Sullivan stronghold
standing on a pedestal of rock two miles to the west;
Sheen Falls, two miles south. Excellent angling in
the Rivers Roughty, Sheen and Dawrose and
magnificent deep sea fishing for tope, pollack, spur
dogfish, bass and grey mullet. Annual regatta in *Aug*
and Sea Food Festival in *Sep*.

Kilkee　　　　　　　　　　　　　**6 D14**
Co Clare. Victorian seaside resort built round a
crescent-shaped beach at the head of a small,
horseshoe-shaped bay. On either side is a
magnificent wall of cliffs and the beach is partly
protected from the Atlantic by a reef called the
Duggerna Rocks. Of interest: numerous sea caves, a
puffing hole, several ruined castles, a ring barrow
and a promontory fort called Doonlicka. Good
deep-sea fishing and skin diving; inland rivers
abound with salmon and sea trout in autumn.

Kilrush　　　　　　　　　　　　　**6 E15**
Co Clare. Pop 2,670. EC Thur. Small sea port and
manufacturing town on the north shore of the
Shannon estuary. Cappagh Pier, one mile south, is
the harbour for boats plying between Limerick and
Kilrush. Of interest: Scattery Island, two miles off
the coast from Cappagh Pier, with remains of early
monastic settlement; large stone fort at Carrowdonia,
three miles to the east; the grave of Ellen Hanley, the
'Colleen Bawn', in the parish church at Killimer, six
miles east, where her murdered body was washed
ashore. This tragedy inspired Gerald Griffin's novel,
'The Collegians'—later adapted by Boucicault for his
play, 'The Colleen Bawn' and by Benedict for the
opera, 'The Lily of Killarney'.

Kinsale　　　　　　　　　　　　　**7 H19**
Co Cork. Pop 1,620. EC Thur. Winding, narrow
streets and handsome bay-windowed Georgian
houses packed tightly on the sloping banks of the
Bandon estuary. One of the chief ports of the British
Navy until the 18thC; the town was granted its
charter in 1333 by Edward III and was later the
scene of a great siege and bitter fighting in 1601–2,
when the Irish and their Spanish allies finally lost to
a powerful English army. The English victory was
followed by the 'Flight of the Earls'. A former
Admiralty clerk of the court in Kinsale, William
Penn, set out from here to found the American state
of Pennsylvania. It was off the cliffs of Old Head, to
the south across the estuary, that the Lusitania was
sunk by a German submarine in 1915, with the loss
of 1,500 lives.

The Old Head, Kinsale, Co Cork

St Multose Church, 12thC building with 17thC–
19thC alterations, has a handsome west tower and
fine north transept and ornamental portal. Also of
interest: remains of a Carmelite friary built in 1314;
Desmond Castle, a 16thC tower house in Cork
Street; Charles Fort, formidable harbour
fortifications of 1677 beside the village of
Summercove, two miles south. Good angling, sailing
and bathing; many fine beaches nearby.

Lahinch　　　　　　　　　　　　　**1 E13**
*Co Clare. Pop 390. EC Sat. 2½ miles W of
Ennistymon*. Popular family resort, fronted by a
promenade and mile of sandy beach at the head of
Liscannor Bay.

Leap　　　　　　　　　　　　　　**6 E20**
Co Cork. Tiny village squeezed in at the head of
narrow Glandore harbour where the River Leap
flows through a deep gorge.

Limerick　　　　　　　　　　　　**7 G15**
Co Limerick. Pop 63,000. EC Thur. Fourth largest
city in the whole of Ireland, it has spread in leaps and
bounds around the head of the Shannon estuary. An
important manufacturing and market centre, it's
really three towns in one: English Town, Irish Town
and Newtown Pery. It's a noisy, joyous town with
buildings as colourful as its people.
History
A 9thC Norse settlement, it was sacked in AD964
by Brian Boru and his brother, who made it their
capital. It was captured by the Anglo-Normans in
the 12thC but quickly retaken by Donal O'Brien
who, having razed the city, began to build a new
town and founded a new cathedral in 1172.
Following his death, the town fell to the Anglo-
Normans. In 1197 it received its first charter and in
1210 the castle, on the instructions of King John,
was built beside Thomond Bridge. Reserved for the
Crown, Limerick became a prosperous English
trading colony rivalling Galway in importance.
Occupied briefly by Edward Bruce, the Scottish
king's brother, in 1315, it was sacked by the

St Mary's Cathedral, Limerick

O'Briens in 1369. Although the Irish were later expelled, their menace was ever-present and an annual tribute was exacted from the town. Captured by a Catholic army in 1642, it was retaken in 1651 after a six-month siege by Cromwellian forces. A centre of Jacobite power during the Williamite wars, it was the last of their strongholds to fall. Following the Battle of the Boyne, William of Orange laid siege to the city with a force of 26,000 men in 1690. The spirited defence included a heroic cavalry raid behind enemy lines, in which a small force led by Patrick Sarsfield destroyed the Williamite siege train; after three fruitless weeks William withdrew. The defenders' French allies, believing the city to be too vulnerable to attack, also withdrew, and the following year the Williamite army reappeared. Hopelessly outnumbered, the defenders capitulated in October 1691. Under the terms of the treaty the garrison marched out with full honours, and set sail for France. Much of the modern town was built by Edmond Sexton Pery (1719–1806), after whom Newtown Pery is named.

Districts

The town centre is divided into three parts. English Town, a tiny grid of antique streets stranded on King's Island, is wedged on a bend of the River Shannon between Curragour Falls and the Abbey River. Irish Town is a catherine wheel of streets shooting out at right angles from the town hall, on the mainland to the south of the confluence of the Abbey River and the River Shannon. Newtown Pery, a more spacious 18thC suburb, runs away south from Irish Town; the main hotels and shops are in this area.

Cathedrals & churches

St Mary's Cathedral, standing on the banks of King's Island in English Town, was built 1172 by the last king of Munster, Donal O'Brien. Only fragments of the original Romanesque church survive, including parts of the aisles, the nave, transepts and west portal. The chancel was rebuilt in the 15thC and numerous chapels added. Of particular interest are the black oak misericords, or choir stalls, carved in 1489; they are the only example existing in Ireland. **St John's Cathedral** in Cathedral Place, is a Gothic Revival design by Philip Hardwick and Maurice Hennessy, 1856–61; its spire, at 280 feet, is the tallest in Ireland. Most of Limerick's churches are modern, although **St Munchin's**, to the north of the castle, is built on a 7thC foundation and is thought to mark the site of the original cathedral. The church itself was built in 1827, and contains the bishop's throne from the earlier cathedral. The **Dominican Church** next to the Tait Clock was built in 1816; there are a variety of 17thC artefacts inside, including a statue of the Virgin Mary known as Our Lady of Limerick, the pectoral cross of Bishop Terence Albert O'Brien and two early chalices.

Castles & palaces

King John's Castle, sandwiched between the cathedral and the south side of Thomond Bridge, was built in 1210. A five-sided structure with one wall rising like a cliff from the waters of the River Shannon, it has three massive round towers and an early 17thC bastion; the entrance, flanked by slender round towers, is on the north side. **Bunratty Castle and Folk Park**, eight miles to the north in Co Clare, is a mighty 15thC stronghold built by the Macnamaras.

Interesting buildings

Fragments of the city walls still stand; beside St John's Hospital is the **'Devil's Battery'**, so called because it was a centre of fierce resistance against the

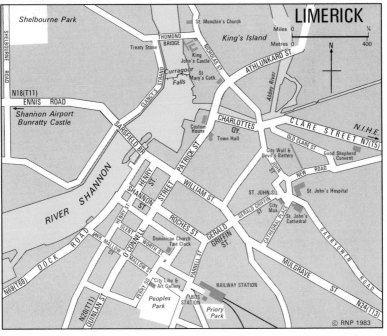

Williamites. The front façade of the **Exchange** is all that remains of the old building and is now incorporated into the boundary walls of St Mary's Cathedral; the exchange was originally built in the 17thC but was virtually destroyed in the Williamite siege and was rebuilt in 1702. The **Treaty Stone**, now mounted on a pedestal at the west end of Thomond Bridge, is said to be the very stone on which the Treaty of Limerick was signed in 1691.

Treaty Stone
Limerick City

Also of interest: **Town Hall**, handsome brick building of 1805; **Custom House**, with elegant pilastered front, designed by Davis Ducart in 1769; balustraded **Sarsfield Bridge**, its design adapted by Alexander Nimmo from that of the Pont de Neuilly, Paris, in 1824–27; statue of **Daniel O'Connell** by John Hogan (1800–1858), the first public monument erected to him in Ireland.

Parks & squares
Several pleasant green spaces, including **Shelbourne Park** and **Priory Park**. The **People's Park** encloses the City Library, Limerick Museum and Art Gallery, and the Spring-Rice Memorial. **St John's Square**, near the cathedral, is a spacious place of fine, stone-fronted town houses designed by Francis Binden in 1751. Many of the buildings had fallen into disrepair but following a preservation order are being renovated.

Museums & galleries
The **Limerick Art Gallery**, next to the City Library in the People's Park, has a good collection of modern Irish painting. The **Hunt Collection**, housed in the National Institute for Higher Education three miles east of the city, has a marvellous assemblage of Celtic antiquities. Of interest: Bronze Age ornaments and weapons; 9thC bronze Cashel Bell, early Christian brooches, medieval Limoges enamels and 18thC Irish porcelain and silverware. The collection was donated to the nation by Mr John Hunt, a noted Celtic historian. The **Limerick Museum** in St John's Square was opened in 1916, and houses a fine collection of archaeological finds dating from 7000BC. There is also a display of civic history, local history and Irish coins since the Vikings.

Special attractions
The **Folk Park** at Bunratty Castle recreates an earlier age through reconstructions of houses typical of the area and displays of traditional crafts. Farriers, basket-makers and bakers are amongst those who demonstrate the old skills. The tradition of the now famous **Limerick lace** was introduced in fact by an Englishman, Charles Walker, in 1824. At one time lacemaking was a major industry, but the sole supporters of the skill are now the sisters of the Good Shepherd Convent; their work can be seen at the convent.

Entertainment
Traditional Irish evenings are held in *summer* at **St John's Castle** and elsewhere in the city, and medieval banquets are served all year round at **Bunratty Castle**. There are several theatres,

including the **Savoy** and the **Belltable Arts Centre**, in O'Connell Street, hosting various events. In *summer*, open-air ballet is to be seen in the **People's Park** and there is a son et lumière at **St Mary's Cathedral**. There are also four cinemas and various cabaret spots.

Liscannor   1 E13
Co Clare, 4 miles W of Ennistymon. Small fishing village huddled on the northern shore of Liscannor Bay. Of interest: remains of an O'Connor castle and house in Castle Street where John P Holland, designer of the submarine, was born in 1831. Glahane Shore is a good bathing beach west of the village and further west are the spectacular Cliffs of Moher which rise to over 700 feet in parts and are one of the wonders of Co Clare. One mile east is St Macreehy's, an early 12thC church built on the site of a famous 6thC school.

Milltown Malbay   1 E13
Co Clare. Diminutive market town planned in an orderly fashion with one main street and secondary streets leading off it at right angles. It stands about a mile inland from the coast. To the south east is the 1,282-foot-high Slieve Callan, on the slopes of which is a large wedge-shaped gallery grave.

Mungret   4 G14
Co Limerick, 3 miles SW of Limerick. Once a leading seat of learning and site of a famous 6thC monastery, it's a straggling four houses lining the coast road south of the River Shannon. The monastery, founded by St Nessan, was pillaged by the Vikings in AD834, 934 and 1080. Destroyed by a band of Ulstermen in 1088, it was pillaged in 1107 by Murrough O'Brien. At the height of its reputation there were six churches, 1,500 students and a large body of priests and teachers. The ruins of three of its churches remain—a large parish church with 13thC chancel and 15thC nave and two small 12thC churches. Also of interest: early 12thC church at Killulta; ruins of Carrigogunnell Castle, a 14thC fortress three miles west.

Parknasilla   6 C19
Co Kerry. Charming resort hidden by woods on the banks of the River Kenmare with the 895-foot Knockanamadare Hill as backdrop. Genial paradise with subtropical vegetation flourishing in the mild, Gulf Stream-washed climate.

Passage East   8 L17
Co Waterford. Picturesque village tucked in at the foot of a steep hill on the wooded west bank of Waterford harbour.

Portmagee   6 B18
Co Kerry. Tiny fishing village scattered in a picturesque jumble of roofs and colour-washed walls around a natural harbour, squeezed in the south west corner of Valentia harbour. There is a bridge from here to Valentia Island. To the south west are Lemon Rock and Puffin Island, thriving colonies of sea birds including fulmar, storm petrels, manx shearwater and puffin. Coomanaspig Pass, three miles to the south, climbs over 1,000 feet through the mountains. Numerous prehistoric remains in vicinity as well as many good beaches and excellent sea angling for skate, bream, pollack, mackerel and shark.

Quilty   6 E14
Co Clare. Small fishing village of weather-beaten houses clinging to the rocky coast for shelter whilst curachs lie beached on the shore. Parts of the beach may be carpeted with drying seaweed, as the village has its own seaweed-processing factory. North of the village is Spanish Point; this rocky hazard has caused many shipwrecks, among them the wreck of several

ships of the Spanish Armada in 1588, hence the name. Two miles offshore is Mutton Island, split in three by a great tidal wave in AD902. On it are the remains of an early Christian oratory.

Ross Carbery 6 F20

Co Cork. Attractive little town raised on a terrace of land at the head of the narrow inlet of Ross Carbery Bay. Site of a 6thC monastery, which later became a famous school. The Protestant cathedral was built in 1612. Also of interest: remains of Coppinger's Court, handsome 17thC mansion with gable façade, burnt in 1641; Castle Freke, Gothic Revival house now a picturesque ruin.

Ross Carbery

Schull 6 D20

Co Cork, 5 miles SW of Ballydehob. Handful of houses snuggling happily together in a gully of land between gentle hills at the head of a picturesque harbour. To the north towers Mount Gabriel, a giant 1,339-foot hill. Good bathing and fishing.

Skibbereen 6 E20

Co Cork. Pop 2,100. EC Thur. Straddling the River Ilen as it pours out into a narrow creek of Baltimore Bay, it was once the seat of the Catholic Bishop of Ross. Two of its bishops joined battle in the wars against the English—Owen MacEgan, slain in battle 1602, and Beotius MacEgan, hanged in 1650 by the Cromwellians at Carrigadrohid. Of interest: remains of Abbeystrowry Abbey, a 14thC Cistercian abbey one mile west; pro-cathedral, handsome Greek-Revival building of 1826; Lough Ine, rich marine life in clear waters. Good angling in the surrounding rivers and lakes. Good sandy beaches within four miles.

Sneem 6 C18

Co Kerry. Pop 290. EC Wed. Attractive little village spread around the head of the Sneem estuary on the north shore of the Kenmare River. There is a tiny green, bordered by colourful two-storey houses. To the north, crumpled peaks rise to 2,240 feet. Good fishing on the River Blackwater and many fine sandy beaches a short distance away. Sneem Regatta and Flower Festival held annually in *Aug.*

Tahilla 6 C19

Co Kerry, 4 miles NE of Parknasilla. Idyllic cove hidden on an inlet of the Kenmare River. Good fishing for salmon and sea trout in the River Blackwater. Deep-sea anglers can catch skate, shark and ray.

Tarbert 6 E15

Co Kerry. Quiet village, once a prominent port, stepping jauntily down the side of a steep hill overlooking a pretty section of the Shannon estuary. Now a terminus for the car ferry operating between here and Killimer, across the water in Co Clare. To the north east is wooded Tarbert Island.

Timoleague 7 G20

Co Cork, 4 miles SW of Kilbrittain. Tiny village at the head of a winding creek of Courtmacsherry Bay. Timoleague Abbey is a Franciscan friary established in 1240 on the site of a 6thC monastery of St Molaga; built along the edge of the sea shore, it was added to

during the 14thC and 15thC. In 1642 it was sacked by English forces. The extensive ruins include a church with chancel, nave and south transept with a handsome tower over the crossing. Also of interest: castle gardens; 20thC Catholic church with fine west window by Harry Clarke; remains of 13thC Abbeymahon Abbey in the seaside village of Courtmacsherry, three miles east. Good bathing and deep-sea angling.

Tralee 6 D16

Co Kerry. Pop 13,260. C Wed. Quiet market town lying inland from Tralee Bay with the peaks of the Slieve Mish Mountains rising to the south and the Stacks Mountains to the north. An 18thC spa town and former sea port, connected to Blennerville at the head of Tralee Bay by a now-disused ship canal, it was also the stronghold of the earls of Desmond until their lands were confiscated with horrifying savagery following the rebellion of 1579. The land was laid waste and in 1583 the 15th Earl of Desmond, hotly pursued by the English, fled into the mountains to the south east; he was finally captured and executed, and his head was exhibited on London Bridge. The castle, granted to an English settler, was taken by a force of the Catholic Confederation in 1641 and later burnt by Jacobites following an advance on the town by the powerful Williamite army in 1691.
The Dominican church, built on the site of an early 13thC friary, was designed by Pugin and supervised by his pupil, George Ashlin. The handsome Court House with graceful Ionic portico was designed 1830 by William Vitruvius Morrison; the portico is flanked by memorials to Kerry men killed during the Crimean War of 1854 and Indian Mutiny of 1860. Also of interest: 1798 memorial, heroic figure of a pikeman sculptured by Albert Power; attractive Georgian town houses in Castle Street and the Mall; Ratass church, remains of Early Christian building with well preserved doorway, one mile to the east; Coghers House, Ballymullen where William Mulchinock, composer of 'The Rose of Tralee', died in 1864; numerous ring forts in vicinity including a huge promontory fort, Cathair Chon-Raoi on a terrace of rock 2,050 feet up Caherconree Mountain; Scotia's Glen, where the legendary sons of Milesius defeated the Tuatha de Danaan in 3,500BC. Scotia, daughter of the Pharoah of Egypt, after whom the glen is named, was among the slain. The Rose of Tralee International Festival is staged here annually in the first week in *Sep.*

Tramore 8 L17

Co Waterford, 8 miles S of Waterford. Pop 3,790. EC Thur. Popular holiday resort tucked in the shelter of hills in the north west corner of Tramore Bay. Fine promenade-backed sandy beach. Good angling in the bay with abundance of mackerel, bass and sea trout.

Union Hall 6 E20

Glandore harbour, Co Cork. Tiny fishing village hidden under an umbrella of trees on the western bank of Glandore harbour. Jonathan Swift lived for a while in Rock Cottage.

Waterford 8 L17

Co Waterford. Pop 34,290. EC Thur. Tight knot of streets on a loop of the River Suir, famous for its glass industry. A 10thC Norse settlement, it was captured by the Anglo-Normans under Strongbow in 1171 in the early years of their conquest of Ireland. The second major Anglo-Norman stronghold, it remained an English colony until the 19thC. Granted a charter by King John in 1205, it remained loyal to the English crown in the English Civil War, withstanding a siege by Cromwell in 1649.

Waterford

There are still traces of the Norse and Anglo-Norman fortifications. Reginalds Tower, a massive circular stone fortress 80 feet high was built in 1003 as a Norse stronghold and became an Anglo-Norman fortress, later a royal residence, army barracks, prison and finally the Civic Museum. In O'Connell Street are the remains of a Dominican friary, established in 1226. French Church, used by the Huguenots in the 17thC, was a 13thC Franciscan friary. Christ Church Cathedral is a Baroque building designed by John Roberts in 1779. He was also responsible for the design of Holy Trinity Church in 1796, the City Hall (1782) standing in the Mall, a handsome Georgian street, and the Chamber of Commerce, an elegant Adam-style building, originally a house, of 1795. Also of interest: Mount Congreve, four miles south west, Georgian house and gardens.

Waterville   6 B19
Co Cork. Meandering series of late 19thC terraces pencilled in diagonal lines along a pebble-backed beach on the eastern shore of Ballinskelligs Bay. Inland, separated by a narrow strip of land, is beautiful Lough Currane, dotted with wooded islands. To the east and south a cliff wall of mountains blocks the horizon.

Youghal   7 I18
Co Cork. Pop 5,450. Aura of a transplanted south-east England holiday resort, with garish terraces wrapped round a bend at the mouth of the River Blackwater. One-time fortified town, it was occupied briefly by the Vikings, then the Anglo-Normans. Sir Walter Raleigh, who lived for a time in Myrtle Grove, a stately Elizabethan mansion, was once the mayor of Youghal. It is said that it was here that he smoked the first tobacco and grew the first potatoes in Ireland. The spacious High Street is spanned half way down by a handsome Clock Gate, a circular arch with four upper storeys, crowned by a cupola with clock built in 1771. Also of interest: St Mary's Church of 1461 with detached belfry; New College House, 1781–82; Red House, 1706–15; 17thC almshouse in North Main Street and nearby 15thC Tynte's Castle, now ruined. Famous for point lace and an excellent touring centre.

clock gate, Youghal
co. Cork.

Islands & peninsulas

Blasket Islands   6 A17
Co Kerry. Once a spartan, Gaelic-speaking fishing community of about 130 souls living a frugal life three miles out into the Atlantic to the west of Co Kerry. Reached by curach from the little harbour of Dunguin, the islands have been uninhabited since 1953. The largest is Great Blasket, a long, narrow raft of rock and gorse rising in a sharp fold some 1,000 feet with a skyscraper wall of cliffs to the north. North of Great Blasket is Inishtooskert, with remains of early Christian oratory and beehive huts; to the west is tiny Tearaght, complete with lighthouse; south are Inishabro and Inishvickillane, the latter with remains of stone oratory and beehive huts. It was in Blasket Sound that the Santa Maria della Rosa, a ship of the Spanish Armada, was sunk in 1588.

Clear Island   6 D20
Cape Clear, Co Cork. Lying an hour's turbulent boat trip from Baltimore, the island has a number of early Christian monuments, including 12thC St Ciaran's Church and a cross-pillar. Also of interest: Dunamore Castle, a ruined O'Driscoll fort to the north west of the island. There is also a bird observatory *open summer*, and fine views from the highest point (500 feet). An annual music festival, the Daonscoil Chléire, is held in the last week of *Aug*. This is the extreme southern tip of Ireland, with the exception of Fastnet Rock, three miles away, and is part of the Gaeltacht. One boat daily from Baltimore.

Dingle Peninsula   6 B17
Co Kerry. A mass of bracken-rusted headlands and hills, this is a frothing tongue of land with great outcrops of rock and beautiful scimitar-shaped bays. A colourful Irish-speaking district alive with folk lore and custom, it is the most northerly of the three Kerry peninsulas. Enclosed in the east by the Slieve Mish mountains, a great wall of peaks up to 2,796 feet high, it runs 30 miles westwards into the fury of the Atlantic. To the north of the peninsula the 3,127-foot-high Brandon Mountain squats on the edge of Brandon Bay like a fat robed monk huddled beside a pool. A Gaeltacht district, the area is also rich in prehistoric and Early Christian remains.

Iveragh Peninsula   6 C18
Co Kerry. The largest of Kerry's three great peninsulas. The Ring of Kerry, a dramatic roller coaster road, circles the peninsula. The 112-mile drive winds from Killorglin in the north via Glenbeigh to Cahirciveen on the westernmost tip, opposite Valentia Island, and round south to Waterville and along the southern coast via Sneem and Parknasilla to Kenmare and back up to Killarney past the Lakes of Kerry. One of the great drives in the world, comparable to that along the Amalfi coast in Italy, the road winds past great wheels of rock with mountain wall on one side and dizzy cliffs dropping into the sea on the other. It crosses countless streams and lovely lakes, like Lough Caragh in the north or Lough Currane, divided by the narrow road from Ballinskelligs Bay and the sea, in the south west. Inland, a series of snaking mountain passes rise sharply skywards or plunge suddenly to the shadow-dark bottom of a valley floor. The roads squeeze past great outcrops of rock and gorse-coloured mountain sides lining scarred valleys crumpled like tin foil.

Sherkin Island   6 E20
Co Cork. A ten-minute trip from Baltimore, Sherkin is a popular resort with good angling and beaches

and the only Outdoor Pursuits Centre in Ireland. Of interest: Franciscan abbey founded 1460 by the O'Driscolls and medieval O'Driscoll castle, both destroyed in 1537 during the sacking of Baltimore harbour.

Skelligs Rocks 6 A19
Co Kerry, 8 miles SW of Bolus Head. Reached by boat from Knightstown, these are three little islands or sea stacks. The largest is Skellig Michael or Great Skellig, a monumental 700-foot-high rock, ½ mile long and ¾ mile wide, rising sharply out of the sea. On a series of stepped terraces carved 540 feet up on the rock are the remains of one of the best preserved of Europe's monastic sites, with numerous oratories similar to that of Gallarus Oratory on the Dingle. Little Skellig is now a bird sanctuary and home of over 20,000 pairs of gannets.

Tarbert Island 6 E15
Co Kerry. A wooded nose of land poking out into the estuary. On it stand a mid-19thC lighthouse and a battery and barracks, remnants of fortifications against the threat of French invasion during the Napoleonic Wars.

valentia Island Co Kerry

Valentia Island 6 B18
Co Kerry. Separated from the mainland by a narrow strait, it's a popular holiday resort and angling centre reached by a modern bridge from the village of Portmagee. A silent world of cormorants, cliffs and epic seascapes, the prow of the island steams south west into the ocean at Bray Head, a 792-foot wall of cliff. In the centre, rich arable land gives way to rock and gorse soaring 888 feet at Jeokaun Mount, its slopes pitted by disused slate mines. The main centre is Knightstown, a secluded harbour on the east coast; the first ocean cable was laid from here in the late 19thC. Numerous prehistoric remains. On Beginish Island, a little to the north, are the remains of an early monastic settlement, including an oratory and beehive cell.

Inland towns & villages

Abbeyfeale 6 E16
Co Limerick. Engulfed in a sea of rolling hills, it's a friendly market town on the border with Co Kerry. There are fragments of a 12thC Cistercian abbey, from which the town takes its name, on the banks of the River Feale and 1½ miles north west are the ruins of Portrinard Castle, a 14thC Geraldine fortress.

Adare 7 G15
Co Limerick. Pop 550. EC Thur. Picturesque, thatched, English-style village set among rolling green hills and woods. It was created with considerable panache by the 3rd Earl of Dunraven (1812–1871), an energetic 'improver' and architectural fanatic, and consists of one wide tree-lined main street of medieval-style cottages. There are some interesting early 20thC cottages by

adare, co Limerick

Detmar Blow, the renowned English arts and crafts architect. It was here that the Normans occupied a castle in the 13thC, on a bend in the River Maigue, which was later rebuilt and considerably enlarged in the 14thC–16thC. In 1230 a Trinitarian monastery was founded, now the Catholic parish church in the main street. To the east of the village, an Augustinian friary was founded in 1325 and in 1464 Thomas, Earl of Kildare, established the Franciscan friary now besieged by the golf course. Also of interest: ruins of St Nicholas, an 11thC church to the north of the castle; 13thC Desmond Chapel, with chaplain's accommodation raised above the east end; Adare Manor, limestone manor house built in Gothic Revival style in 1832 for the 2nd Earl of Dunraven.

Ardfert 6 D16
Co Kerry. Birthplace of St Brendan the Navigator and later important episcopal see, it's a muddle of houses lying inshore from Ballyheige Bay. Fine medieval remains include ruins of 13thC cathedral with Romanesque portal; Temple-na-Hoe, 12thC Romanesque church; extensive ruins of a mid-13thC Franciscan friary; Temple-na-Griffin, diminutive 15thC church; there are numerous ring forts in the vicinity, of which Rathcrihare, 1¼ miles south west, is the most interesting. Mackenna's Fort, a prehistoric fort one mile west, was Sir Roger Casement's hiding place after he landed from a German submarine in April 1916.

Ardfinnan 7 J16
Co Tipperary. Site of a 7thC monastery founded by St Finan the Leper, it was also an Anglo-Norman stronghold; Prince John had a castle built here in 1185. Now a gaunt skeleton hanging precariously on a pedestal of rock commanding a river ford, the fortress was destroyed in the 17thC by the Cromwellians; the remains are largely 13thC. South of the village are the bare bones of a 14thC Carmelite friary, Lady's Abbey. The Suir valley winds south of the village, gouging a deep furrow through the hills.

Askeaton 7 F15
Co Limerick. Small market town by the River Deel on the coast road south of the Shannon estuary. It was here that William de Burgo built a castle in 1199, later extended by the earls of Desmond in the 14thC; standing on a rocky pedestal in the River Deel, remains include a narrow tower, fragments of a tall 16thC house and a magnificent 15thC Great Hall raised above a vaulted ground storey. Beside the town are the ruins of a Franciscan friary, founded in the late 14thC, with lovely 15thC cloister.

Ballina 7 H14
Co Tipperary. Built on the east bank of the River Shannon where it flows grandly through a gap in the mountains to the south west, the town is twinned with Killaloe, joined by a handsome 13-arch bridge.

Ballinascarthy 7 F19
Co Cork. The birthplace of Henry Ford, it's a small village spread out along the Cork Road.

Ballyferriter 6 B17
Co Kerry, 6½ miles SW of Murreagh. Tiny village scrambling for a foothold on the edge of rolling hills

a mile inland from Smerwick harbour. Two miles north west are the remains of 15thC Ferriter's Castle, birthplace of the soldier poet, Pierce Ferriter, one of the last of the clan chiefs to submit to Cromwell. On a rocky outcrop on the edge of Smerwick harbour are the remains of Dún an Óir, an ancient fortress where an infamous massacre of 600 Irish and Spanish soldiers took place in 1580, following their surrender to the English. In the village of Reask, 1¾ miles to the north east, are two cross-slabs and a fine cross-inscribed pillar in the La Tène style. Four miles to the east is the Gallarus Oratory, the best preserved of the Early Christian buildings in Ireland. Also of interest is Teach Siamsa, a rural theatre workshop and Folk Centre.

Ballymakeera   **6 E18**
Co Cork. Tiny village sealed amongst the forests and mountain scenery in the Irish-speaking world of the Gaeltacht. To the north west is its twin village of Ballyvourney. The village Ballingeary to the south west, with an Irish college, is one of the strongholds of the Irish language.

Bandon   **7 G19**
Co Cork. Pop 2,250. Popular angling resort on the banks of the River Bandon, it was founded by Richard Boyle, the Earl of Cork, in 1608 on lands confiscated from participants in the Desmond revolt. Parts of the old town walls survive. Of interest: Kilbrogan Church, built 1610, the first of Ireland's Protestant churches, with the old town stocks inside; Dundaniel Castle, built 1476 on the wooded banks of the River Bandon.

Blarney   **7 G18**
Co Cork, 5 miles NW of Cork. Small manufacturing town on the banks of the River Shournagh, it's famous for the much-kissed Blarney Stone lying at the foot of the battlements of Blarney Castle. The castle, with its huge keep, was built by the MacCarthys in 1446. Nearby is Rock Close, picturesque essay in 18thC landscape gardening. The surrounding countryside abounds in prehistoric remains.

Blarney castle, co.Cork.

Broadford   **4 G14**
Co Clare, 6 miles E of Kilkishen. Attractive town spreadeagled at the foot of the 1,748-foot-high Slieve Bernagh mountains. Good pike, bream and perch fishing in nearby Lough Doon.

Bruree   **7 G16**
Co Limerick. Site of a royal palace and fort from 7thC–9thC, it's a straggling village built at the head of a six-arched bridge crossing the River Maigue. Of interest: remains of ring forts can be seen along the banks of the river; fragments of a 12thC castle built by the Knights Templar, near the church; huge 14thC rampart of de Lacy stronghold; interesting mill-wheel beside the bridge.

Buttevant   **7 G17**
Co Cork. Originally an Anglo-Norman settlement, now a thriving market town packed tightly along the banks of the River Awbeg. A Franciscan friary was founded here in 1251; remains include ruined church of choir, nave and south transept. One mile

south are the ruins of Ballybeg Abbey, 13thC Augustinian priory. Good trout fishing on the River Awbeg.

Cahir   **7 I16**
Co Tipperary. Pop 1,750. EC Thur. Tucked in along the eastern foot of the Galty Mountains, it's a bustling market town straddling the River Suir. Site of 3rdC fortress of Dun Pascaigh and 10thC residence of Brian Boru, it was here that Conor O'Brien built a castle in 1142 standing strategically on a rocky islet in the river. Acquired by the Anglo-Norman Butlers, Earls of Ormond, in 1375 it was gradually rebuilt, becoming one of the largest 15thC castles in Ireland. Thought to be impregnable, it was an Irish stronghold during Elizabethan times and was finally captured in May 1599 by the Earl of Essex, after a three-day battering by artillery. South of the town, along the banks of the river, is Cahir Park, an arcadian place with pretty 'cottage orné' designed by John Nash, the famous Regency architect. Nearby are the ruins of Cahir Abbey, established in 1220 for Augustinian Canons Regular. The Church of Ireland church is a Gothic-Revival building full of cobwebbed quaintness designed 1817–20 by John Nash. Also of interest: fine 12thC motte and bailey on the east bank of the River Suir at Knockgraffon, 3½ miles to the north; ruins of 13thC church in Derrynagreth, 4½ miles east. Good hunting and shooting centre, with exhilarating walks along the Suir valley or round the corner of mountains into the beautiful Glen of Aherlow to the north west.

Cappoquin   **7 J17**
Co Waterford. Pop 870. EC Wed. Quiet market town tucked along the southern slopes of the Knockmealdown Mountains, in rolling woodland on the edge of the Blackwater Valley.

Carrick on Suir   **7 K16**
Co Tipperary. Pop 5,000. EC Thur. It's a cheery market town on the River Suir, with sharp views out west to a long ridge of forest-covered hillside. Originally a 13thC Anglo-Norman manor, belonging to the Le Brets, it was acquired by the Butlers in the 14thC. It was around their castle that the town grew. The castle was rebuilt in the mid-15thC and a handsome Elizabethan-style mansion was added by Thomas, Earl of Ormond, in 1568. Across the river, on the south bank, is Carrickbeg, a suburb of twisting streets with remains of a 14thC Franciscan friary. St Nicholas of Myra, the parish church in William Street, is a Romanesque fantasy of 1880 with a touch of the boldness of the American H H Richardson; the architect, George Ashlin, was a pupil of Pugin's. At Clonea, 1½ miles south west, is a marvellous Gothic-Revival church; by J J McCarthy, considered the Pugin of Ireland, it smells of vampires. At Ahenny, five miles north, are some magnificent sculptured high crosses. Good trout and salmon fishing, and climbing the peaks of the Comeraghs can take you amongst the clouds.

Cashel   **7 I15**
Co Tipperary. Pop 2,690. EC Wed. Ecclesiastical centre of medieval Munster and ancient capital of their kings, it's a colourful town surrounding a spacious square. The Rock of Cashel, dominating the landscape for miles, is a mighty limestone outcrop crowned by a monumental cathedral complex. The seat of Munster kings from the 4thC to 1101 when King Murrough O'Brien gave it to the Church, it was here that Brian Boru was crowned King of Munster. The buildings on the Rock, entered through the 15thC Hall of the Vicar's Choral, consist of the cathedral, a giant cruciform building with central tower, established in 1169 and

Rock of Cashel

rebuilt in the 13thC; Cormac's Chapel, the wonder of Irish-Romanesque architecture built in 1134; 92-foot-high round tower and 11thC St Patrick's Cross, with high-relief figure carvings standing in the green inside the entrance gate. Also of interest: Dominican friary founded in the 13thC at the foot of the rock; 13thC Hore Abbey to the west; Quirke's Castle, 15thC fortified town house in the main street; Bishop's Palace, now a hotel, handsome Georgian mansion designed 1731 by Sir Edward Lovett-Pearce.

Castleconnell   7 H14
Co Limerick. Once a popular 18thC spa with handsome pump house and elegant villas, it is a sublime village set in woods along the east bank of the River Shannon. Below the village are the Falls of Doonass, a series of limestone shelves over which the sedate river throws itself in sudden abandon. Standing on a rocky outcrop above the Falls are the ruins of a de Burgo castle. Renowned salmon fishing centre.

Castleisland   6 E17
Co Kerry. Village-scale market town of blush-red marble built round an early 13thC castle, a shattered ruin to the western end of the town. To the north, the 1,097-foot Knights Hill shoots skywards like a defused volcano. To the east is the 1,441-foot Knockanfune Mountain.

Castlemaine   6 D17
Co Kerry. Small market town originally built round a castle guarding the crossing over the River Maine, just inland from Castlemaine harbour. The castle was destroyed by Cromwellians. To the north west are the Slieve Mish Mountains.

Clogheen   7 I16
Co Tipperary, 9 miles SW of Ardfinnan. Tiny village awash in a channel of green at the northern feet of the Knockmealdown Mountains. Two miles east, on the north bank of the River Tar is a mid-13thC de Bermingham castle. From here a wide plain runs to the foot of the Galty Mountains, a cliff wall of crumpled skyscrapers rising over 3,000 feet. Five miles north west is Shanbally Castle; designed by John Nash, it is a stone skeleton rendered picturesque by a disastrous fire in 1958. Five miles north west are the ruins of Burncourt Castle, a gabled Elizabethan-style mansion.

Clonkeen   6 E18
Co Kerry, 12 miles SE of Killarney. Handful of houses dancing in the Kerry Highlands. Paradise of quiet where the River Flesk flows near the border with Co Cork.

Clonmel   7 J16
Co Tipperary. Pop 11,630. EC Thur. Important river crossing since early Christian times, it's a bustling market and manufacturing town on the banks of the River Suir. Situated on the floor of a gently undulating valley walled to the south by the Comeragh Mountains, Clonmel is the centre of the Irish greyhound world. It was here that Richard de Burgo established a manor in 1243. Granted a charter by Edward I, the town was walled and fortified in the 14thC, became a stronghold of the powerful Anglo-Norman family, the Butlers, in the 15thC and was captured by the Earl of Kildare in 1516. Loyal to the English crown throughout the Middle Ages, it changed sides in the 17thC when it was garrisoned by a force of the Catholic Confederation in 1641. Besieged by Cromwellians in April 1650, the townsfolk capitulated after a spirited defence, their ammunition exhausted and their garrison, commanded by the courageous Hugh O'Neill, forced to retreat. A Jacobite stronghold during the Williamite wars, the town was abandoned by its garrison when threatened by the Williamite army in 1690.

clonmel

Portions of the 14thC town walls still stand, including West Gate, a reconstruction of 1831. St Mary's Church, a 19thC restoration, has a 13thC choir wall and 15thC tower. At one end of Parnell Street is a huge building called the Main Guard; thought to have been based on a design by Sir Christopher Wren, it was built in 1674 as a barracks of the main guard of the garrison and from the early 18thC it was the seat of the royal assizes. The handsome courthouse in Nelson Street was designed 1800 by Sir Richard Morrison. Famous people connected with Clonmel include the author of 'Tristram Shandy', Laurence Stern, who was born here in 1713; Charles Bianconi, an Italian craftsman and mayor of Clonmel, who set up Ireland's first passenger transport system between Clonmel and Cahir in 1815. Anthony Trollope lived here for a while in the mid-19thC. Also of interest: the Falconry, fine collection of birds and falconry demonstrations at Anner House, Twomilebridge.

Cloyne   7 I19
Co Cork. Jolly village nestling in a shadow of hills. It was here that St Colman founded the see of Cloyne in AD580. Of interest: remains of round tower and 14thC cathedral; nearby limestone cliffs.

Corrofin   7 F13
Co Clare. Tiny market village in an undulating swathe of green south east of Lough Inchiquin. Of interest: remains of an O'Brien Castle on the north bank of the lake; remains of 11thC church and round tower at Killinaboy, 2½ miles north west; remains of Romanesque church and 12thC round tower and high cross at Dysert O'Dea, four miles south east. Numerous prehistoric remains in vicinity.

Croom   7 G15
Co Limerick. Small market town on the banks of the River Maigue; the Fitzgeralds built a fortress here in the late 12thC, of which only part of the keep survives. It was in Croom that a group of 18thC Irish poets called the 'Maigue Poets' used to gather. The most famous was Sean O'Tuama, who was buried in the churchyard in 1775. An annual festival is held in

Dysert Church and Round Tower, Croom

the poets' honour in *Oct.* Also of interest: primitive church and 66-foot-high round tower, all that remains of the early 11thC monastic foundation of Dysert, one mile to the west at Carrigeen; remains of a mid-12thC Cistercian abbey founded by Turlough O'Brien at Manister, 2½ miles to the east, including old bridge, abbey mill and church.

Doneraile 7 G17
Co Cork. Tiny town where Edmund Spenser, the renowned English poet, lived between 1588–98. His home was the now-ruined Kilcolman Castle, three miles north west.

Dromineer 4 H13
Co Tipperary, 6 miles NW of Nenagh. Trout fishing centre and popular holiday resort sunning itself on the south west banks of Lough Derg.

Dundrum 7 I15
Co Tipperary. Picturesque village sealed in a wooded plain at the edge of rolling hills. Three miles south east is Killenure Castle, 17thC O'Dwyer fortress.

Dunmanway 6 F19
Co Cork. Pop 1,400. Busy 17thC market town squatting in a rich valley between rolling green hills. To the west of the town is the source of the River Bandon, at the foot of 1,763-foot-high Nowen Hill. To the south east is Ballynacarriga Castle, built along the banks of a lake in 1558.

Ennis 4 F14
Co Clare. Pop 6,000. EC Thur. Thriving county town and industrial centre, spread along the banks of the River Fergus. Shannon Airport, the first customs-free airport in the world, is 12 miles to the west. Near the bridge over the River Fergus stand the ruins of a Franciscan friary, founded by Donough O'Brien in 1241 and added to over a considerable period of time; remains include a beautiful east window of the late 13thC, early 14thC vaulted sacristy and 15thC transept, tower and cloister arcade. The most remarkable feature of the friary is its lovely sculptures. Also of interest: Catholic cathedral, 1831–43, Gothic-Revival building by Dominic Madden; the County Court House, handsome classical building of 1852 with bold Ionic portico; Clare Abbey, an Augustinian priory founded by Donal O'Brien in 1189, 1½ miles south east; late 12thC Killone Abbey built three miles south beside a holy well, which was a centre of religious pilgrimages.

Ennistymon 6 E13
Co Clare. Pop 1,000. EC Sat. Holiday centre built in the shelter of a wooded valley above a cascade on the River Cullenagh. Handsome late 18thC church dominates the town. Good fishing.

Farranfore 6 D17
Co Kerry. Small village seated between the Slieve Mish Mountains to the west and rising ground along the borders with Co Clare to the east. Good salmon and trout fishing a mile away on the River Flesk.

Feakle 7 G13
Co Clare, 5 miles W of Scarriff. Secluded village lying on a sunny slope at the edge of the Slieve Aughty Mountains. The poet Brian Merriman (1757–1805), who was a schoolmaster at nearby Kilclenin and was born in Ennistymon, is buried in the old churchyard.

Fermoy 7 H17
Co Cork. Pop 3,240. C Wed. Straddling a tree-lined stretch of the River Blackwater, it was built by a Scottish merchant, John Anderson, in the late 18thC. To the west are the peaks of the Nagles Mountains. Two miles north west is Labbacallee, a magnificent wedge-shaped gallery grave. Castles of interest in the vicinity include Carrigabrick, Hyde, Licklash, Roche and Barrymore. Magnificent centre for coarse angling with abundance of roach, rudd and perch on the River Blackwater.

Fermoy

Fethard 7 J15
Co Tipperary. Pop 1,070. EC Thur. Once an important 14thC fortified town, now full of cobwebbed corners, including ancient ramparts, several tower houses, ruins of an early 14thC Augustinian friary, town gate, handsome Everard's Mansion. Also of interest: numerous ring forts in vicinity; Romanesque church at Donaghmore to the west; 13thC Kiltinane Castle, perched on a rock above the River Glashawley, three miles south west.

Galbally 7 H16
Co Limerick. Little village in a picturesque setting at the head of the fabulous Glen of Aherlow, with a

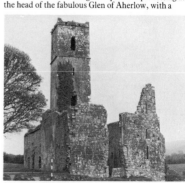

Moor Abbey, Galbally

ruined 15thC parish church. To the east of the village is Moor Abbey, ruins of Franciscan friary founded in the early 13thC. Frequently attacked during the 15thC, the friary was used as a fortress during Elizabethan times and was finally burned by English troops in 1569; remains consist of late 15thC friary church of nave and chancel, divided by a lofty bell tower. Also of interest: wedge-shaped gallery grave at Cordberry, to the north east; chamber tomb crowning the 1,215-foot Slievenamuck.

Glencar   6 C18
Co Kerry, 8 miles S of Glenbeigh. Tiny hamlet huddled in the highlands of Kerry, washed by shafts of sunlight as the mountain peaks of Macgilly-cuddy's Reeks dodge behind a calico canvas of clouds. Good salmon and trout fishing on the upper reaches of the River Caragh, as well as in Loughs Acoose and Cloon. Fabulous centre for climbing and mountain walks.

Golden   7 I15
Co Tipperary, 4 miles SW of Cashel. Quiet village straddling the River Suir with a ruined keep crowning a rocky plinth in the river. One mile south on the west bank is Athassel Abbey, the largest medieval priory in Ireland.

Inchigeelagh   6 F19
Co Cork. Holiday resort and angling centre, it's a small village wandering in a meandering line along the banks of Lough Allua. Several prehistoric remains in vicinity, including a crannog near the presbytery. Good coarse fishing for pike, perch and rudd.

Innishannon   7 G19
Co Cork. Walled town of considerable importance in the Middle Ages, it's now a quiet, pretty spot on the banks of the River Bandon. Of interest: foliage-covered ruins of Dundanier Castle built in 1476 on the banks of the River Bandon; ruins of Shipool Castle, built south east of the village in 1543.

Kanturk   7 F17
Co Cork. Pop 2,050. Small market town straddling the Rivers Allow and Dallow on the northern slopes of the Blackwater Valley. The ruins of Kanturk Castle, a huge fortified house built in 1609, lie one mile south. Numerous ring forts and castle ruins in vicinity. Good trout fishing on the Rivers Allow and Dallow.

Kilbrittain   7 G19
Co Cork. Village cloaked in woods beside the attractive demesne of Kilbrittain Castle.

Kilcash   7 J16
Co Tipperary, 9 miles NE of Clonmel. Tiny village dug in along the southern foothills of 2,368-foot Slievenamon, with the winding Suir valley sweeping past below. The castle, now a ruin, was a Butler stronghold. It was here that Lord Castelhaven wrote his famous memoirs in the 17thC. The ruined church has a fine Romansque portal.

Kilfenora   6 F13
Co Clare. Quiet village in the heart of Clare, it was the episcopal see of Kilfenora diocese in the 12thC, a monastery having been founded there in the early 11thC. The western portion of the cathedral, built on the site of the monastery, is still used. The roofless chancel has fine carved capitals in the window, numerous carved effigies and a handsome sedilia in the north wall. In the churchyard are three stone crosses, the most interesting being the Doorty Cross, with ingenious figure carvings and decorative Urnes work. The area is renowned for its numerous carved crosses, roughly of the same period and of a consistency suggesting that they may have been the

Doorty Cross, Kilfenora

work of a single carver. Also of interest: Lemanagh Castle, an O'Brien fortress 3½ miles south east; it consists of a late 15thC tower house to which a fortified house was added in the early 17thC.

Kilfinnane   7 H16
Co Limerick. Pop 560. EC Thur. Small market village in a forest-walled valley overshadowed by the Ballyhoura and Galty Mountains. North of the village is a gap in the mountain wall running down to the rich dairy pastures of the Golden Vale below. Beside the town is a huge, 150-foot-high mound, the Kilfinnane Motte, a prehistoric ráth 20 feet in diameter at the summit.

Kilgarvan   6 E18
Co Kerry. Idyllic holiday resort sheltering on the edge of the River Roughty in a valley ringed by mountains. Good salmon and trout fishing in the nearby rivers.

Killaloe   4 H14
Co Clare. Pop 900. EC Wed. Small market town in verdant land on the west bank of the River Shannon. Here the Shannon weaves from Lough Derg through the gap between Slieve Bernagh and the Arra Mountains on its way south west to Limerick and the sea. The cathedral town of the Protestant diocese of Killaloe, the town is connected by a 13-arch bridge to the village of Ballina in Co Tipperary on the north east bank. The site of a 7thC religious establishment, it became the stronghold of Brian Boru in the 10thC and later one of the leading ecclesiastical centres of Munster. The town was captured by the Anglo-Irish in 1276. It was here that Patrick Sarsfield forded the Shannon in 1690 to surprise the Williamite siege-train at Ballyneety. The cathedral, built 1185 by Donal O'Brien, descendant of the great Brian Boru, has an aisle-less cruciform plan with fine Romanesque portal from an earlier church on the site. St Flannan's Oratory, standing in the shadows of the cathedral, is a small 12thC Romanesque church with high, pitched stone roof, vault and loft. Standing in the grounds of St Flannan's Roman Catholic Church is St Molua's Oratory; a 12thC church, it originally stood on Friar's Island but was relocated here in 1929 following the flooding of the island for the Shannon hydroelectric scheme.

Killarney
6 E17

Co Kerry. Pop 7,200. EC Mon. A catherine wheel of picturesque streets pinned to the eastern edge of Kenmare demesne in an inspiring landscape filled with lakes in a lush, broad valley edged by mountains. To the west, on the far side of Kenmare demesne is Lough Leane, sometimes known as Lowerlake and the largest of the Lakes of Killarney. Immediately to the south is Lough Muckross or Middle Lake, whilst Upper Lake curves round to the west shadowed by the distant 2,739-foot Purple Mountain. Killarney is a pleasant, unpretentious market town famed for its beautiful lake district rather than its buildings, but featuring a magnificent Catholic cathedral, a Gothic giant with a sky-reaching steeple, designed with reverence by A W Pugin in 1842–55. One of Pugin's great buildings, it's a cliff of limestone with a cruciform plan, much inspired by the ruined cathedral at Ardfert. Also of interest: 14thC Ross Castle, a romantic ruin on a finger of land poking out into Lough Leane; Innisfallen Island, near the northern end of the lough with remains of Innisfallen Abbey, founded in the 7thC; Muckross Abbey, 15thC Franciscan friary three miles to the south; 19thC Muckross House and gardens; ruins of 7thC church and round tower and remains of castle at Aghadoe Hill, 2½ miles north; Dunloe Castle, remains of 13thC stronghold, built to guard the Gap of Dunloe, six miles to the west. Good salmon and trout fishing in the Killarney Lakes and in the numerous rivers and mountain streams. The 11,000 acre Killarney National Park, presented to the nation in 1932 and containing most of the lake district, has fine oak and yew woods, and the arbutus tree is a familiar feature of Killarney Woods. Native Irish red deer and Japanese sika deer roam the park, the latter mainly in the woods, the former in the upland areas.

Killorglin
6 D17

Co Kerry. Pop 1,150. EC Wed. Gateway to the Ring of Kerry on the west bank of the wide, meandering River Laune. Inland, south of Castlemaine harbour, it has the remains of a 13thC castle while to the south is a high rampart of mountains, Macgillycuddy's Reeks. The town is famous for its annual Puck Fair, a three-day event in *Aug* said to date back to pagan times, where a mountain goat is crowned king of the town in a colourful ceremony. Good salmon and trout fishing in the River Laune.

Killorglin

Kilmallock
7 G16

Co Limerick. Pop 1,170. EC Thur. Site of a 7thC monastery and important ecclesiastical centre in the 11thC, the town was fortified by the Fitzgeralds in the late 14thC and sacked by Sir James Fitzmaurice and his clansmen in 1570. The castle was a Catholic arsenal in 1645 and a Cromwellian hospital and depot in 1651. This was a prosperous noble town from the 15thC–17thC, with fine monasteries, castles and elegant stone town houses, but following the fall of the Geraldines the rot began to set in. Frequently sacked and once deserted, albeit for a short time, by the early 19thC its buildings stood broken, a compact, half-forgotten heap of architectural splendours.

Today it is once more a thriving town, sitting on the west bank of the River Loobagh, with the crumpled peaks of the Ballyhoura Mountains to the south. To the east are the Galty Mountains and the lovely Glen of Aherlow in the foothills lies to the north, an undulating valley of grass and boulders washed by the shadows of the towering 3,015-foot Galtymore. John's Castle, a 60-foot-high battlemented tower house was built in the 15thC. There is a 16thC town gate, Blossom Gate, plus a section of town wall, sole survivors of the old town fortifications. The Church of Ss Peter and Paul was built in the 13thC and transformed in the 15thC; an early round tower has been incorporated as a belfry into the west end of the north aisle. The Dominican priory, founded in 1291 and occupying a picturesque riverside site includes a nave, choir and some fine stone carving.

Kilsheelan
7 J16

Co Tipperary, 5½ miles E of Clonmel. Quiet village on the north bank of the River Suir. Of interest: ruins of Transitional-style church with austere Romanesque chancel arch; Gurteen Le Poer, lovely demesne in the foothills along the south bank; ruins of Poulkerry Castle, one mile to the east.

Lisdoonvarna
6 E13

Co Clare. Pop 460. EC Wed. Popular holiday resort and spa with sulphur and chalybeate springs, entrenched on the edge of The Burren, a wild limestone plateau and haunt of geologists and botanists. Numerous caves and potholes, many dangerous; Pollnagollum, at over seven miles the longest cave in Ireland, three miles to the north. Three miles north west is an interesting 15thC O'Brien fortress, consisting of tower and bawn standing on a pedestal of rock.

Lismore
7 I17

Co Waterford. Pop 900. EC Thur. Tiny market town stranded on the south bank of the River Blackwater in a tranquil landscape. It was the site of an early 7thC monastery which grew to a sizeable monastic town in the late 12thC, having withstood the plundering Vikings. It was destroyed by the Anglo-Normans in 1173 and later rebuilt. Of interest: Lismore Castle, built 1185 and once owned by Sir Walter Raleigh, remodelled by Sir Joseph Paxton and Henry Stokes 1812–21; Protestant cathedral, rebuilt 1679–80 by Sir William Robinson.

Listowel
6 D15

Co Kerry. An Aladdin's cave of boozers, one round every corner. Despite such temptations it's a sober, quiet market town on the banks of the River Feale. Its heart is a large, irregular square criss-crossed by roads, with a grey stone spired church sitting imperiously in the middle. Of interest: 13thC Listowel Castle, last stronghold to fall during the Desmond rebellion; Gunsborough, birthplace of Lord Kitchener (1850–1916), four miles north west.

Listowel

Macroom 7 F18
Co Cork. Pop 2,260. EC Wed. Sleepy market town in the fertile valley of the River Sullane. Some fine Georgian town houses; early 19thC Market House; remains of 15thC keep of the castle, traditionally the birthplace of William Penn.

Mallow 7 G17
Co Cork. Pop 5,900. EC Wed. A popular 18thC and 19thC spa, it stands along the banks of the River Blackwater in the midst of rich agricultural land. An old fashioned town with a trace of 18thC elegance in the odd Georgian leftovers in quiet corners of the town. Interesting courthouse and Market House; remains of 16thC Mallow Castle; ruins of 13thC Mourne Abbey, four miles south. Numerous prehistoric and early Christian remains in vicinity. Anthony Trollope lived in Mallow for a while.

Midleton 7 I18
Co Cork. Pop 3,100. Thriving market town, east of Cork, its wide streets clustering at the head of the Owenacurra estuary. Founded by the Broderick family in the late 17thC, it has a handsome 18thC Market House and fine Church of Ireland church, designed 1825 by the Pain brothers. The architect Sir Richard Morrison (1767–1849) was born here.

Millstreet 6 F18
Co Cork, 13 miles N of Macroom. Tiny village in the shadow of mountains south of the River Blackwater. To the north east is an early 13thC castle tower. Numerous prehistoric remains in vicinity.

Milltown 6 D17
Co Kerry, 3 miles east of Castlemaine harbour. There are fragments of 13thC priory, Kilcoman Abbey, and remains of large circular fort and souterrain one mile south west near Fort Agnes.

Mitchelstown 7 H17
Co Cork. Pop 2,790. EC Wed. Rebuilt by the Earls of Kingston during the 18thC and 19thC, it's an important market town and agricultural centre ringed by mountains. To the north east are the Galty Mountains; to the east the Knockmealdown Mountains; to the west the Ballyhoura Mountains with the Kilworth Mountains in the south.

Mountshannon 7 H13
Co Clare, 5 miles NE of Scarriff. Angling haunt on Lough Derg with fine harbour, pier and houses under an umbrella of trees. A mile offshore to the south east is Iniosceatra, a holy island and site of a 7thC monastic establishment founded by St Caimin; remains consist of five early churches, including St Brigid's with handsome Romanesque portal, 80-foot round tower and holy well. Boat from Mountshannon pier.

Murroe 4 H14
Co Limerick, 5 miles SE of Castleconnell. Handful of houses in rolling woodland with a horizon of hills to the east. Of interest: fine Celtic cross standing at the head of the village; Glenstal Abbey, a Benedictine foundation with fabulous gardens in the foothills of the Slievefelim Mountains.

Nenagh 7 I13
Co Tipperary. Pop 5,180. EC Wed. Small town on a fertile plain shuttered by walls of rock and gorse, the Silvermine Mountains to the south and the Arra Mountains to the west. Butler stronghold until the 14thC, when the O'Briens made it the centre of their kingdom. Recovered by the Butlers in 1537, it was burned by O'Carrol of Eile in 1548 and captured for the Catholic Confederation a century later. Of interest: the Butler Castle, a pentagonal fortress with a monumental circular keep 100 feet high with castellations added in the mid-19thC; it has five

Nenagh Castle, Nenagh
Co Tipperary

storeys and massive 20-foot-thick walls. Also of interest: remains of 13thC Franciscan friary in Abbey Street, founded 1250 by Bishop Donal O'Kennedy of Killaloe; Tyrone Abbey, a 13thC Augustinian foundation established by the Butlers, one mile south east of the town.

Newcastle West 7 F16
Co Limerick. Pop 2,550. EC Wed. Bustling market town strung out along the River Dee under a great canvas of sky in the heart of rich, green dairy country. The castle, standing in ruins on the west side of the town, was built originally for the Knights Templar in 1184 and later acquired by the earls of Desmond; remains include part of the curtain wall, circular keep and two 15thC halls. Following the failure of the Desmond rebellion, the castle and lands were confiscated and given in 1591 to Sir William Courtenay; they were retaken in 1598 by the Desmonds only to be lost once more the following year. Also of interest: 15thC Glenquin Castle; Reerassta Fort, an ancient ring fort three miles north at Ardagh, where the famous 8thC gold and silver Ardagh Chalice was discovered in 1868.

Newmarket 7 F17
Co Cork. 17thC village where Sarah Curran, Robert Emmet's sweetheart, lived. She is buried in the churchyard.

Newmarket-on-Fergus 4 F14
Co Clare, 7 miles NW of Sixmilebridge. Large village at the centre of a belt of farmland. Of interest: Ralahine Townland, two miles to the south where, through the influence of Robert Owen, the world's first farming co-operative was established in the 19thC. To the north east is Dromoland Castle, a monumental castellated Gothic mansion designed 1826 by the brothers James and George Pain; now a hotel, it has marvellous formal gardens. Nearby is Moohaun Fort, one of the largest Iron Age hill forts in Europe, covering some 27 acres.

Portlaw 8 K16
Co Waterford. Leather-tanning village in an idyllic landscape setting. Planned as model village and built 1825–1904 by a Quaker industrialist for the workers in his cotton-spinning mills.

Portroe 4 H13
Co Tipperary. Slate-quarrying village on a commanding shelf of land to the south west of Lough Derg. Behind it to the south are the Arra Mountains, whilst across the ocean of water to the north stand the mountains of Clare and Galway.

Quin 7 F14
Co Clare, 6 miles E of Ennis. A village on the banks of the River Rhine, with a remarkably well preserved Franciscan friary, Quin Abbey, built within the ruins of a 13thC castle. Also of interest: 16thC gabled tower house of the McNamara clan at Danganbrack, ¾ mile north east. The McNamaras

ruled the territory around here from early Christian times until well into the 15thC and built 42 castles. To the south east is Knappogue Castle; built in 1467 it has recently been restored. Not far to the east is the Craggaunowen, an outdoor museum with recreated Bronze Age crannog as well as early Christian and medieval buildings next to 15thC tower house of four storeys.

Rathkeale   7 **F15**
Co Limerick. Small agricultural town on the main Limerick–Killarney road, it is an undulating wall of houses punctuated by a skyscraper-tall church spire. There are fragments of a 13thC Augustinian priory and west of the town is Castlematrix, a 15thC tower house and Desmond stronghold where the 9th Earl was murdered by his servants in 1487; once restored by Sir Walter Raleigh. Also of interest: remains of a stone ring fort at Gorteennamrock, four miles to the north; Ballyallinan Castle, ruined O'Hallinar fortress, four miles south. Known as the 'Palatine', the district around was settled by Lutheran refugees expelled from the Rhenish Palatinate by the French in the early 18thC.

Rath Luirc   7 **G16**
Co Cork. Sometimes known as Charleville, it's a handsome market town spread spaciously on a rolling sea of green in the Golden Vale near the borders with Co Limerick. Laid out in the mid-17thC by Roger Boyle, first Earl of Orrery, it has an 18thC market house. Of interest: 15thC Kilbolaine Castle, seven miles west, with part-moat and two circular towers.

Roscrea   7 **J13**
Co Tipperary. Pop 3,860. EC Wed. Prosperous market town cradled between the 1,733-foot-high Slieve Bloom Mountains to the north east and the 1,577-foot-high Devil's Bit Mountain to the south west. The site of a 7thC monastic establishment, the town was of strategic importance to the Anglo-Normans, who built a castle to control the pass in the early 13thC. Of interest: remains of 15thC St Cronan's Friary; 12thC high cross, 10thC round tower and west gable of the 12thC Romanesque cathedral church of St Cronan, with triangular hood crowning the round-headed entrance portal; ruins of Roscrea Castle, built in the mid-13thC and reconstructed in 1332; Damer House, handsome 18thC Georgian town house. Two miles to the south east is Monaincha, the most celebrated pilgrimage centre in Munster during the Middle Ages.

Roscrea, Co Tipperary

Scarriff   7 **H13**
Co Clare. Angling village lying on a green plain near an attractive bay on the south west shore of Lough Derg. In the village of Tuamgraney, two miles south, there is an interesting early Christian church with a 12thC chancel.

Sixmilebridge   7 **G14**
Co Clare. Large village built either side of the River O'Garney on the southern edge of a plain studded with lakes. It's really two villages in one—the old village, built on the west bank and the new village, built in the early 18thC, on the east bank. Two miles to the north is Mountcashel Castle, built by Conor O'Brien in the late 15thC. Three miles east is Mountlevers, a handsome Georgian mansion with ashlar stone front and brick garden façade.

Templemore   7 **J14**
Co Tipperary. Pop 2,180. EC Thur. Small market town stretched out on a fertile plain in the shadows of the Devil's Bit Mountain, a giant hill of rock and gorse lurching skywards with a gap in the peak where, according to legend, the Devil spat out a piece he found unpalatable. The crumb fell further south to form the Rock of Cashel. Also of interest: 16thC Loughmore Castle, with later additions, three miles south; Barna Castle, a five-storey circular keep, two miles south west.

Terryglass   4 **I12**
Co Tipperary, 3½ miles SW of Carrigahorig. Idyllic lakeside village in a landscape rich in legend. Installed on the north eastern banks of Lough Derg, the village was the site of a 6thC monastic establishment and has the remains of a 13thC Norman castle, a square-planned tower with angle turrets, of which only the ground storey survives. At Lorrha village, five miles north east, are the remains of a 13thC Dominican priory and on the site of a 6thC monastic foundation of St Ruadhan stand the ruins of a 12thC Augustinian church.

Thurles   4 **J14**
Co Tipperary. Pop 9,100. EC Wed. Cathedral town of the archdiocese of Cashel and Emly since the 18thC, it is also a thriving market centre astride the River Suir with the fertile plain of Tipperary to the south. The scene of a major defeat of Strongbow's Anglo-Norman army in 1174, the Anglo-Normans finally built a mighty fortress here to control the river crossing. A Carmelite priory was founded in 1300 and the town gradually expanded, nurtured by the Butlers. Of interest: remains of two Butler fortresses—Bridge Castle, beside the bridge on the western bank of the river, and Black Castle, near the main square; Catholic cathedral, an Italianate Romanesque pastiche of 1865–72. Brittas Castle, a 19thC essay in nostalgia of monumental proportions, is a pastiche of Warwick Castle; work was stopped when the client was killed by falling masonry. Also of interest: Kylecrew Mill, mid-19thC timber water mill; historic Holy Cross Abbey, on the west bank of the River Suir four miles south of the town; 16thC Ballinahow Castle, a circular tower house five storeys in height, three miles north west.

Tipperary   7 **I15**
Co Tipperary. Pop 4,720. EC Wed. Market town and dairy-farming centre made famous by the marching song, 'It's a Long Way to Tipperary'. It is cradled in the fertile Golden Vale north of the Slievenamuch Hills. An Anglo-Norman settlement developed round a late 12thC castle, it was burned by the O'Briens in 1339 and torn apart by the Desmond wars. It was virtually a derelict wasteland in the late 16thC but gave its name to the county and figured prominently in the Land League agitation of the late 19thC. It was here that a prominent landlord, Smith Barry, was boycotted by his tenants who set up an alternative settlement on the outskirts of the town called 'New Tipperary'; the boycott proved a failure and the settlement was abandoned. Of interest: remnants of a 13thC Augustinian abbey; Norman motte north of the town.

Toomevara 4 I14
Co Tipperary, 10 miles E of Nenagh. Neat village in a close-clipped landscape. Remains of Augustinian priory established in the 14thC.

Tulla 7 G13
Co Clare, 4½ miles N of Kilkishen. Picturesque village of houses bobbing like curachs in a sea of hills at the centre of the Clare Lakelands. The ruins of an ancient church hang like a skeleton over the roofs. Good fishing in the nearby lakes.

Regional features

Crystal
Waterford Glass Ltd, Kilbarry, Waterford, offers a conducted tour (weekdays), which gives a fascinating insight into the making of this world-famous crystal, from the blowing and shaping to the cutting and polishing. Open all year. Glass blowing can also be seen at Kerry Glass Ltd, Fair Hill, Killarney, Co Kerry. Open all year with showroom selling perfect and imperfect glass.

Making curachs, Mahairees, Co Kerry

Curachs 6 B16
Cloghane, Co Kerry. This small holiday resort on the south west corner of Brandon Bay is a good place to hire curachs, fishing boats constructed of tar-impregnated canvas stretched over a rib-cage of wood. In prehistoric times, animal skins would have been used. The oars are made of a single piece of timber and have a triangular plate fixed near the handgrip with a hole drilled through it, which is used to fasten the oar to a vertical wooden pin in the frame of the boat, making it extremely manoeuvrable in high seas. The high prows are designed to ride the waves safely. Curachs are in constant use throughout the west coast. The nearby village of Ballydavid also has a curach-building industry.

The Gaeltacht
An Irish-speaking nation up to the 16thC, Ireland adopted English as a primary language with the settlement of English planters and the imposition of the English system of land tenure. The government of 1921 stated that the survival and encouragement of Gaelic speaking was an important part of state policy and the Gaeltacht Commission was set up in 1925. Gaeltacht areas in the south include the region known as Corcha Dhuibhne, in the Dingle Peninsula, in a rough line west of the Brandon Mountains. The Gaeltacht area in south Kerry is centred round Ballinskelligs village on the edge of Ballinskelligs Bay, running inland north east along the River Inny valley, through the Ballaghasheen Pass and around Lough Cloon at the foot of the 2,539-foot Mullaghanattin Mountain. In Co Cork, there are two areas: the first is Clear Island, seven miles by boat from Baltimore, where Irish language courses are available between *Jun* and *Aug*; the second is inland, amongst rolling hills around Ballingeary and stretching north west from Ballyvourney to Coolea. It was at Ballingeary that the first Irish College, Coláiste na Mumhan, was established in 1904. The area is renowned for its traditional music and dance.

Jaunting cars
A traditional form of travel around the sights with a story-telling 'jarvey' as guide.

The Kerry Blue Terrier
A friendly, active terrier, it was originally bred for pit fighting. Loved by generations of Kerrymen, the breed became well known in the late 19thC and was said to have descended from the long-haired blue dogs which swam ashore from ships of the Spanish Armada wrecked on the rocky Kerry coast.

Kinsale sweaters
Unique to this area, these are decorative fishermen's sweaters, mostly hand-knitted in traditional patterns.

Limerick lace
The lace industry was introduced by an Englishman, Charles Walker, in 1824. His wife was connected with a lace factory in England. The tradition is carried on by the Sisters of the Good Shepherd Convent, Clare Street, Limerick city; examples of their work can be seen at the convent on weekdays. Lace can also be seen at Convent of the Poor Clares, Kenmore, with a good display of point and other types of lace.

Musical instruments
The traditional bodhran is made in Cork, Kerry and also Dublin. It consists of a goat or greyhound skin stretched over a round wooden frame and beaten with knuckles or drumstick.

Precious metals
There are many small workshops housing silver, gold and enamel metalworkers in the region, particularly in Co Tipperary and Co Cork.

Famous people

Eamon de Valera (1882–1975) 7 G16
De Valera Museum, Knockmore, Nr Bruree, Co Limerick. A tribute to this great statesman, born in New York of a Spanish-Cuban father and an Irish mother but brought up in Ireland, who spent much of his childhood in a cottage in Knockmore. Associated with the resurgence of Gaelic culture and the formation of the Irish Volunteers, he was one of the leaders condemned to death for his part in the Easter Rising, 1916. Spared, no doubt for fear his execution might have an adverse effect on the still-neutral United

Eamon de Valera

States, he became the leading figure in Republican ranks. Elected president of Sinn Fein in 1918, he opposed the treaty and resigned in 1922, following a closely fought election won by pro-treaty candidates. He formed the Fianna Fail party in 1926 and went on to win the 1932 election with a sizeable majority. He remained in power until 1949 and was President of Ireland from 1959–73. The museum, open *Sun*, *Thur* and church holidays, has many personal mementos in addition to local artefacts.

Daniel O'Connell (1775–1847) **4 F14**
O'Connell Monument, Ennis, Co Clare. Monument to
Daniel O'Connell, the Liberator. Unveiled in 1865,
it marks the site in the city centre of the great
meeting in 1828 at which O'Connell was nominated
to stand for election. He was MP for Clare from
1828–31. A lawyer and son of a landowner from
Kerry, he abhorred violence and sought Catholic
emancipation and the abolition of legal
discrimination against Catholics within the
framework of the law.

Jonathan Swift (1667–1745) **6 E20**
Rock Cottage, Union Hall, Co Cork. Home of the
writer, who was born in Dublin in 1667. Studied at
Kilkenny Grammar School and Trinity College and
was ordained in 1694. Author, poet and writer of
political pamphlets, he was the greatest genius of the
new culture. A spirited and tireless fighter against
oppression and unfairness, he was also the author of
'Gulliver's Travels' and Dean of Christchurch,
Dublin. It was in Rock Cottage that he wrote the
poem, 'Carberiae Rupes' in 1723.

Cathedrals, abbeys & churches

Adare Augustinian Priory **7 G15**
Adare, Co Limerick. Built east of the village in 1325
and restored in the 19thC, it is now the Church of
Ireland parish church. Remains include the church
nave, chancel and tall, square central tower. There is
a fine sedilia, some 15thC domestic buildings, now a
school, and tiny, but beautiful, 15thC cloister.

Adare Franciscan Friary **7 G15**
Adare, Co Limerick. Founded 1464 by Thomas, Earl
of Kildare, the extensive ruins stand on a slope of
green overlooking the River Maigue. The church,
which has well preserved windows and a handsome
sedilia, consists of a nave and choir to which a
transept and side chapels were added in the early
15thC. There is a graceful nave and richly
ornamented cloister, with surrounding refectory and
dormitory added in the early 16thC. The friary was
entered by the Killmallock Gate, an elegant gateway
to the west of the church with inset coat of arms.

Adare Trinitarian Abbey **7 G15**
Adare, Co Limerick. Now the Catholic parish church
standing in the main street, it was founded in 1230
for the Trinitarian order, whose work concerned the
liberation of Christians captured during the
Crusades and later ransomed. During Henry VIII's
reign, the monastery was dissolved and the 45
remaining friars put to death. The only surviving
monastery of the order, remains include the tower,
nave, choir and some domestic buildings.

Ardfert Franciscan Friary **6 D16**
Ardfert, Co Kerry. Founded 1253, extensive ruins
include 13thC nave and chancel of church with
elegant lancet windows, handsome 13thC south
transept, tower and two sides of the cloisters.

Ardmore Church and Round Tower **7 J18**
Ardmore, Co Waterford. St Declan established a
monastery here in the 7thC and by 1170 it had its
own bishop with its church recognised as a
cathedral. The church, built in 1203 and known as
the 'Cathedral', has an unusual recessed
Romanesque west window, interior blind arcading
with a fine, pointed arch dividing nave and chancel.
To the east is a tiny building, St Declan's Oratory,
re-roofed in the early 18thC. The 97-foot round
tower, one of the best preserved in Ireland, is built in
four stepped stages.

Ardmore Church and Round Tower

Askeaton Franciscan Friary **7 F15**
Askeaton, Co Limerick. Extensive ruins on the east
bank of the River Deel, north of the town. Founded
1389 by the 4th Earl of Desmond; most of the
remaining buildings belong to the early 15thC. The
church, with a nave, chancel and north transept, has
some fine carved windows, lovely sedilia and
magnificent triple tomb niches. The most impressive
part of the remains is the cloister; built to the south
of the church, it is a unique arrangement
necessitated by the site, which is rocky to the north
but gently sloped to the south. The refectory and
aisled wing added to the north of the church were
built in the late 15thC.

Athassel Abbey **7 I15**
Golden, Nr Cashel, Co Tipperary. Founded by
William de Burgo in the late 12thC for the Canons
Regular of St Augustine, it is the largest medieval
priory in Ireland, covering over four acres. One of
the wealthiest and most important monasteries of
Norman Ireland, its abbot was a Peer of Parliament
and a large town grew up around the priory. The
town, of which little survives, was pillaged in 1319
and 1330 and the monastery burnt in 1447. Remains
consist of a 210-foot-long cruciform-plan abbey
church of 13thC, 14thC–15thC cloisters and
ancillary buildings.

Corcomroe Abbey **1 F12**
Co Clare, 6 miles E of Ballyvaghan. Founded by
Donal O'Brien in 1182. The domestic buildings have
gone but the abbey church, a cruciform plan with a
chapel terminating each transept, is in a remarkable
state of preservation. A fine example of Irish
Romanesque work, with delicately vaulted choir,
fine carvings in the transept chapels and a marvellous
tomb niche in the north wall with an effigy of the
founder's grandson, Donor O'Brien, who died in
1267.

Holy Cross Abbey **7 J14**
Nr Thurles, Co Tipperary. Recently restored for use
as a parish church, it is one of the finest of 15thC
Irish churches. Originally a Benedictine foundation
established in 1169, it was taken over by the
Cistercians in 1186. Little remains of the original
buildings. A popular pilgrimage centre in the 15thC.

Holycross Abbey
Co. Tipperary
(recently restored)

The Cistercians considerably altered and extended the church, which consists of a nave, chancel—one of the finest examples of 15thC Irish architecture—and two transepts. An unusual feature in the chancel is a sedilia, known as the 'Tomb of the Good Woman's Son', with cusped arches crowned with crockets. In the north transept is preserved one of the few medieval frescoes in Ireland. There is a small cloister to the east, recently reconstructed.

Killaloe Cathedral   4 H14
Killaloe, Co Clare. Aisle-less cruciform building on the site of an earlier Romanesque church. The richly carved portal of the earlier church is retained inside the cathedral. The triple lancet windows at the east end, the chief glory of the cathedral, are surprisingly English for a time when the Anglo-Norman-controlled territory was still some distance away. St Flannan's Oratory, which stands in the cathedral grounds, is a small 12thC Romanesque building with stone roof clearly inspired by that of Cormac's Chapel, Cashel. Irish Romanesque church architecture of this period was generally no more than a simple box-like design, enriched by decorative portals and chancel arches.

Killulta Church   4 G14
Nr Mungret, Co Limerick. Small, primitive, rectangular church constructed of large stones with tiny, triangular-headed window in the east gable. Thought to be the earliest church in the county, it was probably built at the turn of the 12thC.

Kilmallock Dominican Priory   7 G16
Kilmallock, Co Limerick. Founded in 1291, the church has a single aisle to which a large transept, divided into two aisles by a single cylindrical pillar, was added in the early 14thC. There is a handsome 13thC west window in the chancel, some fine 13thC and 14thC stone carving, a 15thC tower and some 13thC domestic buildings transformed in the 15thC.

Monaincha   7 J13
Nr Roscrea, Co Tipperary. The site of this monastic settlement, first founded in the 6thC, was originally an island in a bog. A place where no living being of the female sex, either human or animal, might enter without dying immediately, according to a Norman historian, it was taken over by the Augustinians in the late 12thC. Remains include ruins of 12thC nave and chancel church with handsomely carved west portal and beautiful chancel arch; sacristy, north of the church; and abbey cross.

Muckross Abbey   6 E17
Nr Killarney, Co Kerry. Ruins of Franciscan friary begun in 1448. The characteristic nave and chancel church contains fine east windows, handsome sedilia and some interesting tombs. There is a beautiful cloister arcade with an old yew tree at the centre.

Quin Abbey   7 F14
Quin, Co Clare, 6 miles E of Ennis. Well preserved Franciscan friary founded in 1433 by Sioda Macnamara. There had been a church here in the 12thC but this was burnt in 1278 to be replaced two years later by a great square keep with massive round towers. Partially destroyed in 1236, a new church was built onto the ruins in 1350 and when the Franciscans settled at Quin the church was remodelled in its present form. Of particular interest are the fine cloisters with a first floor dormitory. The abbey, built in the Irish Romanesque style, incorporated several of the towers from the earlier castle, which makes it very picturesque.

Rock of Cashel   7 I15
Cashel, Co Tipperary. Limestone rock, nearly 200 feet high, dominating the town. Formerly the seat of

Cormac's Chapel, Cashel, Co Tipperary

Munster kings, it was granted to the Church in 1101 by the King of Munster, Murrough O'Brien. Dedicated to 'God, St Patrick and St Ailbhe', the rock is crowned by a huge cathedral. Largely 13thC, it is an aisle-less cruciform building with a crossing and a three-storey residential castle attached at the west end. This had a Great Hall built over the nave. Cormac's Chapel, tucked at an angle to one side of the cathedral's south transept, is one of the seminal works of Irish Romanesque architecture. Built 1134, it is renowned for its remarkable elegant blind arcading and rich use of ornamentation. It consists of a nave and chancel, with a barrel-vaulted nave with chamber above and high, pitched stone roof.

St Brendan's Cathedral   6 D16
Ardfert, Co Kerry. Ruins of 12thC cathedral remodelled in 13thC with nave and chancel plan. Of particular interest is the Romanesque blind arcading on the west, handsome portal and remains of sedilia. Nearby is Temple-na-Hoe, a Romanesque nave and chancel church with unusual corners articulated by columns. To the north west is Temple-na-Griffin, late Gothic church named after the sculpted griffins inside.

Castles & ruins

Askeaton Castle   7 F15
Askeaton, Co Limerick. Begun by William de Burgo in 1199 and extensively enlarged by the 7th Earl of Desmond in the mid-15thC, it stands on a rocky islet in the River Deel. Remains include a 90-foot-high keep, a bailey enclosed by a curtain wall with a tall tower on the southern face. To the west is a Great Hall, 90 feet long, raised above a vaulted ground storey; built up against the ramparts overlooking the river, it has the remains of delicate traceried windows with built-in seats and handsome blind arcading articulating the southern wall.

Bunratty Castle   4 G14
Co Clare, 4 miles S of Sixmilebridge. Originally an island site in a commanding position controlling the movement of river traffic to and from Limerick. Four castles were built here, the first an Anglo-Irish fortress built in the 13thC. The present castle was built by the McNamaras in 1460. A giant, rectangular keep, it has square towers projecting at the corners. The towers on southern and northern façades are connected by great flying arches not unlike those of the 15thC Hermitage Castle in Scotland, surmounted by a continuous floor above. A large banqueting hall is on the first floor and above it is a magnificent upper hall, 48 feet high and long and 30 feet wide, where the Earl held court; opening off it is a small chapel. Above the hall, to the south,

Bunratty castle, Co. Clare

are the principal living quarters. The collection of
14thC–17thC furniture and furnishings is one of the
best in the British Isles. The castle, open all year, is
used nightly for medieval banquets in *summer*.
Beside the castle is Bunratty Folk Park.

Cahir Castle
7 I16

Cahir, Co Tipperary. Butler stronghold, built from
1375 on the site of an early 12thC fortress of Conor
O'Brien. Recently restored, it stands on a rocky islet
in the river and was thought to be impregnable. It
was the largest 15thC castle in Ireland, with huge
walls with monumental square or rounded projecting
towers. Divided into two irregular courtyards, it has
a huge three-storey square keep with a large,
first-storey hall.

Desmond Castle
7 G15

Adare, Co Limerick. Built on a bend of the River
Maigue. Remains include monumental square keep
protected by a moat and inner ward in the north west
corner of the complex. There is a semi-circular
bastion on the west side and a gate with drawbridge
to the south. The outer ward, enclosing the south
and east sides of the inner ward, contains the 13thC
Great Hall, raised above a ground storey. Attached
to it in the west wall is the main gate. Remains of a
second hall, late 13thC, are to the east beyond a
15thC kitchen and bakery. One of the finest
examples of feudal architecture in Ireland, it passed
to the Fitzgeralds, earls of Kildare, in 1227. Partially
rebuilt by them, it was burned by Turlough O'Brien
in the 15thC. It was confiscated in 1536, following
the ill fated 'Silken' Thomas rebellion, and granted
to the Earl of Desmond in 1541. Besieged by the
English in 1580, it was rendered harmless in 1599
and partially dismantled on the orders of Cromwell
in the 17thC.

Ormond Castle
7 K16

Carrick on Suir, Co Tipperary. Originally a 14thC
fortress, it was rebuilt by the Butlers as a square
enclosure with angle towers, on a bank of the River
Suir. It was Thomas, Earl of Ormond, who added
the most magnificent part, the handsome
Elizabethan mansion; the finest example of its kind
in Ireland, it was built in 1568. Of particular interest
is the Great Hall; beautifully decorated in stucco, it
runs almost the length of the building. The influence
of Elizabethan England was very strong:
characteristic of such mansions is the multiplicity of
gables, the use of string courses and the proliferation
of mullioned windows.

Ross Castle
6 D17

Killarney, Co Kerry. Standing on a promontory
protruding into Lough Leane south west of
Killarney, it was built in the 14thC. Remains include
a huge 15thC tower enclosed by a bawn with
rounded turrets. Held by Royalists during the

Cromwellian wars, it was taken by boat attack from
the lake. It had been prophesied that the castle
would only be taken by attack from the water;
remembering this, the defenders capitulated.

Houses & gardens

Adare Manor
7 G15

Adare, Co Limerick. Gothic-Revival manor house
built by the brothers James and George Pain in 1832
for the 2nd Earl of Dunraven. Marvellous wood and
stone carving, including a fine decorative chimney
piece in the Great Hall, designed by Pugin. Fine
collection of paintings, including works by
Canaletto, Reiysdael and Reynolds. In the pleasure
gardens are five Ogham stones, brought from Kerry.
The landscaping, the work of Hardwick, includes
lovely geometrical box gardens laid out below the
south terrace. *Open summer.*

Anne's Grove
7 H17

Castletownroche, Co Cork. A large woodland garden
with an exotic collection of plants and shrubs,
including Himalayan and Chinese rhododendrons.
Tufted bamboos, large swamp cypress and gunnera
adorn the water garden on the banks of the river
running through the garden. *Open summer. C Fri.*

Bantry House
6 E19

Bantry, Co Cork. Seventeenth-century house
transformed by Richard White, the 1st Earl of
Bantry, in 1771 into a handsome Georgian mansion;
a 14-bay south front was added in 1840. Remarkable
collection of furnishings, Gobelin tapestries, Russian
icons and some fine Irish Chippendale furniture.
Italianate terraced gardens. *Open summer.*

Burncourt Castle
7 I16

Burncourt, Co Tipperary, 5 miles NW of Clogheen.
Ruins of a monumental Elizabethan-style mansion
designed 1641–45 for Sir Richard Everard,
consisting of gabled corner towers and centre block.
Whilst comfort was of primary concern by the
mid-17thC, larger houses such as this still
incorporated some defensive features, such as corner
towers, as protection against local bands of robbers.
The house was burnt by Cromwell in 1650 and Sir
Richard, a member of the supreme council of the
Confederation of Kilkenny, was hanged following
the fall of Limerick in 1651. As the rhyme says, "it
was seven years in building, seven years living in it,
and fifteen days it was burning". It has remained a
ruin ever since. As designed, the castle had 26 gables
and 7 tall, elegant chimney stacks. Parts of the bawn
with corner turret survive. *Open all year.*

Burncourt, Co. Tipperary 1641

Derreen Woodland Gardens
6 D19

Nr Lauragh, Co Kerry. Fabulous gardens with many
fine shrubs and specimen trees, begun 110 years ago
on the shore of Kenmare River. *Open summer.*

Derrynane House
6 B19

Caherdaniel, Co Kerry. The house of Daniel
O'Connell during the busy period of his political life.
Interesting collection of personal possessions and
furnishings. *Open summer.* The grounds belong to
the Derrynane National Historic Park.

Garinish Island 6 D19
Glengarrif, Co Cork. A paradise of rare subtropical plants and beautiful Italianate gardens covering 36 acres. Reached by boat from Glengarrif. Acquired by the Bryce family in 1910 when it was a wilderness, the island was slowly transformed by a landscape architect and has a magnificent series of terraces, belvedere and Palladian-style gazebo with magnificent views out across the waters of the harbour to the ring of mountains beyond. *Open summer.*

Glenstal Abbey 7 H14
Nr Castleconnel, Co Limerick. Benedictine abbey and school since 1926, it was formerly the home of the Barrington family. Designed by William Bardwell between 1837–75, it is a monumental pastiche, part medieval English castle and part Irish Romanesque church. The interior woodwork is enriched by Celtic carvings of leaves and animals. Fabulous rhododendron drives and terraced gardens. Gardens *open summer.*

Lismore Castle 7 I17
Lismore, Co Waterford. Early 19thC castle remodelled 1850–58 by Sir Joseph Paxton and Henry Stokes. Magnificent 800-year-old yew walk and lovely gardens. *Open summer.*

Muckross House

Muckross House 6 E17
Nr Killarney, Co Kerry. Tudor-Revival mansion designed in 1843 by William Burn, a Scottish architect, for Henry Arthur Herbert, MP. Now a museum of Kerry folklife and crafts centre, encircled by magnificent gardens. Many exotic trees and shrubs; magnificent collection of rhododendrons, azaleas and fine rock garden. *Open spring and autumn.*

Museums & galleries

Bunratty Folk Park 4 G14
Co Clare, 4 miles S of Sixmilebridge. Interesting collection of vernacular buildings assembled from Co Clare and the Shannon region. There is also a display of traditional skills, such as basket weaving, farriery and candle-making. In the courtyard of Bunratty House, there is an exhibition of agricultural machinery. *Open all year.*

Burren Display Centre 1 F12
Kilfenora, Co Clare. An appreciation of the Burren area, through a collection of flora and fauna, butterflies, moths, rocks and land formations. *Open summer.*

Cobh Museum 7 H19
Cobh, Co Cork. In a converted church, this little museum will appeal to those interested in the 'Lusitania', which was torpedoed and sunk by a German submarine off the Old Head of Kinsale in May 1915. *Open summer.*

Craggaunowen Centre 7 F14
Nr Quin, Co Clare. Interesting outdoor museum built beside four-storey tower house. The tower house is typical of the fortified houses of the Gaelic and Anglo-Irish aristocracy of the 15thC and 16thC. Nearby is a reconstructed Bronze Age crannog and Iron Age ring fort including souterrain. Within the ring fort are reconstructed vernacular buildings of the late Middle Ages. The entrance lodge contains 19thC cottage furniture and domestic utensils. *Open summer.*

The Hunt Collection 7 H14
National Institute of Higher Education, Limerick, Co Limerick. Over a thousand items collected by the late John Hunt, including weapons and ornaments from the Irish Bronze Age, the 9thC bronze Cashel Bell, early Christian brooches, medieval Limoges enamels, 18thC Irish porcelain and silverware and many interesting Celtic items. *Open summer.*

Nature trails

Farrar 7 G19
Co Cork, 3 miles SE of Coachford. Beautiful scenery in the valley of the River Lee offering some excellent walks. Scenic views, wildlife displays and picnic site.

Glenbower 7 I18
Nr Killeagh, Co Cork. The Glenbower forest lies above the village of Killeagh and covers a large area of hilly land cut through by the River Dissour. Forest walks and nature trail (leaflet can be purchased at the forest). Picnic facilities.

Glengarra 7 I16
Co Tipperary, 8 miles SW of Cahir. Forest and riverside walks. Many unusual species of trees and shrubs can be seen here. Nature trail (leaflet available) and picnic area.

Glengarriff Forest Park 6 D19
Glengariff, Co Cork. Forest walks and nature trail amidst the foothills of the Caha Mountains. Lady Bantry's Look-Out is a well known viewpoint. (Leaflet available.)

Gougane Barra Forest Park 6 E19
Co Cork, 3 miles W of Ballingeary. 1,000-acre park with scenic walks, a nature trail and a car trail. Booklet available.

Killarney National Park 6 E18
Co Kerry. Presented to the nation in 1932 by the Bourn Vincent family of California, this 11,000-acre park contains four separate nature trails of differing lengths; three cut through the wooded lake district to the west of Muckross House. Another, the Blue Pool trail, runs through Clogheren Wood. Japanese sika deer and red deer can be seen.

Birdwatching

Kilcolman Bog 7 G17
Nr Buttevant, Co Cork. A privately owned marsh with a bird observatory, interesting as the only wintering ground of the white-fronted Greenland goose in the county.

Old Head, Kinsale 7 G20
Co Cork. Kittiwakes, razor-bills and guillemots can be seen here in their colonies. Many thousands of sea birds fly past in passage, among them manx shearwaters, fulmers and auks. Skuas have also been sighted and some great and sooty shearwaters.

Gulley Head in the west of Co Cork is also a good viewing point for sea birds.

Forests

Curragh Chase 7 G15
Nr Adare, Co Limerick. A still-developing forest
park. The house (birthplace of Aubrey de Vere, the
poet) was destroyed by fire in 1941, but the grounds
contain an arboretum, picnic area and animal
cemetery, where de Vere buried his pets.

Gougane Barra 6 E19
Co Cork, 3 miles W of Ballingeary. Ireland's first
forest park, these 1,000 acres are surrounded by
mountains on three sides, opening to a beautiful
river valley on the fourth. Coniferous and deciduous
forest with larch, ash, birch and rowan. Arbutus—
the Irish strawberry bush—grows here wild.

St Finbarr's Church, Gougane Barra, Co Cork

Killarney National Park 6 E18
Co Kerry. Extensive park of 11,000 acres of
wonderful walks and lake views, incorporating many
attractions such as the 60-foot-high Torc Waterfall,
one of Ireland's most spectacular views. Muckross
Abbey, House and gardens are within the bounds of
the park, as are Meeting of the Waters, Old Weir
Bridge and Dinis Cottage. Yews, oaks, arbutus and
various mosses grow in profusion and there are three
separate nature trails to follow. Irish red deer and
Japanese sika deer roam the park. The whole estate
was presented to the nation in 1932 by the Bourn
Vincent family of California.

Hills & mountains

The Burren 1 F12
Co Clare. A vast moonscape bounded by the towns
and villages of Lisdoonvarna, Lahinch, Ballyvaghan,
Ennistymon and Corrofin. The haunt of geologists
and botanists, this scarred plateau of giant flagstones
is at the junction of a porous carboniferous limestone
belt and shale system. The cracks and crevices in the
rock floor are full of remarkable wild plants such as
spring gentians, white anemones, yellow primroses
and mountain avery. Below the surface is a
subterranean world of caves, streams, potholes and
numerous lakes which disappear overnight, called
'turloughs'. A populated place in prehistoric and
early Christian times, the area is rich in stone forts
and dolmens. Of particular interest:
Cahermacnaghten stone fort, three miles north of
Noughaval; 100 feet in diameter, it once housed a
famous medieval law school. Cahercomonaun stone
fort, early 9thC and one of the most elaborate forts
on the Burren is five miles north of Corrofin. It
stands on a dramatic cliff-top perch overlooking a
valley and consists of three concentric walls; the
innermost has a number of internal chambers.

Nire Valley 7 J16
Co Waterford. Undulating mountain valley of woods,
lakes and streams bounded on the south and west by
the winding Suir Valley and to the east by the
Comeragh Mountains, a giant wall of rock rising up
to 2,473 feet. Good for pony-trekking and climbing.
Abundance of brown trout in the River Nire.

Countryside

Clare
Co Clare is almost surrounded by water: the estuary
of the River Shannon to the south, Lough Derg to
the east and the Atlantic coast to the west. There are
some good sandy beaches, notably at Kilkee, dotted
along the rocky coastline. The Cliffs of Moher in the
north of the county rise in parts to almost 700 feet.
To the north lies The Burren, a high limestone
wilderness with an unearthly feel. This hilly area is
traversed by rills, ridges and subterranean streams
and is known for its pot-holes and extensive
underground caverns. The Burren plays host to a
number of rare species of plant and is a botanist's
and geologist's dream. On the edge of The Burren is
the spa town of Lisdoonvarna; the spa waters contain
iodine and there are both sulphurous and iron
springs. Around Ennis and Corrofin, in the centre of
the county, there are numerous small lakes and this
area forms a distinct contrast to the arid Burren.

Cork
The largest county in Ireland, split from west to east
by the River Blackwater and the Boggeragh,
Ballyhoura and Galty Mountains. North and east
Cork are characterised by undulating limestone
tracts divided by ridges of sandstone, with many
attractive river valleys. West Cork is an area of
contrasts; there are mountains and lakes and,
perhaps most spectacular, a beautiful rugged
coastline. Ireland's most southerly point is Mizen
Head, within the boundaries of Co Cork. In the
west, mountainous peninsulas with rugged desolate
scenery are divided by Dunmanus Bay and Bantry
Bay, and the Caha Mountains, traversed by deep
valleys, provide excellent hill-walking. South of the
River Lee the land is gentler, until it reaches the
dramatic, rocky coastline.

Kerry
Stiuated in the south west of the country, its main
feature is the rugged coastline made up of three great
peninsulas: Beara, Iveragh and Dingle, the latter
being probably the best known. The southern part of
the county is mountainous and contains Ireland's
highest peak, 3,414-foot Carrantuohill, south west of
Killarney in the Macgillycuddy's Reeks. The
coastline is a mixture of rocky outcrops and sandy
bays. The northern part of the county consists of
undulating plains as far as the River Shannon. The
country surrounding Killarney is especially
beautiful, a spectacular area of lakes, woodland and
mountains. The town of Killarney is close to the
shores of Lough Leane, which is separated from
Lough Muckross by a narrow isthmus. The
surrounding mountains are mainly of red sandstone
although there are some volcanic rocks near Lough
Guitane. The effects of glaciation can be widely seen:
corries in particular abound, such as Horses' Glen
and the Devil's Punch Bowl, and everywhere there
are rocks worn smooth by the ice. The narrow
Dingle Peninsula is straddled by the Slieve Mish
Mountains and to the west lies magnificent coastal
scenery, dotted with hamlets.

Countryside near Glenbeigh, Co Kerry

Limerick

In contrast to the rugged counties of Kerry and Cork, Limerick is mostly low-lying, fertile land. In the east lies part of the area known as the Golden Vale and the Galty Mountains penetrate into the county to the south east. The River Shannon, on which Limerick city is situated, runs from east to west across the north of the county. There are few loughs; the most notable is Lough Gur, south of Limerick city, with natural caves along its shores. Limerick also offers some of the best hunting country in Ireland.

Tipperary

Tipperary lies to the east of the ancient province of Munster and is one of Ireland's more wealthy, fertile counties—a wealth resulting from farming the land to best advantage. The River Suir flows through the centre of the county from north to south and forms the base of the Golden Vale, which runs across into Co Limerick. To the south tower the impressive Galty and Knockmealdown Mountains and the southern half of the county is characterised by hilly country and deep valleys. The town of Cashel stands close to an outcrop of limestone rock known as the Rock of Cashel. It stands 200 feet above the surrounding land and is topped by ancient ruins. The Glen of Aherlow lies to the south of Tipperary, a beautiful valley with impressive views of hills towering over lush farmland, tucked between the ridge of Slievenamuck and the Galty Mountains. The fertile farming areas to the north are among the best in Ireland; sugarbeet is an important crop.

Waterford

The smallest county in the old province of Munster, lying along the south east coast of Ireland, Waterford features a varied coastline of sandy beaches and rugged headlands. The centre of the county is taken up by the red sandstone peaks of the Comeragh Mountains, pocked with corries, of which the most notable is Coumshingaun. There are two important rivers bordering the county: the Suir to the north and the Blackwater, which is perhaps more beautiful here than at any other point, to the south. Lismore is a good centre from which to explore the river valley.

Rivers & loughs

Gougane Barra   6 E19

Co Cork, 3 miles W of Ballingeary. Dark womb of water enclosed by a wall of cliffs and towering mountain peaks, which opens to the east into a long winding river valley. A wild, rugged land covered in a 1,000-acre forest of spruce, larch, pine, birch and ash, this was Ireland's first national forest park and is the source of the River Lee.

Lakes of Killarney   6 D17

Co Kerry. Part of Killarney National Park. The largest is Lough Leane; sometimes known as Lower Lake, it is divided in two by a jagged claw of land poking out from the east bank, Ross Island, on which stand the ruins of a castle. In the northern bay is the largest of the islands, Innisfallen, with the ruins of an abbey founded in the 7thC. Immediately to the south is Muckross Lake, or Middle Lake, divided from Lough Leane by a catwalk of land. Curving south and then west is a narrow passage of water that descends from beautiful Upper Lake.

Torc Waterfall   6 D18

Nr Killarney, Co Kerry. One of the most popular beauty spots in Killarney and one of the finest waterfalls in Ireland, it's a 60-foot-high cascade walled by trees, 4½ miles south of Killarney.

Archaeological sites

Dingle Peninsula   6 B17

Co Kerry. The undulating blanket of land west of the Brandon Mountains and the offshore islands form a treasure trove of prehistoric and early Christian remains, including over 400 beehive-shaped cells, numerous souterrains, several ring forts and many inscribed stones. Of interest: Iron Age promontory forts such as Dunmore and Dunbeg, the latter built on a cliff-edge site with a complex system of earthen ramparts and trenches protecting the mainland flank; the settlement of beehive huts near Glengahan; Cathair na Mairtineach, 108-foot diameter enclosure complete with souterrains and beehive huts; Cathair Fada an Doruis, a triple clochan, rather like one of the Trulli houses of Alberobello, Italy; several cross-inscribed pillars and small stone oratories, especially on the Blasket Islands.

sea road, Dingle Peninsular

Of particular interest is the Gallarus Oratory. Like an upturned boat, it is one of the best-preserved oratories in Ireland and is built of unmortared stone. It has a corbelled roof structure, more roof than wall, with a rectangular plan with square-headed entrance and tiny round-headed east window in the gable end. Built in the 8thC, it stands high up on a sloping shelf of grass a mile inland from the coast. Kilmalkedar Church, part of a monastery founded in the 7thC, is one of the most important ecclesiastical sites in the peninsula, consisting of a handsome Romanesque nave and chancel church built in the 12thC. Modelled on Cormac's Chapel, Cashel, it has a fine carved tympanum over the entrance portal, part of a stone roof and elegant blind arcading.

Lough Gur   7 G15

Co Limerick. Attractive, horseshoe-shaped lake with a remarkable number of Stone Age dwellings and burial places. Remains include wedge-tombs, stone circles, standing stones, crannogs and the foundations of domestic dwellings. Of interest primarily to the specialist, the remains also include some Early Christian buildings. Beside the Limerick road is one of the most impressive stone circles in Ireland, used for both Stone Age and early Bronze Age rituals.

Scattery Island   6 D15

Co Clare, 2 miles from Kilrush. Remains of early monastic foundation established by St Senan in the early 6thC. Pillaged by the Vikings in AD 816 and 835 and occupied by them from 872–975, it was finally recaptured by the great resistance leader, Brian Boru. The remains include five churches, the most interesting of which is St Senan's Cathedral, with antae and huge lintelled west portal. There is a simple, undecorated Romanesque church and numerous cross-slabs. The 120-foot-high round tower is particularly unusual in having its entrance opening at ground level.

Skellig Michael 6 A19
Skellig Rocks, Co Kerry. Perched 550 feet up on a
precipitous series of terraces cut out of a giant sea
stack eight miles into the Atlantic south west of
Bolus Head. The early Christian monastery is
reached by a steep flight of steps and was founded by
St Finian in the 7thC. Remains consist of a group of
beehive cells; two oratories, shaped like upturned
boats with great corbel roofs of unmortared stone; St
Michael's Church; numerous
cross-shaped slabs all
enclosed in a
dry-stone walling.
Pillaged by
Vikings in the
9thC, the
monastery
continued until
evacuated by
the monks in
the 12thC.

Oratory, Skellig Michael, Co. Kerry

Staigue Fort 6 C19
Nr Castlecove, Co Kerry. Crowning the crest of a
quiet valley, it is one of the finest of the early Iron
Age forts in Ireland and is 83 feet in diameter with an
18-foot-high enclosing wall, 13 feet thick at the base
and 7 feet thick at the top. The stairways, which give
access to narrow platforms, are enclosed within the
thickness of the wall and the entrance is via a long
passageway.

Regional sport

Gaelic sports
The Gaelic Athletic Association was founded at
Thurles in 1884 and there is a stadium in the town
devoted to traditional Gaelic sports such as hurling
and Gaelic football, both of which are fast, exciting
spectator sports.

Hunting
Limerick offers the hunting enthusiast a large choice
of packs; the season runs from *Nov–Mar*. The cost of
a day's hunting is high, with not only the hire of a
mount for the day but also the cap fee to be taken
into account. The Co Limerick Hunt, the Scarteen
Hunt and the Stonehall Harriers are active in the
area. Beagling also takes place here and is generally a
more informal affair.

Scuba-diving
Although this sport can be enjoyed virtually all along
the Irish coast, the south west offers the most
spectacular underwater scenery. There are diving
centres or schools at Clare Island, Kilkee, Valentia
Island, Renvyle and Gortahork.

Festivals

All-Ireland Fleadh
A three-day song and music festival and the high
point of Ireland's musical year. Competitions for all
grades of musicians, plus music in pubs, streets and
hotels. Held last weekend in *Aug* at a different town
each year.

Cork Choral & Folk Dance Festival 7 H18
City Hall, Cork. Choirs from Europe and America
compete, with a series of concerts and events.
Apr/May.

Fleadh Nua 7 F14
Ennis, Co Clare. A festival of traditional music, song
and dance. Last weekend in *May*.

Macroom Mountain Dew Festival 7 F18
Macroom, Co Cork. Open-air concerts during festival
week in *Jun*.

Rose of Tralee International Festival 6 D16
Tralee, Co Kerry. Lots of free attractions for all
tastes. Variety concerts, a five-day race meeting and
the selection of the Rose of Tralee. *Late Aug*.

St Patrick's Week
Parades all over Ireland to celebrate the Irish patron
saint's day on the *17th Mar*; lots of festivities all
week.

Waterford International Festival of 8 L17
Light Opera
Theatre Royal, Waterford. A two-week bonanza with
entries from all over the British Isles. Held annually
in *Sep*.

Special attractions

Aillwee Cave 1 F12
Co Clare, 2 miles SE of Ballyvaghan. Dating from
two million BC, this cave was originally a river bed
and was later inhabitated by wild animals, including
bears. Now it has fascinating stalactites and
stalagmites. *Open summer*.

The Blarney Stone 7 G18
Blarney, Co Cork. The famous Blarney Stone, kissed
by thousands of tourists each year, stands at the foot
of the battlements of Blarney Castle. It is said that a
kiss of the Blarney Stone imparts the 'gift of the
gab'. For centuries, until the downfall of the old
Gaelic order, the MacCarthys of Blarney maintained
a bardic school.

The Burren Perfumery 1 F12
Vincent Craft Fragrance, Carran, Co Clare. A very
interesting tour shows how the different subtropical
flora of the Burren make up the Vincent perfumes.
Open summer.

Fish Auction 6 C19
Castletownbere, Co Cork. Lots of varieties of fish sold
every night at 21.00 at the Fishermen's Co-operative
Society.

Gap of Dunloe 6 D18
Co Kerry. A seven-mile trip through this
breathtaking pass on horseback or by jaunting car
begins at Kate Kearney's cottage, an original
coaching inn.

Medieval Banquets 4 G14
Bunratty Castle, Co Clare. A 15thC fortress with
14thC–17thC furnishings, where diners are
entertained by the Shannon Castle Singers.
Knappogue Castle, Co Clare. Banqueting
accompanied by attractive historical pageant. *Open
summer*.
Also at: Ballyseedy Castle, Tralee, Co Kerry.

Pleasure cruises 8 L16
*Galley Cruising Restaurant, Bridge Quay, New Ross,
Co Wexford*. Lunch, tea, high tea and dinner cruises
among others on fully licensed vessels. Fresh local
produce is served. Tel (051) 21723.

Shell Cottage 7 J17
Abbeyside, Dungarvan, Co Waterford. Pretty and
colourful designs made with seashells decorate this
cottage; worth a visit.

The Wheel of Fortune 7 F20
Clonakilty, Co Cork. A water pump, still in use,
erected in 1890 by the Earl of Shannon as part of the
town's waterworks.

Index

Abbeyfeale, Co Limerick **139**
Abbeyknockmoy, Co Galway **74**
Abbeyleix, Co Laois **103–4**, 119
Achill Island, Co Mayo 28, **72**
Achillbeg Island, Co Mayo **73**
Act of Union **24–5**, 56, 93
Adare, Co Limerick 33, **139**, 148, 150, 152
Aghanaglack, Co Fermanagh **61**
Aghavannagh, Co Wicklow **104**, 122
Ahascragh, Co Galway **74–5**
Aillwee Cave, Co Clare **154**
Anascaul, Co Kerry **129**
Annaghdown Priory, Co Galway **82**
Annaghmore, Co Armagh **61**
Annalong, Co Down **40**
Annamoe, Co Wicklow **104**
Anne's Grove, Co Cork **150**
Annestown, Co Waterford **129**
An Tostal, Co Leitrim **88**
Antrim, Co 17, 29, 37–62
Antrim, Co Antrim **46**, 54, 58
Aran Island, Co Donegal 66, **73–4**
Aran Islands, Co Galway 28, 31, 64, **73**, 81, 86
Ardagh, Co Longford **104**
Ardamine, Co Wexford **92**
Ardara, Co Donegal **65**
Ardee, Co Louth 90, **104**
Ardfert, Co Kerry 128, **139**, 148–9
Ardfinnan, Co Tipperary **139**
Ardglass, Co Down 39–40
Ardmore, Co Waterford 128–9, 148
Ardrahan, Co Galway **75**
Ardress House, Co Armagh **55**
Ards Forest Park, Co Donegal 66, **85**
Arklow, Co Wicklow **92**, 126
Armagh, Co 17, 19–20, 35
Armagh, Co Armagh 19–20, 35, 39, **46–7**, 52–3, 55, 57
Arthurstown, Co Wexford **92**
Ashford Castle, Co Mayo 77, **84**
Askeaton, Co Limerick **139**, 148–9
Athassel Abbey, Co Tipperary 33, 143, **148**
Athboy, Co Meath **104**
Athenry, Co Galway **75**
Athleague, Co Roscommon **75**
Athlone, Co Westmeath 90, **104**
Athy, Co Kildare **104**, 121, 124
Augher, Co Tyrone **47**, 61
Aughnacloy, Co Tyrone **47**
Aughrim, Co Galway 23, **75**
Aughrim, Co Wicklow **104**
Avoca, Vale of, Co Wicklow 115, **122**
Avondale House, Co Wicklow 91, 112, 115, 121
Avondale Forest Park, Co Wicklow **121**

Bailieborough, Co Cavan **104**
Balbriggan, Co Dublin **92**, 125
Balla, Co Mayo **75**
Ballaghaderreen, Co Roscommon **75**

Ballina, Co Mayo **65**, 88
Ballina, Co Tipperary **139**
Ballinafad, Co Sligo 63, **75**, 82, 84, 87
Ballinamore, Co Leitrim **75**
Ballinascarthy, Co Cork **139**
Ballinasloe, Co Galway 64, **75**, 88, 124
Ballindoon Friary, Co Sligo **82**
Ballinrobe, Co Mayo **75**, 81
Ballintober, Co Mayo **75**, 82
Ballintober, Co Roscommon 33, **76**, 84
Ballintoy, Co Antrim **40**, 45, 58, 62
Ballintra, Co Donegal **65**
Ballybay, Co Monaghan **104**
Ballybofey, Co Donegal **76**
Ballybunion, Co Kerry **129**
Ballycastle, Co Antrim 29, **40**, 45–6, 53, 57, 59, 61–2
Ballycastle, Co Mayo **65**
Ballyclare, Co Antrim **47**
Ballyconneely, Co Galway **65**
Ballyconnell, Co Cavan **104–5**
Ballycopeland Windmill, Co Down 55
Ballycotton, Co Cork **129**
Ballycroy, Co Mayo **65**
Ballydehob, Co Cork **129**
Ballyferriter, Co Kerry **139–40**
Ballyhack, Co Wexford **92**
Ballyhaunis, Co Mayo **76**
Ballyheige, Co Kerry **129**
Ballyjamesduff, Co Cavan **105**
Ballylickey, Co Cork **129**
Ballyliffin, Co Donegal **76**
Ballylongford, Co Kerry **129**
Ballymahon, Co Longford 90, **105**, 125
Ballymakeera, Co Cork **140**
Ballymena, Co Antrim **47**
Ballymoney, Co Antrim **47**, 52
Ballymoney, Co Wexford **92**
Ballymote, Co Sligo 76, 84
Ballynahinch, Co Down **47**
Ballynoe, Co Down **61**
Ballysadare, Co Sligo **65**
Ballyshannon, Co Donegal **65**
Ballyvaughan, Co Clare **129**
Baltimore, Co Cork **129**, 138
Baltinglass, Co Wicklow **105**, 121, 125
Banagher, Co Offaly **105**, 123
Banbridge, Co Down **47**
Bandon, Co Cork 128, **140**
Bangor, Co Down 39–40, 48
Bann Valley, Co Antrim 18, 38, 59, 60
Bantry, Co Cork 21, 128–9, 133, 150, 152
Bar Mouth, Co Londonderry **58**
Barna, Co Galway **65**, 81
Baronscourt, Co Tyrone **55–6**
Beaghmore, Co Tyrone **61**
Beckett, Samuel 26, 49
Behan, Brendan 26, **114**
Belleek, Co Fermanagh **51**
Belfast, Co Antrim 17, 28, 35, 37–8, **40–4**, 53–7, 61–2, 124
Arts Council Gallery **57**
Botanic Gardens 35, 43
Castle 43, **54**
City Hall 43, **55**
Crown Liquor Saloon **55**
Custom House 35, 43

MacArt's Fort 38
Queen's University Festival 62
St Anne's Cathedral 42, **53**
Transport Museum 43–4, **57**
Ulster Museum 44, **57**
Zoological Gardens 42, 44, **62**
Bellacorick, Co Mayo **76**
Bellevue, Co Wicklow **121**
Belmullet, Co Mayo **65**
Beltra, Co Sligo **66**
Belturbet, Co Cavan **105**
Ben Bulben, Co Sligo 67, 70, 86
Berkeley, George 113–4
Bettystown, Co Meath **102**
Birr, Co Offaly **105**, 119
Black and Tans 25, 96, 131
Blacklion, Co Cavan **105**
Blackrock, Co Dublin **92**
Black Rock, Co Louth **92**
Blackwater, Co Wexford **92**
Blarney, Co Cork 128, **140**, 154
Blasket Islands, Co Kerry 133, **138**, 153
Blessington, Co Wicklow **105**, 120–1
Bloody Foreland, Co Donegal 73, **80**
Blue Stack Mountains, Co Donegal 67, 76, **85**
Boa Island, Co Fermanagh **46**, 52
Bonamargy Friary, Co Antrim **53**
Book of Durrow 19, **114**, 116
Book of Kells 19, 90, 98, 109
Borris, Co Carlow **105**, 118
Borris-in-Ossory, Co Laois **105**
Boru, Brian 20, 25, 39, 90, 93, 128, 134, **140**, 143, 153
Boviel, Co Londonderry **61**
Boycott, Captain Charles 72, 75, **81**
Boyle, Co Roscommon 33, 64, **76**, 82
Boyne, Battle of 23, 48, 104, 107, 121, 124, 128, 135
Brandon Bay, Co Kerry 130, 138, 147
Brandon Mountains, Co Kerry 130, 133, **138**, 153
Brandy Pad, Co Down **57**
Bray, Co Wicklow 91, **92**, 120, 122
Brendan, St 64, 74, 82, 87, 133, **139**
Bricklieve Mountains, Co Sligo 64, **75**, 87
Broadford, Co Clare **140**
Browne's Hill Dolmen, Co Carlow **106**, 125
Bruce, Edward 22, 38–9, 40, 70, 75, 93, 101, 104, 108, 111–12, 134
Brugh na Bóinne, Co Meath 112, **125**
Bruree, Co Limerick **140**, 147
Bunbeg, Co Donegal **66**
Bunclody, Co Wexford **105–6**
Buncrana, Co Donegal 66, 68, 74, **84**
Bundoran, Co Donegal 66, **88**
Bunmahon, Co Waterford **129**
Bunratty Castle & Folk Park, Co Clare 135–6, **149–50**, 151, 154
Burke, Robert O'Hara **81**, 84

Burncourt Castle, Co Tipperary 33, 141, **150**
Burren, Co Clare 127, 129, 144, **151–2**, 154
Burrishoole Abbey, Co Mayo 71, **82**
Burtonport, Co Donegal **66**, 73–4
Bushmills, Co Antrim **47**
Butt, Isaac 24, 76, 78
Buttevant, Co Cork **140**, 151

Caher Island, Co Mayo **73**
Caherdaniel, Co Kerry **130**
Cahir, Co Tipperary **140**, 150
Cahirciveen, Co Kerry **130**, 138
Caledon, Co Tyrone **47**, 56
Callan, Co Kilkenny **106**
Camp, Co Kerry **130**
Camphill, Co Tyrone 57
Cappoquin, Co Waterford **140**
Carlingford, Co Louth **92**
Carlow, Co 89–126
Carlow, Co Carlow **106**, 118
Carna, Co Galway **66**, 81
Carndonagh, Co Donegal **76**
Carraroe, Co Galway **66**
Carrick, Co Donegal **66**, 81
Carrick-a-Rede Lion Park, Co Antrim 40, **46**
Carrickart, Co Donegal **66**
Carrickfergus, Co Antrim 21, 23, 37–8, 42, **45**
Carrickfergus Castle, Co Antrim 21, 33, 38, 45, **54**
Carrickmacross, Co Monaghan **106**, 114
Carrick on Shannon, Co Leitrim 63, **76**, 87
Carrick on Suir, Co Tipperary 34, **140**, 150
Carrigaholt, Co Clare **130**
Carrowkeel, Co Sligo 63, 75, **87**
Carrowmore, Co Sligo 63, 72, **87**
Carson, Sir Edward 25, 96
Carton House, Co Kildare 91, 110, **119**
Casement, Sir Roger 101, 128, 139
Cashel, Co Galway **66**
Cashel, Co Tipperary 27, 33–4, **140–1**, 146, 149, 153
Cashel, Rock of, Co Tipperary 27, 127, 140–1, **149**, 153
Castle Archdale, Co Fermanagh **54**
Castlebar, Co Mayo **76–7**
Castleblakeney, Co Galway **77**
Castleblayney, Co Monaghan **106**
Castle Caldwell Nature Reserve, Co Fermanagh **57–8**
Castle Carra, Co Antrim **54**
Castlecomer, Co Kilkenny **106**
Castleconnell, Co Limerick **141**
Castlecoole, Co Fermanagh 39, 48–9, **56**
Castlecove, Co Kerry **130**
Castlederg, Co Tyrone **47**
Castledermot, Co Kildare **106**
Castlegregory, Co Kerry **130**
Castleisland, Co Kerry **141**
Castlemaine, Co Kerry **141**, 144
Castlepollard, Co Westmeath **106**, 121
Castlerea, Co Roscommon **77**

Castleruddery Transport Museum, Co Wicklow 105, **121**
Castlestrange Stone, Co Roscommon 31, 64, 75, **87**
Castletown, Co Kildare 34, 91, 106, 118, **119–20**
Castletownbere, Co Cork **130**, 154
Castletownshend, Co Cork **130**
Castle Upton, Co Antrim **56**
Castle Ward, Co Down 46, **56–7**
Castlewellan, Co Down **47**
Castlewellan Forest, Co Down 45, **59**
Causeway Coast Lion Park, Co Antrim **62**
Cavan, Co 31, 63, 89–126
Cavan, Co Cavan **106**, 114
Celbridge, Co Kildare **106**, 118–20, 124
Churchill, Co Donegal **77**
Ciaran, St 90, 110, 116
Clandeboye, Co Down 48, **56**
Clara, Co Offaly **107**, 123
Clare, Co 24, 28, 32–3, 127–54
Claregalway, Co Galway **77**, 82
Clare Island, Co Mayo **73**
Claremorris, Co Mayo **77**, 88
Clarinbridge, Co Galway **66**, 88
Clear Island, Co Cork 28, **138**, 147
Cleggan, Co Galway **66**, 74
Clew Bay, Co Mayo 70–3, 88
Clifden, Co Galway 64, **66**, 88
Cloghane, Co Kerry **130**, 147
Clogheen, Co Tipperary **141**
Clogher, Co Louth **92**
Clonakilty, Co Cork **130**, 154
Clonalis House, Co Roscommon 77, **84**
Clonard, Co Meath **107**
Clonbur, Co Galway **77**
Clondra, Co Longford **107**
Clones, Co Monaghan **107**
Clonfert Cathedral, Co Galway 14, 64, **82–3**
Clonkeen, Co Kerry **141**
Clonmacnois, Co Offaly 26, 90, **116**
Clonmany, Co Donegal **77**
Clonmel, Co Tipperary 127, **141**
Clontarf, Battle of 20, 39
Clontuskert Abbey, Co Galway **83**
Cloyne, Co Cork **141**
Cobh, Co Cork **130**, 151
Coleraine, Co Londonderry **47**, 56
Collooney, Co Sligo **77**
Colt Island, Co Dublin **103**
Columba, St 38, 40, 48–9, 67–9, 74–5, 77, 79, 90, 109, 113–4, 116
Comber, Co Down **47**
Comeragh Mountains, Co Waterford 128, 152–3
Cong, Co Mayo 33, **77**, 83–4
Connacht 17, 19–21, 36, 63–4, 68, 87, 127
Connemara, Co Galway 28, 64, 79, 81, 86, 88
Connolly, James 25, 96, 107
Connolly, William 91, 106, 118–19

Conolly's Folly, Co Kildare 106, **118**, 120
Cookstown, Co Tyrone 38, **48**, 55, 57, 61–2
Coolaney, Co Sligo **77**
Coole Park, Co Galway 80–1, **84–5**
Cooley Peninsula, Co Louth 90, 102–3, 123
Cootehill, Co Cavan **107**
Copeland Islands, Co Down **58**
Corcomroe Abbey, Co Clare 129, **148**
Cork, Co 33, 127–54
Cork, Co Cork 21, 34, **130–2**, 133, 154
Cormac's Chapel, Co Tipperary 20, 32, 127, 141, 149
Corrofin, Co Clare **141**, 152
Corrofin, Co Galway **77**
Costelloe, Co Galway 67, 81
Courtown, Co Wexford **93**
Craggaunowen, Co Clare 146, **151**
Craigavon, Co Armagh **48**, 51
Crawfordsburn, Co Down **48**, 56
Creeslough, Co Donegal **67**, 83, 88
Creevykeel, Co Sligo **87**
Croghan Valley, Co Wicklow **122**
Crookhaven, Co Cork **133**
Croom, Co Limerick **141**
Crosshaven, Co Cork **133**
Crossmaglen, Co Armagh **48**, 61
Crossmolina, Co Mayo **77–8**
Cruagh, Co Dublin **121**
Crumlin, Co Antrim 53, 61
Cuilcagh Mountains, Co Fermanagh 38, 59, 87, 90
Culdaff, Co Donegal **67**
Curlew Hills, Co Sligo 64, 75–6, 84
Curlieus Castle, Co Sligo 75, **84**
Curracloe, Co Wexford **93**
Curragh, Co Kildare 91, 109, 111, 123, **126**
Curragh Chase, Co Limerick **152**
Cushendall, Co Antrim **45**, 52, 59
Cushendun, Co Antrim **45**, 54, 59

Daingean, Co Offaly **107**
Dalkey, Co Dublin 89, **93**, 103, 115
Davitt, Michael 24, **81**, 115
de Burgo, Richard 68–70, 76, 79, 82, 84, 141
Derragara Museum, Co Cavan **121**
Derreen Woodland Gardens, Co Kerry **150**
Derrymore House, Co Armagh **56**
Derrynane House, Co Kerry 130, **150**
Desmond Castle, Co Limerick **150**
de Valera, Eamon 25, 96, 100, **147**
Devenish Isle, Co Fermanagh 39, **46**, 53, 55, 60
Devil's Glen, Co Wicklow **121**
Dingle, Co Kerry 128 , **133–4**

Dingle Peninsula, Co Kerry 28, 31, 128, **138**, 147, 152–**3**
Donaghadee, Co Down **45**, 62
Donard Forest, Co Down **59**
Donegal, Co 17, 32, 36, 63–**8**
Donegal, Co Donegal 63, **67**
Doneraile, Co Cork **142**
Doolin, Co Clare **133**
Dooney Rock, Co Sligo **85**
Down, Co 17, 34–5, 37–**62**
Downings, Co Donegal **67**
Downpatrick, Co Down 21, **48**, 52–3, 55–6, 58, 61
Dowth, Co Meath 89, 124–**5**
Drogheda, Co Louth 23, **93**, 102, 124
Droichead Nua, Co Kildare **107**
Dromahair, Co Leitrim 63, **78**
Dromineer, Co Tipperary **142**
Dromore, Co Down 21, **48**
Dromore West, Co Sligo **78**
Drumcliff, Co Sligo 63, **67**
Drumena, Co Down **61**
Drum Manor Forest Park, Co Tyrone 48, **62**
Drumshanbo, Co Leitrim **78**, 88
Drumsna, Co Leitrim **78**
Dublin, Co 89–**126**
Dublin, Co Dublin 17, 19–21, 23, 25–6, 29, 33–5, 37, 39, 87, 89–91, **93**–**101**, 112, 114–6, 123–6
  Abbey Theatre 26, 81–2, 89, 96–7, 101, 115
  Christ Church Cathedral 33, 96–7
  Four Courts 25, 34, 96, 98
  Marino Casino 34, 99
  Parliament House 34, 98
  Phoenix Park 24, 34, 99, 100
  St Patrick's Cathedral 33, 97
  St Stephen's Green 34, 99
  Trinity College 19, 25–6, 34–5, 87, 96, 98, 114–6, 121
  University College 115
Dublin Horse Show **126**
Duiske Abbey, Co Kilkenny 108, **116**
Duleek, Co Meath **107**
Dun A'Ri Forest Park, Co Cavan **121**
Duncannon, Co Wexford **101**
Dundalk, Co Louth **101**, 119
Dundrum, Co Down 21, **45**, 54
Dundrum, Co Tipperary **142**
Dunfanaghy, Co Donegal **67**
Dungannon, Co Tyrone 38, **48**, 62
Dungarvan, Co Waterford **133**, 154
Dungiven, Co Londonderry **53**, 55, 61
Dunguaire Castle, Co Galway 33, 70, **84**, 88
Dunkineely, Co Donegal **67**
Dun Laoghaire, Co Dublin 35, 96, **101**, 101–**2**, 115, 120, 122
Dunlap, John 51–2, 55
Dunluce Castle, Co Antrim 47, **54**
Dunmanway, Co Cork **142**
Dunmore, Co Galway **78**
Dunmore Cave, Co Kilkenny 109–10, 126
Dunmore East, Co Waterford **133**

Durrow, Co Laois **107**
Durrow Abbey, Co Offaly 114, **116**
Duvillaun More, Co Mayo **73**
Dwyer, Michael 114–**5**

Easky, Co Sligo **68**, 81, 88
Easter Rising (1916) **25**, 82, 84, 96, 100, 107, 110, 128, 147
Edenderry, Co Offaly **107**
Edgeworthstown, Co Longford 107–**8**
Elphin, Co Roscommon **78**
Ennis, Co Clare **142**, 152, 154
Enniscorthy, Co Wexford 35, 91, **108**
Enniscrone, Co Sligo **68**, 81, 88
Enniskerry, Co Wicklow **108**, 120
Enniskillen, Co Fermanagh 39, 46, **48**–**9**, 54, 56–7, 60, 124
Ennistymon, Co Clare **142**, 152

Fahan, Co Donegal 63, **68**, 71
Fair Head, Co Antrim 40, **45**
Falcarragh, Co Donegal **68**, 81
Fanad Peninsula, Co Donegal 71, **73**
Farranfore, Co Kerry **142**
Farrar, Co Cork **151**
Feakle, Co Clare **142**
Fenagh, Co Leitrim **83**
Fenians **24**, 81, 100, 131
Fenit, Co Kerry **133**
Fermanagh, Co 17, 37–62, 123
Fermoy, Co Cork **142**
Ferns, Co Wexford **108**, 118
Fethard, Co Tipperary **142**
Fethard, Co Wexford **102**
Fianna Fáil 25, 147
Fintown, Co Donegal **78**, 81
Fleadh, All-Ireland 28, **154**
Fleadh Nua, Co Clare 28, **154**
Flight of the Earls (1607) 37, 40, 49, 67, 71, 134
Florence Court, Co Fermanagh **56**
Fonntrai, Co Dublin **126**
Fore Abbey, Co Westmeath **116**
Fournocks Hill, Co Dublin **125**
Foynes, Co Limerick **133**
Frenchpark, Co Roscommon **78**
Freshford, Co Kilkenny **108**

Gaelic League 25, 27, 52, 78, 81, 89, 96
Gaelic sports **62**, **154**
Gaeltacht 28, 68, **81**, 114, 138, 140, **147**
Galbally, Co Limerick **142**–**3**
Gallarus Oratory, Co Kerry 31, 128, 140, 153
Galway, Co 17, 29, 31–3, 36, 63–**88**
Galway, Co Galway 21, 29, 33, 64, **68**–**9**, 88
Gap of Dunloe, Co Kerry **154**
Garinish Island, Co Cork **151**
Garron Plateau, Co Antrim **58**
Geragh, Co Dublin 35, **120**
Giant's Causeway, Co Antrim 27, 38, **45**, 47, 54, 58–**9**
Giant's Ring, Co Antrim **61**
Giles Quay, Co Louth **102**

Glandore, Co Cork **133**, 137
Glaslough, Co Monaghan **108**
Glenarm, Co Antrim **45**, 52, 59
Glenbower, Co Cork **151**
Glenbeigh, Co Kerry **133**, 138
Glencar, Co Kerry **143**
Clencar Waterfall, Co Sligo **81**
Glencolumbkille, Co Donegal 63, **69**, 81, 85
Glencree, Co Wicklow 91, 115, **122**
Glendalough, Co Wicklow 31, 91, **116**–**7**, 118, **121**–**2**, 126
Glenealy, Co Wicklow **108**, 121
Glengarra, Co Tipperary **151**
Glengarriff, Co Cork **133**, 151
Glen of the Dargle, Co Wicklow 92, **122**
Glen of the Downs, Co Wicklow **122**
Glens of Antrim, Co Antrim 17, 38, 52, **59**
Glenstal Abbey, Co Limerick 145, **151**
Glenties, Co Donegal **78**
Glenveagh Castle, Co Donegal **84**
Glin, Co Limerick **133**
Golden, Co Tipperary **143**, 148
Golden Vale, Co Tipperary 127, 143, 146, 153
Goldsmith, Oliver 26, 90, 104–5, **115**, 125
Goleen, Co Cork **134**
Gorey, Co Wexford **108**
Gort, Co Galway **78**, 80, 84
Gougane Barra Forest Park, Co Cork 128, **151**–**3**
Gowna, Co Cavan **108**
Gowran, Co Kilkenny **108**
Gracehill, Co Antrim **49**
Graiguenamanagh, Co Kilkenny **108**, 116
Granard, Co Longford **108**
Grand Canal 104, 107, 109, 112–3, 123–**4**
Grange, Co Sligo **70**, 74
Great Famine **24**, 37, 69
Greencastle, Co Donegal **70**
Greencastle, Co Down 54
Green Island, Co Down **58**
Greenore, Co Louth **102**
Gregory, Lady 80–1, **85**
Grey Abbey, Co Down **53**
Greystones, Co Wicklow 92, **102**, 120, 122, 126
Grianán of Aileach, Co Donegal 50, 63, 74, **87**
Gweedore Peninsula, Co Donegal **73**
Gweesalia, Co Mayo **70**

Hacketstown, Co Carlow **108**
Hazelwood House, Co Sligo **84**
Headford, Co Galway **78**, 83
Heaney, Seamus 26, **52**
Hezlett House, Co Londonderry **56**
High Island, Co Galway **74**
Hill of Knockaulin, Co Kildare 125
Hill of Tailte, Co Meath 125
Hillsborough, Co Down **49**, 52–3
Holy Cross Abbey, Co Tipperary 33, 146, **148**–**9**

Holywood, Co Down 39, **45**, 57
Home rule 24–5, 78, 96, 115
Howth, Co Dublin **102**, 120
Hunt Collection, Co Limerick
  151
Hyde, Douglas 25, 27, 78, 96

Inch, Co Kerry **134**
Inch Abbey, Co Down 48, **53**
Inchigeelagh, Co Cork **143**
Inishbofin Island, Co Galway 66,
  74
Inishglora Island, Co Mayo **74**,
  87
Inishkea Island, Co Mayo **74**,
  85, 87
Inishmaine Abbey, Co Mayo **83**
Inishmurray Island, Co Sligo **74**,
  87
Inishowen Peninsula, Co
  Donegal 50, 70, **74**, 76
Inishturk Island, Co Mayo 74
Inistioge, Co Kilkenny **109**
Innfield, Co Meath **109**
Innishannon, Co Cork **143**
Inniskeen Folk Museum, Co
  Monaghan 106, **121**
Irish Horse Museum and
  National Stud, Co Kildare
  109, **120–1**
Irish language 26, **27–8**, 69, 74,
  81, 96, 133, 147
Irish Republican Army 25, 82,
  114
Irish Volunteers 25, 52, 147
Irvine, Alexander **52**
Irvinestown, Co Fermanagh **49**,
  54
Island Magee, Co Antrim **46**
Iveragh Peninsula, Co Kerry
  128, 130, **138**, 152

Jamestown, Co Leitrim 78
Jerpoint Abbey, Co Kilkenny
  33, 91, 113, **117**
Jigginstown House, Co Kildare
  111, **120**
John F Kennedy Park, Co
  Wexford 112, **122**
Johnston, Francis **52**, 93, 97,
  101, 109, 112–3, 121
Johnstown, Co Kildare **109**
Johnstown Castle Gardens, Co
  Wexford **120**
Joyce, James 26, 97, 101, **115**

Kanturk, Co Cork 33, **143**
Keady, Co Armagh **49**
Kells, Co Kerry **134**
Kells, Co Kilkenny **109**, **117**
Kells, Co Meath 90, 118, 125
Kenmare, Co Kerry **134**
Kerry, Co 21, 30–1, 127–54
Kerry Blue Terrier **147**
Keshcarrigan, Co Leitrim 78
Kevin, St 31, 91, 116–7
Kilbeggan, Co Westmeath **109**
Kilbrittain, Co Cork **143**
Kilcar, Co Donegal 28, **70**, 81
Kilcash, Co Tipperary **143**
Kilclief Castle, Co Down **54**
Kilcolman Bog, Co Cork **151**
Kilcullen, Co Kildare **109**, 125
Kildare, Co **34**, 89–126
Kildare, Co Kildare **109**, 118,
  120–1, 126

Kilfenora, Co Clare **143**, 151
Kilfinnane, Co Limerick **143**
Kilgad Lake Fishery, Co Antrim
  62
Kilgarvan, Co Kerry **143**
Kilkee, Co Clare **134**, 152
Kilkeel, Co Down **45**
Kilkenny, Co 89–126
Kilkenny, Co Kilkenny 23, 26,
  33, **109**, 118, 120
Kilkieran, Co Galway **70**
Killadeas, Co Fermanagh 60–1
Killala, Co Mayo **70**
Killaloe, Co Clare **143**, 149
Killarney, Co Kerry 17, 128,
  138, **144**, 147, 149–51, 153
Killarney National Park, Co
  Kerry **144**, **151–2**
Killimer, Co Clare **134**, 137
Killiney, Co Dublin **102**
Killorglin, Co Kerry 138, **144**
Killoughternane Church, Co
  Carlow **117**
Killulta, Co Limerick **149**
Killybegs, Co Donegal **70**, 88
Killykeen Forest Park, Co
  Cavan **121**
Killyleagh, Co Down **49**, 53–4
Kilmallock, Co Limerick **144**,
  149
Kilmore Quay, Co Wexford
  102–3, 122
Kilruddery, Co Wicklow **120**
Kilrush, Co Clare **134**, 153
Kilsheelan, Co Tipperary **144**
Kingscourt, Co Cavan 110, 121
Kinlough, Co Leitrim 79
Kinnegad, Co Westmeath **110**
Kinnitty, Co Offaly 110, 122
Kinsale, Co Cork 34, **134**, 151
Kinsale sweaters, Co Cork **147**
Kinvarra, Co Galway **70**, 84, 88
Knappogue Castle, Co Clare
  146, 154
Knock, Co Mayo **81**
Knockmany, Co Tyrone **61**
Knockmealdown Mountains
  127–8, 140–1, 145, 153
Knowth, Co Meath 89, 124–5

Lace 136, **114**, **147**
Lady Dixon Park, Co Antrim **56**
Lahinch, Co Clare **134**, 152
Lambay Island, Co Dublin **103**,
  122
Lambegging, Co Antrim **52**
Lammas Fair, Co Antrim **62**
Land League 24, 81, 115, 146
Lanesborough, Co Longford
  110
Laois, Co 89–126, 127
Laragh, Co Wicklow **110**, 121–2
Larne, Co Antrim **45**, 57, 59
Laytown, Co Meath **102**
Leap, Co Cork **134**
Leenaun, Co Galway **70**
Leighlinbridge, Co Carlow **110**
Leinster 17, 19–21, 89, 106,
  110–1, 118, 123, 125
Leitrim, Co 63–88
Leixlip, Co Kildare 119
Leprechauns 18, 27, 52
Letterfrack, Co Galway **70**
Letterkenny, Co Donegal **70**
Lettermore, Co Galway 28, **70**
Lewis, C S **52**

Liffey, River 89, 93, 96, 106–7,
  110, 122–3, **124**, 125–6
Lifford, Co Donegal 79
Limavady, Co Londonderry 38,
  49, 52
Limerick, Co 127–54
Limerick, Co Limerick 20, 23,
  33, 114, 128, **134–6**, 147, 151
Linen 38, **52**
Lisburn, Co Antrim **49**, 62
Liscannor, Co Clare **134**, **136**
Lisdoonvarna, Co Clare **144**
Lismore, Co Waterford 128,
  144, 151, 153
Lisnakea, Co Fermanagh **49**, 57
Lissadell House, Co Sligo 67, **84**
Lissoy, Co Westmeath 90, 115
Listowel, Co Kerry 128, **144**
Londonderry, Co 17, 37–61
Londonderry, Co Londonderry
  38, **49–50**, 53, 55
Longford, Co 87, 89–126
Longford, Co Longford 35, **110**
Loughs
  Allen 78, 86–7
  Arrow 75–7, 86
  Ballynahinch 86
  Belfast 38–40, 43, 45, 60
  Carlingford 17, 39, 46, 54,
    58–60, 90, 92, 102–3
  Carra 75, 81–2
  Conn 65, 77, 79–80
  Corrib 28, 64, 69, 77–9, 81,
    85, 86
  Derg 63, 79, **86–8**, 127,
    142–3, 145–6, 152
  Derravaragh 106, 111, 123
  Ennell 111, 123–4
  Erne 46, 48, 53–4, 57, **58–9**,
    60–2, 105, 123–4
  Foyle 70–1, 74
  Gill 17, 63, 72, 78, 84–**6**, **88**,
    130
  Gowna 90, 108, 123–4
  Gur **153**
  Key 76, 85–**6**
  Leane 144, 150, 152–3
  MacNean 39, 59–60, 105
  Mask 75, 77, 83, 85–6
  Navar **59**
  Neagh 17, 20, 27, 38, 46,
    50–1, **58–9**, **60**, 62, 124
  Oughter 105–6, 121, **124**
  Owel 111, 123–4
  Ree 87, 90, 104, 110, 125
  Strangford 45–9, 51, 53,
    56–7, **58–9**, **60**
  Swilly 66, 68, 70–1, 73–4
Loughbrickland, Co Down **50**,
  52
Loughcrew Hills, Co Meath **125**
Lough Cultra Castle, Co Galway
  78, **84**
Lough Island Reavy, Co Down
  61
Lough Key Forest Park, Co
  Roscommon 76, **85**
Lough-na-Cranagh, Co Antrim
  61
Loughrea, Co Galway 79, 85,
  88
Loughshinny, Co Dublin **102**
Louisburgh, Co Mayo **70**
Louth, Co 33–4, 39, 89–126
Louth, Co Louth **110**
Lucan, Co Dublin **110**, 120

Curgan, Co Armagh 48, **50–1**
Lusk, Co Dublin 103, 118

Maam, Co Galway **79**
Maamturk Mountains, Co
  Galway 70, **85**
Macgillycuddy's Reeks, Co
  Kerry 134, 143, 144, 152
MacMurrough, Dermot 20, 63,
  91, 105, 108
MacNeice, Louis 45, **52**
MacNeill, Eóin 25, 27, **52**, 96
Macroom, Co Cork **145**, 154
Magherafelt, Co Londonderry
  51
Maguire's Castle, Co Fermanagh
  54
Malachy, St 20, 32, 39, 117
Malahide, Co Dublin **102**
Malin Beg, Co Donegal **71**
Malin More, Co Donegal **71**
Mallow, Co Cork **145**
Manorhamilton, Co Leitrim **79**,
  88
Marshall, William 106, 108, 116,
  118
Maynooth, Co Kildare **110**, 119
Mayo, Co 17, 26, 63–88
Meath, Co 21, 89–126
Meeting of the Waters, Co
  Wicklow 91, 115, 122
Mellifont Abbey, Co Louth
  32–3, 82, 90, 105, **117**, 124
Midleton, Co Cork **145**
Millford, Co Donegal **71**
Millisle, Co Down 55
Millstreet, Co Cork **145**
Milltown, Co Kerry **145**
Milltown Malbay, Co Clare 127,
  136
Mitchelstown, Co Cork **145**
Moate, Co Westmeath **110–1**
Moher, Cliffs of, Co Clare 127,
  133, 136, 152
Moira, Co Antrim **51**
Molaise, St 39, 55, 74, 87
Monaghan, Co 39, 47, 89–126
Monaghan, Co Monaghan **111**
Monaincha, Co Tipperary 146,
  149
Monasterboice, Co Louth **117**
Monasterevin, Co Kildare **111**
Monea Castle, Co Fermanagh **54**
Moneymore, Co Londonderry
  56–7
Monicknew Woods, Co Laois
  111, **121**
Monivea, Co Galway **79**
Moone High Cross & Church, Co
  Kildare **117**
Moor Abbey, Co Limerick
  142–3
Moore, George 26, 75, **81**
Moore, Thomas 26, 91, **115**
Mountcharles, Co Donegal **71**
Mount Kennedy, Co Wicklow
  34, **120**
Mountmellick, Co Laois **111**
Mountrath, Co Laois **111**
Mountshannon, Co Clare **145**
Mount Stewart, Co Down **56**
Mount Usher, Co Wicklow 103,
  120–1
Mourne Mountains, Co Down
  40, 57–**9**, 90, 92, 103
Moville, Co Donegal **71**

Moy, Co Tyrone 38, **51**, 53
Moycullen, Co Galway **88**
Muckross Abbey, Co Kerry 144,
  149, 152
Muckross House, Co Kerry 144,
  151–2
Muine Bheag, Co Carlow **111**
Mularanny, Co Mayo **71**
Mullaghbane Folk Museum, Co
  Armagh **57**
Mullaghmore, Co Sligo **71**
Mullingar, Co Westmeath **111**,
  123–5
Multyfarnham, Co Westmeath
  111, 119
Mungret, Co Limerick **136**, 149
Munster 17, 19–20, 23, 127–8,
  135, 140, 143, 149, 153
Murlough National Nature
  Reserve, Co Down **58**
Murroe, Co Limerick **145**
Music, Irish **28**, 69, 107, 114,
  126, 147
Mussenden Temple, Co
  Londonderry 55

Naas, Co Kildare **111**, 120
National Steam Traction Rally,
  Co Laois **126**
Navan, Co Meath **111**, 124
Navan Fort, Co Armagh 31, 39,
  55, **61**
Nenagh, Co Tipperary **145**
Newbliss, Co Monaghan **111**
Newcastle, Co Down 39, **45**, 58
Newcastle West, Co Limerick
  145
Newgrange, Co Meath 89,
  124–5
Newmarket, Co Cork **145**
Newmarket-on-Fergus, Co Clare
  145
Newport, Co Mayo **71**, 82, 88
New Ross, Co Wexford 33, 91,
  111–2, 118, 154
Newry, Co Down 21, 39, 46, **51**,
  60–1
Newtownards, Co Down **51**
Nire Valley, Co Waterford **152**
North Antrim Cliff Path, Co
  Antrim **58**

O'Brien, Conor 140, 146
O'Brien, Donal 134–5, 143
O'Casey, Sean 26, 80, 96, **115**
O'Connell, Daniel **24**, 96, 99,
  130, **148**
O'Connell Monument, Co Clare
  148
O'Conor, Rory 20–1
O'Donnell, Red Hugh 64–5, 67,
  77, 98, 110
O'Donnell, Rory 37, **71**
Offaly, Co 89–126
Oldcastle, Co Meath **112**, 125
Omagh, Co Tyrone 37, 38, **51**,
  57, 59
O'Malley, Grace 71, 73–4
Omeath, Co Louth **102**
Omey Island, Co Galway 74
O'Neill, Hugh 22, 37, 39–40,
  71, 141
Oranmore, Co Galway **71**
Ormond Castle, Co Tipperary
  150
Oughterard, Co Galway **79**, 88

Our Lady of Bethlehem Abbey,
  Co Antrim 53
Oxford Island Nature Reserve,
  Co Armagh **58**

Pale, The 21–2, 93, 101, 104,
  106–7, 111
Parkes Castle, Co Leitrim 78, **84**
Parknasilla, Co Kerry **136**
Parnell, Charles Stewart 24, 91,
  96, 104, 112, **115**, 121
Partition (1921) **25**, 37
Partry Mountains, Co Galway
  70, **86**
Passage East, Co Waterford **136**
Patrick, St 19, 39, 46, 48, **52**, 53,
  65, 72, 75, 86, 90, 92–3,
  103, 112, 154
Pearse, Patrick **81–2**, 110
Pettigoe, Co Donegal **79**
Pontoon, Co Mayo **79**
Portacloy, Co Mayo **71**
Portadown, Co Armagh 50–1,
  55, 59, 60
Portaferry, Co Down 35, **45**
Portarlington, Co Laois **112**, 116
Portglenone, Co Antrim 53, 58
Portlaoise, Co Laois **112**, 118
Portlaw, Co Waterford **145**
Portmagee, Co Kerry **136**
Portmarnock, Co Dublin **102**
Portnoo, Co Donegal **71**
Portroe, Co Tipperary **145**
Portrush, Co Antrim **45**, 54,
  62
Portsalon, Co Donegal **71**
Portstewart, Co Londonderry
  38, **46**
Portumna, Co Galway **79**, 85, 88
Powerscourt, Co Wicklow 91,
  108, **120**, 122
Prosperous, Co Kildare **112**
Punchestown, Co Kildare **126**

Quilty, Co Clare **136–7**
Quin, Co Clare **145–6**, 149, 151
Quoile Pondage Nature Reserve,
  Co Down **58**

Raghly, Co Sligo **71**
Randalstown Forest and Nature
  Reserve, Co Antrim **58–9**
Raphoe, Co Donegal **79**
Rathcroghan, Co Roscommon
  87–8
Rathdowney, Co Laois **112**
Rathdrum, Co Wicklow 91, **112**,
  115, 121, 122
Rathgory, Co Louth 121
Rathkeale, Co Limerick **146**
Rathlin Island, Co Antrim 40,
  46, **58**
Rath Luirc, Co Cork **146**
Rathmelton, Co Donegal **71**
Rathmullan, Co Donegal **71**
Rathvilly, Co Carlow **112**
Ravensdale, Co Louth **121**
Recess, Co Galway **79**
Robertstown, Co Kildare **112**,
  124, 126
Rosapenna, Co Donegal **71**
Rosbeg, Co Donegal **71**
Roscommon, Co 31, 33, 63–88
Roscommon, Co Roscommon
  79–80
Roscrea, Co Tipperary **146**

Rose of Tralee International
  Festival, Co Kerry 154
Rosguill Peninsula, Co Donegal
  66–7, 71, **74**, 86
Rosmuck, Co Galway 81–2
Ross Abbey, Co Galway **83**
Ross Carbery, Co Cork **137**
Ross Castle, Co Kerry **150**
Rosserk Abbey, Co Mayo 33, **83**
Rosses, The, Co Donegal **74**
Rosslare, Co Wexford **102**, 120
Rossmore Forest Park, Co
  Monaghan 111, **121**
Rossnowlagh, Co Donegal **71**,
  85, 88
Rostrevor, Co Down **46**, 52
Rostrevor Forest Nature
  Reserve, Co Tyrone **58**
Rothe House, Co Kilkenny **120**
Roundstone, Co Galway **71**–2
Roundwood, Co Wicklow **112**
Rowallane, Co Down **56**
Royal Canal 107, 110, **124**–5
Rush, Co Dublin **103**, 122
Russborough House, Co
  Wicklow 34, 105, **120**–1

St Cleran's, Co Galway 81, **84**
St Cooey's Wells, Co Down **55**
St MacDara's Church, Co
  Galway 31, 66, **83**
St Mullins, Co Carlow **118**
St Patrick's Island, Co Dublin
  103
Saltee Islands, Co Wexford
  102–**3**, **122**
Sarsfield, Patrick 23, 131, 135,
  143
Saul, Co Down 19, 48, 52, 55
Scarriff, Co Clare **146**
Scattery Island, Co Clare 134,
  153
Schull, Co Cork **137**
Seatown Windmill, Co Louth
  101, **119**
Seskinore, Co Tyrone **59**
Seven Arches, Co Donegal **81**
Shane's Castle Nature Reserve,
  Co Antrim 46, **58**, 62
Shannon, River 17, 64, 76, 78,
  86–7, 90, 104–5, 107, 110,
  116, 123–5, 127–30, 133–7,
  139, 141, 143, 152–3
Shaw, George Bernard 26, 80, **115**
Sheep Haven Bay, Co Donegal
  67, 74, 83, 85–6
Sheep Island, Co Antrim **58**
Shenick Island, Co Dublin **103**
Shercock, Co Cavan **112**
Sheridan, Richard Brinsley 26,
  115
Sherkin Island, Co Cork **138**–9
Sinn Fein 25, 96, 131, 147
Sixmilebridge, Co Clare **146**
Skellig Michael, Co Kerry 31,
  139, **154**
Skerries, Co Dublin **103**, 126
Skibbereen, Co Cork **137**
Slane, Co Meath **112**–3, 124

Slieve Bloom Mountains, Co
  Offaly 90–1, 110, **122**–3
Slieve Gullion Mountains, Co
  Armagh 39, **59**, **61**
Slieve Mish Mountains, Co
  Kerry 130, 134, 137–8, 152
Sligo, Co 30, 63–88
Sligo, Co Sligo 33, **72**, 85
Sneem, Co Kerry **137**, 138
Sperrin Mountains 38, **58**–9, 60
Spiddal, Co Galway **72**
Springhill, Co Londonderry
  56–7
Staigue Fort, Co Kerry 30, 130,
  154
Stormont Parliament 25, 37
Strabane, Co Tyrone 37, **51**–2,
  55, 60
Stradbally, Co Laois **113**, 121,
  126
Strandhill, Co Sligo **72**
Strangford, Co Down **46**, 54
Strokestown, Co Roscommon **80**
Strongbow 20–1, 103, 108–9,
  118, 137, 146
Struell Wells, Co Down **55**
Swift, Jonathan 26, 106,
  113–14, 137, **148**
Swinford, Co Mayo **80**
Swords, Co Dublin **113**, 118
Synge, John Millington 26, 86,
  91, 96–7, **115**

Tahilla, Co Kerry **137**
Tandragee, Co Armagh **51**
Tara, Co Meath 19, 31, 89, 108,
  111, 124, **126**
Tarbert, Co Kerry **137**
Tarbert Island, Co Kerry **139**
Teelin, Co Donegal **72**
Templemore, Co Tipperary **146**
Terryglass, Co Tipperary **146**
Thomastown, Co Kilkenny
  113–4
Thoor Ballylee, Co Galway 82
Thurles, Co Tipperary **146**
Tibradden, Co Dublin **121**
Timahoe, Co Laois 118
Timoleague, Co Cork **137**
Tipperary, Co 27, 127–54
Tipperary, Co Tipperary **146**
Tirnony, Co Londonderry **62**
Tobercurry, Co Sligo **80**
Tollymore Forest, Co Down 45,
  59
Tone, Theobald Wolfe 23, 38,
  42, 66, 70, 97
Toomevara, Co Tipperary **147**
Torc Waterfall, Co Kerry **153**
Tory Island, Co Donegal 28, **74**,
  81
Tourmakeady, Co Mayo 28, **85**
Townley Hall, Co Louth **121**
Tralee, Co Kerry 128, **137**, 154
Tramore, Co Waterford **137**
Trim, Co Meath 33, **113**, 118
Trollope, Anthony 78, 105, 141,
  145
Tuam, Co Galway **80**, 85

Tulla, Co Clare **147**
Tullaghan, Co Leitrim **72**, 86
Tullaghoge Fort, Co Tyrone **55**
Tullamore, Co Offaly 107, 109,
  113–4, 116
Tullow, Co Carlow **114**
Tullycross, Co Galway **72**
Tullynally Castle, Co
  Westmeath 106, **121**
Tulsk, Co Roscommon **80**
Turlough, Co Mayo **80**
Turoe Stone, Co Galway 79, **88**
Tweed **52**, **80**, 101, **114**
Twelve Bens, Co Galway 64, 66,
  70, 85–**6**
Tyrrelspass, Co Westmeath **114**
Tyrone, Co 17, 37–62

Ulster 17, 19, 21–2, 24–5,
  36–63, 90
Ulster American Folk Park, Co
  Tyrone 51, **57**
Ulster Folk & Transport
  Museum, Co Down 39, 42,
  44–5, 52, **57**
Ulster Way **58**
Union Hall, Co Cork **137**, 148
Upperlands, Co Londonderry 57
Urlingford, Co Kilkenny **114**

Vale of Avoca, Co Wicklow **122**
Valentia Island, Co Kerry **139**
Valley of Diamonds, Co Sligo **81**
Virginia, Co Cavan **114**

Warrenpoint, Co Down **46**, 57,
  60
Waterford, Co 21, 31, 127–54
Waterford, Co Waterford 20, 22,
  35, 128, **137**–8, 154
Waterville, Co Cork **138**
Wellbrook Beetling Mill, Co
  Tyrone **55**, **57**
Westmeath, Co 89–126
Westport, Co Mayo **72**, 84, 88
Wexford, Co 33, 89–126
Wexford, Co Wexford 20–1, 23,
  91, **103**, 112, 126
Whitehead, Co Antrim **46**
White Island, Co Fermanagh **46**,
  52, 60, **62**
Whitepark Bay, Co Antrim **58**
Wicklow, Co 31, 34, 89–126
Wicklow, Co Wicklow **103**
Wicklow Mountains, Co
  Wicklow 17, 90–3, **122**, 124,
  126
Wilde, Oscar 26, 49, 99, **115**
Wild Rose Festival, Co Leitrim
  88
Woodenbridge, Co Wicklow
  114, 126
Wyatt, James 72, 112, 119–20

Yeats, W B 26, 63, 67, 70, 78,
  80–2, 84, 96–7, 99, 115
Youghal, Co Cork 33, 128, **138**